# PRAISE

"*Lion Dad* serves as a practical guide for parents on how to balance the pressures of academic excellence with both encouragement with compassion; all while instilling worth which transcends 'grade point average' and standardized test scores. I was able to witness how this approach nurtured a confident, kind, and happy child resulting in admission to a prestigious Computer Science program in an Ivy League school. Lucky would be any community who welcomed him- wisdom and maturity beyond his years."
- Karl J Mueller, Superintendent, Coronado Unified School District

"Contrast little soldiers, obedient, compliant, controlling in every way, the- ends-justify-the-means of the Tiger Mother with physically, socially, spirituality and scholastically balanced and the unconditional love approach to child rearing of the *Lion Dad*. Which would you choose for your child? This book provides the substrate for admission to any school, not just the Ivy league, and most importantly results in a child who will understand work-life balance. A must read for any parent."
- Joseph C. Maroon, M.D., F.A.C.S., Clinical Professor and Vice Chairman, Department of Neurological Surgery, Heindl Scholar in Neuroscience, University of Pittsburgh Medical Center, Team Neurosurgeon, The Pittsburgh Steelers

"*Lion Dad*, written by a long term colleague, is a fascinating commentary on modern day parenting, elite college admissions, and much more. It also integrates a functional medical component. I strongly endorse the author and this book for parents and children."
- Robert M. Goldman M.D., PhD, D.O., FAASP, World Chairman-International Medical Commission, Co-Founder & Chairman of the Board-A4M, Founder & Chairman-International Sports Hall of Fame, Co-Founder & Chairman-World Academy of Anti-Aging Medicine, President Emeritus-National Academy of Sports Medicine (NASM), Chairman- U.S. Sports Academy's Board of Visitors

"*Lion Dad* is Greeat!!. The natural essential and nurturing benefits of a father's love has been decreasing over the last few generations with disastrous effects. Dr Roark, a longtime colleague, gives the RX for the cure."

- Ronald Klatz, M.D., D.O., Founder of the new clinical specialty of anti-aging medicine, Best-selling author/editor of 36+ books with over 2 million copies in print, Founder of A4M, coined the term "Anti-Aging"

"The competition students face securing a position in an elite ivy league school has become overwhelming. Dr. Roark has written a very important book providing a strategic outline for both students and parents in preparing for admission to elite colleges and universities in the United States. This is a must read for any family who desires admission in these oversubscribed and popular universities and who wishes to have emotionally healthy children as well."
- Steven Sinatra, M.D., Fellow, American College of Cardiology, Fellow, American College of Nutrition, Board Certified, American Board of Internal Medicine, Certified, American Board of Anti-Aging Medicine

"Finally!! THE guide to help a parent develop a healthier, more practical style to enhance their child's chances of success! As a psychiatrist, I've treated the sequelae of the authoritarian parent who demands submission and accepts nothing short of perfection, excellence, and high academic success. Now, thanks to Dr. Roark's comprehensive book, so many children may have a chance of achieving their goals and grow into a more emotionally balanced adult."
- Mathew Geromi, D,.O., Clinical Assistant Professor, Department of Psychiatry, Philadelphia College of Osteopathic Medicine

"The Roark's really are "successful" parents. Theirs is a happy, productive family capable of addressing all kinds of issues and opportunities that life presents. I love their son, not because he's an "Ivy Leaguer," but a genuinely compassionate individual with the interpersonal skills to engage and inspire others. He continues to utilize the empowerment

instilled in him by touching others in meaningful ways along his path in life."
- Richard and Mary Ann Pantella, Parents and Grandparents

Dr. Roark may be the new "Dr. Spock" in regard to successful parenting especially as it pertains to elite school admissions. If you are serious about your child's education, this is a must read. I have seen many children damaged by demanding parents with misguided methods. What are we doing to our children?? I knew some of the people entangled in the recent bribery scandal which only shows the absurd length people will go to get into elite schools."
- John Hunt, M.D., Author, Entrepreneur, pediatrician, pulmonologist, allergist/immunologist

"For every parent who aspires to gently guide their child's educational future, you'll find the "Lion Commandments" incredibly helpful. You'll come away touched by the strong bonds of love and support that underpin the best of father-son relationships."
- Mark J. Tager, M.D., ChangeWell Inc., Co-Author Enhance Your Presence: The Path to Personal Power, Professional Influence & Business Results

"This book is a real tour de force and a labor of love. It's really two books in one: a charming and inspiring memoir while also a detailed 'how to' book of actionable steps for preparing a child for college admission. It gives parents a clear path they can confidently follow regardless of their budget." It is very practical!!"
- Todd A. Scott, M.D., F.A.C.S., Double Board certified in Ophthalmology and Anti-Aging Medicine

"Finally someone who thoroughly provides parents step by step advice to get their kids into an Ivy league college. Filled with practical advice, encouragement and real life anecdotes, it's a must read for any parent who has kids going through the competitive and stressful process of college admission."

- Laura Gomez Freeman, M.D., O.D., member of the AAO, ARVO, ASCRS, and The National Association of Professional Women

"This is a roadmap to successful college applications. We raised 5 children with very similar methods outlined in this excellent book. They all attended elite schools. I am thrilled Dr. Roark put these methods into print since they are seldom talked about by elite parents."
- Stephanie and Hadar Wietzman, Member of the Israel State Bar, Member of the California Bar

"*Lion Dad* reaches new heights in demonstrating the best ways to educate, inspire, and motivate our children in preparation for entry into our country's top schools, in today's unique environment. Dr. Roark provides the best guide available for giving our kids a shot at the Ivy League. It goes beyond education and provides a fundamental manual for good parenting."
- Doug Krell, M.D., OBGYN

"As the mother of 2 children, currently in medical school, I found *Lion Dad* to be an interesting book about how to raise a child. Unlike *Battle Hymn of the Tiger Mother*, this book provides a refreshing story about how to support a child's academics and life. *Lion Dad* provides a blueprint to helping children grow with supportive parents."
- Allsion Selko, J.D., Member of the Michigan State Bar

"This book is packed with sensible advice on how to guide your child into a top college. Some of it is what one would expect, but a lot of it is contrarian. The step-by-step plan it presents works best early in your child's education, so get it NOW, before it's too late!"
- Robert W. Bly, B.S. in chemical engineering, University of Rochester, Author of 100 published books

I have known Dr. "Roark" for over 40 years and his son since he was born. I have witnessed the amazing results of his parenting methods along with his wife's. His story is unique, transformative, and will be essential advice for any parent.
- Erwin Omens, M.D. Ophthalmologist

"As a registered dietitian, it is heart warming and so refreshing to hear that Dr. Roark includes nutrition as a foundation for nurturing children. It has been my ultimate quest to get more and more focus on nutrition in the earlier stages of life to be sold as a corner stone of development both physically and emotionally.
- **Lisa Delaney Camhi, R.D., M.S., L.D., Healthwise, LLC**

"I have known Dr. "Roark" for over over 45 years dating back to medical school. He, like many parents, struggled with justifying the process and high costs for his son to matriculate to an Ivy League university. His book takes an analytical and anecdotal approach to help make that decision."
- **John A. White, M.D.**, Board Certified Orthopedic Surgeon

"I have known Dr. "Roark" and his son for many years. His story, as well as deep parental involvement , illustrates the primary value of nurture in elite school admissions. This book is a must read for all parents at any stage including prenatal."
-**Felice Gersh, M.D.**, Board-certified in OB-GYN and Integrative Medicine, Princeton Graduate

# LION DAD

## How to nudge your cub into the Ivy League

J K Roark, M.D.

# Publisher's Information

EBookBakery Books
Book Cover Design by 100 Covers

ISBN 978-1-938517-95-2
Library of Congress Control Number: 2020905042
© 2020 by Lion Dad, LCC
Web: LionDad.com
Author contact: DrRoark@Lion-Dad.com

ALL RIGHTS RESERVED

No part of this work covered by the copyright herein may be reproduced, transmitted, stored, or used in any form or by any means graphic, electronic, or mechanical, including but not limited to photocopying, scanning, digitizing, taping, Web distribution, information networks, or information storage and retrieval systems, except as permitted by Section 107 or 108 of the 1976 United States Copyright Act, without the prior written permission of the author.

Disclaimer: The author's opinions expressed herein are based on both his personal observations and his research and readings on the subject matter. The author's opinions may not be universally applicable to all people in all circumstances. The information presented in this book is in no way intended as medical advice or as a substitute for medical or other counseling. The information should be used in conjunction with the guidance and care of your physician. The publisher and author disclaim liability for any negative or other medical outcomes that may occur as a result of acting on or not acting on anything set forth in this book.

# DEDICATION

*For my mother, who showed me how to be a loving parent. I think of you every day. You would be so proud of your grandson, Max.*

*For my wife. The reason Max and I thrive.*

*For my sister, Ellen, who taught me the meaning of courage.*

# TABLE OF CONTENTS

**Foreword**
By David Brownstein M.D. ................................................... xiii

## Part A - Our Basic Thinking

**Preface**
Why I Wrote this Book ............................................. xvii

**Introduction, the Philosophy**
How is a Lion Dad is Different from a Tiger Mother ............... xxv

*Chapter 1*: **Why an Ivy League or Elite College?**
And is it really hard to get in? ..................................... 1

## Part B - Our Story - What To Do

*Chapter 2*: **Birth Through Pre-K.**
The Foundation of an Excellent Life ............................. 21

*Chapter 3*: **Elementary School**
A Three-step Method to Set Your Child on the Successful Path. 37

*Chapter 4*: **Middle School**
The Warm Up ..................................................... 61

*Chapter 5*: **High School - I**
Boot Camp – Now It Counts ..................................... 73

*Chapter 6*: **High School - II**
The Extras - How to Knock It Out of the Park .................. 87

*Chapter 7*: **Standardized Tests**
Life is Graded on a Curve ........................................ 103

*Chapter 8*: **Counselors and Consultants**
How to Hire Your Support Team ................................ 121

*Chapter 9:* **Extracurricular Activities**
Who Are You? ........................................................................... 131

*Chapter 10*: **The Essay**
A Window into Your Student's Mind ...................................... 143

*Chapter 11:* **Admissions Tactics**
The Details that Matter ........................................................... 153

*Chapter 12*: **Film, Travel, Volunteering**
A Deep Dive into Three Significant Differentiators ................ 165

### Part C - How To Choose Schools - Pre-K to College

*Chapter 13*: **Which College?**
Know Your Values and Beliefs ................................................ 181

### Part D - What We Learned That Will Help You

*Chapter 14*: **The Three Mental Capacities For Success** ............ 195

*Chapter 15:* **Putting it All Together**
The Bird's Eye View ................................................................. 207

*Chapter 16:* **Our Mistakes** ........................................................ 217

*Chapter 17:* **Summary and Conclusions** ................................... 233

*Chapter 18:* **Education & Parenting in the Pandemic Age**
How the Virus is Altering the Scene ....................................... 239

**Epilogue**
The Results .............................................................................. 250

## Part E - Questionnaires and Important Comparisons

**Parent Questionnaire**
Are You a Lion Parent or a Tiger Parent?................ 256

**Cub Questionnaire**
Does Your Child Think You're a Lion Parent or Tiger Parent?. 264

**Acknowledgments**................................................. 269

**Appendices**......................................................... 276
   I - Value Hierarchy Worksheet for college choice.......... 276
   II - Max's Essays for his Ivy League applications......... 285

**Resources & Websites for Tutoring, College Admissions and Counseling**............................................... 287

**Notes on Select Chapters**........................................ 305

**References**......................................................... 350

**Index**................................................................ 381

**About the Author**................................................. 405

# FOREWORD

By David Brownstein, M.D.
Medical Director Center for Holistic Medicine, Author of 15 books and "Dr. Brownstein's Natural Way to Health" newsletter

*Lion Dad* is a much-needed book. It is a story written by Dr. Roark, a colleague and close friend, about how he and his wife raised their son, Max. After enrolling Max in an exclusive private school, they attended a parent-teacher conference and were told Max did not pay attention well and was not as intelligent as the other kids. The teacher advised Max's parents to adjust their expectations since "not every kid can go to college" and that perhaps Max would be better suited for manual labor.

Max's parents did what any good parent would do—they pulled him out of that negative environment. Dr. Roark makes it clear that no parents should allow their children to be negatively framed. This story culminates with Max overcoming such negativity and being admitted into an Ivy League university.

I am a parent of two daughters, both in medical school. I am incredibly proud and honored to be their father. My wife, Allison, and I shared a *Lion Dad* philosophy similar to the one described in this book when raising our children. Reading each chapter made me reflect on my own parenting skills. The main message in each chapter, from my perspective, is that parents need to provide a safe and stable environment for their child, show unconditional love and support, and know that their child should be their number one priority.

When my girls were young, around five and six, I remember taking them to a friend's house on a lake. These friends had older children who were away at college. We spent a glorious day boating, swimming, and doing all the summer things that kids should do. At the end of the day, as we were getting ready to leave, our friends stated, "It is so nice to see how much you enjoy being around your children."

I was stunned. I asked, "Why wouldn't I enjoy being around my children?"

They replied, "Most people find children a bother; that is why many have nannies and take vacations without their children."

I have thought more about our friend's comments since then. Allison and I have always loved being around our children. We are still amazed that, in their twenties, they want to go on vacation and be with us. I guess we did something right. Lion parents like to be around their children. In fact, Lion parents live to be around their children. That is a central message in this book.

What did Allison and I do right? I think we employed the *Lion Dad* philosophy for raising children. We always respected and listened to our children. We did not accept, nor did we evoke negative remarks about our children. We were actively involved in our children's lives without over-parenting them. We supported them and are still their biggest cheerleaders, and we fully embraced our children being able to make their own decisions about how to succeed in life. And succeeding they are.

Comparing the parenting styles of Amy Chua's *Tiger Mother* and Roark's *Lion Dad* is illuminating. One method is harsh, the other loving. One method demands subservience; the other promotes independence. Our modern world has become too fast and too hard on kids. Children are pushed to learn more at an earlier age. As a consequence, we have children with more and more problems. A large percentage of children have a psychiatric diagnosis, and over 10 percent of children in the US are on ADHD medications. I think if parents adopted the *Lion Dad* philosophy of listening and being supportive, without causing undue stress about academic achievement, their children would be more successful, both academically and emotionally, leading to happier, better-adjusted adults.

To conclude, *Lion Dad* is a book about parenting by nurturing. A child can be treated as an object or as an independent, sensitive individual. Our kids are overstressed because of many pressures coming at them from all sides. This book should be read by parents and parents-to-be so they can give their children the tools needed to address these pressures and succeed in life.

# PART A
# OUR BASIC THINKING

# PREFACE

## Why I Wrote This Book

*"It is a wise father that knows his own child."*
- **William Shakespeare**

*"Childhood is not a rehearsal for the rest of their lives. Children have their own thoughts, relationships, and emotions."*
- **Sir Ken Robinson** - You, Your Child, and School, 2018

Many parents think that getting their child into an Ivy League school—Harvard, Yale, Princeton, Brown, Cornell, Columbia, Dartmouth, or the University of Pennsylvania, is the ultimate symbol of success and guarantees their child's future prosperity. Is that true? The short answer is maybe. The long answer is much more nuanced and is, in large part, what this book is about.

For those who think the ROI of an Ivy League education is valuable, this book will provide detailed advice on how to achieve it. For those who are on the fence about this, this book will guide you through this important decision. High school students worldwide clamor for one of these coveted acceptance letters. What is all the fuss about?

When we visited the East Coast Ivy League schools in the summer before Max's senior year, we took the usual student-run walking tours and attended lectures given by articulate senior admissions officers. We sat next to other prospective students, and I even leaned in to ask one about his stats. Surprisingly, he shared them, and they were impressive to say the least. But the question was: do we measure up?

It was raining after one of the tours, so we dropped into the bookstore to browse and savor our visit since we truly thought we would never see this campus again. It was such a long shot. I have two physician friends who are Ivy alumni, and neither one got their child into any Ivy. Other very successful people have confided in me that the Ivy League was also their first choice, but they too could not get in. The enormity of the task of gaining admission to any Ivy League school was, at the time, too great to even contemplate. What was the secret sauce?

I just wanted to see the campuses since I had never been and to experience first hand what all the fuss was about. While at the bookstore, we were looking at swag and overheard a young woman talking to her grandparents. She mentioned that she was starting school there in a couple of months, so I started a conversation and eventually got to my main question: how did she get in? It's not every day you get to speak to a rising freshman. Her response?

"I have no idea!"

I was dumbfounded. She seemed like any normal teen, but she must have had some idea. Perhaps she was being modest or just did not want to get into her entire story in the brief time we had. Then again, maybe she really did not know. Getting accepted is an amalgamation of talent, academic prowess, character, and luck I suppose. But what was this mix?

Someone had to know. I looked around for books written by parents from outside the college industrial complex (admissions officers, counselors, tutors, deans, etc.) and found none, even on Amazon. I was puzzled and curious at the same time. Was the answer a deep secret, or did people really not know? I had to find out.

The college application process is a minefield. The industry that has grown around it is daunting, and the choices can make your head spin. To complicate this further, the Ivy League has particular requirements because, well, they look for different things. Parents may be unaware of this and make the mistake of thinking there is only one path to prepare for every college. Indeed even different Ivy League schools can have dramatically different expectations. Unfortunately, well-meaning counselors and professionals working with your child in high school don't have the benefit parents do of knowing your child's background. Counselors do their best, but what they have to work with depends on what your child has been exposed to prior to high school. Guiding your child from an early age is crucial and will have the greatest impact on creating quality options when choosing colleges.

Most books on the subject of college admissions are written by college counselors trying to attract business, ex-admissions officers, or consultants who meet with students briefly, late in high school. Some are written by teachers or students who have achieved elite school admissions. These authors have unique perspectives and valuable insights, but they do not know your child from day one. They do not have skin in the game as you do. They don't necessarily share your values, they certainly don't love your child as you do, and in many cases, they are being paid quite handsomely to please you, their client. Their agendas can be different from yours, and it's important for a parent to know this. They have a job to do—you have a child you love and know intimately. These consultants can be used, but make no mistake: you are the ringleader. You have a front row seat. You are the focus of decision making. You are the cheerleader.

Only you will instill the values to achieve the goal of the Ivy League or more importantly, the goal of a successful life. The mindset that the parent establishes early on is the limiting factor in most cases.

I make no claim as an expert. I have just one 'client'. I will show you how we planned, what we valued, and how we chose tutors, schools, counselors, test prep services, doctors, lawyers, books, and much more. Although all families have unique values and goals, successful Ivy League applicants can be remarkably alike in many ways. I have spoken to many of them. They did not follow any blueprint or guidebook but rather customized their approach to their individual child.

The choice between public, private, and home high school education will be covered as will the pros and cons of sports participation. Extracurricular activities will have a chapter as will standardized test prep and strategy. As you can see, getting into an elite school is an enormous undertaking that requires intelligent planning, execution, and feedback. It does not happen by luck, and in most cases, does not happen by sheer intelligence. Nurture trumps nature in this effort by a long shot. I don't believe 99 percent of the Ivy League students get in on their own . . . without a team effort. The captain of that team is you, the parent. **Take charge!**

The academic process is inherently unfair, many times favoring the privileged. It is not, nor should be, a meritocracy, although that is the illusion, and there are court cases currently pending trying to make it 'fair'. The current bribery scandal involving elite school admissions

(Varsity Blues) illustrates how far some will go, risking everything to achieve admission for their child. Life is not fair. Some people have advantages that others do not, rightly or wrongly. More often than not, dealing with these facts of life is what separates the successful applicant from the herd. We still live in a free country so it is nonetheless possible to achieve great things coming from a modest background. In fact, most high achieving people did just that. We are one example.

Getting into an elite school is a byproduct of a great parenting, grooming, intrinsic (versus extrinsic) motivation, and providing a safe environment for your child to make mistakes, learn, develop grit, curiosity, and enthusiasm.

I have changed my son's name and have taken out much of the identifying details out of respect for his privacy and at his request, as he is modest. However, everything else in this book is factual and accurate. I have written under a pen name for the same reason—privacy and the ability to tell all. The pen name "Roark" was chosen since Howard Roark is the protagonist in *The Fountainhead*, written by Ayn Rand, also a pen name.

As Bob Dylan said, *"Give a man a mask and you will hear the truth."*

I have used the name 'Lion Dad' or 'Lion Parent' to contrast our methods with the Tiger Mother Paradigm. A Lion Parent or a Tiger Parent can be male or female, any nationality, any religion, any race, and can come from any socioeconomic class. It is a philosophy, not an indication of gender, nationality, religion or wealth.

You have one chance at this. There are many books on parenting and thousands of mom blogs, but this book is unique in its focus, point of view, and tell-all attitude. This is written from the male parent perspective but any family member will benefit.

## Who will be helped by this book?

While this book can be useful for prospective college students—and indeed I often wrote sections with that audience in mind—it is primarily intended for the parents of school-aged children before significant college planning begins. I know what kept me up at night, what I asked myself along the way, and what the pivotal choices are. Intelligent, proactive parents will read and devour this book early in their child's life and likely again and again, right up until their child's senior year.

## Why am I writing it?

For several reasons. To carefully examine this amazing experience in detail before moving on, to help other parents make good choices, and to develop a new paradigm for achieving elite school acceptance that is fun and respectful of the childhood experience. You do not have to take your child's early years away from him or her in order to be successful.

## How to use this book

Some books are reference books, meant to be used in a non-linear manner, skipping to whatever chapter suits your current interests. Please read it cover-to-cover in the order it was written. Then, and only then, should you refer to individual chapters for refreshers, bullet points (Lion Commandments) and specific topics.

This subject does not lend itself well to reductionism, quick fixes, and easy formulas. What I am attempting to do in this book is to change the parent paradigm, challenge parenting attitudes, and motivate you to interact with your child in the most effective ways possible. The discussion surrounding parenting must be changed in this country, and I hope this book contributes to this before we take away the precious childhoods from more generations. Read it slowly, think about it deeply, and refer to it often. Discuss it with family. You will not regret it when your child is admitted to an elite school and thrives there.

We are proud parents. I imagine you are as well. I hope this Lion Dad philosophy will be of use to you in ensuring that you enjoy your child's growth as you guide him or her to a meaningful life.

# Roots and Wings

# INTRODUCTION

## HOW IS A LION DAD DIFFERENT FROM A TIGER MOTHER? THE PHILOSOPHY

*"There are two things children should get from their parents—roots and wings."*
—**Johann Wolfgang von Goethe, author/philosopher**

"Remember to look up at the stars and not at your feet."
—**Stephen Hawking, theoretical physicist**

In January 2011, Yale law professor Amy Chua released a book entitled *The Battle Hymn of the Tiger Mother.* In it, Chua discusses her successes and failures in embracing a parenting method emphasizing the strict promotion of academic excellence (only 'A's are allowed) and the musical study of the piano or violin. With this parenting style there are no sleepovers, and unquestioning obedience to authority is expected. Rewards, even basic positive reinforcement, are predicated solely on scholastic achievement. Under the Tiger Mother model, as Chua calls it, the ultimate decision maker is the parent, and there is little consideration for a child's wishes. Meant for all parents, not just mothers, Chua's book was controversial upon its release, and even though Chua never intended it as a parenting manual per se, it has gained widespread cultural cachet.

Chua, ethnically Chinese, linked the Tiger Mother strategy to Confucian norms, resulting in the modernization of an ancient parental style relevant for parents raising children in competitive school systems. Confucius stressed a top-down model of authority: the son does what the father demands, the wife does what the husband demands, and the ultimate way for a child to show respect for their parents or teachers is to succeed in school.

Extending these Confucian roots, Tiger Mothers (and Fathers) are frequently involved with their children's activities as a full-time job, tend to associate with other Tiger Mothers, and follow a strict set of rules. They discipline their children at a very early age and only allow them time for non-academic activities (as rewards) if compliance is high, academic achievement stellar, and if the activities will contribute to a child's resume.

Tiger Mothers are also less likely to compliment their children and may yell at them in public (even to the point of name-calling or physical punishment) or be otherwise demoralizing—anything to achieve their goal. Concerns about self-esteem, happiness, child development (outside of school) are hardly entertained. These humanistic notions are superfluous to the Tiger Mother. Creating little soldiers, obedient and compliant in every way, seems to be the sought-after result . . . the ends justify the means. (This is further written about in *Little Soldiers* by Lenora Chu and *Beyond the Tiger Mom* by Maya Thiagarajan.) Childhood is thought of as a "preparation" or dress rehearsal for adult life, not as a period to be celebrated or enjoyed.

In the Tiger Mother model, all aspects of a child or young adult's life are controlled, even decisions about friends and dating. Slacking off, free time, self-discovery, most social events, and childhood spontaneity are not valued or at best tolerated poorly. Is it any wonder that Tiger Mother cubs can be socially awkward? The child's conditioning (or should I say indoctrination) begins at birth. Competition for the best pre-K, best private elementary schools, best high schools, and of course the Ivy League is at the forefront of every Tiger Mother's mind.

There was a recent article in the local paper about a five-year-old from China who "wrote" a fifteen-page resume to gain admission to a preschool! In it, the child bragged about not crying, having wide-reaching goals, and working very hard. This reflects the obsession with education and upward mobility in China, which also exists in the US.

Problematically, the majority of the scientific evidence shows that raising a child like this can do harm, sometimes leading to parental resentment, depression, and other psychological problems, even suicide. For every Tiger Mother cub "success" story, there are dozens of lives wrecked by trying to meet another Tiger Mother's standards. Some consider it, especially the tendency toward humiliation, child abuse.

While my wife and I also wanted our child to have the most stimulating and promising academic opportunities, we guided him in a far gentler manner. Academic achievement is important, but we certainly did not want it to be a source of pain during his childhood. I value and love my son too much to ever call him 'garbage', force him to practice a musical instrument, or metaphorically chain him to a chair to do homework. I only hoped for him to become a happy, well-adjusted, socially aware, independent thinker with a fulfilling life. Fortunately, my wife and I agreed this ideal should be central to our teaching philosophy. Our values were consistent with the core competencies outlined by Ken Robinson's book *Your Child and School: curiosity, creativity, critical thinking, citizenship, collaboration, compassion, communication, and composure*. Notably, these are also the attributes of respected citizens in our country, so nurturing these values as parents can enable a child to become a positive member of a free society, not a totalitarian dictatorship.

Before our family moved to the West Coast, the Tiger Mother only seemed like a mythical creature to us. But upon arrival, they were clearly real. We saw them on a daily basis in our child's elementary and middle school. At first, I thought it might be good to be surrounded by such well-meaning, disciplined peers. But when we noticed the unhappy faces of the young Tiger cubs, we quickly ruled out the Tiger Mother parenting strategy. Max was, and is, fun-loving, social, compassionate, and respectful. There was no way my wife or I wanted to change that.

There were two public high schools in our community—one with a very high percentage of students raised by Tiger Mothers, the other with a smaller concentration. We were warned by friends not to attend the former school since academic competition would be too fierce. We chose the latter which luckily turned out to be a top-rated school on the national level. It was highly competitive but also respectful of the well-being of children.

The Tiger Mother approach does not work in our culture. Not only did Max outperform the vast majority of his peers (with and without Tiger Mother assistance), he had fun doing it, was intrinsically motivated, never had to be pressured, and is now as happy and well-adjusted as you can imagine. How did we achieve this? Read on.

Part of the Tiger Mother philosophy seems to be that a child must be taught to suffer early on to prepare them for more suffering, pain, and hard work later. This coincides with the modern-day myth that in order to be an expert at something and master it fully (like a musical instrument, an academic course, or a complex skill), all you need to do is practice ten thousand hours. Malcolm Gladwell, the public intellectual credited for popularizing various social scientific theories, is famous for touting this idea. The problem is that it's not true.

Detailed psychological studies have shown that practice only counts for about 12 percent of success. Other factors, such as the early adoption of a skill, childhood interest (thirty times more important than practice hours), collaboration, ability, and enjoyment are much more significant in achieving success than mind-numbing, repetitive practice. In other words, a child doing what he likes and what he chooses will be far more competent in a relevant skill than one who was told to practice that skill hour after hour.

As we raised our son, the local public library was filled with elementary-school-aged Tiger cubs, sitting for hours after a long school day under the watchful eye of their "trainer." It seemed cruel and in stark contrast to how my son was enjoying himself at the skate park, baseball field, surfing beach, or just hanging out with his friends. Making children work double shifts by forcing them to study for another four to six hours after a full day at school is as counterproductive as making an adult work two jobs for eight hours each. Any philosophy that hopes to achieve a child's optimal performance, both physically and mentally, must consider the child's natural interests, curiosity, and vitality. Pain does not prepare children for future pain. Resiliency, confidence, happiness, parental love, and achievement do.

Similarly, American education researcher Alfie Kohn talks about the detrimental effects that punishments and rewards can have on a child. However, rewards and punishments are the main tools of a Tiger Mother: reward academic success and punish everything else. A student or cub motivated by a reward will stop performing once the reward is gone.

Once you link any behavior to a reward, the behavior (which was previously done for free or just for fun) is extinguished.

> A simple story illustrates this. Once there was an old man living alone who was mercilessly teased by a group of ten-year-olds as they walked to school. Every day they taunted him with verbal insults, like "Your lawn is bad," "You're bald," "You're too old," or "Your house is falling apart." The man was at his wit's end and could not figure out how to stop it. The more he reacted, the more they delighted in upsetting him.
>
> One day he stopped the kids and said, "I want you to tease me again tomorrow, and I will give you each a dollar." The kids did as instructed and got one dollar each. The next day they did the same thing, but the man said, "I can only pay you twenty-five cents each."
>
> They said, "Fine, it's still money."
>
> The following day, however, the man said, "Sorry, but today I can only pay you one cent each."
>
> The kids looked at each other and said, "No way! I am not doing this for one cent," and they never came back again.

That is why we never rewarded Max, only celebrated his own intrinsic value as a person. This is a key component to the Lion Dad philosophy and exactly the opposite of what Tiger Mothers do. Since high school, I've seen overbearing parents: fathers who push their sons into football in order to revisit their own high school athletic fantasies and parents who boast about how smart their children are to impress others at dinner parties. You may have seen the same. Perhaps my greatest concern about the Tiger Mother model is how it can legitimize these thoughtless or selfish parental behaviors, allowing parents to excuse their overbearing actions as "tough love" for a child too young to know what she wants.

Even as parents around the country decry the Tiger Mother model, some may secretly ask themselves whether it might be worth using it to help ensure their child's academic success. After all, isn't a prestigious and top-notch education perhaps the best gift parents can provide their children? Beyond this, there is an "arms race" factor to consider: if the children of Tiger Mothers are snatching up the best academic spots, parents may think they have no choice but to adopt the same parental style.

Certainly, Tiger Mothers are a fact of life, and an intelligent parent must be prepared to compete with them. But this does not require parents to adopt the Tiger Mother approach. The exact opposite is true. The Lion Dad paradigm, a name that responds directly to Tiger Mother parenting, is an alternative path that incorporates the virtue of compassion to ensure a child's future.

## Introducing Lion Dad—The Anti-Tiger Mother

- A Lion Dad is more interested in his cub's happiness and health than his cub's academic success.
- A Lion Dad makes a point to have fun with his cub at all ages.
- A Lion Dad wants his cub to develop his or her own values, not those of the parents.
- A Lion Dad keeps his cub safe in all circumstances.
- A Lion Dad stresses thinking as opposed to blind obedience. The child does not raise himself or herself, but a Lion Dad is the guide on the side, not the sage on the stage.
- A Lion Dad knows that once the cub figures out why he or she is doing something, the cub will automatically figure out how it's done. Internal motivation is strong, especially with young, high-energy children. This is a primary focus of the Lion Dad: to harness internal motivation, values, and confidence so the cub can use them to thrive throughout life.
- A Lion Dad does not withhold love and does not use threats, time outs, physical punishment of any kind, insults, or manipulation. They don't use common gimmicks like gold stars, syrupy "good jobs," or other conditional reinforcement in an attempt to control behavior. When the child does something well, they are acknowledged and celebrated but not rewarded externally. The Lion Dad cub's reward is knowing that the a

# TIGER VS LION PARENTING

## Tiger Parents

This is the typical Tiger Parenting model with the parent in a higher position in relation to the child dictating most of the decisions

## Lion Parents

This is typical Lion Parenting with the parent and child on equal ground

Lion Dad is pleased, not an increased allowance, extra dessert, or other kind of bribe.

- A Lion Dad is never surprised at a good outcome, but he is always happy about it.
- A Lion Dad is not interested in training his child to comply in order to earn a living. He wants his child to design a life based on his or her own values and beliefs.
- A Lion Dad wants his cub to spread his or her wings, but he knows that the cub first must first develop the muscles to have functional wings. That's the Lion Dad's responsibility, at least in the beginning. A Lion Dad wants to get inside his cub's head and harmonize with them, not simply control behavior. Once the Lion Dad is allowed in, on the cub's terms, the real magic happens.

Our child is loved unconditionally, and by the time he was ten years old, he knew it in his bones. Our love and acceptance were not dependent on what he did or achieved. It has been a constant. We frequently hugged him, told him we loved him, and reinforced his self-confidence at times other than when he achieved. He did not have to perform like a trained seal to get our love, and now he knows this absolutely. He does not need other external proofs that show he is worthy. He knows this as an inherent foundation of his being. Yes, we are happy when he achieves, and we celebrate accordingly—not because life's a competition but because that happiness is a natural expression of how we feel about him.

A pair of Tiger Mothers lived across the street from us when we first moved to the West Coast. They were professionals and well educated, and I have no doubt they were convinced they were doing the right thing as Tiger Mothers. Max hung out with their child when they allowed their cub to play. Such moments were rare, as their cub endured frequent time outs while Max spent time outside with someone else.

## KIDS

Kids are people

Kids have their own thoughts

Kids have their own emotions

Kids have their own goals and dreams

Kids think

Kids are curious

Kids want to be heard

Kids know lies are bad

Kids like money

Kids learn faster than adults

Kids do not like to be imprisoned (time outs)

Kids will inherit the earth

Kids expect honesty

Kids see and hear everything

Kids can handle the truth better than adults

Kids crave respect

I found myself getting angry at these parents since it interfered with Max's play plans. I can only imagine how the child felt! That child always appeared angry and borderline scary. Although he was always in some academic after-school program, and we were constantly told how smart he was, that cub wound up at an average college. I fear, in the end, he will become an angry, resentful, and unhappy adult.

We also got to know another family in which the father stressed the importance of sports to his child. Once, Max and I went to the field to play football with them. I was shocked to see how the Tiger Dad berated, pushed, and threatened his child in front of us.

It was clear that this Tiger Dad considered himself "above" the child, acting like an iron-willed coach, demanding compliance and performance rather than treating his son as an equal. I just wanted to have fun with Max, joke around, throw the ball, and strengthen our relationship. It's true, the other child was better at football than Max, but at what price?

I always treated my son as a peer, although I was fully aware that I knew more than him and wanted to keep him safe. When he looked to me for guidance, I provided it as an equal, not an authority figure. Occasionally Max would say, "Dad, sometimes you have to be the parent." Nowadays he feels safe with me, tells me everything (almost), and is secure in his position in the world. Max does not take advantage, respects me fully (as I do him), and frequently asks for my advice, which I give respectfully. Many people comment on what a great relationship we have and ask how we were able to achieve this. I really don't know if the Lion Dad attitude was the cause or simply correlated with Max's success, but I'm sure it played a part. Maybe he would have succeeded with any parental style, but perhaps not as spectacularly. Certainly, it would not have been so enjoyable for both of us. He had only one childhood, so I wanted it to be a happy one.

Make no mistake about it, Max was a hard worker growing up. The Lion Dad philosophy is not a formula for a quick fix or free lunch, but it can help encourage children like Max to develop skills based on a child's own drive, values, and beliefs. Max scheduled his own tutors (although I helped select them). He scheduled his time, planned his courses, and seemed to find a groove that resulted in self-confidence, great study habits, and amazing time management. Hopefully what worked for us will be helpful to you as well.

I believe that real human beings will prevail against robots, and perhaps our story will inspire others to respect their children as people rather than treat them as objects to be manipulated. I do not consider my child my creation, my alter ego, or my shadow. He is his own person with his own thoughts, beliefs, and values. He will paint his own life canvas with whatever paint he chooses and about whatever subjects suit him. He will be able to display critical thinking, engage in enthusiastic learning, make ethical choices, be a deep thinker, and a productive member of society. I have no doubt about any of this. As a Lion Dad, I want the parental voice in my child's head to be one of support and love, not fear and criticism.

Even if your goals for your child do not include the Ivy League, or if you have certain limitations financially, the advice given here will help your child become a more successful student with a better chance of getting into a great school and, more importantly, having a great life.

| Traits, Values, Methods | Tiger Parenting | Lion Parenting |
|---|---|---|
| **TIGER VS LION PARENTING - GOAL OF THE PARENTS** | | |
| Motivational methods and rewards | Extrinsic - leads to internalization of parental values | Intrinsic - leads to self-actualization |
| Value of happiness | Not important | Very important |
| Parental love | Conditional on academic success | Unconditional |
| Child's values | Not considered | Considered seriously |
| Chilld's beliefs | Irrelevant | Relevant |
| Academic success | Primary value | Secondary |
| Primary parent goal | Control | Connection |
| Parental positioning | On pedestal | On equal ground |
| Parent actions | Doing to | Doing with |

| Traits, Values, Methods | Tiger Parenting | Lion Parenting |
|---|---|---|
| **TIGER VS LION PARENTING - EFFECTS ON THE CHILD** | | |
| Punishments | Frequent | Never or rare |
| Rewards | Only with academic achievement | Not linked to school or any behavior |
| Child's emotions | Resentment, anger, dutiful compliance | Many friends, happiness, achieving own goals |
| Cub towards parents | Obedience, outward respect | Love and respect are intrinsic |
| Cub refers to mother as | Mother | Mom or Mama |
| Cub refers to father as | Father | Dad or Daddy |
| Friendship | Few | Many |
| Usual result | Well-trained student | A leader |

INTRODUCTION

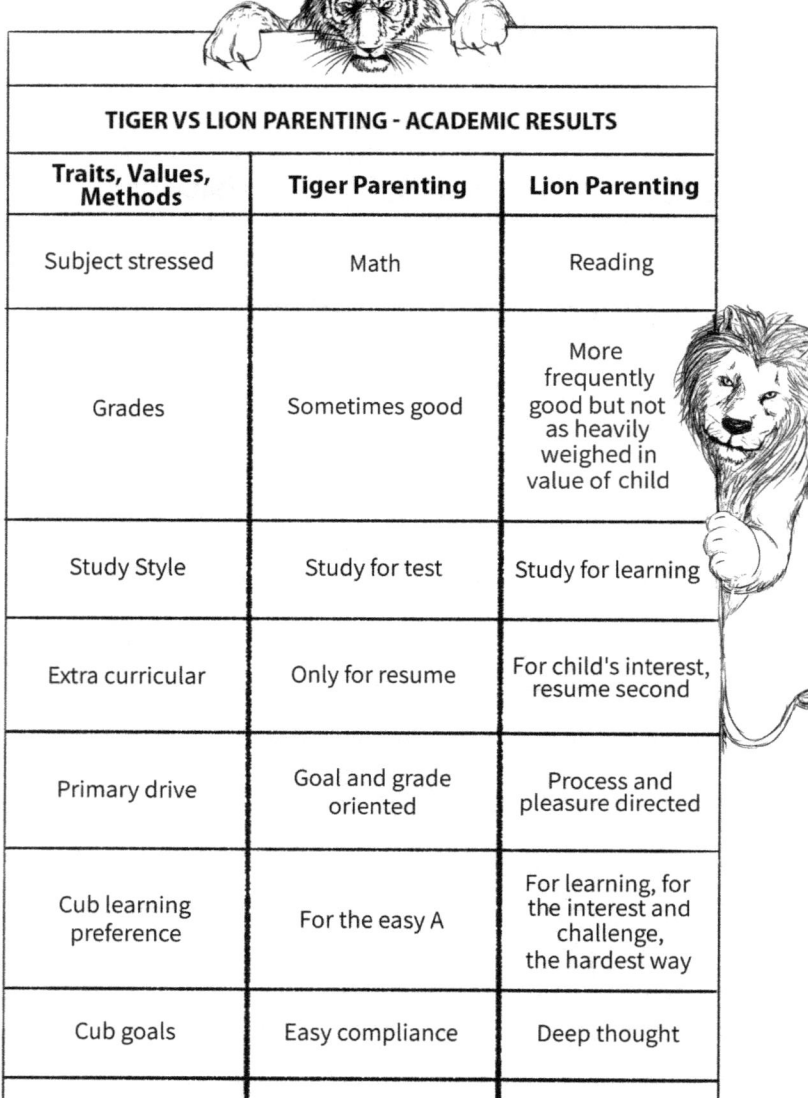

| Traits, Values, Methods | Tiger Parenting | Lion Parenting |
|---|---|---|
| | **TIGER VS LION PARENTING - ACADEMIC RESULTS** | |
| Subject stressed | Math | Reading |
| Grades | Sometimes good | More frequently good but not as heavily weighed in value of child |
| Study Style | Study for test | Study for learning |
| Extra curricular | Only for resume | For child's interest, resume second |
| Primary drive | Goal and grade oriented | Process and pleasure directed |
| Cub learning preference | For the easy A | For learning, for the interest and challenge, the hardest way |
| Cub goals | Easy compliance | Deep thought |
| Cub attitude towards school | A big test | An opportunity |

J K Roark M.D.

## TIGER VS LION PARENTING - OTHER DISTINGUISHING FACTORS

| Traits, Values, Methods | Tiger Parenting | Lion Parenting |
|---|---|---|
| How parent wants cub to communicate | Listen | Talk |
| Life goals | Earn a living | Design a life |
| Self image | What others think determines self image | What cub thinks determines self image |
| Teacher goals | Tell what to do Tell how to do it | Encourage the cub to discover the "why" of any action |
| What parent tells cub about how to evaluate a purchase or activity | Ask what it costs | Ask what its worth |
| Does parent apologize to cub | Never | Frequently |
| Thinking style encouraged | Shallow and wide | Deep thought |
| Competence | In school | In life |
| Comfort with themselves | Low | High |
| Final product | Excellent sheep | Thoughtful humans |
| Goals for childhood | A race for the top | A time for discovery |
| Goals at college or high school | Doing the homework Getting the answer Aceing the test | Using your mind Thinking for yourself |

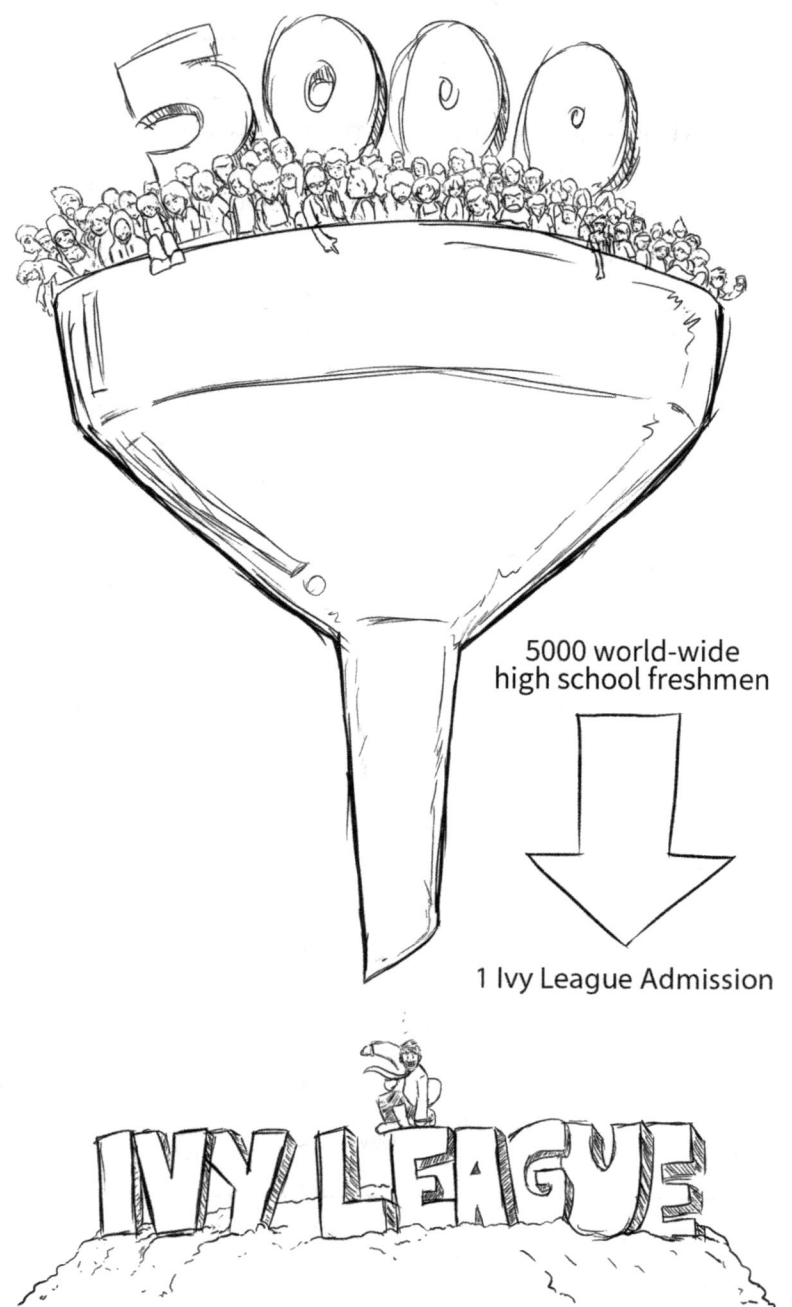

# 1

# WHY AN IVY LEAGUE OR ELITE COLLEGE?

## Is it Really Hard to Get In?
## Is It Worth All the Trouble?

*"Education is the best provision for life's journey."*
—Aristotle, philosopher

When our son was five years old, we submitted an application for the local elite private school (pre-K–12). Yes, it required an application, an interview, testing, and profiling. He got in but not for the year he applied for. They said he did not "test out" for kindergarten, so they offered him a spot in the pre-K class. Can you imagine? I still think it had nothing to do with my child's abilities at that tender age but rather had to do with needing another body in pre-K and having too many in kindergarten that year. After a great deal of debate, we decided to take the offered spot since we were convinced it was the best school (as they repeatedly told us) and that getting in at the ground level was preferable to not being there at all. Let the stress and insanity of college prep and childhood education begin!

In many areas of this country and abroad, childhood education creates a frenzy that has become uncontrollable. As we've seen in the 2019 Ivy League entrance scandal, people will do almost anything for their children and become swayed by crowd psychology and heavy marketing. Whether or not a particular family buys in to this frenzy depends on their values and vulnerability to mass hysteria. The book, *Extraordinary and Popular Delusions and the Madness of Crowds*, by Charles Mackay speaks to this phenomenon. So does *Excellent Sheep*, by William Deresiewicz and the 2009 film *Race to Nowhere*. These references are well worth checking out, and the earlier in your child's education, the better.

As it turned out, most students left our elite private school along the way, and soon the school had trouble filling spots at all. My son was born in the summer, so this made him one of the oldest in his class. The extra year ended up giving him a great advantage later. The maturity, experience, and extra time helped him. Among his peers, he was seen as a leader, an identity that became forged into his personality. Becoming a leader early on can pay huge dividends later in life.

During the first week of pre-K, I made an appointment with the headmaster, introduced myself, and asked him, somewhat tongue in cheek, "How do we get Max into Harvard?"

He laughed and said, "Just leave it to us. We will handle everything."

I guess that's what the parents at an exclusive private school want to hear, so that's what they are told. It was terrible advice, and fortunately, I did not follow his recommendation. Parents are the cornerstone of a child's education for many reasons. Handing over responsibility to someone else or some institution is a big mistake. You cannot simply write a check and delegate this. Remember what Mark Twain said: "I have never let my schooling interfere with my education." Wise words.

We made Max business cards with this quotation on it when he was three years old. He handed them out. He still has them and lives by those words. Max appreciates what school has to offer but does not limit his vision to whatever curriculum happens to be presented.

One conclusion that could be drawn from Twain's words is that college is a massive waste of time and money. This is not necessarily the case, but attending college certainly can be wasteful if not done intelligently. If you major in underwater basket weaving (yes, there is such a class), you may not be happy with your job prospects upon graduation.

For the purpose of this book, I will assume that the decision to go to college has been based on what is appropriate for your child and your family. If that subject has not been deeply probed, then please do so. Sometimes it's perfectly okay not to go to college. Many students and families borrow money they do not have to attend college and to take courses that don't matter in order to qualify for jobs that don't exist. This choice has significant ramifications, so consider it rationally and over a period of years, not minutes.

Whether or not the difficulty of admission, high tuition, and competitive peers of the Ivy League is worth the price is something each family must decide. Sometimes the lower-priced model works just fine. Some say that you can get just as good an education at almost any college, or even online, as you can get at an Ivy League school. Going to an Ivy League university, however, involves far more than academics, just as driving a Rolls Royce is far more than mere transportation. It's about style, choice, standards, and who you want to associate with.

In his book *Where You Go Is Not Who You'll Be*—An Antidote to the College Admissions Mania, Frank Bruni cites case after case of very successful people who went to obscure colleges that few people know about. Of course, that is possible and even likely, given the fact that there are only eight Ivy League schools and almost 4,000 others. However, the percentage of highly successful people coming from Ivy League schools is far greater than from other schools. There is no guarantee of future success, but going to an Ivy League school certainly stacks the odds in your favor.

The benefits of any college education have been discussed in many studies and books. On the other hand, there are more college graduates than ever before. In 1870, there were nine thousand students in college, most of them becoming ministers. Compare that to the 20 million currently attending about 3,600 schools today. With a college degree becoming commonplace, the employment market following graduation has gotten exponentially more competitive. A college education is no longer a guarantee for future financial success. So, counter to Mr. Bruni's assertion, I'd venture that where you go and what you major in are vital to career success. But with college education now as a growing business, the competition to get into elite schools is tougher than ever.

## DOWNSIDES OF THE IVY LEAGUE

There are a few key factors that may make Ivy League schools seem unappealing. The first is financial: they have sky-high tuition and no merit-based financial aid. Location may also be an obstacle to some since all of the schools are located in the northeast. Then, of course, there's the difficulty of gaining admission and then feeling like a small fish in a big pond if accepted. In other words, at an Ivy League school you will most likely not be considered the best student, but just one of many smart people.

Some parents and counselors advise that the opposite strategy—being a big fish in a small pond (i.e., being at the upper end of the class at a college)—helps distinguish a student. In other words, they recommend Ivy candidates apply to an average school so they can be considered the school's genius, graduate magna cum laude, etc. This, they argue, will make it much easier to get into graduate schools and give students time to enjoy the extracurricular activities that colleges offer. Going to such schools also opens up opportunities for merit-based financial aid.

## BENEFITS OF THE IVY LEAGUE

The original Ivy League schools were Harvard, Yale, Princeton, and Brown. Since there were four institutions (Roman numeral IV), they were dubbed the IVY League: pronounced "I-V." It's not due to the ivy-covered walls as many people think. As time progressed, four additional schools were allowed to enter the League: Columbia, Dartmouth, Cornell, and the University of Pennsylvania. The Ivies were founded between 1636 (Harvard) and 1865 (Cornell), with all but two founded before the Revolutionary War. The Ivy League was initially an athletic alliance meant to promote sports competition, but they have since grown to symbolize academic excellence, social elitism, selective admission, prestige, and wealth.

Once admitted, 80 to 90 percent of Ivy League students graduate in four years. This percentage is much higher than in second-tier schools and is a factor that should be considered no matter which school your child attends. The high graduation rate for the Ivies is likely because admission standards are so high and because the educational support is deep. No one slips through the cracks (although grade inflation may push some students through that might not have graduated otherwise.) When we visited the campus for our first parent weekend, I was very impressed with the multiple levels of counseling services, health services, food services, religious organizations, and other support services right on campus. You feel very taken care of.

The benefits of an Ivy League education include world-class facilities and resources that are second to none, including libraries and an alumni network that includes past presidents, CEOs, billionaires, and celebrities. Further, since Ivy League schools have multi-billion-dollar endowments, they can afford to hire faculty from the highest echelon of academia. The salary for an Ivy League president can be as much as $4 million per year! Much-lauded professors compete for positions at these schools, and many are Nobel laureates, celebrity professors, and persons with political clout. After being in such an environment, it's no wonder that Ivy Leaguers also earn higher salaries, easily get into graduate schools, and improve through academic rigor.

Some companies only recruit out of Ivy League schools. Why not? The screening is already done for them. In Barry Caplan's book *The Case Against Education*, he clearly points out the "signaling effect" that an elite school broadcasts for its graduates. It essentially a lifetime label that you are smart.

The amount of academic, social, and personal support is unlike that of any other collegiate institution. Recently, Max became ill with a high fever and was bedridden for almost a week. As expected, multiple friends and his RA (resident assistant) checked in on him, but he was also able to see two physicians at the on-campus health center close to his dorm, had food delivered to his room by the food services department, got a call from the Dean of Student Affairs, visited with a rabbi who came with soup, and had his meds delivered by the onsite pharmacy. The

Ivy League school he is attending is like a family. This may not happen elsewhere. We were also told that emergency medical services would respond within minutes if needed. You feel your child is being looked after by the top professionals, which was reassuring to us parents.

## How to Choose?

How does one weigh the benefits versus expenses? Here is an illustration of my own value system related to this choice. The other day, I was parked at a shopping center when the car next to me opened its door, hitting my car. Had I been in a Rolls Royce, I would have been upset. But in my ten-year-old car, I barely cared. Sometimes, the high maintenance costs of the Rolls causes too much stress and worry to be worth it. Then again, the values I used to choose which car to drive are different than the values I used to choose where to send my son to school. I economized on the car and liked its safety features, but we felt that money spent on a good education among elite students was worth it.

Other parents want their children to go to the most challenging school they can get into, regardless of the cost, and worry about graduate school later. They claim that being around a highly intelligent and accomplished cohort, the kind you find in an Ivy League school, provides ineffable benefits to students. At an Ivy League school, the people you meet and the groups formed are combustible in a good way. Ideas "ignite" in ways that might not happen elsewhere. Look at Google coming from two Stanford undergrads, or Facebook and Microsoft coming from two undergrads from Harvard.

Your child will definitely have an easier time of it academically if they rule out Ivy League schools, although that's entirely dependent on the field of study. (I am told the easiest pre-med program is at Harvard.) Some people want an easy life and others want to be challenged. As JFK once said: "We chose to go to the moon in this decade and other things, not because they are easy but because they are hard." You frequently become like the people you most often associate with, so being in the Ivy League definitely puts your child around inspiring peers who will likely spur them on to actualize their greatest potential.

J K Roark M.D.

## NUMBER OF STUDENTS IN THE USA OVER TIME

|  | Number of High School Students | Number of College Students | Percent of adults less than age 25 graduated 4 years of college |
|---|---|---|---|
| 1870 | 50,000 | 9,400 | 11% |
| Now | 56.6 million (k-12) 16 million (9-12) 3.7 million graduates/year | 20 million Includes part time, community colleges, and extra years to graduate | 31% |

Note: these numbers are approximate and vary by the sources. Use them for relative comparison not absolute values

Going to an Ivy League school is like going to Disneyland instead of a local park. One is a world class destination and the other is just for play. Yes, you can play in either one, but with who and with what?

Nevertheless, there are highly selective and excellent schools that are not Ivy League, such as Duke, Stanford, Vanderbilt, Rice, Wash U, Northwestern, and MIT. They are ranked in the same category but do not have the history, the cachet, the instant prestige, and generally the selectivity of the Ivies. However, individual tastes vary, and for many, other factors predominate: financial concerns, campus life, geographic location, alumni ties, etc. Not all parents aspire to send their child to the Ivy League or even think it's desirable. Then there are legacies themselves who have firsthand experience with the benefits. No matter where you fall on this spectrum, I say: set your sights high for your child. If you don't, who will? If they don't apply, guess what, they won't get in. There are dozens of very selective schools that provide an excellent education and are perfect options to consider.

## But let's face it, there are only eight Ivies.

Let me be perfectly clear on this next point: what you do with your education is much more important than where you go. I am sure that a student can have a wonderful life without going to an Ivy League school. There are many exceedingly successful people who did not attend Ivy League schools or who dropped out of college altogether. Having clear-cut goals and making good decisions are far more important than which school your child goes to.

That said, there's no reason not to aim for the top and do well there! Your child might as well have it all. He or she can still make good decisions and do well at an Ivy League school and benefit from everything it offers. Is it "worth" the effort, cost, and stress to go to an Ivy League school? It depends on how you define worth and what your family values are.

Ivy League schools spend an average of $92,000 per student as opposed to the $12,000 per student other second-tier schools spend. Ivy League graduates earn 39 percent more over a lifetime than second-tier grads, and 11 percent of Fortune 500 CEOs graduated from Ivy League schools.

This should not be ignored. Neither should the overwhelming number of Rhodes and Fulbright Scholars that were educated in the Ivy League or the high percentage of department chairmen who come from the Ivies.

It is obviously a privilege and of benefit to attend schools that offer the ultimate higher education experience. Figuring out if your family wants to put the time, energy, and money into applying to an Ivy League school is an individual choice and requires great inner knowledge. How many seventeen- or eighteen-year-olds can say that they know themselves well enough to chart a course for the rest of their lives? Ivy League schools are great places to discover passions and develop talents, but your child will need your support to get there.

If you want your child to be a part of the bastion of prestige, authority, tradition, and influence, try for the Ivy League. There are no guarantees in life, but you certainly tilt the scales in your child's favor by attending an Ivy League school. Just go for it! You only live once.

## IS IT REALLY HARD TO GET IN? *YES!*

Here is a seldom-discussed secret: Getting into an Ivy League school is extremely hard, but once you are in, you basically have to just show up. Ivies consistently rank among the top-fifteen schools in the country by *US News and World Report* magazine. Most are in the top ten, so an Ivy League education is synonymous with excellence in academics.

Enrollment ranges from 6,000 to 20,000, including graduate students. Freshman class acceptances are between 700 and 2,000 students. Since there are 3.6 million high school graduates per year in the U.S. (3.3 million from public schools, 0.3 million from private schools), the chances of a high school graduate attending an Ivy League school are about 16,000/3.6 million, or 0.4 percent. Since about 30 percent of high school freshman fail to graduate on time, the chances of a high school freshman attending an Ivy League school is about 0.3 percent. In other words, if you look at your high school freshman just starting out, and his typical class has thirty students in it, he would have to be the best student in 12 of those classes combined in order to be admitted into an Ivy League school.

## INTERESTING FACTS ABOUT IVY LEAGUE

| | |
|---|---|
| Number of Ivy League Colleges in the world | 8 |
| Number of other colleges in the U.S. | 4,000 |
| Number of other colleged worldwide. | 23,729 |
| Number of public hight school graduates in the U.S. | 3.3 Million/year |
| Number of private high school gradutes in the U.S. | 0.3 Million/year |
| Chances of a U.S. high school freshman going to an Ivy League (Assuming 70% high school graduation rates) | 3/1000 |
| Chances of a U.S. high school freshman going who is not also a legacy, recruited athelete, billionaire donor, faculty child or celebrity child going to an IVY League. (Assuming 70% high school graduation rates) | 1/1000 |
| Chances of a high school freshman worldwide who does not have a "hook" going to an Ivy League. (Assuming 70% high school grfaduatioh rates) | 1/5000 |

If you are not a legacy, recruited athlete, celebrity offspring, rich donor, faculty child, affirmative-action candidate, or international student, your chances are even less. How much less? Consider this: athletes can take up to 10 to 25 percent of the spots! Remember, Ivy League schools offer about thirty different sports, and they need players. Many of these sports (polo, fencing, water polo, equestrian sports, crew, gymnastics) are only played at prep schools for the rich.

Although football and basketball are also present in the Ivy League, they are no match for the Big Ten schools. (If attending these Big Ten games is a priority for you, don't go to the Ivy League. These football games and the school spirit they engender are definitely things I miss.) If your child has no exposure to or talent in these sports, their chances of getting into an Ivy League school are greatly diminished—regardless of their GPA and SAT results. In fact, Harvard rejects over 50 percent of applicants with perfect SAT scores, and there are only about 850 students per year who achieve that amazing result in the US.

Legacies (relatives of prior graduates), can also take up 10 to 25 percent of the class spots, although that percentage is changing at some schools. It even matters whether you are a first-degree relative (parent, sibling) or second-degree relative (uncle, aunt, grandparent, cousin). While on campus recently, I met a graduate who bragged that three generations of family members had attended this school. It's hard to believe that all of them would have gotten in without that connection.

The administration likes to downplay the percentage of legacy admits, but my son informally polled his friends and found that only about one out of twenty-five of the students he knows got in without some kind of "hook." Sometimes these hooks have to do with money, which often trumps merit in the Ivy League. They may be need-blind when it comes to admissions, but they are not wealth-blind when granting preferential admission to the wealthy. Is there any wonder that Ivy League admissions committees are frequently bribed with large sums of money even though, for the most part, it is considered crass?

Still, there are only three colleges in the US who admit students strictly on academic merit (no legacy, celebrity, athletic, donor, or minority preference): CalTech in Pasadena, Cooper Union in New

York, and Berea in Kentucky. They are not rated as highly as the Ivies, but more on the rating system later. None of the Ivy League schools are strict academic meritocracies, yet this is minimized due to the fear of this knowledge affecting the schools' reputation. The reason everyone wants to go to an elite school is the reputation of meritocracy and academic excellence being second to none.

If that reputation gets challenged or is doubted by the public, there will be fewer applicants and less money for the school. Schools have to strike a balance, but by the numbers, it's clear that money matters. Development cases (children of billionaires who have the potential to be big donors) can take 2 to 5 percent of the spots, and faculty children can take 1 to 3 percent of the spots. Celebrity children also make up another 1 to 2 percent of admits. People like Danny Devito, Kevin Costner, George Harrison, Ringo Starr, Sophia Loren, Jimmy Carter, Robert DeNiro, and Carly Simon have been associated with the Ivies. Some say that being a celebrity child is worth one hundred SAT points. Combine that with legacy status (another one hundred SAT points) and you have a real advantage. And while one can appreciate the benefits of affirmative action, as touted by researcher Leah Shafer of the Harvard Graduate School of Education, qualifying minority students often fill between 10 to 15 percent of class spots.

However, it's likely more correct to say that the Ivy League uses affirmative action for the rich and famous. The rich need more support and recognition as far as I am concerned. After all, many of them are responsible for great contributions to society, so they should be honored, not rejected. Yes, there are initiatives in place that grant large need-based scholarships for a carefully controlled percentage of the class, but no school can afford this aid for more than about 50 percent of the class. Personally, I see nothing wrong with the rich being able to use their hard-earned or inherited wealth to purchase things that others cannot afford, if done legally. That is the way life is. Some people or groups have things others do not. Deal with it.

The 2019 college admission scandal involving Felicity Huffman and Lori Loughlin shows that some parents are willing to pay millions to get their child into top schools. I do not agree with that practice, and both

## THE HOOKS

| Preferential Admission Categories | Percentage of Freshman Admissions |
|---|---|
| legacy | 10-25% |
| recruited athlete | 10-25% |
| celebrity offspring | 1-2 % |
| rich donor | 2-5% |
| faculty child | 1-3% |
| affirmative action candidate | 10-15% |
| Total Percentage | 34-75% |

the parents of these children and the institutions (with poor checks and balances in the admissions process) are at fault. Bribing is certainly not what's needed, but if you are a billionaire legacy donor who is on the faculty, and you or your child is a celebrity, and your child can play polo, your child will surely get in. Unfortunately, if your child has none of these hooks into the Ivy League, their chances are automatically reduced by at least 50 percent. Without any of that, your student's chances are about 1.5 in 1,000 (instead of 3 in 1,000), if that.

The Ivy League may seem to take a much higher percentage of students from private schools than public schools, but the percentage of freshman Ivy League admissions from public schools is actually 58 percent. That means if your child attends a public school, his or her chances of getting admitted to an Ivy League goes down to about 0.25 percent, or 1 in 400. Without any of the aforementioned hooks, it is more like .0015 percent. However you slice and dice these numbers, they are daunting and intimidating.

Still, the raw percentages can be misleading since the overall number of college applications are up by 30 percent since many more schools have started accepting the Common App. If each of the current 3.6 million high school graduates applies to ten schools, the number of college applications equals approximately 36 million per year. Frankly, we never knew or considered these facts until after Max was admitted. Luckily, since there are eight Ivy League schools which want to maintain full enrollment, it is still possible for the "hookless" to get in. There is always room at the top if you present yourself well and prepare accordingly. The code can be cracked, and our family is proof of that. We had no hooks at all.

According to many Ivies, 97 percent of admitted students are in the top 10 percent of their high school class. I am not sure how that is possible, especially when you consider the various special categories, but that is the figure published. That means that even with the advantage of the previously mentioned "hooks," the student still has to have stellar academic records. I recently spoke to the Dean of Admissions at an Ivy, and he disagreed with me about these percentages which I got from *The Price of Admission* by Daniel Golden. The dean pointed out that most of the legacy admits had higher grades and SAT scores than the average admits. Of course, they had the genetic and environmental benefits of being raised by one or two Ivy League parents, so it makes sense.

The published admission rates of the Ivy League schools range from 6 percent to 10 percent. Considering that only the top students even bother to apply, the 6 percent figure is somewhat deceiving. It's actually much less, as I described above. Also, since most Ivy League schools admit about 50 percent early admission, a regular-decision applicant (like my son) only stands about a 3 percent chance of gaining acceptance. Remember: that is 3 percent of the top 10 percent in the country who have the nerve to apply.

It may seem that the numbers are stacked against your student, but working to achieve this goal may not be in vain. Virtually all students admitted to the Ivies have a team behind them. You are the captain. Ivy League admission is not based on luck. It takes planning, skill, teamwork, and good decisions. Max got in without any hooks. He was not an athlete, celebrity, rich donor, minority, faculty, or legacy.

## LION DAD COMMANDMENTS FOR CHAPTER ONE

1. College choice is a family decision.
2. Take a hard look at what you can afford.
3. Research the differences among Ivy League schools as early as possible.
4. Make sure your child knows why he or she is going to college before going.
5. Visit all of the schools you are considering—in person.
6. What your child's education is worth is more important than what it costs.
7. Gather information, but decide as a family. Don't delegate this choice.
8. Do not rush life decisions.
9. Your child's academic major and work ethic is more important than where he or she goes.
10. Think deeply about your values relative to your college choice.

J K Roark M.D.

## PART B
# OUR STORY - WHAT TO DO

# 2

# BIRTH THROUGH PRE-K

## The Foundation of an Excellent Life

*"Experts tell us that 90 percent of all brain development occurs by the age of five. If we don't begin thinking about education in the early years, our children are at risk of falling behind by the time they start kindergarten."*
—**Robert. L. Ehrlich, Former Governor of Maryland**

It was the summer of 2001. Max was three years old. We were in the habit of spending the summers in Manhattan since he was still not in school. We loved the city and all it offered, and we needed to get out of the Southwest's heat, which sometimes reached 115 degrees. Strongly considering moving to New York City as a primary residence, we started looking for real estate and researching schools. Those plans ceased after 9/11. However, prior to that we were seriously investigating pre-K programs.

If you think the rest of the world is crazy when it comes to private school education, admission, competition, childhood pressure, and expense, then just try NYC! It's truly insane. Think $40,000 pre-K programs, $100,000 college counselors, exclusive elementary schools that make getting into Harvard look like a cakewalk, and parental planning starting years before pregnancy.

I am not kidding. It's an arms race fueled by mass hysteria if you ask me. Parental thought is controlled by their limbic system not their frontal lobes. The limbic system governs the sympathetic nervous system, among other things. It's part of the reptilian brain, and when it's in charge, emotion, not rational thought, controls behavior. In other words, it's fight or flight, kill or be killed.

We chose to move as far away from that atmosphere as possible. If elite school admission is one of your goals, know that the top ten schools want geographic diversity. With that in mind, moving out of New York City is smart since you'll face less fierce competition in another area.

Yes, very good schools and some very good counselors with connections to the higher ups are in NYC, but students are small fish in a big pond at almost every school in such a competitive atmosphere. I think elite schools have their quotas for NYC students, and they definitely have (and brag about) their geographical diversity when it comes to the number of countries and states represented in their class. The advantages of being around impressive students in high school should be balanced against the disadvantages of the same group of peers who are all trying for the top schools.

Even though Max was three, we felt we were already behind when we heard what other parents were doing for their children. Thinking it would be advantageous for Max, we had him interviewed and tested at the Hunter College School for Gifted Children. When we called, they asked, "What are you noticing with your child that makes you think he is gifted?"

"Well, he isn't composing symphonies, reading Japanese, or writing code—yet!" I replied. "But he seems bright to us." A full day of testing revealed that he was in the forty-third percentile! I was shocked. Below average! Were they kidding me? Not possible. How could they test a three-year-old with that much precision anyway?

Max did not get admitted, and I dismissed the whole thing as absurd. I was, however, disappointed even though I tried to rationalize it. It meant nothing to Max; all he wanted to do was dress up as a knight in shining armor and walk around Manhattan with his sword. I tell this story to make a point: Max was not born a genius with savant-like talent. He developed his skills, personality, and brilliance through sheer willpower, passion, guidance, confidence, and parental love. I believe any normal child can do the same. The concept of intelligence is overrated. It is so intertwined with environmental factors that it is becoming an outdated metric. No college asks for an IQ test, and for good reason.

The idea of an IQ test originated in 1912 and was meant to quantify an individual's memory, attention, and speed, similar to the SAT or how we quantify computer performance (processor speed and memory capacity). Two-thirds of people score between 85 and 115, and 2.5 percent score above 130 or below 70. These scores are estimates at best and are very dependent upon environment, especially within the "normal" range. Raw scores have also been rising dramatically, reflecting educational exposure. In addition to these failings, IQ tests, and tests like the SAT, do not measure emotional intelligence, grit, executive function, social skills, and other factors vital in determining future college or life success.

I believe that any child who does not have a neurological defect can achieve whatever they want as long as the proper opportunities, support, and parental love is present. Do yourself and your child a favor by not taking an IQ test. Once a child is labeled (especially if labeled deficient in some way), it can be hard for parent and child alike to overcome negative outcomes to the psyche.

On the other hand, if your child does get tested, results could have an opposite, positive effect, perhaps offering a placebo that raises self-concept and confidence. When I was ten years old, my dear mother took me for intelligence testing with the goal of steering me in the most appropriate direction. The testing was rudimentary by today's standards and in retrospect was ridiculous.

However, one thing about that experience stuck with me throughout my life. The "expert" told me, in front of my mother, that I was "very bright" and that I could do anything I wanted in life as a result. We felt relieved and, of course, proud. I used this "knowledge" as a foundation for my intellectual self-image for the rest of my life. If I did not do well on a test or challenge, I knew in my bones it was not because I had some cognitive defect. Either I was not interested, or there was a problem with the test. End of story.

Consider what a child who is told he has a low IQ thinks in those circumstances. It's night and day. In one sense, testing your child like this can be good if the "expert" and you clearly understand how it will be used and what the child will be told. This may seem like hocus pocus to some or even make you feel uncomfortable about lying to your child. In that case, don't take the IQ test at all. In my experience, however, this really works. The child will live up to their identity and the expectations of those around them. It is almost magical.

When my son was about four years old, we were walking to the park, talking about a variety of things, including what he might do with his life and what a great kid I thought he was. It was very casual and carefree. Then, out of the blue, he looked up at me in the middle of the conversation and said: "Dad, I really have a bright future ahead of me, don't I?" I could only agree profusely.

This is exactly the attitude you want your child to have: one of positive expectations. Creating that feeling takes time, but soon they'll feel it deep down, and that confidence will well up spontaneously. If that happens, you'll have done a good job in their first few years.

## **SHAPING CHILDREN FOR THE FUTURE**

The early years are the foundation for the rest of your child's life. There is now an enormous interest in quantifying adverse childhood experiences (ACEs) since it is becoming clear that distressing events from birth to age five have a significant impact on the future for certain diseases, both mental and physical. Social problems, depression, anxiety, early death, and many other pathologies can result from ACEs.

A young child can be compared to a pluripotent stem cell which is a cell that can differentiate into a number of different fully functional cells. In other words this kind of stem cell, when exposed to the appropriate epigenetic and environmental factors can become a liver cell, a skin cell, a brain cell, or any other kind of cell found in the human body. Once the change into a more differentiated cell occurs however, it cannot change back. A young sensitive child can likewise be steered into many different directions resulting in totally different endpoints. Once however they do so, it is extremely difficult for the child to revert back into a person with many potentials. This is the power of early childhood. In my opinion this period of development is very powerful if respected and exposed to the proper guidance and environment. The earlier the better.

The developing brain at that early age is much more sensitive to insult than it is later in life. A child who is exposed to pain, stress, yelling, chronic illness, or a negative environment that is dangerous or leaves them feeling unloved and resented will have a dramatically different life than a child who is pampered, kept smiling, well-fed, free of pain, and surrounded by love, smiles, and pleasure. In either case, deep-seated attitudes toward life develop which are extremely challenging to change.

You get one shot at this. Before age five is when their fundamental, life-guiding attitudes form. This is not the time to teach them about the "harsh realities of life" or how to "suffer the pain for the future." Nothing like that. There is plenty of time for that later, if you choose. It is also not the time to drill them with math or force piano lessons. This foundation is what they will tap into when all else fails. Make it a good one. We all know people who seem to always be happy and cheerful no matter the circumstance. This is why—they have a solid, happy foundation to stand upon. On the other hand, there are people who are always serious and intense. Now you know why.

This is a large subject with a great deal of current research efforts; it is an evolving field. Look at what happened to Romanian orphans in the late 1980s. The dictator Ceausescu enforced austerity laws which made conditions harsh for families. This led many to put their children in orphanages that became their homes throughout their childhood. They were neglected: never touched, loved, or cared for by anyone. Almost all have suffered from lifelong physical and mental problems, some even dying young. They were born normal but as a result of severe neglect in the first years of childhood they became permanently injured, cognitively impaired, and suffered from all kinds of diseases.

These orphans represent one extreme on the continuum of early childhood treatment, but it relates to situations that are more familiar. It is no coincidence that 95 percent of foster children do not graduate college, 50 percent do not graduate high school, and 85 percent of current prisoners in this country were involved with foster care at some time in their lives. There are now 500,000 children in foster care in the US. Childhood poverty is also a significant factor in early childhood development. It can place four-years-olds a full 1.5 years behind their peers since they are usually sitting in front of the TV, even with their own parents!

Does anyone doubt that early childhood matters? The die is cast in early childhood, for better or worse. Your job as a parent in the early years is to make your child happy. Period. I have heard that before, but it never struck home as strongly as when I experienced it with my son. The time, money, and energy you spend on your child during this period will pay off more than any other time in their lives. You have a golden opportunity as a parent during this period to have massive influence in a positive way if you do the right things, but always remember that the opposite is also true.

My mother once told me a story that I will never forget. It concerned a couple she knew who adopted a three-month-old child from Mexico and brought her back to the US. The new parents were concerned since the child never smiled, laughed, or reacted to much of anything. The doctors could find nothing wrong and were beginning to think the child was autistic. Then, by chance, the new parents hired a maid who spoke Spanish to the baby. She immediately smiled and lit up! It was the language she'd heard since birth. The baby felt at home and did well from then on as long as Spanish was spoken regularly. You must speak your child's language, verbally or nonverbally.

The successful child is the one cared for by loving parents, provided with every possible advantage, respected, appropriately stimulated, encouraged to have friends, given toys, music, played with, etc. This does not require being in a family with a lot of money. As Deepak Chopra would say: it's the "consciousness" of the parents that matters—the intention and the attention. A good example of this is Arnold Schwarzenegger, who became a world-class bodybuilder, real estate developer, movie star, and governor of California. He grew up with a stay-at-home mom and a father who regularly coached him in school and sports.

If neglected, orphans are on one end of the how-one-is-parented spectrum, Schwarzenegger is on the other. In between these two extremes

Age appropriate fun!

is everyone else. Where your child sits on this continuum will, in large part, determine his or her future. You have a direct pipeline to your child's unconscious mind when he is young, particularly when he is non-verbal. Don't miss this opportunity. It is during this period that the child's unconscious attitudes toward life, people, and the world are formed. It is during this time that the child "decides" if the world is a friendly, safe place or if the world is hostile, scary, and dangerous. If you want a successful child, make their first few years happy, and they will see the world as a happy place. They will have a success-driven attitude. This is a huge advantage. Remember: one chance.

## THE RIGHT ATTITUDE

How you feel about your child is perhaps more important than what you say. Children sense this and will evolve accordingly. They will prove you right, one way or the other. If you feel disappointed in them, they will be disappointed in themselves and perform accordingly. If you are hopeful, respectful, and admire them, they will feel that way about themselves. Make no mistake, your child's lifelong attitudes, for better or worse, will form in early childhood. And attitude is everything.

What is *attitude* anyway? As a pilot, I learned that the attitude of a plane is its position in relation to the horizon. A level attitude is when the plane is flying at a stable altitude, not pointed up or down, flying straight and steady. A nose-up attitude is exactly as it sounds; the front of the plane is pointed higher than the rest of the plane. This happens during takeoff or when more altitude is required. A nose-down attitude is when the nose of the plane is pointed down when descending or landing. It is much harder to take off (although possible) with a nose-down attitude rather than a nose-up attitude. And it is much harder to descend and land with a nose-up attitude than with one's nose down.

Your child is taking off in life. Give them the gift of a nose-up attitude: positive expectations and a happy, stress-free childhood. No pain, minimal crying, no hunger, attention, and a loving atmosphere. This will pay off in ways you cannot imagine. The time, money, and energy spent on your children during this critical period is likely worth ten times

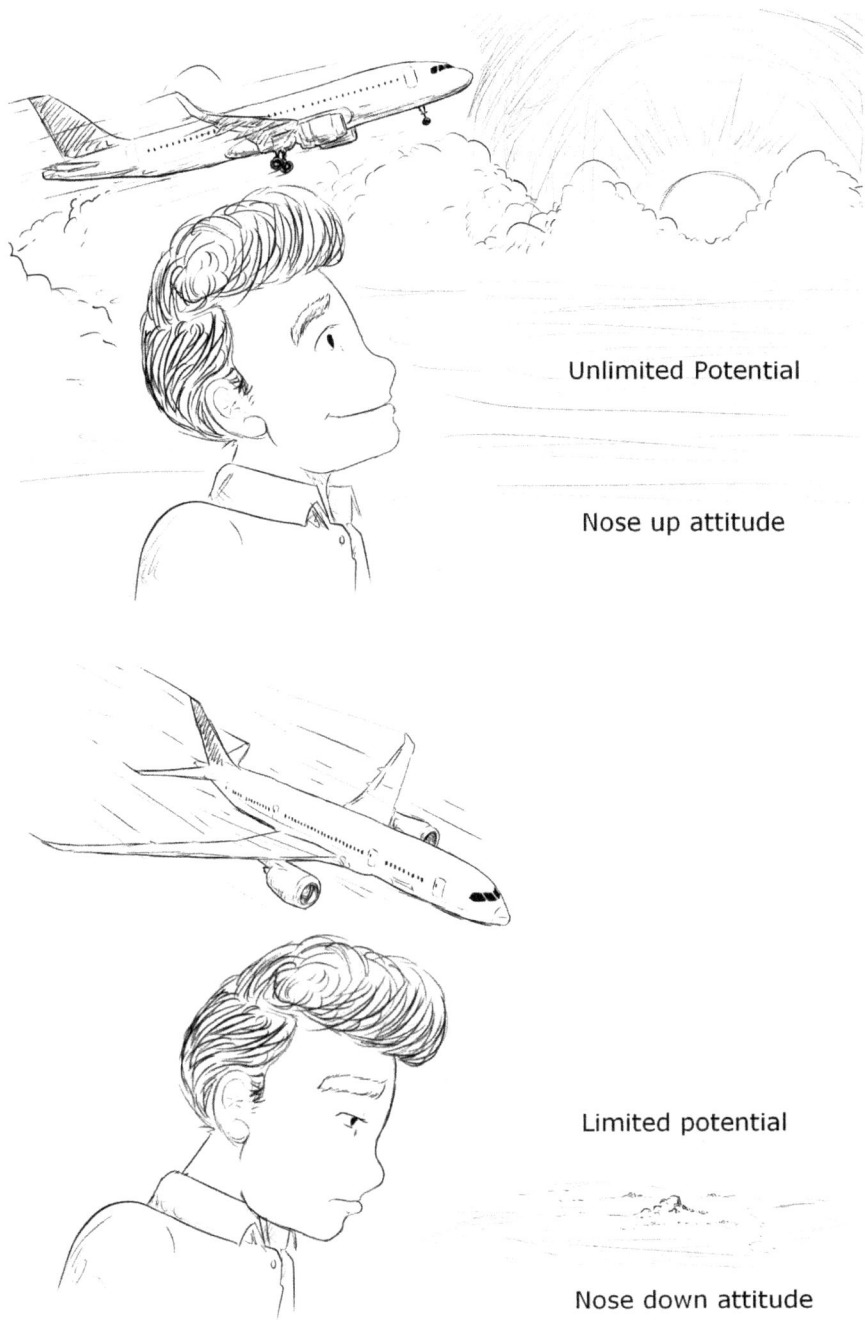

more than the same attention later in life, and it's far more valuable than SAT prep, college counseling, or extracurricular activities.

Today, how we raised our son is referred to as attachment parenting, and I fully subscribe to it. He slept with us for the first few years. He was breastfed for several years. We did not let him "cry it out" but rather figured out what he needed and provided it. We were careful about his food, his medical care, his environmental exposure (much more on this later), and his mood. He grew up laughing, happy, and curious. We started getting comments from other parents when he was four years old about how well adjusted, confident, and engaging he was. He maintained that attitude throughout childhood and to the present, even though he has had plenty of adversity. His high school teachers commented on how implacable he always was and how he was "comfortable in his own skin." This kind of emotional intelligence cannot be learned from a book or taught easily later in life. It has to happen when they are very young.

I recently spoke to Max and he commented that there are many students he knows who face mental health challenges like depression, even at an Ivy League school. He has none of that. This is one reason I am so appalled at the Tiger Mother way. None of this is considered when they berate, punish, and force their children to do their bidding, producing kids manufactured from a checklist. The Tiger Mothers defend this brutal behavior with two main rationales: 1) sometimes they are "successful," and their kids get into Harvard or the like; and 2) they claim their kids still love them and are even grateful for this kind of upbringing. That is erroneous logic.

Children who are abused by their parents still say they love them. Is that a justification for child abuse? The terror these children faced, and still face, in terms of fear of abandonment is almost impossible to overcome. If the only possible source of love that children have is a Tiger Mother, they will say they love their parent. Kids do not have the same frontal lobes as adults and are truly a captive audience. It's a variant of the Stockholm syndrome that describes how a hostage can bond with their captors. If a Tiger Mother acted toward another adult like they do to toward their child, they might wind up in prison, but somehow society tolerates this aberrant behavior toward children.

Max's current preparation for adversity stems from his happy, pleasurable childhood, not because we punished him or purposefully made him suffer in order to "prepare" him for future pain (as so many Tiger Mothers do to their own cubs). He has developed and maintained the triad of passion, curiosity, and grit that's so important in today's world. Again, I am not a child psychologist nor do I consider myself an expert in this area. I am simply telling you what worked for us. We fell into this pattern by instinct and then read about it after the fact, which confirmed this strategy as being effective.

Here is an analogy that may bring home the point that thoughtful and kind early parenting is worthwhile. Imagine a football player standing at the one-yard line facing ninety-nine yards to the goal line. A small five-degree change in direction will massively change where he winds up a hundred yards later. If, however, that same player makes the same five-degree change in direction at the fifty-yard line, the effect is much less, and if they are within five yards of the goal, it's negligible.

In the early years, your child is at the one-yard line with the entire field right there. Pointing your child in the right direction is not only easier at this time but much more effective. Mindfully protect them from undue stress. They have recently moved from the womb into the real world. Make it a gentle and happy experience. As a parent, you have a tremendous responsibility and are typically the one who determines what your child is exposed to. Take full advantage of this wonderful opportunity.

## **EARLY AGE NURTURING**

We read to our son, provided him with toys to play with that were safe and stimulating, and made sure his friends came from families who shared our values. We spoke to him and played classical music for him in utero. I will never forget when he was two days old, being breastfed in his mother's arms. I entered the room and said something to my wife. He immediately turned his head and looked at me right in the eye, showing clear recognition of a voice that he had heard in utero. It was magical. He was listening to me before he was even born, and he continues to listen to me.

Be careful about exposing your new child to loud noises or music. They have an immature, developing brain that needs to be cared for. Be respectful of it. I am including these details since you cannot fully explain how a child reaches the pinnacle of academic achievement (the Ivy League) without considering his environment at every stage, including prenatal. I could write several chapters on this subject alone, talking about vaccinations, lead exposure, chemicals in foods, GMOs, cow's milk, pharmaceuticals, nutrition, water, and many other factors, but in the interest of the primary subject of this book, I will be brief.

Suffice it to say that these elements are much more important than most people think, and whatever you can do to optimize your child's physiology will optimize his or her brain function. The Ivy League is actually a proxy for the real goal—optimal brain function, physical health, and psychological strength. Getting into an elite school is an indication of peak performance up to that point and should be celebrated and savored. Maintaining that level of achievement becomes easier when surrounded by similar peers, but it is up to the child to persist in excellence going forward.

At age three or four, many parents begin some form of pre-K experience. Be careful when selecting who and in what capacity will have this kind of contact with your child. This is not just babysitting. We rarely had a babysitter, and when we did it was a relative. Pre-K environments are variable. Some have enough staff, some do not. Some are clean, some aren't. Some serve healthy food, some do not. Some have a loving and patient staff with the time to attend to a few children, some do not. Occasionally you hear horror stories of children getting sick or being severely neglected in these facilities. It's up to you to carefully choose the environment in which your child will spend time.

We chose to send our child to a wonderful Jewish Community Center's (JCC) pre-K program. With adequate staffing, a safe environment, and like-minded parents, it was a perfect fit for us and our child. There was even a "graduation" with a cap and gown. The next time our son wore a cap and gown was at his high school graduation. It was a formative time; he did not get sick, had good socialization, and above all, looked forward to going. After the short day was over, I would ask him about his day, and he'd usually tell me about one activity or another. One day, however, he looked at me and said: "Dad, I have my own life."

He certainly did, and from that moment on I knew he would be fine. Few Tiger Mothers would say that.

There was one moment at a different pre-K program that illustrates a very important point. After the JCC pre-K semester, we enrolled our son into what we thought was an exclusive private school pre-K. He was only four and a little younger than most of the other students. I noticed that he did not like going to school every day, and it was disheartening to drop him off while he looked so dejected. Then we had our first parent-teacher conference. We had no idea what to expect and were shocked at what we heard. The teacher, and I use this moniker loosely, told us that our son was not quite as intelligent as the other kids and did not pay attention well. She also said that maybe we should adjust our expectations of him since "not every kid can go to college" and "maybe he would be suited as a manual laborer or something like that."

Can you imagine that?

I have replayed this event hundreds of times in my mind, fantasizing about my response. When it occurred, I said nothing. We did, however, immediately withdraw our son from that horrible place. It is absolutely amazing what some of these characters will say about your child when they are put into a position of power. The point is this: never, and I mean never, tolerate this kind of framing of your child, especially at an early age. Young children look at most adults as authority figures, so negative words coming from them get incorporated deep in a child's psyche and will stay with them for years, if not a lifetime.

Nowadays, I continue to experience a feeling of anger at how misdiagnosed Max was. This anger, I suspect, is a consequence of realizing just how momentous this occurrence was: if I had followed their advice, Max would be living a very different life. At the time, however, all I felt was shock and dismay. As I describe later, we faced this kind of situation a few times in the future, and other parents have talked to me about similar experiences with their own child. It's not that uncommon, and most parents try to keep quiet about it, or worse yet, take the advice to heart.

As a parent, you stand between your child and the world. You are the key person who influences your child's beliefs, values, attitudes, and self-confidence. Their goals are a direct reflection of you, good or bad. A child listens very carefully to their parents and other adults they have close contact with. They assimilate your values automatically. Think of them as little tape recorders, and be mindful of what you say around them because that's what they will say around others. It's a big responsibility, especially early on. Don't ignore it. A small child looks upon anyone bigger than them with wide-eyed openness and vulnerability. They can't discriminate as adults can.

When Max was age three and hugged Mickey Mouse at Disneyland, he reacted as if the Disney mascot was real, not an actor dressed up in a Mickey Mouse suit. He hugged Mickey Mouse as if he was a member of the family. Never mind there were fifty other actors dressed in Mickey Mouse costumes running around the park. As far as that three-year-old was concerned, that was the Mickey Mouse. Children of this age are open to everything, tend to take most statements literally, and soak it all up like sensitive recording devices. A Lion Parent is very careful with whom and with what their cub is exposed to. In the jungle, danger lurks behind every bush. An experienced Lion Parent watches closely.

When I see Max get straight As at an Ivy League school, feel excited about his future, and be fully engaged with people and events around him, I can't help but conclude that this started in early childhood. He was loved for who he was as opposed to what he did and became confident in the family and in the world. The pattern was established and is now almost impossible to break.

I dedicated an entire chapter for this topic because it is so important and frequently overlooked when parents are scrambling to find the right SAT tutor, the correct AP classes to take, the right college counselor, and the like. Bricks are laid in these early years, the foundation set. Without a good foundation, the house will not last, no matter how fancy the furniture, decorations, or flooring. Building a good, solid foundation in the early years will make it so much easier to achieve Ivy League admission and, more importantly, an Ivy League life.

## LION DAD COMMANDMENTS FOR CHAPTER TWO

1. Breastfeed as long as possible.
2. Carefully select who has contact with your child.
3. Minimize and avoid pain, hunger, crying without responding, loud noises, and toxins.
4. A strong foundation sets the stage.
5. Never accept negative remarks about your child.
6. Have positive expectations at all times.
7. Point your child in the right direction early.
8. Attitude is everything.
9. You are the captain—act like it.
10. The payoff for time spent with your child when they are young is far greater than when they are older.

# 3

# ELEMENTARY SCHOOL

## A Three-Step Method to Set Your Child on the Ivy Path

*"Every child deserves a champion—an adult who will never give up on them, who understands the power of connection and insists that they become the best that they can possibly be."*
—**Rita Pierson, teacher**

Max spent six years (pre-K to grade 4) in an exclusive private school that cost a great deal of money. This school was filled with over-indulged, spoiled, and wealthy kids. Most of the parents thought this was natural and did not give it a second thought. To them, their child was like any other possession: something to brag about and showcase. Yes, he had yet another year of pre-K since that was what the school recommended. But that extra year turned out to be a lucky break since he had an extra year to develop. He was also seen as a leader among his peers at school by virtue of his age. I believe this put him at a competitive advantage later in high school and therefore with college admissions.

Many psychologists and educators have written about how children who are older than their classmates develop confidence, leadership skills, and an entirely different self-image based on the physical and mental advantages of being further along in growth and development. This has been proven not only in academics but also in sports. Older children (compared to their peers) achieve more in sports and with college recruitment success than their younger counterparts.

Many parents are competitive and want to see their child propelled out of the gate as fast as possible, thinking they appear more intelligent if they are the youngest. That might be appropriate for some, but in my opinion, most children would benefit from the competitive advantage of being slightly older. Parents must weigh the psychological and academic advantages several months would give their child.

The first few years in this private school were great. There were exclusive parties where we got to know attentive teachers, administrators, and families who shared our values. There were expensive trips where we were pampered and got to mingle with the rich. It almost felt as if we were in an Ivy League elementary school, an attitude that pervaded throughout the school. It really felt as though we were in a feeder school for the Ivy League. We assumed your child was getting a much better education than the other kids in the neighborhood.

Was that true?

Absolutely not! I slowly learned that the real client at a school like this was the parent. They were the ones paying the bills. They were the ones being asked for donations on a regular basis. They were the primary focus of attention, not the students. I believe that most students would have done better in a good public school or with homeschooling. Naturally, the private school did not say this, but it was intuitively obvious to the most casual observer. There are some private schools that do get a high percentage of their graduates into Ivy League schools (Harvard Westlake and Pacific Ridge come to mind). This is how it should be if you are paying that much money. The school Max attended until the fourth grade, however, got only a small percentage into elite schools, really no more than average. In my opinion, they underperformed.

There is one school, however, that gets over 33 percent of their students into Ivy League schools. I found out about it from listening to a lecture by an investment guru. He moved to Puerto Rico a few years ago for the tax benefits primarily, lived in a gated community, and enrolled his kids into this private school. Why do they get such a high percentage into the Ivy League? Because their students can check the box that says they are Puerto Rican, which gives them an affirmative action edge. That's gaming the system. Whenever there is a system in place, some people will learn how to take advantage of it. I see nothing wrong with that, and most people do this one way or another for items big and small throughout life. That makes them smart, not unfair. They did not make the rules, the institution did. This is not the same as illegally bribing someone at the school for an undeserved acceptance.

In my experience, children with these advantages are suddenly rubbing shoulders with highly intelligent peers and do just fine after they get adjusted. You become like your closest associates, and as I have said several times in this book, that is perhaps the main advantage of an elite school.

Small private schools do not have the concentration of really smart, motivated students that select public schools have, nor do they have the ability to provide a wide selection of AP classes. The competition that develops among a cohort of smart kids at a public school will do more for your child than any fancy private school will. I suspect that private schools attract wealthy families with parents who attended elite schools and have raised intelligent kids. These kids will succeed wherever they go.

Private schools, however, use this success as proof that their school is great even though they likely have little to do with it. I know several private school parents who are disappointed in their school's methods and have to prepare their child outside of the school curriculum. As Mick Jagger once said: "It's the singer, not the song." Likewise, I say it's the parents, not the school.

When Max finally left that school to enroll in an excellent public system in another state, he was behind academically. In fact, they recommended remedial work in some subjects. It was a difficult transition since the curriculum at the private school was so flawed and the new public school was so much better. Private schools are all different, but they share a fierce commitment to maintaining their own reputation and the bottom line. This may be at your child's expense and is definitely at your expense. Sometimes they experiment with pedagogical techniques that are new and unproven in an effort to appear cutting edge. The Exeter math system is an example. I wonder if anyone understands it.

The earlier in your child's education that you transfer out of a flawed school, the better. It's much easier if done early. Transitioning to another school, school system, or state can be traumatic and at times require a major adjustment. It's not like eating at two different McDonald's, where you are likely to get the same hamburger in any city. Different schools can have dramatically different standards. We knew one child who attempted to finish the last year of high school in another school out of state and could not do the work. He had to move back to the system he was used to. The lesson is to choose your school system well the first time, and if that is not possible, transition as early as you can and into a school that's better. If we had waited until Max was in the eighth grade or beyond, he might not have been able to handle the switch.

## Spending Time, Not Money

When you have a child, he or she should be your number one priority. I have overheard many parents complain about their children and what they are "forced" to do for them. I feel sorry for that child. Others think of school as a babysitting service and spend no time with their child on homework or provide little support in helping them navigate the college application process. These children, for the most part, will not be competitive, will not get into elite schools, and will be handicapped going forward.

Once again, having a child is an enormous responsibility as well as opportunity. Take it seriously but have fun. There are plenty of wealthy parents who spend little time with their child. They think they can delegate everything, pay large tuitions, buy them expensive things, or hire the "best" counselors. These "strategies" rarely work. Wealthy professionals who have achieved a great deal have an opportunity to pass that knowledge on to their children, but only if they spend time with them, not money. Time and effort trump money.

I followed a simple three-step plan which I learned from Tony Robbins, the undisputed leader in self-improvement, to chart a course for

Time with your child is more important than money

my son. It's simple but powerful, and I've learned a great deal from him as well as from similar authors.

> **Step 1** – Know Your Outcome. In this case, it's getting your child into an Ivy League school or similar college. The outcome could be anything, however.
>
> **Step 2** – Take Massive Action. In other words, do whatever you know how to do even with incomplete knowledge. Try everything.
>
> **Step 3** – See What You Get. Once you've acted, evaluate the results and make the appropriate adjustments.

Keeping this strategy in mind, especially with something that takes many years to achieve, it will almost always result in success. Jet pilots taking off for a destination three thousand miles away know their goal. They start off with certain instrument settings, make hundreds if not thousands of changes along the way, and then land on a dime. They don't get stuck on the initial course if it's not working or the winds change. There's constant surveillance, constant learning, constant feedback.

Every child is unique, reacting differently to the environments they're exposed to. Your child will require your loving oversight to guide them along the way. You are the producer and the director of this film. This is what we did in a nutshell. The rest are just details, adjustments, and faith.

## Affluenza

When we first moved to the West Coast and Max was entering the fifth grade, I frequently went to a local gym with a dry sauna. In that sauna, I often had interesting conversations with the other men. One told me he had recently sold his business for $50 million. He was only forty years old and had three school-aged children. I asked him where he lived, expecting to hear about some exclusive enclave worth at least $5 million. He told me he had purchased a very modest house in a working-class neighborhood that cost about $150,000—in other words, well below his financial ability. When I asked why, he said that he wanted to give his three children a normal childhood.

Without them knowing how rich they really were, he thought they would develop good values, a stable work ethic, and become friends with their neighbors. He felt the kids would benefit much more from this experience than living in a large luxury home in an isolated, gated community. Well, his plan worked. All three children became enormously successful by any measure, went to excellent colleges, and had families of their own.

I don't know if they ever actually found out how well off their parents were, but sheltering them from that knowledge obviously helped them. It's important to immunize your children against "affluenza." Affluenza is a communicable disease and seems to affect children the most. There is a movie about affluenza which concerns a spoiled rich child who was indulged in every possible way and winds up getting drunk and killing several people in an auto accident. The public was outraged when he got a minimal sentence, claiming he was mentally ill from abuse as a child. We know people in our community with kids who brag about their "unlimited" piggy banks, expensive cars, and credit cards. This is not good for them in my opinion.

It appears to me as if growing up rich is actually a handicap for childhood development, as counterintuitive as that sounds. I have known a number of well-off kids sequestered in their fortresses, secure in their financial future, who drive expensive cars, and have unlimited credit card use. Many of them wound up doing nothing with their lives, a major symptom of affluenza.

As with any disease, prevention is primary, so just as you would wash your hands to prevent influenza, I would advise living modestly to prevent affluenza. Sadly, there's no vaccination. Max has friends with affluenza, some of them seem terminal. Maybe they lack motivation since everything is provided for them, or maybe they cannot imagine earning enough money to match their parents' lifestyle, or maybe it's something else altogether. I don't really know. The kids with their backs against the wall, who either have to do it on their own or not do it at all, somehow find a way.

The kids without wealthy parents are the ones with the fire in their belly and something to prove. They are the ones who start businesses, give out jobs, and live in big houses by their own labor. Then they usually spoil their own kids. That is why many have noticed that achievement seems to happen to every other generation. I myself grew up in a lower middle-class environment. I never thought of myself as poor, but I knew it was up to me and only me to make my way. I had no safety net. In my first semester at a state college, on a full scholarship, my mother sent me $100 for spending money. I sent it back. I was fiercely independent from age seventeen forward. If I did not have the money for something (which was often), I did without.

Private college was out of the question even though I could have gotten in. I was unwilling to take out loans. The same applied when I went to medical school on a full scholarship. In fact, I spent more on my son's private school pre-K year than I spent on my entire education through medical school. I spent more on the trip to take Max to his Ivy League school in travel expenses than I spent on my entire education. Different times. Different generations. I often reflect on that and wonder if Max was better off or not.

The best ground to grow a child who will knock it out of the park financially, socially, and spiritually is a modest, middle-class environment. Even though I spent money on Max's tutors, counselors, prep classes, and travel, I still spent far less than I would have for twelve years at a private school.

Still, I recently apologized to Max for providing him those advantages other kids might not have had. I told him it was a handicap he must overcome. He understands this. I could not help myself. I am not perfect. Max fully understood this and accepted my apology. He now attempts to be as independent as possible, thinks of ways to economize, and visualizes a time in the future when he earns his own way. It is far more gratifying to achieve in life based on your own choices and actions as opposed to inheriting it. The view from the top is so much better when you climb there yourself as opposed to being dropped off in your parents' helicopter.

So, yes, I do apologize to Max if it is warranted. I am not too proud. This is one thing a Tiger Mother would never do: apologize. Lion Parents do it as frequently as it is needed. Good values are learned by example, not by forced lectures.

I had a unique and painful childhood which I believe shaped my attitude toward parenting and will shape my son going forward. When I was eight years old, my five-year-old brother died of leukemia. When I was a teenager, I shared a bedroom with my younger, mentally handicapped sister. I tried to sleep with earplugs, but since we slept in the room next to my parents, I could still hear our father screaming in pain from lung cancer for months. I lost him at fifteen (when he was forty-one).

My sister has required lifetime care and is now in an institution. She had a seizure at age two that resulted in irreversible brain damage. I am her guardian and only living support. She has multiple medical, social, and financial problems which I do my best to manage. Coincidentally Max also had a seizure when he was two but had no lasting effects. Max sees all this and knows how lucky he is. He is extremely grateful for all he has. This is why I was so focused on savoring my only child by doing the best I could for him. It is one reason I developed the Lion Dad paradigm. Living through all this trauma gave me a very different outlook than most of my peers. It also shapes Max.

After the three kids of the rich man I met in the sauna moved out, he finally bought a big house. I thought about this encounter many times and modeled my own family around it. I was not in the same league as this man, but I had choices. I decided to rent in a modest neighborhood where kids played in the streets and we had significant contact with the neighbors. It was good for Max but difficult for my wife and me since we were living below our means and were not used to it. It taught my son good values about money, and I think this experience is a significant reason why he has accomplished so much. He is humble, respectful, and definitely not spoiled. This will serve him well. The neighbors where we lived had significant contact with Max, and their comments about him were helpful. They frequently said he was sincere and attentive, always looking them in the eye. He learned to be part of a community in a way that would not have been possible in a luxury compound.

## FOCUS ON SELF-EFFICACY, NOT SELF-ESTEEM

We have a family pet—a Labrador retriever—who worked her way into all of our hearts. She is a full-fledged member of the family and is especially important for Max, an only child. She is still living as we speak, and we do everything possible to make her comfortable in her old age. We love her even though she is on multiple medications and can barely walk. We frequently give her treats when she does something right or performs a trick. That's good for a dog, but not my son. I frequently praise my dog for no reason at all, and she seems to love it. She has great self esteem. I consider my son different from my dog, so I treat him as a thinking human, not an animal to be trained.

As you raise your child, remember that self-efficacy is much more important than self-esteem. Self-esteem, which is valued today more than ever, is a child's opinion of himself or herself. The prevailing theory seems to be that if a child has high self-esteem, they will use that as a basis for achievement later. But this theory has been proven wrong and does not work. It's always hard to fight reality and objectivity. Trophies for just showing up, constant and formless praise, frequent rewards, and enough "good jobs" can turn a child into an entitled, lazy snob. Just look at the millennial generation that was unfortunate enough to be conditioned like this, all with the good intentions of their parents. The road to hell is paved with good intentions. Good intentions are not enough.

Self-efficacy, on the other hand, allows your child to develop a positive self-image based on actual objective reality and achievements. They are praised when they do something well after working hard, overcoming obstacles, and achieving at a high level (compared to their peers). The key to this is a dirty word: competition. Somehow competition has become taboo, and we are told not to compare one child against another since it might hurt their fragile self-esteem. I believe that only incompetent people resist competition. Competition is good. There is no better way to learn and achieve. It's all about attitude. Give them roots and wings.

Achievement in the future is based and encouraged by achievement in the past, not by meaningless praise. If you are careful about when you praise your child, your child will develop the attitude that success is possible because of their hard work and effort. Therefore, try to limit your praise for things they actually do. Be as specific as possible. I am not saying limit your love. Love them unconditionally at all times. However, praise them conditionally. Don't give them trophies for just showing up. Sometimes distinguishing praise from love can seem like a fine line, but they are two different things. If you can communicate the difference between praise and love to your child, you will be doing them a big favor.

There are many excellent books written about the nature of elementary school education, many of which talk about how traditional education depends on rewards to function. In my opinion and experience, these first few years in school should not stress homework and should be fun for children while instilling in them a love of learning rather drilling specific facts or skills. Grades, rewards, and accolades based on certain behaviors are counterproductive, although that is what is usually done. Alfie Kohn has a recent book on the myth of rewards and punishment in school and in life. Neither practice has been proven to work, and they seem to even make things worse for child development in the long term. When you give a child an extrinsic reward for a certain behavior (like giving them an A for doing well on a test), it conditions them to the reward rather than fostering an intrinsic motivation to do well. Learning becomes only a vehicle to the reward rather than a primary motivation. Learning and, more importantly, the intrinsic motivation to learn should be the real goals in the first elementary school years.

You want your child to have their own drive and reasons to do well in school and in life rather than the extrinsic carrots you or the school provides. That is what will carry them the distance. You want them to discover their own why. Once that's done, they will easily figure out the how. However, most schools do this in reverse, teaching only about the *hows* through external rewards, hoping or not even considering whether the students formulate a *why*.

Try sending your child to a school that stresses teaching them the *why* rather than the *how*. Then, when the rewards are gone, your child's good performance will persist instead of disappearing as it does with reward-based learning.

ELEMENTARY SCHOOL

# Rewards and punishments are good to train animals but not your child. Treat them as people.

If a student discovers his own why, then he can figure out the how in any new environment. This perspective on the reward/punishment cycle is a major difference between a Tiger Mother and a Lion Dad. If you, as a parent, harness and understand this critical concept, your child will soar. It may seem counterintuitive, but it's powerful. There was an experiment done with preschool children that illustrates this perfectly. There were two groups of children. One group of ten was told that if they played with a certain toy, they would get a reward of some kind, which they got. The other group was just given the toy to play with but were offered no reward. After a rest, both groups were placed back inside the room with the same toy, told there would be no reward, and secretly filmed. In the group that previously received the reward, nine out of ten did not touch the toy at all, but all of the children in the group that received no reward continued to play with the toy. In short, the ones who did not get the reward found their own internal motivation and persisted in the behavior once they had a chance. The others lost interest since there was no reward.

## **The Prison of Time Outs and Forced Compliance**

Some of the parents in Max's exclusive private school were very competitive and wanted their child to surpass all the others. They not only paid the hefty tuition but hired tutors and made their poor children sit and do another three or four hours of homework after a long day at school. They stood over them and made them practice violin, do math exercises, play chess, and do anything except what they wanted to do, which was to play with their friends. Can you imagine the resentment these children must eventually feel? It's as if they were imprisoned for most of the day. Combine that with the time outs that are so prevalent today, and you can easily see how children come to hate school (not to mention their parents). How would you feel if you were imprisoned against your will, even if that prison is your room. Is it any wonder that many burn out and look at school negatively?

How did we "discipline" Max? Believe it or not we rarely did. Occasionally we would take away his phone for a period of time, but I cannot remember ever banishing him to his room (prison cell) or docking his allowance. I just could not bring myself to do it. I fully admit that at times we acted like Tiger Mothers, and I regret that. Sometimes we lost our patience. But he did not seem to need the kind of discipline his friends frequently received. I think it's more likely his friends received it unnecessarily. Just think about how a prisoner feels about their warden or prison guards. Do you want your child to feel that way about you? When some people hear this story they comment that we were just "lucky." I never discount any luck I may have in my life, but in this case, I think luck has little to do with it. I am not and never was Max's warden.

When he was still young, Max did something that was not too bright, dragging mud inside the house. He looked at us and said, "Okay, give me a consequence. I have never had any consequences!" I realized he was right. I never gave him "consequences" for his missteps. As parents, we talked and reasoned with him as if he was our equal, but we never punished him. Was I a bad parent? Should I have punished him for bad behavior or rewarded good behavior to "train" him into compliance? I just could never bring myself to do that. It seemed wrong, controlling, and a misuse of power.

I never wanted him to see me as some authority figure to fear while being totally dependent on my wife and me for his food, shelter, and security. I could easily have done this, as many parents still do. But I did not have the stomach or the heart to send him to his room, take away his allowance, or bar him from an event he looked forward to. He now trusts me unconditionally, tells me things that most parents never hear, and has a solid foundation underneath him. That is exactly how I want it.

Your children will do what you tell them. You are the center of their lives. They assume you are telling them the right thing. They don't question it, but that does not mean they will not suffer the effects of bad decisions. Our focus with Max during this time was to have as much fun as we possibly could. We traveled frequently as a family, had deep conversations, and explored many topics. As we traveled, we constantly pointed out curious facts, unusual environments, observed behaviors, and learned a great deal. (Some people think travel is the best education.) We played every kind of game, had our own special language (which we still use now at times), watched some TV, went to all kinds of events, and basically had a blast. We used to watch certain TV shows (like *Breaking Bad*) together and discussed them. I vividly remember when Max got engrossed in his schoolwork, I would literally beg him to come down for an hour to watch a TV show rather than study. He usually refused. He loved his work.

The key is to have fun with your child. Play with them rather than tell them what to do. Let them discover their own passions, not yours. Let them live their own lives, not yours. It's so much more meaningful when they do this, and you will have a much better relationship with them. They will have better, happier lives, be more creative and free, and thank you instead of resent you later in life.

This, more than anything I can think of in retrospect, is why Max did so well in spite of many obstacles in his life. I was his best friend, on his level most of the time. He confides in me and still does. I was never "above" him, watching for every mistake, and giving him time outs or "consequences" for every misstep. I would not force anything on him, only encourage the completion of certain educational milestones to satisfy school requirements. I was happy about his successes, especially the ones that stemmed from his own interests, but never rewarded him and never acted surprised when he did well. He knows he is loved unconditionally, and always has us to rely on. This gives him the space to design his life, not just earn a living or follow directions from the boss (who can be a surrogate parent).

## EDUCATION IS MORE THAN CURRICULUM

Ensuring your child has the freedom to develop an intrinsic desire to learn and succeed is vital, but that does not mean you should forgo your responsibilities as a parent and guide. A Lion Dad cannot ignore the demands of the real world including grades and comparative performance. But recall that we adhered to the famous words of Mark Twain: "I have never let my schooling interfere with my education." What he probably meant by that was that his education was innately designed and mapped out. The scope of it and the content was not dependent on a "school." In fact, we made Max a little business card when he was three with Mark Twain's quote on it. Eventually, he knew what it meant and is now an independent thinker. He has this card in plain view in his room today.

A Lion Dad believes it is far better to have questions you cannot answer as opposed to answers you cannot question. There is a difference between learning, education, and school. Sometimes they all happen at the same place, but in my opinion that's rare. Learning is like physical activity and going to the gym. You can go to the gym all day long but never develop physically if all you do is casually use the equipment or talk to your friends. Learning takes effort and internal motivation, just like training your body. An education is dependent on a good curriculum, and the school is where that happens. A good school provides the environment, peers, and examples to foster learning. The internal drive to learn is what makes school and education succeed.

It became clear to me when Max was in third grade that his private school was not good. There is research now that says third grade performance is pivotal in predicting future success in life and in school. I did not like the direction he was headed in the third grade at all. One day after school, Max turned to me and asked, "Dad, am I stupid?"

It was like a knife in my heart. Where did he get that? At our next parent-teacher conference, the elderly teacher who had been at that school for decades told us Max was in the bottom third of his class (there were only thirty students in the class). What was she talking about? I saw a very bright, engaging, fun-loving child who was confident, curious, enthusiastic, and intelligent. Was I going to buy into this assessment? After all, they were the experts, right? We were paying them the big bucks, so they must have known, right? Wrong.

Once again, we were facing an opinion that was not only contrary to our own observations but had the potential of harming our child so much that he was coming home questioning if he was "stupid." Obviously this environment was bad for him. Now that I reflect back on it, they were just trying to solicit a donation or foster a dependence. What I mean by that is that there always seemed to be regular fundraising efforts on the part of the private school, and it appeared to me that higher grades were dependent on higher donations. I have no proof of that, and I'm sure the school would deny it.

Still, we had so much invested in this school and hung on for another year before we got him out of there at the end of the fourth grade. Leaving it was the best decision we ever made, although it took years to figure this out and to undo the damage that this private school did. Max succeeded in spite of this private school, not because of it. It was a toxic environment, and we had the courage to walk away. Have confidence in your own observations and do not be overly swayed by the institution or the faculty's credentials. We have proven them wrong many times. Max has also learned from these experiences and has confidence in himself based on self-efficacy, not baseless utterances designed to increase self-esteem. Perhaps he performed poorly (as defined by the school) because he was bored or because there was a faulty curriculum or, more likely, an atmosphere so stuffy it could choke a horse. This school fostered an abrasive and intimidating group, making it such a relief to leave.

If you face a similar issue, make a change. Never buy into a negative assessment of your child, no matter who it comes from. Not from a teacher, administrator, doctor, neighbor, family member, or anyone else. Your child's self-image, confidence, and future values are at stake. Be careful with them and have the confidence, faith, and courage to take a stand. You will eventually be proven right.

## What's the Best Type of Schooling?

The choice between public and private school is a difficult one and very dependent on a family's circumstances, including the availability of both kinds of schools, finances, their child's psychology, and personal preferences. Many times these decisions are based more on the parents' likes and dislikes rather than what is objectively good for the child. The home school choice is also very viable, and I have known several families who made that choice. One of them had a child who waltzed right into Harvard after being homeschooled for twelve years. I cannot make conclusions about all private schools based on our near-disastrous experiences, but here are some general lessons:

- Private schools have their own agendas, and they usually revolve around their own survival and funding as opposed to what's best for your child, although they all claim otherwise.
- The small classes and individual attention you receive at a private school may be important up until about grade four. After that, the quality of the teacher and curriculum are more important. Generally, both are better at good public schools.
- Teachers at private schools stay for long periods of time and they brag about that. This is not a sign of meritocracy.
- Try not to compare your child with others in the same class, especially if the parents brag about them. More often than not, the quiet ones come out on top.

The teachers at the excellent public school Max attended were much better than anyone at his private school. Some of them were truly outstanding, having impressive backgrounds and great talent. Max did much better in the public system we were lucky enough to attend, but other public school systems are not as good, so be careful. We chose where to move, in part, based on the school system. Many parents did the same, which made the real estate prices much higher. As the center of your child's life and the director of their education, you should choose the school system and individual school carefully. If you do not have a great public school choice (like much of the country), then perhaps private school or homeschooling is better.

Homeschooling should be carefully considered since this can be ideal, cost-effective, and very time-efficient since you can handpick the teachers who come to your house and provide a curriculum at your child's speed. You also avoid putting your child in a class that teaches to the lowest common denominator and wastes time. Of course, your child will miss out on the socialization in public or private schools, but there are plenty of other social opportunities for homeschooled children to enjoy. In particular, they have the time to develop deep talent and interests in extracurricular activities.

One downside to homeschooling is the inability of the elite schools to objectively evaluate GPA since homeschooled children frequently get all As from the instructors you hire. My friend's homeschooled daughter had the time to develop her fencing skills, which helped her gain admission to the Ivy League. This would not have happened in either a public or private school setting since most do not have fencing as an elective, and the time demands of formal school would have prevented her from this activity altogether.

Boarding schools can provide a great educational environment, but some parents use them to get their child out of the house, not because it's what is best for them. We could not bear the thought of sending Max to a boarding school, even one that was a feeder school to Harvard. We enjoyed each other's company too much to even consider that option.

## TUTORS: REINFORCING YOUR CHILD'S EDUCATION

An individual tutor can tune into your child and know what needs reinforcement or what needs a cursory glance. We supplemented Max's attendance in a first-rate public system with tutors who taught Max one-on-one based on the excellent curriculum supplied by the school. We lived next to a large university with very competitive students, so I put out an ad for a tutor around campus and got back several responses, including CVs from a number of college students. We picked a very bright college junior who was an English major, graduated college in three years, and is now getting his PhD. He was amazing and taught Max many excellent things, especially in writing. He also helped us get two other tutors when he left, ensuring we had tutors for Max from grade seven through high school.

We had one tutor who got a perfect 2400 on the SAT on his first try and got an early decision admittance to Stanford. How would you like someone like that coming to your house and tutoring your son one-on-one? He was a fellow student at Max's school and approached him about the tutoring job. Another one was a physics genius getting his PhD and won many international competitions. He was good for AP Physics and AP Calculus. Then there was the student who graduated from Washington U in 3.5 years, got a full-ride to the University of Chicago Medical school, and started his own tutoring business in the six months between college and med school, which he sold to another tutor. He also got a 35 on the ACT. We became friends, and he has helped Max many times along the way. He stays in touch and will undoubtedly be a department chair one day. How is that for a good influence?

It was like our own private home school education combined with public school. He loved it and would do all the scheduling himself. These tutors became friends and mentors to Max, and they held him to the same high standard they had for themselves.

I did not stand over Max and make him spend time with those tutors after he spent a long day at school. We introduced him to this way of learning, and he took to it hook, line, and sinker. He repeatedly said the main reason he did so well in school was the tutors. Had he rebelled, I would have backed off. I also never gave Max extrinsic motivators like extra allowance, gifts, or other rewards for his performance in school. These extrinsic rewards are counterproductive and would have hurt him, contrary to what most parents think. I wanted him to have the chance to develop his own intrinsic motivations which would take him much farther, as it has. Extrinsic motivators would have hampered this.

Tutors cost between $15–$25 per hour, a true bargain. I would have paid much more, so I usually gave them generous bonuses when they departed to express my gratitude. I also had a specific bonus schedule for the tutors based on Max's performance, but Max did not know about this.

The word spread among the tutors, and I received many applications, having my choice in any subject I wanted. I was not concerned with the long-term effects of these extrinsic motivators for the tutors since they were all short-term parts of our lives, and they seemed to enjoy the bonuses. Plus, I was not parenting the tutors. Max, however, was learning to motivate himself, which he continues to do. He seemed to rise to the level of the tutor and eventually outgrew most of them. Some had to be let go since he didn't feel they were worth his time. Again, see what you get and make the change.

Max had a custom-made, one-on-one education that supplemented his excellent public curriculum. The results speak for themselves.

There are many opportunities to hire tutors like this for your own child: local colleges, bulletin boards around town, online sources (see appendix), and of course word of mouth. Here is where your maturity, practical skills, and experience as the parent can make a big difference for your child. Interview potential tutors, observe a session, and stay in contact with them. Know what they are doing and develop a friendly relationship with them. People work with and for others who they like. Make the tutors like you, whatever it takes. Pay them more than what they ask, on time, and with gratitude. Your attitude toward tutors will pay large dividends for your child.

Any properly motivated Lion Parent can follow the advice in this chapter. Remember that a Lion Dad can come in any race, color, sex, religion, or creed. So can a Tiger Mother. It's not about what they look like—it's about how they think.

ELEMENTARY SCHOOL

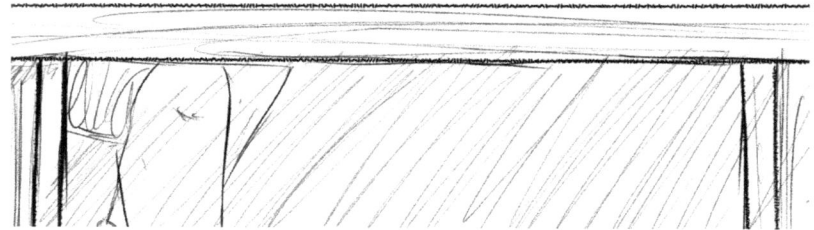

Tutors

## LION DAD COMMANDMENTS FOR CHAPTER THREE

1. Give your child the extra year if possible.
2. Never accept a teacher's or school's negative proclamation about your child.
3. Hire well-screened tutors yourself.
4. Constantly talk with your child and probe their minds.
5. Give bonuses to the tutors, not your child.
6. Follow the three-step plan for success.
7. Do not let school interfere with your child's education. Take control.
8. Observe your child's stress level. Customize your approach.
9. Harness intrinsic motivation, not extrinsic motivation.
10. Unconditionally love your child, no matter what the result.
11. Have faith in your child. They will prove you right.

# 4
# MIDDLE SCHOOL

## The Warm-Up

*"I had a science teacher in middle school who inspired me . . .
simply because she acknowledged me and made me feel
that what I had to offer was worthy."*
—**Marcia Gay Harden, actress**

*"What I'm really addicted to is getting people to understand
that if their kids aren't competent readers coming out of middle
school, it's really going to be hard for them in high school."*
—**James Patterson, author**

We moved into an excellent new school system in a new state after 6 years in the private school. Max entered the public system in grade five at the elementary level. Right around that time, our family experienced a life-changing event. We were on our way to the West Coast for the summer when, just a few blocks from our home, a drunk driver in a stolen car, driving on the wrong side of a divided road, broadsided us at sixty miles per hour. Our car spun around and was totaled. The other car burst into flames, flipped over, and the driver had to be extracted mechanically. It was a miracle none of us suffered significant physical trauma. The only reason we were not instantly killed was that we were hit in exactly the right location on our vehicle (a six-thousand-pound SUV). Six inches one way or the other would have meant instant death. It was a wake-up call. Life is precious.

Mary and I were both taken by ambulance to the ER, with Max coming along for the ride. He appeared unharmed but suffered considerable PTSD for months afterward. The other driver, an illegal alien, was deported after serving her jail sentence. The psychological effect of this experience likely compounded the difficulties Max had at his new school due to his poor private school education. Max also developed an endocrine disorder, most likely the result of the rapid deceleration and spinning from the impact. The pituitary gland, located in the brain, can be traumatized by the sudden deceleration during an auto accident. He needed thyroid supplements after that, and my wife and I both had physical and psychological trauma, which took years to resolve.

## PROFESSIONAL OPINIONS

Due to all these factors, we had Max evaluated by a highly recommended developmental psychologist who specialized in children's education. We also had concerns that Max might have attention deficit disorder (ADD). My wife has some tendency toward it, and Max was not doing well in school. The psychologist ran a suite of tests on Max, had interviews with him and us, and wrote up a comprehensive report. She said a few things that were shocking:

1. "Max is not very bright."
2. "He would never get into a UC school since no one gets in those schools." (University of California schools like UCLA, Berkeley, UCSD, etc.)
3. "He has not accumulated the knowledge that most kids his age have."
4. "He needs a special education plan (or even attend a special school altogether). You should notify his school so they can place him in a 'special' class."

We were devastated. Max was in tears, not because she said these things in front of him, but because of the heavy-handed way she talked to him. While I discussed special accommodations for him with the middle school counselor, we decided to see how he did without them.

As school progressed, Max did fine and got mostly A's after adjusting to the crowded classes and working with his tutors. Not only did Max get into several UC schools—including UC Berkeley, which is considered the fourth-best school in the world—he got into many other very highly rated schools including the Ivy League school he now attends and thrives at. He showed no signs of ADD, did not need a special education plan, was never medicated, and was considered one of the top ten students in his class. He graduated with so many honors and accolades that it was hard to keep up with all of it. Now, if anyone knew what this psychologist predicted he'd become, they would not believe it.

The psychologist's advice was completely wrong but left us with lingering doubts throughout the rest of his schooling. The whole experience was damaging. I wrote her a letter informing her of Max's accomplishments and how wrong she was. There was no reply. For her to issue predictions like that was unprofessional and obviously inaccurate. People with power can ruin a child's life if you let them. If we would have bought into her advice, our son's life would be completely different. He would have been in a special class, developed an identity like his peers', and would have never set his sights so high. I knew in my heart he was not as she described, did not want to burden him with that identity, and refused to accept it. We prevailed, and so did he.

Please do not delegate the opinion of your child to someone else. You know them better than anyone, even more than a so-called expert. How you look at your child is how your child will see himself or herself. Eventually, this is what the world will see, too.

This shows how careful you must be if you encounter the industry of neuropsychology. Its practitioners feed on the fears of distraught parents, charge a great deal of money, and justify the expense with lengthy reports that predict negative outcomes and prescribe special treatment for children. We got a second opinion from an MD who did not agree with the Ph.D. psychologist. Thank God we did, but even without it, I would not have incorporated her negative opinion into my psyche and never allowed it into Max's. People who make negative predictions about your child are as dangerous and evil-minded as a doctor who predicts early death. Stand by your child. If you are convinced that your child needs help with ADD or other neuropsychological problems, it's best to get several opinions. These problems are real but very over-diagnosed and over-treated, so be careful.

Fortunately, Max shrugged the whole thing off, but I can't say the same for myself. Whenever I think of it, I fume, even now. Discussing the damaging advice of other so-called medical professionals will likely be the subject of my next book. The lesson is this: believe in your child. Trust what you see and have a clear vision for him or her. If someone, even a so-called professional, disagrees with your positive expectation and tries to lead you down a negative path—walk away. Do not buy into it, and do not expose your child to these false beliefs. I had deep guilt about doing this to my child.

The fact that I am an MD gave me the confidence to ignore negative predictions and continue to have faith in my son because I am used to hearing inaccurate advice given to patients from all sorts of specialists, but I shudder to think what would have happened without my medical training. Children are put on powerful psychotropic meds and are labeled as deficient every day. The drugs and labels are harmful, frequently do not work, and are part of a misguided industry. It is corruption on an institutional level.

There are several good books on this subject, including those by Robert Whitaker, Irving Kirsch, Nortin Hadler, and Gilbert Welch. Whitaker's book, *Anatomy of an Epidemic*, proposes that psychotropic drug use changes the neurotransmitter receptors and leads to an increase in symptoms over time. This conclusion is reinforced by the dramatic increase in mental disease after the introduction of these drugs into society.

Kirsch's book, *The Emperor's New Drugs*, proves that most psychotropic drugs work no better than a placebo. Both Hadler and Welch's books speak about overdiagnosis and overtreatment being a much greater problem than undertreatment. In fact, the US accounts for 90 percent of Ritalin use in the world, and there has been a 700 percent increase in the use of these drugs (Ritalin et al.) since 1990. There are several other distinguished researchers, physicians, and authors writing along the same lines, and I'm sure the drugging of our youth will someday be seen as comparable to using leeches to cure diseases. This is a very large subject, and in the interest of the main subject of this book, we will move on, but it illustrates how careful you must be in guarding your child against environmental dangers, including "medical care," neuropsychological "evaluations," and psychotropic drugs.

I firmly believe that people like the neuropsychologist we encountered represent a clear and present danger to children, and as your child's advocate, you need to discern who those people are and avoid them at all costs. Your child's future is at stake. I have known more than one child whose life, school performance, and personality were ruined by legally prescribed drugs and bad advice. Many times drugs are used to zombify children because parents don't have time or interest to spend time with them. Once these drugs are started, they are almost impossible to discontinue, creating the impression that they are really "needed." They are addictive, change brain chemistry, and can make patients truly dependent on them for their functioning.

A veritable industry has emerged around getting students extra time on tests, special accommodations, powerful drugs, and educational programs. I am not saying these are never needed, but they are way overused. There are some private schools where 80 percent or more of the students are on psychotropic drugs and get extra test time to try and game the system. To get these "benefits," paying a fee is all you need to do. Don't do it. It's dangerous and not Lion Dad behavior. There are safer ways to optimize brain function.

## JOURNALS AND JARS

Gratitude and the commitment to lifelong learning are two keys to ensuring a successful life. Max has both in spades. When he was in middle school, I bought Max a "gratitude journal," which he took to willingly and eagerly. Every night before going to bed, he would write in it three things that he was grateful for during the day. They did not have to be big things, and often they were just notes about little moments that happened throughout the day. This practice helped develop an attitude of gratitude which he still maintains. Many people mention that Max always thanks people for things big and small. He is so appreciative of his life.

We also put an expensive glass jar next to his bed and called it the Jar of Awesome. On a small paper, he would write down something he noticed that was remarkable or awesome to him. This honed his sense of curiosity and observation big time. These are small things that I believe helped to make him the incredible human being he is today.

## MIDDLE SCHOOL, THE GATEWAY TO HIGH SCHOOL

Max did average to well in middle school, which is essentially a preparatory time for high school. Fortunately, he was in the feeder school for one of the best high schools in the country. It is now rated very highly on the US News rankings, both nationally and locally. The high school required a lottery to get in since people in the know rush to claim spaces for their children. Parents from all over the country and the world move here to try to get into this school, which has strict residency requirements. There are several excellent public school systems in the country, as well as several highly ranked individual schools. There is an enormous difference in the education your child can get at a top-two hundred school versus a bottom-tier school. Is it worth the time and effort to position your child into one of these schools? You bet it is!

The best teachers compete to get into top schools, the best students flock to them, and your child will be surrounded by inspiring peers. Elite colleges know which schools fit into this category. Do your research. If there are no excellent public school choices in your area, then consider homeschooling. This modality has several advantages, including better control of your time, increased efficiency, and easy tutor integration. A good homeschooling program is far better than attending a mediocre public school or a mediocre private school.

People are often constrained by their circumstances, but when a child's education is at stake, I believe a parent has an obligation to seriously consider their options.

If you have an excellent public school choice, then take it. If not, move to a place that does. If you can't do that, then investigate private options or homeschool. There is always a way. One of the reasons Max's high school was so good is that it attracted top-level students. Getting into a peer group with those students improves the chances of meeting higher standards than being in a small private school with fewer top students to interact with. The positive effect of a good peer group cannot be overestimated and that is one reason the Ivy League is so important. When you live, eat, and study with elite students for four years, you become a different person. Max has a poster in his room that says "Your life is a direct reflection of the expectations of your peers." I couldn't agree more. Give your child the gift of great peers whenever you can. It's one of the best things you can do for your child.

## **Finding Room to Grow**

In middle school, Max got his first exposure to film as an academic class when he took an elective that taught how to use editing software. This sparked something in him. He already had a basic interest in film but took it up in earnest after that. This turned out to be a major influence on his life. He won many awards for his filmmaking, enrolled in the film conservatory at the high school, developed two websites to showcase his films and advertise his film business, and won large scholarships as a result.

Middle school years are pivotal in a child's life, but they're not just for high school prep. It's a time when children grow physically and psychologically, when they develop a unique self-image, inner goals, and confidence. When Max started middle school, he said, "I will do the best I can in school and accept whatever grade I get."

By the end, he changed that philosophy to "I will get an A, whatever it takes."

This mantra stayed with him throughout high school, and it obviously paid off. This may sound like a Tiger Mother thought, except it came from Max, intrinsically. At the end of middle school, he had a fundamentally different self-image, which served him well later on. This self-image was based on efficacy, not brainwashing.

Your inner voice is incredibly important, and the younger your child develops a positive inner voice that doesn't limit goals and is accompanied by grit, passion, and curiosity, the better off they will be. Most people never develop these things. Max has all of it, and I am proud to say we fostered that in him consciously. What you tell yourself becomes what you tell others, which in turn becomes what they tell you. We always expected great things but did not pressure him. When he received a good grade, we never acted surprised but celebrated with him and were happy about it. The good grade just reinforced what we already knew about him, not an unexpected aberration.

Here's the key point: when your child succeeds, act happy—not surprised. If your child falters, remember that it's a learning experience, not something to punish or dwell on as Tiger Mothers do. It is in middle school that these lifelong values, beliefs, and identities are firmly established in your child's psyche. It's not a time that is as unformed and unconscious as the earlier years, but it's nevertheless very important. Max did not incorporate these values immediately. It took many years of positive reinforcement until he made them his own. Once a child does that, the sky's the limit. You will not believe what they are capable of. At times, other adults would hear about what Max had done and say "you are so lucky" or "he is so smart." It had nothing to do with luck, and although Max is intelligent, he is about average. This is one of the primary messages of this book. A child raised by attentive parents can achieve the same results.

In China, no matter how small an apartment is, a child has his or her own desk. This is not true in most US households. Students study at the dining room table or in the living room in front of the TV. It's very important for your student to have their own desk and study area. Max not only had his own desk but an entire room with tables, bookshelves, files, and chairs. He decorated it with his favorite posters. If a separate study room is not possible, try to establish a separate study area or time that the rest of the family knows is "study time."

I would wander into Max's office when I could not sleep, and sometimes I would look through his class notes. They were so neat, organized, and complicated. I was blown away. I couldn't remember doing that kind of high-quality work in high school, never mind middle school.

Where was this excellent work coming from? I could no longer help him with his homework after about the seventh grade. It was just too hard for me to understand, yet he was able to do it. I knew right away that he was in the right school, with the right peers, and getting the right tutors. Again, Max essentially had a one-on-one private home school education while going to a top high school with amazing peers. Is there any wonder he is thriving at an Ivy League school now?

The middle school years were the basis for high school. He was ready. The Lion Dad always has an eye for the future, has a bird's-eye view that no child can possibly have, and carefully monitors his cub's progress, always ready to make the adjustments necessary to land on a dime.

## The Power of Identity

Another very important event that occurred in the middle school years was Max's Bar Mitzvah. For those who do not know, this is a rite of passage from childhood into adulthood occurring at age thirteen. It is not just a symbolic ritual. It requires many years of study in Hebrew school and intense preparation for six to eight months. Max had to read Hebrew, chant verses, and basically lead an entire service in another language. He had several tutors, practiced intensely, and did a wonderful job.

The religious ceremony was followed by a large, extravagant party complete with over 150 attendees (including 65 of his friends) along with music, performers, a personalized *New York Times* issue, and lots of fun. Why do I bring this up? Because I am convinced that the rigorous academic work he put into preparing for this rite of passage at such a young age put him ahead academically. A strong connection to a cultural or religious group can definitely contribute to a child's success. It does not matter what the group is as long as their values are positive. It's not just about being well rounded or doing the right thing. It's about having an identity to live up to. It's about associating with people you are proud to be around.

Amy Chua wrote a follow-up book to *Tiger Mother* called *The Triple Package*. In it she attempts to codify the reasons exceptional students and groups outperform others. According to her, the key is a unique combination of: (1) identifying with and considering yourself a member of a special, "superior" group; (2) a sense of insecurity; and (3) impulse control. These are not necessarily Tiger Mother values but rather observations of successful kids. The list is a Tiger Mother's attempt to figure out what is going on with exceptional children.

Clearly Max had all of these. There's not room to explain the nuances of Chua's book, but being a member of a respected cultural group, going through a rite of passage into adulthood, a touch of insecurity as a result of his modest living circumstances, and impulse control could explain his spectacular success. Obviously, there is no magic-bullet as to why Max did so well—that is one of the key messages of this book—but there is magic buckshot.

## LION DAD COMMANDMENTS FOR CHAPTER FOUR

1. Protect your child from drugs, legal or otherwise (this includes tobacco and alcohol). They are neurotoxins and not consistent with optimal brain function.
2. Be very careful about selecting an "expert" to examine your child.
3. Believe your own observations, not those of people who pull you down, no matter their so-called credentials.
4. Be a member of a cultural group you respect.
5. Pick your child's school(s) well. Move if necessary.
6. Encourage the best possible peer group for your child.
7. Try to develop curiosity, gratitude, and wonder in your child.
8. Keep a close eye on your child's school work and know the terrain.
9. When your child succeeds, act happy—not surprised.
10. Have faith in your child.

# 5

# HIGH SCHOOL - I

## The Fundamentals - Now It Counts

*"I went to a high school reunion a couple years ago and realized that the kids who were the most unusual in high school are the ones who are the most interesting now and the ones who were popular are dull and boring."*
—**Anderson Cooper, CNN host**

Two friends were walking in the woods together. After some time, they noticed a giant grizzly bear just one hundred yards away charging toward them. They both turned and ran as fast as they could. One turned to the other and said, "We will never outrun this bear!"

The other replied, "I don't have to outrun the bear. I just have to outrun you."

Remember, your child has to outrun his peers. Think about this carefully since it may make a difference between the Ivy League and a second-tier school. Competition is a reality in high school and life. It's not usually life or death, but only an incompetent person avoids competition. This may seem like a Tiger Mother attitude, but it is shared by Lion Dads as well. The approach and methods are just different.

## High School - I

Everything before ninth grade was just a warm up for the real thing, high school. Now is when the rubber meets the road and careful choices must be made about which high school to attend (including which type of high school to attend) and what courses to take. You'll also need to know how to investigate and vie for the right teachers, how to select tutors to supplement each curriculum, what extracurricular activities should be encouraged, how close to the school to live, what to do over the summer, and how to establish lifestyle habits that optimize brain and body function, etc.

Just a little to think about.

Navigating all of this requires adult guidance, hopefully from a well-grounded Lion Parent. No student, unless they are very unusual, has the perspective, life experience, or judgment to make these decisions by themselves. I have known parents who have a let-them-figure-it-out-themselves kind of attitude. Lion Dads know this is a big mistake. It rarely works. Yes, the student needs to be involved and respected, but that's a far cry from throwing them overboard to sink or swim. You should not hover over your child (as a Tiger Mother would) to the point that your child makes few real choices. Rather, gradually let them go while gently guiding them along the correct path. Part of being an adult is to take advantage of the advice and judgment of those around you, especially parents.

Think of the pre-high school years as the context for the content in high school. Content is important, but without context, the content can be harder to understand. Content without context is hollow. It's like a house without a foundation. Always keep the context in mind when making choices for your child. What is appropriate, what are their talents, what are their interests, how does it fit with the family values, etc. Think about what your child can do in relation to what your child will do. The can in this equation is a function of skills, education, and abilities. The *will* is a function of preferences, motivation, and what excites your child.

## SELECTING A SCHOOL

I've talked some about choosing a high school for your child in previous chapters, but there's more to say. Before picking where to send Max, we looked at all the local schools, private and public. We toured them, interviewed, took admissions tests, spoke to parents, read blogs, reviews, and ratings, and labored over this extremely important decision. Consider your child's future just as seriously. The peer group you choose for your child will lift them up or hold them down. Do you want your child in a peer group that they have to live up to or live down to? This decision can be made rationally to put the odds in your favor.

By the time you are ready to choose, your family will likely be established in a community already and have a finite number of choices. Every situation is different and choices vary. Fortunately for us, we made the right choice, but we were not fully confident in our decision right away. It took time to develop over a year of investigation. The rating systems that appear on the internet are a starting point, but many of them consider aspects of the schools that may not be important or you and your family, such as a school's focus on a particular sport. Talking to other parents can supplement this research, but know that values don't always align, so don't be overly swayed by their opinions either.

Considering your child's goals should be central to this search. How much do you want your child to "stretch" himself? This requires astute observations combined with realistic goals that are consistent with potential. What do you really think your child is capable of? Err on overestimating your child's abilities rather than the other way around, but be careful about putting your child in a situation that's too difficult. There are no rules for this choice, but the relationship built over many years between parents and child will in large part inform this key decision. Your cub will ask for your guidance, so be clear. This is real pressure that will keep you up at night if you are doing it right. All of your knowledge, wisdom, experience, and parental skills will be needed.

In my opinion, the peer group that goes to the school is the primary consideration, followed by the curriculum, level of academics, teaching excellence, and proximity to the home. The first items on the list should be self-evident at this point, but subjecting your child to a lengthy commute both ways is not good and should be factored in. I have known parents who are so enamored by a famous private school that their child must make an hour-long commute each way just to attend. In most cases, that's counterproductive and even harmful. There is definitely something to be said for the neighborhood school, especially if it measures up in ratings and other factors. We hit the jackpot with Max's high school—close and highly rated, with great peers and a film program. I would compare the quality of education at this school favorably to the best private schools.

The peer group your child will encounter at a private school can be highly variable. Max stays in touch with peers who graduated from his high school, even visiting them when they come home from colleges like Yale, Princeton, Berkeley, Northwestern, Brown, and Harvard. They compare notes and hold each others' feet to the fire. They all know that they will see each other for many years. They are doing great things in the world and will continue to do so because of the standards set in high school, maintained by peers at college, and reinforced by each other. Excellence has become part of who they are. None of them are working at the local 7-11. In a sense, Max gets to benefit from the years of positive parenting most of his peers have been exposed to at home. It's one giant family in a way. You become like your peers, especially the closest five.

Private schools often attract families with money as opposed to excellent students. I still believe the highest concentration of excellent students (and teachers) are found in well-run public schools, not private schools. Of course there are exceptions, and a parent must figure all this out. Combined with the custom-made homeschooling program that we designed and implemented, it was a home run! The private tutors were only possible since our school was so close by and because we had that time.

If you think your options are limited, think again. Tutors of all levels can be easily obtained on the internet, and one-on-one interviews can happen via Skype or over the phone. There are websites (see resources) that have highly vetted tutors accessible from anywhere in the world! Local high schools, local universities, and word of mouth are all great resources. Even if your high school is not ideal, you can structure your child's education. Full-time homeschooling is a viable solution, as mentioned earlier. There are online curricula fully mapped out with standardized tests that are excellent. If we did not have such an ideal setup where we lived, I would have opted for homeschooling, and if that did not work out, online programs. There are some futurists like Ray Kurzweil and Peter Diamandis who think education will be dematerialized, demonetized, and democratized in the near future due to the internet. Why not be taught by the best talent online as opposed to the local ones? If you ever have the thought "we just can't do that in our circumstances," think again. There is always a way. *(Please visit resource section starting on page 305 for more on this topic.)*

When you hear the true story of a homeless girl who managed to get a full scholarship to Harvard while living on the streets (see the movie *Homeless to Harvard: The Liz Murray Story*, 2003), you realize your obstacles are minor in comparison. When colleges hear about a student immigrating to the US who cannot speak a word of English yet manages to get a perfect SAT score and good grades, they take notice. The SAT has recently established an adversity score that attempts to quantify hardships the child may have overcome. (Although it's a good idea, I do not believe that the way its being implemented is good. There are many factors not taken into consideration, and most of these adverse events can be described in the essay portion of the application.) Your child can do anything he sets his mind to as long as your goals align. It's a matter of cultivating your child's intrinsic motivations from the very beginning.

## Picking the Right Courses

As much as possible, plan your child's four years of high school up front, before the ninth grade. We hired an excellent college counselor for this. She carefully developed Max's resume, discussed course selection with the entire family, and made adjustments along the way. She was a vital component to Max's success and was not prohibitively expensive—far less than a private school would cost for even one semester. We had many other consultants, but the general college counselor was key to our process.

You want to select courses that are challenging and appear so on the transcript. Honors courses are not as important as AP classes since they are not weighted, but they still look good on the transcript. Each quarter-long class covered a semester's worth of material, allowing Max to take many more classes than a typical school and at a faster pace. Colleges noticed this big time. Elite universities want "sure things" from those they admit as much as possible. Picking rigorous courses at an already rigorous school is about a "sure" as you can get. If your high school has had students admitted to elite universities who have done well, you stand a much better chance of gaining admission. (See Naviance talked about later in the book.)

I made it a priority to personally introduce myself to every one of Max's teachers early in the quarter. Making that personal introduction to every teacher is key. It lets the teacher know you are deeply involved with your child's education and creates a partnership between you, your child, and the teacher. Teachers love this and will respect you for taking the trouble to do so. The best teachers root for and keep an eye out for the student who has a family like this. I believe it made a big difference for Max's grades in several key classes. Max made the same kind of personal contact by himself and continues to do that in college. This behavior says to the instructor, "I respect you, I am interested in your class, I want to do well, I am approachable for corrections, and I matter." This confidence and openness form an attitude (again, attitude) that is optimal for learning.

## THE RIGHT TEACHERS

Now that you are in the school of your choice and have selected the courses you want your child to take, it's time to get into selecting individual teachers that your child gets. Though this process is easier at private schools, you can still do some research and lobbying for your cub even at public schools. The right teacher selection can make a tremendous difference for your child. There are usually local websites with student ratings of teachers that talk about things like homework, testing, likability, accessibility, grading style, subject knowledge, etc. Sometimes there are great differences between two teachers teaching the same course. Unfortunately, many teacher rating websites focus on how easy it is to get an A as opposed to how talented the teacher is. This is a reflection of the conditioning all students are subjected to so they value the grade (reward) over knowledge. This can be insidious.

Max got a teacher for AP Chemistry (the class most students at his high school thought was the hardest) who was considered bad by most of the students, especially compared to the teachers available. Even the principal said he hoped his children did not have this teacher when they took AP Chemistry. I begged the principal to let us change, but no dice. We were stuck, and Max got a B. Our only option was to drop the class, which Max always refused to do (grit). At the beginning of her course, this teacher told the class that the course would "destroy all your dreams." Always think strategically. Outrun the bear.

## **WHAT A THING TO TELL HIGH SCHOOL SOPHOMORES!**

Lobbying for the good teachers means getting down to the nitty-gritty details. The techniques vary according to circumstances, but in general, make your wishes known as far in advance as possible rather than after the selection process occurs. You will be amazed at what can happen with the right attitude, preparation, and respect. We were not perfect at this, but we tried. It's kind of like picking out the best insurance company, bank, mortgage, house, or vacation. Careful choices work out better in the end and can prevent much heartache.

It was an unlucky break to have that AP Chemistry teacher, but we made the best of it. We made a point to meet with her several times, and Max did get one of the few As in the second quarter of the class. I think our lobbying helped, even though working with another teacher would have been better. If you can exert some control over who teaches your child, you can improve your child's GPA and make life easier. Of course, if you homeschooled you would have total control over who you hire, but the disadvantage is that there would not be an arms length distance between the teacher and your family. As a result, some colleges will have a more difficult time evaluating the GPA.

This same talent can be applied in college much easier. It's not just about the grade but the passion of the professor that makes a huge difference. Sometimes certain teachers seem to have a chip on their shoulder and want to prove to the world that their class is hard. At the same time, I have found these teachers to be less effective at teaching the course material. There is an art to effective teaching in high school, and I have the highest respect for a job well done. The ones who do it well truly enjoy the process, the subject matter, and the students. I still recall some of my favorite high school teachers from fifty years ago! Somehow they stick in my mind more than my college professors or even my medical school professors. Odd.

## Getting the Most Out of Tutors

We did not wait to see how Max would do without tutors. This was a primary component of his education and in many ways more important than classroom time. In a way, it was an apprenticeship in high school excellence, with the master craftsmen being students who had already achieved what he was trying to do. We started each quarter by finding tutors, and we incentivized them based on Max's grade in their subject.

The incentivization method evolved over time, like anything else. At first, I just gave them a lump sum at the end of every quarter if Max got an A. This worked at times, but later, we customized their pay depending on the class, interim goals, assignments, etc. Max was not involved with any of this. The tutor presented his bill to me every two weeks, and I handled the bill and the bonus (if any) directly to the tutor. That gave me a chance to talk to the tutor as well. I paid them on the spot. This also had a motivating effect. Some tutors wanted payment in cash every time they came over. It was inconvenient for me, but if that's what they wanted and what would keep them coming enthusiastically, that's what they got. Intermittent reinforcement seemed to work just fine as far as the bonuses were concerned.

The incentives encouraged the tutors to prompt Max to plan for tests, papers, time management. It worked, although he did get a few Bs. We used each time that happened as a learning experience, not a battering ram (as a Tiger Mother would). Tutors also taught Max how to collaborate with someone closely. This was huge. Collaboration skills are stressed by Lion Dads and almost ignored by Tiger Mothers who stress only competition instead. The attitude of the parents is as important as the attitude of the student. There is a balance between competition and collaboration that must be struck.

The best tutor is a student who did well in the same school and class as your child within the past five years. The subject is fresh in these tutor's minds, and they are less expensive, flexible, and will generally come to the house. Being an excellent student is not the same as being able to teach, however. Your child's tutors must have communication skills and be able to dive into your child's mind to discover hidden strengths and weaknesses. This combination of skills can be determined most efficiently by the parent. The tutors must have academic knowledge, communication skills, empathy, insight, and relationship skills. Sometimes, professional, full-time tutors with offices can be used for specific subjects. We tried all of them, leaving no stone unturned. Like our initial formula, we took massive action, saw what we got, and made adjustments.

## Grades: Letters that Matter?

Max's school had an online system called Aeries, which allowed parents and tutors to follow along with the class. There were about fifty entries per quarter for each class—every quiz, test, assignment, participation, and formative lesson tracked and weighted. It was an excellent system that allowed for frequent feedback. You knew where your child stood all along the way—no surprises. You could calculate what your child needed to get an A and work for it. Although the entire subject of grades could be debated, they are a fact of life that must be considered when you are trying to funnel your child into an exclusive school. Grade inflation is rampant, but nevertheless, it means something to get an A in an AP class or a challenging subject.

In some ways, an occasional B validates the As since it shows colleges that your child's high school isn't handing out As like candy. Grade inflation is everywhere, and colleges watch for it. I graduated college with a 3.2 GPA, which at the time was considered excellent and got me into several medical schools. Now I could not get into a community college with that GPA due to systemic grade inflation. Everyone gets As. The reputation of the school offsets this somewhat, but not entirely. Grade inflation increases the importance of the SAT and extracurricular activities. Grade inflation has been talked about since the early 1900s, so it is really nothing new. It seems as if each generation thinks the current generation is spoiled. It's still about outrunning the bear, so just deal with the current terrain.

This system of grading and tracking in a public school is far better than in most private schools, where grades are more subjective and require kissing up to teachers or the administration (in other words, donating extra money to the school). Unlike with Aeries, there is sometimes no feedback until the final grade, at which time you get a narrative about your child. I experienced this in the private school we attended early on. It was almost a blatant bribe solicitation. After a while, I am sure the big donors expected the private school administration to do anything they requested, including giving their children impressive academic accolades. Of course, this did not prepare the children of these rich donors for the real world, where they would eventually have to compete. This can hurt the child since they never learn to make it on their own, or worse yet, they get the idea that money can buy them anything they want. (Think of the recent bribery scandal.) It's always better to climb to the top on your own steam as opposed to being dropped off there in a helicopter. The view and experience is so much more gratifying.

I was always impressed with and respected how hard public school teachers work. My own mother was a public school teacher in NYC, and I frequently heard stories about her experiences. There are, of course, drawbacks to government-funded schools with top-down guidelines that can be inflexible. The textbooks, standardized tests, and milestone tracking can be cumbersome and a big distraction to learning. It is very hard to generalize about all public schools or all private schools. Use the best option you have available in conjunction with hand-selected tutors. To repeat, when I refer to a Lion Dad I do not mean to imply that only a father can do this. You can be a female Lion Dad, of any race, religion, or nationality. It's a philosophical orientation.

To make fifty entries per student per quarter, with over forty students per class, and teaching five or six classes is amazing. But somehow they do it. Still, sometimes mistakes in grading can happen, so a parent must be on top of this. It could make the difference between a B and an A. I watched this like a hawk (or should I say lion?). If there was a class in which Max was on the borderline for an A, I always met with the teacher to strategize and put them on the same page (it also let them know I was watching). Max did the same. It made a difference in several classes. I never acted in a disrespectful or threatening way and never assumed anything when dealing with them. That didn't keep me from joking with my son, though. When he'd ask what I said to the teacher, I'd say, "I gave them an offer they couldn't refuse."

I used the Aeries app, looked at it frequently, and put my two cents in when needed. This kind of micromanaging works big time if done right. You can achieve this without pressuring your child, depending on the relationship established early on. I completely disagree with parents who say, "I will let them figure it all out." To me this seems like an excuse to not be involved, and it's kind of like throwing them overboard with weights on their feet instead of fins, hoping they will learn to swim. Most likely they will sink. No child, no matter how smart, can figure this all out themselves and be competitive for the Ivy League. This technique is somewhat different than helicopter parenting since it's focused on school strategy.

A Lion Dad needs to protect his cub on the savanna. Eventually they will learn to prowl on their own. Now, Max does many of these things by himself, has no tutors except under rare circumstances, and is well known in the community. He is getting high As at a top school. He has learned how to learn, how to assert himself, and what to value. I fully understand that many parents have long work schedules, some with multiple children, and they can have limited time even if they are wealthy. Being wealthy in regard to time is more important. We all have three basic commodities to spend in life in order to achieve our goals: time, money, and energy. What you buy with those commodities is a function of your goals and values, but accumulating these basic commodities can give you great power. Think of your time, money, and energy as your "nucleus" of power. Once that nucleus becomes strong, it can be used to create a great life based on carefully considered beliefs and values.

## LION DAD COMMANDMENTS CHAPTER FIVE

1. Know the terrain.
2. High school choice is vital—start one year in advance.
3. Tutors are central, not just remedial.
4. Form cooperative relationships with all your child's teachers.
5. Course selection is strategic.
6. Micromanage grades, events, and schedules.
7. Use the school's online resources.
8. Give your cub the benefit of your own life experience and spend time with them.

# 6

# HIGH SCHOOL-II

## The Extras - How to Knock It Out of the Park

*"As you start your journey, the first thing you should do is throw away that store-bought map and begin to draw your own."*
—**Michael Dell, founder of Dell Computers**

There is no getting around it—a competitive student must be in good physical shape. The hours spent studying, the stress, extra-curricular activities, and the extreme pressures of elite school applications make good health habits essential.

Ideally, this means no smoking, drinking, drugs of any kind (legal or illegal), eating organic food, drinking clean water, no exposure to environmental toxins, regular exercise, etc. If you think you are getting your child into the Ivy League without considering all of this, you are wrong. What we are really talking about here is a lifelong standard of behavior that your child takes to every aspect of their life—not just school. In that sense, the Ivy League is just a proxy, a public announcement of who you are, your sense of life, your unwavering commitment to excellence, now and forever. It's not just about those four years.

I have seen parents ignore their child's drinking, pot smoking, obesity, and blatant disregard for food choices. Now the country is filled with overweight kids who cannot focus and have chronic diseases usually only seen in older adults (diabetes, hypertension, heart disease, etc.). Their youth will only carry them so far. In fact, they struggle to keep up with their healthy peers.

Parents who feed beautiful children microwaved, plastic-laden, processed, packaged "foods" or chemical concoctions not suited for human consumption are doing their children great harm. We have several close friends and relatives who appear to be on a lifelong path to ill health, obesity, and mental dysfunction all based on junk food.

I cannot stress enough the importance of healthy food choices. They will not only improve your child's brain function but also allow him or her to have a long, healthy life. You will be at a competitive advantage for the Ivy League and beyond if you establish good eating habits early on that the entire family follows. This is not the place for a long discussion on the details of this.

In general, no processed foods, no dairy, no chemicals, no GMOs, no animal products, no soda, no alcohol. Basically, follow a plant-based, whole-food, organic diet when possible. I have written only a few sentences on this subject, but this is by far the most important lesson you can teach your child.

Nutritionfacts.org is a wonderful resource produced by Michael Greger, MD. It is a free, evidence-based website that offers hundreds of short videos, articles, and opinions about food. I find this site to be a tremendous resource. Lifestyle is often underemphasized in conventional medicine since it does not involve drugs and surgery, but it is far more effective than most other interventions.

Looking around at the students at Max's college, it is obvious that many of them have adopted this healthy style of eating by how thin they are. There is no other way they could have achieved that level of excellence. I also noticed the same general good health and weight among the alumni, even years after they graduated. They have learned Ivy League eating habits and know that to stay competitive they must maintain them. If there is one thing and one thing only you should teach your child, it is how to eat. Most schools (including medical schools) do a very poor job of this, so the responsibility falls directly on the parents.

## Getting Physical: Exercise and Sports

Regular exercise is also a must, but competitive and brain-threatening sports like lacrosse, football, and soccer should be avoided. Never let you child headbutt anything. Sports like tennis, swimming, track, table tennis (our favorite), and the like are fine. Competitive sports may be good for some, but they require time and can become an additional source of stress. Some parents use their kids as proxies for athletic achievements they could not accomplish themselves. They push them to the limit, and for what? The chances of an athletic scholarship? That is much harder to obtain than you think. Fewer than 2 percent of high school athletes get recruited, and less than 1 percent of those (which translates to .02 percent of high school athletes) go pro. But if you don't mind those odds, and it's right for your child, go for it.

You have a better chance of getting into the Ivy League by straight academics than winding up a professional athlete recruited from high school or even getting on a college team. Second-tier schools have better odds, so if your child is good at sports like golf, hockey, or something other than baseball or football, then this may be the way to go. But it's still a long shot.

Please also consider the substantial amount of time spent in sports practice—sometimes four days per week after school, and that does not include the weekend meets. Remember, your child is supposed to do their homework after all that! Sports take significant time away from academics, and your child's grades will show it. The draw of high school athletics is strong and tempting. Parents like to attend events, students get to blow off steam, and sometimes it helps a child look "well rounded" on a resume. That's all fine and good, but I had a math teacher in high school who always talked about the "well-rounded idiot" in his usual sarcastic manner. I understood what he meant. Fortunately academics still rule. God help us if that changes.

Many people justify school athletics with hours of practice, drills, competitions, tryouts, and stress by thinking this is how their student can "stay in shape." It is true that a benefit of high school sports is fitness, plus there is the benefit of having team experience. However, if staying healthy and developing a lifelong habit of exercise is the main goal, there are more efficient and effective ways of doing so. Regular gym visits, weight training, interval training, ten thousand steps per day, or just push ups at home can be very effective. The point is seeing the results and developing the habit. It does not have to take a lot of time and can be a great way to develop friendships with exercise buddies. Staying in shape is a lifelong, daily requirement of peak performance, so try to have your child develop this habit while they are still living with you and by emulating your behavior. So many high school or college athletes wind up obese later in life since good habits were not established early or they got conditioned to the reward of trophies, accolades, and gold stars. Once those are removed, athletic behavior can vanish. Life is a marathon, not a sprint.

Academics is still the most important aspect of high school and college admissions so why take time away from that just to get a slight edge as an athlete? It made no sense to me, although I know Max could have been good in some sports, especially track. He made a point to regularly visit the gym and stay in great shape without the rigors of team participation. I did miss showing up for team competitions, but that is primarily an elementary and middle school experience. You are in the big leagues now (pun intended).

## Avoiding Toxins

The subject of environmental toxin exposure is a large one and also frequently overlooked. Diet goes a long way to address this, but air quality and water quality are both very important. If you can, don't live near a freeway or in a polluted city. We also have a whole house water filtration system that was worth every penny and keeps even the water we shower with free of pesticides, herbicides, pharmaceuticals, heavy metals, fluoride, particulates, chlorine, and much more. These chemicals absorb through your skin as efficiently as drinking, so be careful about what you put on your skin. Many of them are neurotoxins, like mercury or lead. Don't make the mistake of relying on the government to protect you. Again, this is a large subject, and I am barely scratching the surface here.

Max developed hypothyroidism as a child as a result of the car crash, but also because of toxic exposure. He started to gain weight, lose focus, and perform poorly in school. At age ten, there was a time he looked like a forty-year-old man with a pot belly. We had to see several professionals before getting on top of it. A few said he did not need to be treated, but I knew better and persisted until he received the treatment he needed. As a result, his school performance shot through the roof, he lost all his extra weight, and he looked and felt great. He still takes thyroid supplements and probably will for the rest of his life. Those tiny pills have helped him more than any tutor, SAT prep class, or counselor. Keep in mind he was replacing a deficiency and is carefully monitored. There appear to be many undertreated and under diagnosed children with thyroid disorders, metabolic syndrome, and diabetes today. If you compare a picture of children from fifty years ago with a picture of children today, you'll realize how obese and sick looking many children today are. If you know in your gut that there is something wrong and your doctor says there is not, I urge you to get other opinions until you find a physician with the background to properly treat your child. Supplementing a nutritional or hormonal deficiency is different than covering up symptoms with a strong drug.

## Creating a Healthy Balance

Along with diet, exercise, detoxification, and nutritional supplements, endocrine health is vital to proper brain functioning. An overweight, unhealthy body does not support optimal brain function, and you will never really know what your child is capable of until these five areas are fully addressed and optimized: diet, exercise, detoxification, endocrine health, and nutritional supplements.

The subject of childhood vaccines is a contentious one that I hesitate to mention in the context of this book. There are strong opinions on both sides, and I certainly have mine. All I will say here is that parents should be careful and make their own decisions based on research they do themselves. With the availability of the internet, it's not that hard. Max had some vaccines but signed exemptions for others. In general, evaluate the risk-benefit ratio for each vaccine. Make your own mind up on a case by case basis on this subject, but try to educate yourself so you can choose rather than delegate this to others. I see no benefit to injecting neurotoxins like aluminum and mercury into a healthy child. Herd immunity is a myth.

A brief word about supplements. We do not have the same quality of food that we had fifty years ago, even if it is organic. It simply is not possible to obtain the required nutrients without supplementation. I usually recommend at least a multivitamin, vitamin D, fish oil, magnesium, and probiotics. Many others can be helpful on an individual basis, depending on the clinical situation. There are tests available now that can determine individual nutrient needs as well as toxic exposures. Don't ignore this. Supplements can definitely propel your child much higher. Max takes a number of supplements daily, the combination of which took several years to customize, but it was well worth it. He takes no pharmaceutical brain stimulants, even before exams unlike so many students these days. He doesn't even drink coffee. He has learned how to optimize brain function without artificial stimulants, which offer short-term benefits and long-term harm.

How did we customize his supplements? This is one area of the book where I can claim to be an expert. I am board-certified in anti-aging medicine and holistic medicine, so supplements are very familiar to me. The Natural Medicine Comprehensive Database is one of the most comprehensive and reliable natural medicine resources for those without the training that I have. I would caution any lay reader to enroll with a functional medicine practitioner when developing a course of therapy for your child outside of the fundamentals mentioned before. As the saying goes, don't try this at home. Use a professional. It can require specific testing, monitoring, and observing clinical results. But to answer the question, we assessed specific deficiencies as well and focused on areas we wanted to optimize. After the initial studies, however, it was a matter of trial and error. It's truly amazing what concentrated nutrients can do. Alan Gaby, MD, and Jonathan Wright, MD, are two other credible sources. Gaby wrote the comprehensive book *Nutritional Medicine*, which took ten years to write.

Some say that as many as 50 percent of college students (as well as high school students) take psychostimulants like amphetamines to gain an edge on exams or help them stay up all night. Some of them do this illegally by obtaining them on the black market, usually from other students. These drugs are very dangerous, and hopefully you, as a parent, counsel your student long before college so that he or she can make good choices. They're simply not necessary if your child stays healthy. Kids who have a health program firmly in place will naturally steer away from this subculture, so that's another reason for addressing the aforementioned areas.

After working with Max over many years to design a nutraceutical and exercise program, I'm encouraged to know he's still following it and ordering his own replacement supplements (which I see online). That also assures me that he is not taking drugs or drinking, which would be completely out of character and inconsistent with his own values at this point. He also tells me spontaneously about others who take drugs when he was present. He has tried some of these substances, as any curious teen would, and he did not like any of them. He immediately noticed a decrease in his cognitive abilities, which is something he would never want to repeat. I have sent him many articles about neurotoxicity and drugs.

Again, working with your child from an early age, having them develop their own set of standards for their own reasons (intrinsic motivation) is more reassuring to a parent than any "promise" to be good would ever be.

## Counselors

Most applicants to elite schools have many counselors and consultants. If you think you can compete with them on your own, you are simply wrong. The playing field has changed, and you must have the same good equipment and advice as your competitors. Yes, your child will eventually have to make life decisions independently, but I do not think high school is the time to completely pull back. The intelligence, life experience, common sense, strategy, and organization you can add as an adult is invaluable. Your student should eventually fly solo, but not in high school when the stakes are high. Believe me, other parents are doing this, so if you want your child to compete at the highest level academically, you must do this as well. Do it respectfully, make the teachers, administration, and counselors your friends and allies, and do it in a way that your child understands and agrees with. But do it. It will make a big difference when you see that admission letter.

Counselor selection is a critical step and will be covered later in the book. It appears to me that other parents who have a hands-off approach to high school seem to think that watching their child sink or swim is the best way. As mentioned before, that is like throwing your child overboard with weights attached to their feet instead of flippers. Give them good flippers, a good mask, and a spear gun while you are at it. Their competition will have this gear. If you want to swim with the sharks, know the terrain. If you were playing a football game and everyone else had helmets and shoulder pads on, you'd want to wear them, too. The same goes for applying to elite schools. Provide good equipment and advice.

It takes a village and you are the chief. Judging by the parents I met going to Max's Ivy League school, they all agree and are deeply involved in their child's life at every level. These are children who have been successful and will achieve great things in life. They have the wisdom to understand that their parents are allies who can benefit them in many ways. They have the confidence in themselves to take advantage of their parent's guidance without it affecting their self-image or autonomy.

Yes, most students want to spread their wings and be independent. That's natural and healthy. It should even be encouraged, in stages. Part of being independent is knowing where and how to get guidance. Parents are a vital source of that guidance. Ivy League families tend to establish contiguous dynasties with intergenerational communication and respect. This is one of their secrets to success. This illustrates one key difference between the East and the West. The East worships the elderly, the West worships youth. Tiger parenting does have some benefits. The Ivy League will put you in contact with like-minded families you can learn from and collaborate with. Max's school has a Facebook group just for parents, and I can tell from the intelligent and enthusiastic conversations in that group that parental involvement is a key factor in getting a child into the Ivy League. His new school has students from over one hundred countries and almost every state. These families don't send their students far away from home at considerable expense, travel ten hours one way or more multiple times per year, or give up having their child close to home for no reason. They clearly see the benefits of an Ivy League education and are willing to pay for it with their time, money, and energy.

## **Extracurricular Activities**

What your child does outside of school is just as important for college applications as it is for your child's life. A good school wants to see that the child has something extra going for them besides grades and test scores. Extracurriculars give a sense of a student's life and the choices they make about their free time. I believe this—more than any other factor—is what distinguished Max from the pack.

To be clear, GPA and the SAT/ACT comes first. Don't think you can wow the admissions committees with great extracurricular activities to make up for low grades—this is very unlikely unless your child is the star quarterback or something comparable. Once the baseline scores and GPA are achieved, the extracurriculars rule.

Many Ivy League students have resumes that would knock your socks off. You wonder how it is even possible for anyone to do all the things they do. It is both intimidating and encouraging at the same time. You hear about the achievements of Max's colleagues and feel proud that your child is surrounded by such students, but at the same time, you have to guard against feeling inadequate by comparison. Someone who can be inspired by having high-achieving friends while avoiding jealousy and resentment will grow and benefit from such an experience. You certainly will have plenty of this opportunity at an Ivy League school, and this attitude will propel a student to ever greater heights as they progress through life.

But don't think that you can impress admissions committees with a laundry list of activities that are numerous but shallow. Your child's engagement in activities should be deep and narrow, not wide and thin. This means fewer activities over a long period of time, especially the unique ones. Something unusual that indicates passion, grit, curiosity, and creativity are golden. It cannot be faked or even planned too much since that would appear contrived. It should ideally stem from the student, organically and spontaneously.

What extracurriculars are valued? That's the wrong question. Elite schools want to see whatever the student is passionate about, continues over several years, and achieves recognition for. They want to have a variety of personalities and interests on their campus. A Tiger Mother would decide on an activity for her child based on her perception of what the school values. A Lion Dad lets the child choose based on his or her passions and then figures out a way to make it unique.

Ivy League admissions officers want to create a community that is balanced in its collection of unique individuals. They do not want the same profiles over and over again. That is one reason why many Asians students think they are being treated adversely in the admissions process, and there are currently class action lawsuits pending about this very issue. It seems to me that many of the Asian students have great scores, grades, extracurriculars, etc. This is all good and a reflection of extreme effort, but elite schools want unique individuals. That's one reason 50 percent of perfect SAT applicants are rejected at Harvard. They could fill up the entire class with perfect SAT scores or even with valedictorians, but how boring would that be?

There are roughly 37,000 high schools in the US, which means there are 37,000 valedictorians. Even if each one applied to the Ivy League, 40 percent would be rejected since there are not enough spots in the freshman classes of all eight Ivies combined! Who would want to live in a community with only valedictorians anyway? This is the fatal flaw of the Tiger Mother and why this mode of parenting is rapidly losing popularity. US schools value individuality not egalitarian conformity. Same with the rest of American society.

Max had a deep and unusual interest in film, which he maintained throughout high school. His awards, film websites, national recognition from several sources, and deep community service all stood out. He was a leader who was asked to speak at large, well-attended events many times. He had multiple press articles written about him. When he moved into his dorm, he met the school website photographer, who spent an hour with him taking hundreds of photos for a feature article that appeared on the school website. Only five students were highlighted out of the whole freshman class. When we were moving Max into his dorm, I got separated from him and my wife since I had to retrieve some items left on the sidewalk. As I was doing so, one of the other families looked at Max, the photographer, and then me to ask, "Who is that student that they are taking pictures of?"

I proudly said, "That is my son!"

The point is this: if you want to get your child into the Ivy League, have them do something new, innovative, unusual, creative, and important. Encourage them to do it over a long period of time. Help them stand out, not blend in. Ivy League schools do not want to miss the next Bill Gates, JFK, Zuckerberg, Supreme Court justice, president, actor, or celebrity. They want movers and shakers, not followers. They want leaders, original thinkers, not cogs in a wheel. It's your job to show admissions officers your child has this potential. It really is not as hard as it seems.

This type of person is consistent with what I would like to see my child become—an individual who can think on his own, has well-founded and thought-out opinions, and can influence others but get along with them at the same time. Such an individual respects others and thinks critically. He reads widely because he wants to, not because he has to. He achieves for his own sake, not to get a grade or someone's approval. He is more interested in giving the gold star than getting one. He has passion, grit, curiosity, and the self-confidence to achieve his goals. Yes, high school students can demonstrate all these qualities in their resume and essays, and they don't have to be the next Albert Einstein to do so. Consultants can definitely help you craft your resume to better showcase your child, but it is the student who is doing the heavy lifting.

The best way a parent can encourage a child to become an Ivy individual is to be introspective, stress long term goals, value relationships, ask questions rather than talk, be flexible, focus on connection, and value who they are as opposed to what they do. Never say "do this, and you will get that." Try to bring out your student's qualities as opposed to shaping him in your image. Recognize who your child is rather than molding him into what you think he should be.

## Social Media

A serious applicant simply must monitor and control their social media presence. I can assure you, any Ivy League applicant who is being considered is searched for on Google, Facebook, and other sites. Your media presence will affect an admissions committee one way or another. It can make or break an applicant's chances. Nothing turns a committee off more than a negative press release about a clash with the law, a snarky comment, or a photo of your child drunk at a party. A positive article or two can help a great deal. Max already has several pages of hits on Google—all positive. This communicates "mover and shaker" to the Ivy League, which is not something that can be said flat out in a resume. It's something schools piece together on their own. So make sure your child is cognizant of his or her online presence. Schools look.

## Summer Activities

An often overlooked aspect of a child's development—summer activities—allow the Ivy League to consider what decisions potential students will make when free time presents itself. Do they hang around and play video games, or do they volunteer in Zimbabwe? Do they value their time? Ivy League schools understand that not all students can afford exotic travel. Costly activities are not the point anyway. It's the mind of the child that they are interested in.

Max had already visited several foreign countries (many of them more than once) by the time he graduated high school. He produced films in Italy, Spain, France, Israel, and India. This took a lot of work, focus, and commitment. He was selected as the leader for a trip to Israel and he guided forty mixed-culture teens throughout Israel under very stressful circumstances, which meant he had three free trips to Israel. He met the mayor of Jerusalem and introduced Randi Zuckerberg (Mark's sister) in front of six hundred international attendees. A film crew from NY was flown to our house to produce a film about him, which was shown in San Francisco when he accepted a merit scholarship. These are just some of the highlights of his resume. Your child can make a local impact just as easily if foreign travel is not possible. Be creative.

Max did not slack off during his senior year or during the summer. Most of his colleagues have similar accomplishments. It is a rarified group. While Max was doing all this, however, he was not thinking about the "rewards." He sincerely enjoyed doing it and created the necessary time and energy himself. Of course, we supported him in any way we could, but they were his ideas.

Don't be intimidated by all this if your child has not done things like this. Be inspired, be supportive, and most of all, hold these things as possibilities for your child. How the parent holds the child in their mind is how they will come out. Think of your child as great and capable, then they will prove you right. Think of them as mediocre or average, and they will also prove you right. It's truly in the mind of the parents. The child will figure out how, while the parent sees the possibilities, supports the how, and thinks of the why. Always talk about why as opposed to how. And above all, try to teach your child positive self-talk. If you catch them in any form of negative thinking, try to nip it in the bud. Remember, what a child tells himself is what he will tell others, which in turn will be what others wind up telling the child. Be careful about what you say.

## LION DAD COMMANDMENTS FOR CHAPTER SIX

1. Be very careful about what goes in your child's mouth.
2. Be mindful of your child's physical health. Get second opinions.
3. Be aware of toxins.
4. Find the right nutritional supplements for your child.
5. No psychostimulants.
6. Use a college counselor as early as possible as part of the team.
7. Go deep and long for extracurricular activities, not shallow and short.
8. Help your child stand out, not blend in.
9. Be wary of dangerous sports that take up a lot of time. Choose wisely.
10. Keep your child thinking positively. No negative self-talk.
11. Never let your child headbutt anything.

J K Roark M.D.

# 7

# STANDARDIZED TESTS

## Life is Graded on a Curve

*"Not everything that counts can be counted and not everything that can be counted counts."*
**—Albert Einstein, physicist**

Now, let's get to the nitty-gritty—the last two to three years of high school and a subject that has as many opinions as there are parents: the SAT/ACT. Except for a few schools, these tests are required for admissions and used to filter out (or in) applicants. One can argue all day long about the validity of these standardized tests and whether they predict future college success or correlate with intelligence. But the fact remains that they are very important for admissions to select universities. Right or wrong, they are a fact of life. It's the single most important test in your child's life to date. Make no mistake about it, it's big. Don't treat it casually. Yes, they are surrogate markers and may not accurately predict success in college or even success in life, but their existence is real, so you must deal with it. Somehow, some way you and your child should figure out how to do well. If it means preparing four years in advance or six months in advance, figure it out.

Standardized tests are much more important in China than in the US. In China, they start much earlier. The PSLE sixth-grade test, for example, is a pivotal test for children there. Some parents take a year off from work to prepare their students, and most hire tutors. Japan spends $12 billion a year on tutors, and a good tutor in Hong Kong can make over $1 million per year! In China 16–18 million students take high school entrance exams for the 8 million spots in good schools. There is nothing like that here. Maybe that's why a 2012 study published in *The Lancet* medical journal calculated the prevalence of myopia (nearsightedness) to be 80 percent in Asia, as opposed to 20 percent in the US. While rigorous study may not be the source of such medical issues in the US (yet), the SAT/ACT is the first exam with real stakes that most students face.

The SAT and ACT are the only objective tools the universities have to screen for literacy and numeracy. The reading and vocabulary sections, of course, address literacy, and the science and math sections address numeracy (the same concept applied to numbers). Innumeracy is much more rampant in today's college applicants than illiteracy. In fact, it's rampant in many professions, including medicine. The ability to read graphs, have a basic conceptualization of number relationships, and think numerically is sorely absent in many spheres. The introduction of the calculator and computer has made this even worse. Many high school students can't do simple math facts without these devices, never mind think in terms of orders of magnitude.

In China and other Eastern countries, math is stressed much like reading is in the West. Children in the East are brought up with math from an early age. Perhaps this has something to do with the dominance that India and China have in the computer world, artificial intelligence, programming, etc. Many of the tech jobs go to them.

Nicolas Carr covers this very well in his book *The Shallows*. His argument is that technology like the calculator, computer, automation of every kind, and even artificial intelligence is creating a population of shallow thinkers who cannot put ideas into perspective. When London cab drivers started to use GPS to find their way around rather than by memory, their hippocampal size shrunk. The hippocampus is the area of the brain associated with memory. When commercial pilots get used to using autopilot, their piloting skills decrease. There are many other fascinating examples described in Carr's book, but the point is that technology should be used carefully, and users should be mindful of what they may lose as a result. (Cal Newport's latest book, *Digital Minimalism*, speaks more about the importance of controlling tech use in your life.)

Attention span may be a casualty of an addictive use of technology. Reading is a primary color as far as our family is concerned. Consumed via the printed word or an audiobook, books are as vital as food. Blogs, surfing the web, and hyperlinks do not count and are discouraged. It rots your mind by destroying your attention span and ability to think deeply. I believe your child's academic success is inversely proportional to their use of social media and hyperlinks. The less they use them, the more successful they will be. You may consider this "old school," but short, attention-grabbing pieces will limit their attention span and condition them in ways that can harm.

Such internet content can be used constructively if your child is in control and is working toward a goal. In addition to Nicholas Carr's book *The Shallows,* Cal Newport's book *Digital Minimalism* speaks to this very point. Your child must have time to develop this context on their own. If not, the web will be in control, becoming the context. Beware. Some predict the web will eventually be integrated into our very biology (Kurzweil's singularity) and result in *Homo Deus* (Harari), or humanity 2.0. Maybe, maybe not, but in the meantime, I believe those who can control or resist the temptations of the infinitely clickable internet will have a competitive edge. They will be able to think as opposed to react. Social media, web surfing, TV surfing, video games, constant smartphone use—all of it can condition your mind to the quick fix and result in a decreased attention span. This is not conducive to deep thinking, creativity, or leadership skills. Once a mind is wired like this, it is very hard to reverse. As Walter Issacson said in his book on da Vinci: "Creativity requires time for ideas to marinate."

When it comes to objectively evaluating a student's ability to focus, the SAT levels the playing field. Scores are prominently displayed on application folders that admissions committees see, providing a simple metric to weigh one student against the other. It's not everything, but it gets you in the door. *Getting into a Top College* by Pria Chatterjee—a former Harvard admissions officer who now has a service she claims has 100 percent success in placing students in elite schools—states that the main categories listed on the top of every application is a student's race, home region, legacy status, country of origin, and income level. The SAT has its own special box. These categories are used to fill certain buckets the universities design and are sometimes supplemented by athletics and special accomplishments that are unique (such as being a filmmaker or winning a prestigious award). If your child identifies with a race, geographical region, legacy family, country, and/or financial bracket a school wants, then your child stands a better chance of admission. The SAT, however, helps filter out students within each of a school's selected buckets.

The effect of the SAT adversity score remains to be seen. It does not change the actual SAT score, but it is reported to the colleges as a background metric. The adversity score is based on about fifteen items about where a student lives, which is then compared to socioeconomic data. It does not, however, tell you if a student takes care of a disabled sibling (like I had to), lost a parent while in high school (like I did), works after school, or other factors that would indicate adversity. The score, therefore, is still incomplete. There is no doubt that this adversity score will be gamed by savvy counselors, especially if *US World News* somehow takes it into consideration and ranks schools accordingly. For now, however, it is only one item in the black box of admissions that may influence the admissions committee.

Should the adversity score even exist in the first place? I usually do not like commenting on things I have no control over, but my opinion is that there needs to be at least one objective number used to compare students across the board. *The SAT is it.* Any other factors can be revealed if the student and family desires, but that should be optional. What if you don't wind up with a high adversity score (e.g., if your family lives in an expensive zip code)? You are out of luck, I suppose, and it may count against you.

You ideally should have a plan of attack for standardized tests set years in advance. Try to start preparing the summer before sophomore year and accelerate the intensity of this preparation until your child gets the score you want. This plan varies, of course, according to the student. An entire industry has evolved around these tests involving books, tutors, classes, summer programs, counselors, and the like. Part of your responsibility as a parent is to emphasize the importance of the exam to your child, motivate them to prepare, and research the options. How did we do this? We started to mention the SAT to Max in middle school, at first just casually. Then as the time approached, we ramped up the rhetoric. By the time he was a sophomore in high school, he was prepared psychologically. Some parents downplay the importance of this test in an effort not to pressure their kids. They do not stress rigorous preparation, and the scores reflect that. I do not believe anyone (no matter how smart) can do well on these tests without serious attention, practice, and taking it a few times (even if only in practice).

The importance of these exams has risen in direct proportion to the devolution of the grading system in this country. Grade inflation is rampant, as I mentioned before. From a college's point of view, the interpretation of GPA is dicey at best. Most colleges say GPA is more important than the SAT/ACT—and it should be. But I am not sure how they can interpret GPA in light of grade inflation.

The pressure on teachers—from students, parents, administrators, and even governing boards—to hand out As is enormous and unfair. It must be very frustrating for the teachers since they probably feel manipulated and devalued. Many of them say they do not teach to the test or emphasize the grade over learning, but inflated grades are inevitable since external pressures exist beyond their control—namely, the need to get into college. Colleges put pressure to do well on these tests by publishing their average scores and ranges. This makes it all very black and white. The score appears on the front page of an applicant's dossier, in plain view for all to see.

If an occasional teacher resists giving out As in high school, they are avoided by students, face hours of meetings with the parents, and risk being fired if enough complaints come in. It's simply easier for them to get along and go along with giving most student As. It's a matter of self- interest and survival.

## Standardized Tests

> The entire discussion of extrinsic versus intrinsic rewards (grades versus internal motivation) is a very interesting one, but I must be brief. In short, extrinsic motivators (gold stars, grades, parental rewards, money, incentive plans, etc.) actually diminish the natural intrinsic motivations students have to learn and perform. This creates an entire population of students who work for the grade, the reward, and learn to do so for the rest of their lives. They eventually need to be told what to do by someone else their entire lives as a result. They become trained to the reward and usually trained to be factory workers of one kind or another, even if the factory is, say, a hospital. Physicians, as a group, are very controlled and must do as they are told. They're essentially high-level factory workers who, in most cases, cannot think on their own. That hurts everyone, and it all started with a school system that teaches to the reward rather than creating independent thinkers. I am a physician and see this daily. It's very sad. In general, they practice by protocol, algorithm, and legal constraints as opposed to independent thought. It's cookbook medicine in most cases.

The entire grading system is counterproductive in my opinion, but until someone thinks of an alternative that is widely accepted, we are stuck with it. A top student is usually defined by these grades and scores, unfortunately. Curiosity, grit, passion, focus, and interests are difficult to measure, so evaluation comes in the simpler format of grades and standardized tests. Emotional intelligence and executive function are also not measured, both of which, I'd argue, are far more important than test performance. More on this later.

SAT/ACT prep involves many issues that must be addressed in a short period of time—which test to take, how to prepare, how many times to take the test, when to take the test, and which books to use. Let's dive in.

## Which Test(s) to Take?

Generally, the ACT is the more science-based of the two, lacking a vocabulary section. However, the SAT recently lost its own vocabulary section, so the two tests are more alike than ever. The ACT is more dependent on speed, which can be a disadvantage for a slow, deliberate thinker (which is exactly the type of thinker that is most needed today). Max did a sample of each test and decided to emphasize the SAT after seeing the initial results. It is my impression that elite schools prefer the SAT over the ACT even though its not stated in their printed materials. Just the fact that the SAT is graded over a much wider range (1600 versus 36) makes it better from their point of view.

As a result of the practice tests and careful thought, we prepared exclusively for the SAT. I believe the SAT is easier for a certain type of mind compared to the ACT. For example, Max had a close friend throughout high school who was a highly intelligent, voracious reader. For her, the reading sections of the SAT were easy and she scored highly. I thought the reading sections were the hardest on the test, even though I read quite a bit. Being able to quickly comprehend the context and specific content of an SAT passage is a real skill. On the other hand, the complex and varied graphs and charts on the ACT favor the technically minded.

The only way to really tell which is best for your child is by trying two timed samples of each test. If the results are close, then it's a matter of personal preference. But if they differ by a lot, then you have your answer. At first Max thought he would do better on the ACT because of the reading section, but he switched early on when he took another two practice tests. After a few weeks of study and practice, you may have to reevaluate the choice of test, as we did. Some people take both tests for credit, but that is rare.

The PSAT, taken earlier, is not considered for college admissions, but it helps determine National Merit Scholarship awards. Less than 1 percent of students become semi finalists, and maybe .1 percent are finalists. It's not so much about the money awarded but the prestige of having it on a resume that matters. Still, it's better to eventually do well on the SAT, which is "superscored" (taking the best score on each section) by some colleges.

AP tests, graded on a one-to-five scale, are used to grant or deny AP credit in college. AP credits are primarily a badge of honor used for college admissions, and students compete on the number of AP classes taken. Some think it's better to go to a high school that offers fewer AP classes to avoid having to compete with other students over the number of APs. Max's school had too many AP classes, in my opinion, which created another arms race of sorts. It was brutal. How can you really compare a student from a small school offering five AP classes total with a student from a school offering thirty? I believe the colleges still look at the absolute number of AP classes taken and favor the higher numbers, even though they say that smaller (sometimes private) schools are not discriminated against. Private high schools simply cannot afford to offer too many AP classes since there are not enough students to take them. This is another disadvantage of private high schools.

Ivy League schools do not grant AP credit for the most part and usually don't even advise taking a higher level class if you took an AP class in high school. There are scholar designations, like AP Scholar and AP Scholar of Distinction, that depend on the number of AP classes taken and grades of four or five on the AP exam. Max was an AP Scholar of Distinction and took thirteen AP classes. In his junior year, he took six AP classes (all his classes) and got As in all of them, resulting in a weighted junior year GPA of 4.65. I am sure this weighed heavily in his elite school acceptances. This is not easy. He definitely had it going on in junior year, arguably the most important high school year. The SAT II tests are subject tests, and most colleges like to see two or three of these as well.

There are separate prep books for AP tests as well as the SAT II subject tests. We had all of them. Max became a test-taking machine, complete with pretest rituals, like careful diet, sleep, exercise, meditation, self-talk, etc. We had a pact between us that I would drive him back and forth to all these big tests, which I did gladly. (I saw other kids driving themselves.) It gave us a chance for a final moment of confidence-building, but we did not talk about the test material during those drives. We learned a great deal about the various prep programs and had discussions on promoting optimal brain performance, which I knew about from my functional medicine background. Max became good at noticing which activities enhanced his mental performance and which ones hampered it. Sleep, a vegan, whole-food diet, targeted supplements, exercise, and stress reduction all helped him. Alcohol, conflict, video games, almost any pharmaceutical, lack of sleep, and overwork hurt his performance. He was learning what worked for him.

## How to prepare.

Review books, tutors, practice tests, and online prep are all important. We found the Barron's review books most helpful, although the practice tests we used were once real tests, not fabricated ones. Expensive online tutors can be good on a case-by-case basis, but we did not get much from them, although we tried. I think in our case, one-on-one, face-to-face tutors worked best. There was a very expensive local tutor who charged $175 per hour, but she claimed to be so tuned-in to the test that her fee was worth it. It wasn't. We actually tried two expensive tutors like this. I was curious. Maybe they knew the secret sauce. Neither one did. Somehow they kept their clientele coming, but I think that was largely because the parents were wealthy and delegated this task to the highest bidder without really looking at what they got. This is another example of misguided thinking, similar to the belief that sending kids to the most expensive private school means giving those kids the best education. You cannot delegate your child's education as if you are buying a product rated in *Consumer Reports*. It's a hands-on affair.

There are online tutors who "guarantee" any score you are shooting for if you pay their large fee and give them enough time. Others charge by the hour (ranging from $15 to $175 per hour), claiming one-on-one is the only way to go. Some people are disciplined enough to just read a review book, take the practice tests, review the results and repeat. That is the most cost-effective option but is reserved for highly intelligent, disciplined students. (I think that method is rapidly becoming an urban myth.)

But if you think you can go into this test unprepared, you are simply wrong. That is how I did it in the 1960s. I did not prepare at all. There were no classes or review books (except rudimentary ones), and certainly no individual tutors.

Maybe that's why no one from my high school with over eight hundred graduates was admitted to an elite school. The playing field was different. There was no grade inflation, so your GPA mattered. Nobody prepared, so you were on a level playing field. And the results were not considered as important as they are today. I don't even remember what I got years ago, but I bet students today will have that number emblazoned in their memory for life. We tried everything. Max had at least five different tutors just for the SAT. He attended two in-person group classes and took about thirty practice tests (over three hours each). He took the actual test five times and nailed it on the last attempt. I'm grateful that Max could combine some of the privileges/extras we could afford with his own determination in order to achieve his goal. That's grit.

## How Many Times to Take the Test?

Most students give up long before achieving Ivy League scores, and the Ivy League knows this. We knew students that achieved perfect scores on the first try, but those are few and far between. Our general college counselor advised taking it only three times, in part because preparations for the exam are grueling. It is a trial by fire.

What score is "good enough?" That is defined by the student and the parents. The ones who don't give up after getting an average score are the ones the Ivy League wants. They know how hard the test is and how much grit it takes to get a great score. Which type of student is preferred by the Ivies? One who easily gets a great score without trying very hard on the first attempt, or one who has to work hard to achieve the same results? Which type of student will work harder in college and in life? I say the latter, and I think the colleges think the same way. I think that is one reason the admissions committee does not ask how many times you took the test and why they superscore your results (taking the highest score from each section, no matter how many times you took the exam).

Flash-cards: A family affair

Most students take this test two or three times. It's fine to be naturally gifted, but if this gift is not paired with the ability and willingness to work hard at something until it's achieved, that gift is wasted. Hard work, perseverance, grit, and passion will surpass innate intelligence every time. It's best to have both, but frequently, highly intelligent students who can knock it out of the park on the first try get frustrated if they encounter an obstacle and quit before their objective is reached.

Most Ivy League schools see highly intelligent applicants all day long. What they want to see is harder to find: students who can stick to a goal until it is achieved, no matter what. It's harder to screen for this, and that's why the SAT score is so valuable. They know these tests are hard—almost no one nails it on the first try—so it becomes essentially a screening tool for grit. Max had a motto: "I don't quit when I am tired. I quit when I'm done."

## **THE BENEFITS OF STANDARDIZED TESTS**

Preparing for these tests created stress and pressure, but there were some unexpected benefits. Vocabulary was one of them. Having a large vocabulary is very important for future success, especially if it is used. This is rarely taught in high school, and the SAT gives a student the opportunity to learn words and use them in the proper context. Max still uses many of these words today. We had flashcards and played games trying to use three to five new words in the same sentence. Studies have shown that prisoners represent the demographic group with the smallest vocabulary (in terms of number of words known). The larger your vocabulary, the more complex thoughts you are capable of. From those thoughts come complex actions. I caught Max reviewing his SAT vocabulary flashcards after his freshman year at college just for fun!

Shakespeare had a vocabulary of about 20,000 words, and he is often considered the most intelligent person who ever lived. Some of those words he only used once, of course. Most people have a total vocabulary of about 1,000 words, of which 500 are used regularly. After the SAT, your vocabulary should be about 5,000. How much you use it is up to you. The SAT was unique in that it stressed vocabulary, and in my opinion, it was a mistake to eliminate it from the new SAT. Max took both the old and the new SAT, so he still benefited from an expanded vocabulary, a predictor of future success and earning capacity.

Another benefit of the SAT is reading comprehension. Yes, there are English classes that teach this, but the kind of reading comprehension you must master with the SAT is unique and valuable. The largest benefit of the SAT, however, is writing skills. Max got a perfect 800 on the writing section of the old SAT. His writing is excellent now and was central to getting him into the Ivy League. There is no one in an important position in industry, academia, or in any of the professions who cannot write well these days. The ability to put your thoughts into proper English cannot be overemphasized. Good grammar, spelling, vocabulary, syntax, sentence structure, overall composition is extremely valuable, and unfortunately I know of no other place besides SAT prep that teaches this so well.

Another benefit of standardized tests are the analytical skills needed to interpret graphs, charts, and tables. Using these skills is stressed on the SAT, and although they are covered in some science classes, they are not always covered well or in detail. The analytical skills developed to do well on the SAT/ACT can be critical in a student's development—independent of getting into a good school. These exams are very hard, take focus, intelligence, and grit.

## **Staying on Track**

To review, standardized tests are a fact of life, so take them seriously. Encourage your child to prepare for them in earnest no later than the summer between freshman and sophomore year, and prepare him or her psychologically before that. This test is by far the most important test of a student's high school career. It will make or break them. I have known brilliant kids who just did not take this seriously enough and suffered as a result. That is the parent's fault. Parents establish the mindset and values their children strive for. If something is important to the parents, it will be important to the child in most cases.

## Standardized Tests

Although some people say you only need a few months of preparation, waiting that long may leave you out of luck. Keep in mind that what your child learns during test prep is valuable in its own right, so it's not just about studying to get a good score. We purchased review books at first and went through a set number of pages weekly. It was really fun for us as a family. As time progressed, we enrolled Max in classes, which gave him high-level peers, reviewed what he knew, and provided structured practice tests, graphs of his progress, and standards to live up to. It's important that your child not do this alone.

We had fun with this preparation and made a game out of it. It was a family event, as was all of Max's schooling. We were constantly quizzing each other and enjoyed it. Had Max showed any sign that he was not having fun, I would have stopped immediately. He frequently said to me I should push him even more than I was, and I often asked him permission to do so. Again, I was not the sage on the stage—I was the guide on the side. I did it with his full consent and encouragement. He was intrinsically motivated to learn, and that came from the early years. The fact that his parents valued and enjoyed learning made it so much easier.

This is just one example of how deeply involved parents can make an enormous difference in a child's life. It has been shown that the number of books in a family's home is directly linked to the academic success of the child. We have a library of over six thousand volumes, which Max grew up around. If your child is not eager to learn or shows signs of stress during the process, then I would advise backing off. If your child resists too much, you risk losing your relationship with your child. Yes, these tests are important, but not more important than your child's well-being.

I actually think there should be courses within the high school curriculum that teach to the SAT and ACT since the material is so important for life skills and future use. Most schools do not have this, and neither did Max's. Take the test as many times as necessary in order to achieve a good enough score to qualify for the Ivy League (usually above 1,500 on the SAT, and 34 to 36 on the ACT). This is far from easy but will get you past the first screen. It will definitely not be enough to get you in, but it will put you in a different pile and keep you in the running.

Once you are considered "smart enough" for the Ivy League, then they look at other things like your extracurricular activities, AP classes, essays, etc., but if you do not have the score, you can forget the Ivy League, unless you are a legacy or a recruited athlete.

Legacy admissions are becoming much harder to achieve, no matter how much money is donated by a past graduate. I think that's a good thing. It keeps the standards high. I know low-scoring legacies still exist, but there are fewer than before. The same goes for recruited athletes in most cases, especially in the Ivy league. Those two groups may give you a slight edge, but less so in the Ivy League than second-tier schools. Merit still matters in the Ivy League, at least for some of the spots. That is yet another reason to strive for these schools since you are assured your child will be in the company of quality peers.

## LION DAD COMMANDMENTS FOR CHAPTER SEVEN

1. Take the SAT/ACT seriously.
2. Prepare early.
3. Don't give up until you get your score.
4. Use every method to prepare—tutors, books, classes, etc.
5. Enjoy the journey. You will learn from it.
6. Hard work and persistence trumps innate intelligence.
7. Practice with actual old tests, not drills from books.
8. Research the best classes and tutors.
9. Ensure your child rests well the night before and tries to relax. Make it a family affair.
10. Have fun with this, and focus on the benefits, not the cost.

J K Roark M.D.

# 8

# COUNSELORS & CONSULTANTS

## How to Hire Your Support Team

*"It had long since come to my attention that people of accomplishment rarely sat back and let things happen to them. They went out and happened to things."*
—**Leonardo da Vinci, painter**

The industry that has grown around college admissions is enormous. Fifty years ago, there were hardly any of the services for college admissions that are available today. The standard then was to sit down with your parents over dinner, take about ten minutes to decide which five local colleges to apply to, complete the written applications in one afternoon, put a stamp on them, and hope for the best. The whole thing was very matter of fact and casual.

Nobody in my class of about eight hundred went to an Ivy League school, although several became famous and wealthy. Most of the applications did not require an essay and required little more than demographics, GPA, and SAT scores. They did not require a resume (no one even knew what that was), and most were about three pages long if that. Most kids did not graduate high school at that time, and only about 20 percent went to college. Going to college at all was a big deal. It didn't matter where. College also cost about $1000 per year. Ah, the good old days.

Today, 65 percent of high school graduates go to college, and 90 percent graduate high school eventually (thanks in part to No Child Left Behind legislation). Only 70 percent graduate in four years, however. Still, only about 25 percent of the US population graduates college. This demographic shift meant increased competition for the Ivy League and other colleges in a major way. Now, a college degree is like a high school degree was fifty years ago—it's very hard to navigate life without it. Even a college degree is becoming devalued, making graduate degrees necessary to move up economically and socially. The more people want something, the more watered down and less valuable it may become. Some say the high price of a college education is not worth it economically at all. It can cost $70,000 to $80,000 per year in some cases! How can anyone justify that expense? It's not all dollars and cents, that's how. And a degree has become almost mandatory, not elective.

Sometimes starting your own business right out of high school makes more sense. It's become the cultural norm to go to college, which was not the case fifty years ago. Combine this with inflated prices largely resulting from cheap government loans, and you get tuition costs that are, in a word, ridiculous. The government has created student debt of over $1.5 trillion—more than all credit card debt combined. They did this by offering what appeared to be free money. They did the same thing to the housing market, inflated real estate by offering mortgages to unqualified people, which drove the prices up. Then the whole thing collapsed in 2008.

College graduates cannot get jobs as easily now, have large amounts of debt, and can be trapped in a life of poverty if they are not careful. Choose wisely. Currently, you cannot declare bankruptcy to avoid education loan repayment even though politicians always talk about student loan forgiveness. If student loan debt is wiped out by some future draconian law, I think it would be a mistake and would devalue education. It would also prejudice the students and families who paid in full. Like I said before, many students borrow money they do not have to take courses they do not like, only to apply for jobs that do not exist. That's why parents need to play a big role in determining students' choices and guiding them to eventual success. In Caplan's recent book entitled *The Case Against Education*, he summarizes the economic studies, which prove how devalued education currently is and how careful you must be in choosing its various options.

## FINDING THE RIGHT HELP

The application process has become increasingly more complicated, time-consuming and costly. Applications are also all online now, and navigating this process and being competitive can greatly be aided by expert advice. Most top students have this kind of expert help—because it is needed. Even if a student got a perfect SAT score, had a 4.5 GPA, and was the class president, he or she would be foolish to attempt to navigate this maze without strong support from counselors. I am not talking about school counselors who have hundreds of students they barely know. I am talking about paid, outside counselors. Yes, there are some people who navigate the process on their own, and some are even successful, somehow. More power to them, but I bet if they had the kind of advice we are talking about here, they would have done even better.

There are even sub-specialties among college counselors, and a general counselor functions much like a general practitioner in medicine who refers clients to specialists. Sub-specialists in college counseling focus on individual aspects of the application process, including essays, SAT prep, financial planning, resume writing, interview help, social media, PR, and motivational support. Many firms claim to do all of it or have individual specialists within their services. I generally like services that specialize in one area, but occasionally, a general counselor can do it all.

Consultants all have their opinions, but what is most important is how successful have they been in getting students into an Ivy League school. Many consultants have never achieved admission for even one of their clients, so buyer beware. The ones that do regularly get clients into top schools usually charge very high fees, which some might not be willing to pay.

Remember, your child is doing the heavy lifting. You tell them what to lift. Everyone else is cheering on the sidelines, hoping to take some credit and sometimes a fee. You must be a careful consumer of these services if you don't want to waste your money and time. Some of these services can lead you down the wrong path, so it's a double whammy. First, a bad counselor is costly in both time and money, but worse than that, they have you follow an ill-advised path that can take time to correct if it can be corrected at all.

As the parent, you have control of the purse strings, but more importantly, you have the life experience and judgment to know specifically what is required for your child and how to obtain it in a way that's consistent with your goals as a family. Try to be careful about pushing your student into a situation that is not right for them just because you want bragging rights. This happens all the time in the race for college acceptances or in sports participation.

We hired an excellent general counselor in ninth grade. She took on only a handful of clients and charged a flat fee for the entire time. She met with Max every two weeks in the beginning and then almost weekly during the last year. She built a resume bit by bit during this time, and it turned out to be very impressive. She knew what to put on the resume, where to put it, and how to word it. She added items as they happened so we were not scrambling to assemble it at the last minute when there are plenty of other things to focus on. We never could have done this on our own, or it would have required the type of organization we did not have early on. This counselor, however, did not ever achieve Ivy admission for her clients as far as I knew. We did not have this on our radar in the ninth grade, and while she was good, we needed more.

We hired another generalist to supplement our first and who helped with test prep and high-level strategy. He also tracked important deadlines, helped Max decide which schools to apply to based on many hours of discussion and investigation, planned course schedules based on Max's goals, and many other things. He became like a member of the family, and we communicated with him regularly. He was a dignified individual who wrote beautifully and had a large vocabulary, so an additional benefit was just interacting. I frequently sent him articles and books about the college process, and was always ready to have a discussion with intelligent remarks. He would respond back with long, thoughtful emails.

How did we find this person? Word of mouth. We interviewed three or four others who, for one reason or another, were not right for us. Some did not have the track record, others did not follow up with emails or calls, and more than one could not provide credible references. Some were simply overbooked. We made the right choice, but it was a time-consuming process, requiring multiple interviews, conversations with references, and gut reactions. There is no shortcut, no website, no Yelp, that can make this easy for you. Sorry. The best advice I have is to find out which kids were admitted to elite schools from your area, ask about the consultants and counselors they used, and when you have a list of about five, interview them all in person. Then check them out online for reviews. This is a critical decision. Remember, five minutes with an intelligent, successful consultant is worth hours with an average one.

There are remote counselors who live on the East Coast or elsewhere who claim to do great work, but I don't advise working with them. Some of them charge exorbitant fees (up to $100,000) and claim to have inside information and connections to the Ivy League. I spoke to one of them who wanted to charge me $10,000 just to write one letter to a college to reconsider an early decision rejection. I said, "No thanks." That early decision rejection, it turns out, was a blessing in disguise. (I will write about the pros and cons of early decision and early action later in the book.) Not only were the East Coast super-specialist counselors expensive, but they were arrogant, acting as if the one minute spent on the phone was a waste of their time since they had so many clients willing to hire them.

There are people with so much money that these kinds of fees mean nothing to them. This is your competition. Remember the bear chasing the two friends? The college admissions process is like outrunning your competition. Make no mistake about it. The more you know who your competition is and the better equipped you are with consultants, the better chance you'll have to outrun the competition. It's that simple. It's not, however, about throwing money around, even if you can afford it. There are plenty of rich parents paying large fees to counselors who are still not successful. It's about the quality of the hire that's most important.

## Choosing a Specialist

As good as the general college counselor was, we needed to find specialists to address his weaknesses. We needed an essay specialist, several SAT specialists, course tutors, financial consultants for the extremely complicated financial forms (FAFSA and CSS), and even a voice teacher who prepped Max for interviews.

The second generalist we hired, as mentioned, was an excellent addition in Max's junior year. He was the primary consultant for two other college counseling firms before he started his own firm. He was also responsible for more perfect SAT scores than anyone else in our state! With a list of college admission stats about his office that would knock your socks off, he was highly intelligent, personable, and had a deep understanding of the entire process and connections at the highest levels. The cohort of students he attracted was worth the price of admission all by itself. Max was rubbing shoulders with students who'd earned perfect test scores, applied to Ivy League schools, and gotten in. You learn a lot from others with the same goals as long as you can keep from becoming intimidated by them.

This second generalist gave us one piece of advice that proved essential for Max's application. I produced a video that highlighted his accomplishments, complete with special effects, interviews with teachers, interviews with Max, and clips of his lectures and speeches. I thought it was powerful and would be an exceptional addition to the application. After spending considerable time and money on it, I showed it to our consultant, and he advised against including it, saying it seemed like bragging since it was not a standard part of the application. He turned out to be correct since Max did not get into the one school he submitted it to (Harvard), though he got into many other highly rated schools. I think Max would have gotten into Harvard if we had followed his advice. People like this have their finger on the pulse of the admissions process minute by minute. They are invaluable.

## Taking Charge

We spent a lot of time selecting and interviewing these consultants in an effort to make the best choice possible. There are scores of consultants available in just our community. So how do you choose? Word of mouth, careful interviews, online reviews, gut instinct, and trial and error are the best methods that exist. Some of the consultants we tried we later fired. We followed our original formula: know your goal, take massive action, see what you get, then make adjustments. You can consider remote counselors for some things like SAT advice or maybe even essay advice (much more on this important subject later). However, advice that requires a deep knowledge of your student requires face-to-face contact, availability, and even a cohort of fellow students trying to achieve the same goal.

This last factor is very important, and I think made all the difference for Max not only with college applications, but in high school too. He had excellent peers who taught him a great deal. This is probably the most important reason to choose an Ivy League school. It is far better to be in the bottom 10 percent of an excellent school with high level peers than in the top 10 percent of a second-tier school. The level of conversation at the Ivy League is different. I know others may disagree. I did not think of these consultants and the time spent with them to be totally about the college process. Max learned a great deal from them along the way—writing, planning, test taking, critical thinking, organization, tactics, and much more—all of which will help him in the future. Working with consultants was an integral part of his education, providing a private component to supplement his public school curriculum. Plus, we spent far less money than it would have cost to keep him in private school for all of his schooling.

Deciding on which type(s) of consultants to look for, which ones to hire, how to monitor them, whether or not to switch, and what to pay are all crucial decisions. This is where parental judgment (and money) really helps. It would be a mistake to hire the first consultant you meet, pay them their fee without shopping around, and just let them handle everything from then on. You as a parent simply must be on top of these key people. They can make or break your child's chances. Everyone has an opinion, but a seasoned, proven track record is important.

However, that's not enough. You must judge for your own situation what works and what does not. Remember, this is still a business, and you are the client. If you act appropriately and respect them, you will get a better result. But you are in charge. It's a different relationship than you have with a teacher or with a private or public school. Don't rely on what your neighbors or friends are doing. That may be part of the calculus, but try to make your own independent choice based on the intimate knowledge of your student and family that only you have. You are in charge.

I had an instinct about the second counselor we hired. It turned out to be right, but I had my doubts along the way. These kinds of decisions can keep you up at night, and frankly, they should. In retrospect, I can identify a few pivotal decisions and moments along the way which clearly made the difference. Combined, they resulted in Max getting into an Ivy League school. I have gotten to know several of the parents of freshmen, and many of them say the same thing: "I never expected my child to get into an Ivy League school." It was clear to me after speaking to these parents that they shared the same team approach, the same unwavering commitment to their child, and the same values as we did. They valued being with other like-minded families and felt elevated by the experience. There was no question that attempting to achieve at this level was hard work. The students and the families understood this. They didn't want an "easy" life. They wanted the rewards that a hard-earned accomplishment can bring.

## LION DAD COMMANDMENTS FOR CHAPTER EIGHT

1. Use a general college counselor starting in the ninth grade.
2. Use specialty counselors along the way as needed.
3. Build your student's resume early and on a regular basis.
4. Submit your application with what is asked for and no more.
5. Get to know other Ivy League applicants and their families early on.
6. Know your competition and the playing field.
7. Assert yourself in the application, but be humble.
8. Don't be afraid to fire your consultant if a better one comes along.
9. Good consultants are valuable, but bad ones can be harmful.
10. Monitor your consultants the same as your student's tutors.
11. Remember: you are paying, so you are boss. This is different than with teachers.

# 9

# EXTRA CURRICULAR ACTIVITIES

*"When I was a teenager, I began to settle into school because I'd discovered the extracurricular activity that interested me: music and theatre."*
—**Morgan Freeman, actor**

*"Please God, please, don't let me be normal."*
—**Sigourney Weaver, actress**

When I was in seventh grade, I had an interesting classmate and friend. His name was Steven Tallarico. I used to look forward to going to school just to be entertained by him. He would do all manner of things to torment the teachers, tease the fellow students, tell jokes, and generally disrupt the orderly progression of the day. It was great fun. He was kicked out of high school. He also never went to college. Academics never interested him but music did. He started a band as a drummer but soon discovered he wanted to be out front, so he developed his singing skills. He worked at this incessantly.

By the time high school came around, he was performing with his band at several school dances and eventually at our senior prom. No one thought he would amount to anything. No one, except himself. He had a passionate commitment to his band and his music, kept at it, and when he changed his name, he really took off. What did he change it to? Steven Tyler. His band? Aerosmith. He was a born entertainer, had unlimited energy, and was incredibly creative with his antics. Today he would probably be labeled with ADHD, medicated, and forced to conform. What a loss that would have been. This shows you the power of extracurricular activities (ECs).

When Max was about eleven, he developed an interest in film. He started taking his small camera to the skate park and created movies with his friends. He filmed from all angles, with and without a tripod, and he had filters, microphones, assistants, and lighting. It was remarkable. He used advanced editing tools I could not possibly understand. Most importantly, his hobby kept him from just hanging out at the shopping center like so many of his peers. It kept him from excessive video game use or TV. It was a passion he could focus on and show a product. This eventually led him to make films all over the world, create his own business and website, and accumulate exotic equipment that we lugged to every destination. He did this not because he "had" to or because he was getting a grade. He did it because he loved it and he owned it. Now he makes extra money and has a full team that reports to him, even as he attends college.

ECs are a key component of a "killer app." Why? Aren't straight As, a high if not perfect GPA, great letters of recommendation, a perfect SAT, and ten or more AP classes enough? In a word, no. The Beatles expressed it perfectly when they said "Oh, that magic feeling, nowhere to go." What does a student do when nobody is telling him what to do or when he has "nowhere to go?" That's when the magic happens.

When I applied to colleges in the '60s, ECs were very much a secondary, if not tertiary, consideration. The only thing I recall doing along those lines was being in the chess club. No sports, nothing unusual, and I am not even sure I mentioned chess club on my application. Yet I was admitted easily to a state school. I was not an athlete, president of the class, or anything like that.

### Extra Curricular Activities

Things are very different now, however, and ECs are almost on par with GPA, SAT, and teacher recommendations. Things change, but like I said before, you have to outrun your hiking partner when a bear is chasing you. Part of that is knowing the terrain, and now that the terrain highly values ECs, you must as well.

When Ivy League schools (and most other highly regarded schools) look at ECs, they ask some key questions:

1. **Does the student have anything extra in his or her tank, and if so, how much?** If all a student does is study, then they will struggle when the work gets harder. If a student has time for a few EC activities, especially those that take many hours per week, then this will be the "fat" they can trim when the going gets tough at college. I know a student who was a great high school athlete. Sports took up a lot of his time, but he was recruited and admitted to UPenn. Once he started to attend, he found the academic work so time consuming and difficult. He had to drop out of his sport, which was the right decision. Once he trimmed the fat, he did fine in school.

2. **What makes the student tick?** Colleges want to see the passions of a good student. What do they do with their spare time? If there isn't any spare time (there should be!), why not? Sometimes there are legitimate excuses for a child to have no extra time for ECs, like if they are taking care of a sick relative or providing childcare for a sibling. Colleges want to know that. Is the student hanging out at the skateboard park, loitering at the shopping mall, or doing something constructive with their time and life? Whatever the answer, this is most likely how they will conduct their lives in the future (or so the colleges think).

3. **Is the EC about polish or passion?** Colleges are very adept at discerning if an EC is being done to polish an applicant's resume or if it stems from an intrinsic motivation and passionate interest. Are there a few activities that are pursued deeply, or are there many one-time events scattered over many

areas? This is a very important distinction that many parents and students do not take into consideration. It's far better to have fewer, deeper interests than many shallow ones.

4. **How common are the ECs?** Volunteering at a homeless shelter, although certainly worthwhile, is very common and will not raise any eyebrows. But becoming a Big Brother to an at-risk youth over many years can lead to an engaging story and looks better. The latter is, of course, harder to do and more time consuming, but it stands out. It feels unique by comparison. Note that ECs do not necessarily need to involve volunteering. A good student can start a business, and some have not only done that, but also scaled their businesses to the international level.

I know one student who had the creative idea of recycling used soap from luxury hotels in foreign countries by repackaging and distributing them to the homeless and other poor people in the community. This required a great deal of logistical skill, cooperation with hotel management, fundraising, distribution channels, and press coverage. It was also especially difficult to do remotely in another country, but this unique idea was thought up by the student and implemented throughout high school. This student is now attending Dartmouth, and I can assure you that this EC had a great deal to do with it. She demonstrated leadership, business skills, and the grit to pull it off. These qualities are exactly what Ivy League schools look for in an EC.

Another student had a developmentally disabled sibling, so she designed a comic book project to distribute to other siblings of disabled children to help them cope with this unique situation. I also have a disabled sibling and have lived a life that is very different from my peers. I am now her legal guardian, and the challenges that this presents can be daunting and time consuming, requiring creative thinking and certainly emotional energy others don't have to expend. My sister recently fell and broke her back, so the entire family (including Max) made an unplanned trip to NYC to visit her. The experience of having to care for a disabled member of the family is a major responsibility that can stretch a family in many ways. There are support groups and services aimed at caregiver siblings; I can certainly appreciate this student's drive to do something along those lines. She is going to Yale. Believe me, Yale noticed this EC big time.

The point is this: Ivy League schools do not want to miss admitting the next Bill Gates, Mark Zuckerberg, or JFK. They look far into the future and know that having a famous person, a mover and a shaker who graduated from their institution, will improve their reputation and ranking. When applying, it is your job as a parent to help your child show admissions committees that he or she has the potential to be that kind of person. The key word is potential. There are some applicants who have already achieved great status or press coverage sufficient to make their name well recognized, but that is not necessary to catch the eye of an admissions officer. Those people are few and far between. When you are the daughter of a sitting US President, showing up to your tour with the Secret Service in tow, that will catch their attention. If you are an Olympic gold medalist, discover a new test for cancer, are working at a high level on a relevant research project, have won the Intel science fair, or the like, you will have a much better chance of admission. There's no guarantee, of course, since you must have the baseline grades, GPA, and APs, but ECs certainly add favorably to the picture. These spectacular achievements are not necessary for the Ivy applicant however. It's the potential that they are interested in.

## Finding Inspiring Peers

One of Max's peers is now attending Harvard and was voted the smartest student in the world after discovering new treatments for influenza. President Obama even honored him at the White House. That is what we are talking about. This was all done in his "spare" time. How is that for good peers at your school? Intimidating or inspiring? That choice is pivotal.

Start planning early. Think big. You just might hit it out of the park. This last example also points out the benefit of being at a highly rated school with high-level peers. These will be your child's role models. It is a well-known fact that like begets like, so surrounding yourself with high performers will bring out your child's best traits. If you are the parent of a middle school student with the goal of the Ivy League or other elite schools, then I would seriously consider moving to a place with a high school like this. It's a big sacrifice but well worth it.

There are several schools like this, and you are likely to find one not too far from you, but you have to look. Don't think the neighborhood school, public or private, is as good as a top-twenty high school. That is simply not true. It is more difficult to analyze private schools since they do not release their statistics, like student SAT scores. I believe this is purposeful since they want to carefully craft their reputation, and these scores may not measure up. There are really no rankings per se of private high schools like there are of public schools (*US News* rankings), so you have to evaluate carefully constructed reputations from private school PR departments. Be careful. Know they're biased. That doesn't mean a school is not good, but just know that public school rankings are much more objective.

In general, most public high schools in this country are not good. In fact, most are mediocre. It's a big problem in this country and has stimulated interest in private schools. That said, the top-rated public schools are way better academically than most private schools for a number of reasons. The difference is that private colleges are included in national ratings whereas private high schools are not. A top-rated public high school has better curricula, better teachers, better peer groups, and better counseling than the great majority of private schools. You don't get the expensive school trips, the hand holding, fancy classrooms, cachet, or exclusivity, but you will get your child a better education in an environment with top peers who will motivate your child. If you then supplement with tutors as needed, you'll have the best of both worlds.

When Max attended the exclusive private school through the fourth grade, we were surrounded by millionaires and even billionaires. I frequently asked myself what we were doing there, but it was kind of fun hanging out with them (as if their success would somehow rub off). Some of their children would brag to Max about how much money their family had (they were too young to know better). Good for them. They will most likely live off of that money the rest of their lives as opposed to creating their own lives, businesses, and relationships. Affluenza is a handicap that must be overcome if you want to design your own life.

I have been asked about what parents can do if their local school does not measure up. If possible, move. If it's not possible to move due to job commitments, family, or other reasons, then search out tutoring options, online instruction, homeschooling, private schools, or whatever will work in your particular circumstance. If you think all this is too hard, then think about the homeless student who got into Harvard or the immigrant who did not speak English. They had problems—you have a choice. Is supplementing your child's education with handpicked tutors enough to make up for a poor school? No! The school, curriculum, and teachers all mean more. Your priorities, values, and decisions will determine what happens to your child. Take a good look in the mirror and ask yourself what is more important: you or your child's future? Sometimes it comes down to that.

What did Max do for ECs? Film schools rarely see a STEM student with excellent credentials since film takes so much time and usually attracts a different kind of mind. Also, top-twenty universities rarely see applicants with a deep experience in film. Max decided not to make film a career even though he intends it to be a lifelong hobby. He made over twenty films, had two websites showcasing his films, and a film business. He also had a YouTube channel, multiple articles in the press about him, and won prestigious national awards for film. This included a large award given to only fifteen students nationwide. He is now flown back to San Francisco yearly to participate in the awards ceremony and mingle with his peers. He made films in several international locations like Italy, France, Israel, Spain, and India.

Max started making films in elementary school with his friends. He then graduated to filming skateboarding since he enjoyed that activity for a time. This shows deep involvement in an activity rarely seen by the Ivy League. It also shows grit, passion, business skills, commitment, and accomplishment within the industry. Max loved to skateboard from an early age. So do many other kids, but he took this very common activity and made his way into the Ivy League by integrating it with film. Think about what your child likes doing anyway and get creative. This is far different from forcing them into an activity you think would look good.

In conclusion, ECs must be planned out in advance of high school based on your student's interests. This will not work if the activity is contrived or put upon the child. It must come from them. A Tiger Mother would select the activity themselves and force cubs into compliance by threatening to withhold love. A Lion Dad knows better. No three-hour-long, forced violin lessons just to look good for college for my cub! Seek out the appropriate venue for this unique activity and pursue it with passion, grit, and purpose. You and your student will reap the rewards.

Extra Curricular activities

## LION DAD COMMANDMENTS FOR CHAPTER NINE

1. Talk to your child early about their interests.
2. Encourage the development of a few passions.
3. Support these interests with your time and money.
4. Seek out guidance and programs for these interests.
5. Never force your child to "practice."
6. Be flexible.
7. Celebrate your child's accomplishments with ECs.
8. Develop intrinsic motivations, not extrinsic motivations.
9. Do not do these activities for the resume.
10. Have fun with it.

# 10

# THE ESSAY

## A Window into Your Student's Mind

*"Writing is the painting of the voice."*
—**Voltaire, writer**

When Max was about twelve years old, we were walking in the downtown area of our new city. It had the feel of Haight-Ashbury in San Francisco, with coffee hangouts and old record stores. We had just come from an international car show at the nearby convention center, and we went into a hippy shop so I could show him the kinds of things I valued as a teenager.

Inside was a long-haired man dressed in robes and a turban. He was visiting from India and led an ashram for people seeking enlightenment. Max was fascinated by him and asked him how long it would take to become enlightened. "Ten years," the guru responded. Max continued to press him and asked how long would it take if he tried really hard and studied more than the average student. He said, "In that case, it would take twenty years."

"How about if I came in to see you every day?" Max asked.

"Then it would take thirty years."

"Why," Max asked. "Would it take longer if I worked harder?"

## THE ESSAY

"Because when you have one eye on the goal instead of the process, you will not progress as fast."

It's fine to have a stated goal, but it's not fine to be constantly focused on it or graded, tested, and self-conscious about it. This, in a nutshell, is the basic problem with education today—a problem that relates directly to the college essay.

Part of learning to be a leader and to create complex concepts is developing the skill of writing. Once the mechanics of writing are mastered (grammar, spelling, composition, etc.), then creative thought can evolve. But it has to have something to evolve from. Writing stems from thinking, and thinking stems from your inner world, your vocabulary, your experiences in life, and the breadth of your reading. This is one reason why reading is so important. As Mark Twain said, "Those who do not read are no better than those who cannot read."

The printing press is arguably the most important technological invention in the history of mankind. It allowed the widespread distribution of knowledge which was previously almost impossible. Prior to the printing press, books were handwritten, very few in number, and almost always on religion. Almost no one read. Gutenberg's introduction of the commercial printing press in 1450 was an enormous pivotal point in communication, making texts readily accessible to anyone. Exposing yourself to as many thinkers as possible expands your own thoughts and leads to better writing. It's all related. Writing is a reflection of your inner mind, the quality of your thoughts, and your ability to integrate many aspects of your memory.

That's why the essay is the most dreaded part of the application for many students. Some start working on their college essay a full year in advance. Why is that? I think it's because most students are focused on the multiple choice test, the fill-in-the-blank questions, and the rote memory required of them in today's schools. They are not used to thinking on their own and pulling thoughts out of the air. They need prompting. Many students also rarely read books. These two deficiencies do not lead to independent thinkers, leaders, creators, or innovators. Rather, students are being taught to do what they are told. When faced with a blank sheet of paper in front of them and asked to produce a coherent, enjoyable story, they freeze. They need to be told what to think, how to do it, and provided a rubric and formula.

The essay is the only part of the application that's not formulaic (although it's getting there). It's meant to showcase applicants, in their own words, and distinguish them from other candidates. It should demonstrate parts of themselves not evident in the rest of the application. The essay is a chance to show colleges that your child can think without being told specifically what to think or how. It's the subjective part of the application and a tall, stressful order to do well. Think about this. By the way, most adults do not know how to write well since they have been conditioned by the multiple choice test and the "boss" telling them what to do every minute. That "boss" could be an individual, a governmental agency, or an institution.

## How to Write a good essay

Essay prompts vary by school. They can be 150 to 650 words long and will be read by "readers" who somehow plough through hundreds if not thousands of applications. How do you stand out? Use big words? Catchy titles? Racy subjects? There is so much advice floating around on this subject that is seems everyone has to weigh in. However, the essay is part of the whole presentation and above all should be consistent with the rest of the parts. It must also be written by the applicant, not the parents or the consultant. A good consultant will coach applicants by bouncing ideas off them, but they will not write an essay themselves or drastically edit one to the point that they are basically writing it. I have known parents or consultants who do just that.

The readers know which essays are written by the student and which are not. In fact, it's one of the most important considerations. If they suspect your essay was essentially written by someone else, you can forget getting into that school. It's just not worth the risk. Admissions officers have been known to compare the application essay to the style, vocabulary, and flow of an applicant's SAT essay if they suspect the college essay has questionable authorship. If they think your child's essay drifts too far from your SAT essay, he or she's out. Period. This does not happen very often, but keep it in mind. It's better for your child to write a bad essay in his or her own words. Colleges know your child is not a Pulitzer Prize winner, so unless your child has written that quality of work in the past, don't submit it here from someone else. It would look absurd and dishonest.

## Essay Consultants: Worth It?

There are consultants who work solely on the essay—that's how competitive this process has become. These consultants would not exist if there were not worried parents and students willing to pay them large fees. They would not exist if students were taught to think on their own instead of following directions and prompts. Most of these specialists are a waste of money and time, however. They can lead you down the wrong path, edit your work beyond recognition, and make your essay so inconsistent with the rest of your application that it will be a net negative. Most of them do not even look at the rest of your application since that is not their "department." There are of course good essay consultants as well, but it's difficult to know who they are.

If you pay a large amount of money to an essay consultant, there is a great deal of pressure from both sides for the essay to "turn out good." In many cases, this means the essay is essentially written by the consultant. As I've said, that's far from ideal. It's another reason why I do not advise an essay consultant. It rarely can be done effectively and is too risky. At the most your student should have light editing done and nothing more. By that I mean spelling, grammar, and sentence structure. No content edits, no rewriting.

If an essay consultant is hired, they should help your student talk about his or her passions, personality, unique attributes, and style. The essay will flow from that. An essay consultant is, therefore, different from a writing tutor. The good essay consultant takes the rest of the application into consideration and draws out a consistent presentation. Writing tutors usually just focus on technique, which should have been in place years before thanks to your child's teachers and reading history.

Essay consultants can be helpful in subject selection, however. Sometimes a student might want to write about an especially meaningful experience that they hope illustrates a certain character trait to the reader. Be very careful about that. Many times that can come across as self-aggrandizement, which is a no-no. There is a subtle difference between bragging and self-expression. Colleges don't like bragging. I recall one student who produced a brief and poorly made video of himself talking about his high GPA, test scores, ECs, etc. These were all things already in the application, and it made him look bad. He got rejected from many schools as a result. That's probably why our counselor advised against sending the video we made, even though it was artfully made and had things in it not in the application.

## Picking a Theme

Please, please, please do not write about a special trip or a sports injury. These subjects are way overdone and totally boring to an admissions officer. You do not want your admissions officer groaning about any part of your application.

Decide what theme your child's application presents. Serious STEM students shouldn't write about a recent trip to the art museum, for example. Likewise if your child is an artist, don't have them write about playing baseball. Tangentially related topics to your theme are fine, but the key is to be consistent with the chosen theme.

When conveying your story, make sure your child keeps in mind the following tips:

1. ***Show, don't tell.*** Show, through your words, what you are trying to convey. Don't lecture or describe, even if the words are flowery.
2. ***Get personal, but not too personal.*** Don't tell a total stranger your innermost secrets. It looks ridiculous. This is not a true confessions article. Talk about feelings and the impact the subject of the essay had on you.

3. *Craft a title and introduction that grabs the reader.* This is very important. You want to pull your readers into the story, keep them there, and punctuate their reading experience with a harmonious conclusion—harmonious to the essay, your application theme, and you.

4. **Be yourself.** That's who they want to see in the essay. Show off parts of yourself not evident in the rest of the application, so do not brag or rehash what is already in the application. Be sincere.

5. *Use language that's natural to you while meeting the requirements.* Of course, make sure the grammar, spelling, punctuation, and length is correct, but do that while fully communicating your ideas. Sounds easy, right? Not really. It's a process of continual rewriting, thinking, brainstorming, and middle-of-the-night insights. Have fun with it, but don't think you can do it in one sitting the night before the application is due.

## Putting the Applicant into Words

One of the best essays I read from an applicant was about a trip to Costco when she was ten years old. It was so engaging and entertaining. Nothing dramatic, but it clearly showed who this woman was and that she knew how to write. She didn't use big words from a thesaurus (another no-no), but her skill was evident by the analogies she drew while weaving an entertaining story through the eyes of a ten-year-old. Remember, the essay is a slice of life, not the whole thing. Don't try to tell your life's story in 650 words.

I think Max's essays were a key component of his admission to his current university. I have included versions edited for privacy in the appendix. He wrote them entirely on his own, and I did not even see them until the application was submitted. He tried using consultants for essays to other schools with limited success. These included everything from specialists to general counselors to friends who claimed to have writing skills and did it for free. They all had their opinions, but none of them sounded like Max.

As I wrote this book, I solicited opinions and comments from a variety of sources, each contact had original suggestions not thought of by the previous readers. I have no doubt if I solicited another dozen readers, I would get twelve more suggestions—at least. The point I am trying to make is this: The essay is not about the "right" answer. It is not a voting contest. It's also not objective. Certain writing conventions should be followed, but at its core, the essay is a sincere expression of who the applicant is in their own words, without pretense, self-aggrandizement, big words, or content from other parts of the application.

An experienced admissions reader will be able to sort through all this. When you read thousands of essays, meet thousands of students every year, you can quickly know who is sincere and who is not. Sincerity, clarity, likability, and flow is much more important than fancy vocabulary, spectacular or odd subject matters, and dazzling prose. I know most students are dying to try out their newfound vocabulary words, but this is not the time or place. Perhaps one or two well-placed words would be appropriate, but that's it. Pretend you are reading the essay yourself. If you like it, others will.

## Be a Researcher and Advocate

Every year there are winning essays published in books and websites. Reading these can be helpful at the start of your process. It might help stir up some qualities or stories unique to your student. For a fee, admitsee.com will let you see the key stats for top students, including SAT scores, GPA, college acceptances, and full essays. I found this site very helpful and certainly interesting, but I don't think Max looked at it very much. Some of these websites, pages 291-308, are very helpful. Check them out. The amount of information available on the web now for college applications is overwhelming, which makes the whole process somewhat transparent but also confusing. An intelligent read of some of these sites can give you an advantage. Look deeply and spend time on them. The more background

THE ESSAY

you have, the more you know the current terrain (remember the bear story), the better off you will be.

There is a difference between what you think colleges (or certain colleges) require and what actually works. I have known more than one intelligent parent assume that they know what's important at a certain school only to be shocked by a rejection letter. Be sure to do the work necessary to figure out what really works at a particular school.

You are your child's biggest advocate. Do the research to be the best advocate you can.

> **SUGGESTION: PLEASE SKIP AHEAD TO THE RESOURCES SECTION ON PAGES 287-304 FOR VALUABLE COMMENTARY AND WEBSITES ON COLLEGE ADMISSIONS, TUTORING AND COUNSELING.**

## LION DAD COMMANDMENTS FOR CHAPTER TEN

1. The essay should be written solely by the student.
2. Pick a topic consistent with the theme of the application.
3. Use very few $100 words, if any.
4. Don't brag.
5. Write from the heart.
6. Use consultants sparingly for the essay.
7. Value writing since it will propel your student higher, no matter his or her field.
8. How you write is how you think.
9. Try to write about something not in the application.
10. Clarity, clarity, clarity.
11. Don't exaggerate, but keep the reader hooked.
12. The essay is a slice of life, not the whole thing.

# 11

# ADMISSIONS TACTICS:

## The Details that Matter

*"Do not train a child to learn by force or harshness; but direct them to it by what amuses their minds, so that you may be better able to discover with accuracy the peculiar bent of the genius of each."*
—**Plato, philosopher**

On a recent visit to Max for parent weekend, I met several students and parents. What a great opportunity for research on this book. These are people who have succeeded at the very thing this book is about (sometimes more than once). I met one couple in their late fifties during a breakfast event. They had a freshman in Max's class, so I asked them why they chose this school. In a thick Russian accent, the mother told me that they had one child go to Harvard and another go to Max's school, so they decided to send their third child there as well. The school's name is deleted for privacy reasons, as are many other details. This is a family who has figured it out. When I asked them how they achieved this, they were somewhat reserved, and I knew it was too broad a question to receive a rational answer in that setting. I don't think their three children got into Ivy League schools because they inherited intelligence genes. The parents seemed normal in every way.

ADMISSIONS TACTICS:

I think they all learned how to think, what decisions to make, what to value, and what actions to take over many years in order to wind up at the highest level of education possible.

This illustrates a general principle that's important in life and specifically for college acceptance. When you want to achieve a certain goal, study the people who have achieved that goal, not the ones who failed. Learn from success, not failure. It's a simple and intuitive method, so it makes you wonder why so many do just the opposite! They try to learn from their mistakes or the mistakes of others, thinking that avoiding all the pitfalls will let them stumble into where they want to go. Rather, learn from the parents of successful Ivy League applicants and pick their brains whenever possible. Hopefully they will tell you.

Do the same with Ivy League applicants. Most will likely avoid the question out of modesty or since they know it is too complex a question to answer simply. Besides, they are already on to the next thing. It's the ones who say to themselves "I am as good as anyone on the planet, so there is no reason I should not be thought of that way" that succeed. They find a way and learn from others who have succeeded, not from the ones who have failed. Most parents of students like this do not write about this experience for several reasons, including concerns for privacy. This is one reason I took great pains to anonymize the story as much as possible. The names, locations, and some details have been changed, but the essence of the story remains intact. It is hard work to write a book about getting a child into the Ivy League, especially a tell-all like this one.

It has always amazed me that medical schools and medical education in general study every aspect of disease in order to achieve health. What they should be focusing on is healthy people, their habits, decisions, lifestyle, and social settings. Study the people who are healthy and living past ninety. Of course you need to treat people for various diseases, but not having one illness or another is not the same as being healthy or living long. Medical schools study disease to achieve health, they say, but that's not really what they're all about. They are focused on treating disease, so don't think the average doctor will teach you anything about health. Focus on what you want, not what you don't want.

## Letters of Recommendation

Letters of recommendation (LORs) are important components of a killer app. If done right, they can be very important. Ask someone who knows your child well as opposed to a big name or influential person. These details are important. However, the ideal situation is to ask a powerful, influential person who knows your child well to write the LOR. This rarely happens, but it happened to us when the superintendent of Max's school district, originally Max's high school principal, volunteered to write a letter for Max. He said he only writes two or three letters per year and always handpicks the students. We were flattered that he chose Max. We never saw the letter he wrote, since that is the custom (the student must sign a statement that says they will not read the letter), but I am confident it helped. This superintendent was charismatic, popular, positive, and well respected in the local educational community.

This kind of letter is the best you can do. How did we get to know this person so well? Surely there were other worthy students, but he did not know them as well as Max and his family. We made it our business to get to know him from day one, not because we were thinking about an LOR, but because he was in a position of influence, and we wanted him on our side. Besides, he was such a nice person. I made an appointment with him the first week of Max's ninth grade year and went to his office to get off on the right foot. It paid off.

Some have celebrities or wealthy well-known people write letters for their child but do not know the child very well. This is a mistake, and it tells the admissions committee that they are supposed to be impressed that the student's family knows someone famous. Don't do it. It could backfire. We know several people in this category who could have written an LOR for Max, but I am glad we resisted. The admissions committee members know that you probably know some celebrities, and you look better by limiting your LORs writers to people who have had significant contact with your child, even if they themselves are not famous or well-connected. The Ivy League sees celebrities all day long and they will not be impressed that you know one.

ADMISSIONS TACTICS:

The knowledge these individuals have about your child should come through in a well-written, non-boilerplate letter. It should hopefully compare your child to their peers in a favorable light. This is the most important aspect of this letter. Admissions committees read these letters by looking for statements that favorably contrasts students to others, not just general accolades. Letters that stress leadership, character, participation, and personality are usually impressive. Whatever you do, do not write these letters yourself and present them to the teachers for signature. Not only is this insulting to the teacher, but admissions committees will see through this in a heartbeat. Unfortunately, some high school teachers who have had extensive contact with your students are not also good LOR writers. It might be a good idea to ask your school counselor who writes the best letters, and if there is one who knows your student well, choose that one.

Most students have to request letters from selected teachers. Do this well in advance, do it respectfully, and give them the opportunity to say no. Provide them with all the information needed to write the letter without telling them what to write, and thank them (with a formal, handwritten thank you note) after they write the letter, even if you don't see it. In Max's school, they encouraged the child's family to design a "brag sheet," which is basically bullet points of the child's key achievements (not a full resume). This is a great help to the writers. How many letters should you submit? Follow school guidelines, but generally two or three at maximum.

Typically, an admissions committee wants an LOR from your child's guidance counselor, which can be a problem since many of guidance counselors have hundreds of students they are responsible for and may not know your student very well. How do they write hundreds of letters like this? Can you say "copy and paste?" It's up to your student to make sure the guidance counselor knows them as much as possible. What about asking a private counselor you hired for a letter like this? No. Don't do this. They want to hear from the school counselor, not someone on your payroll.

Finally, students who try to impress a committee with ten or more LORs will do just the opposite—turn them off. It will make you look desperate. Remember, it's what is said in the letter that is more important than who writes it. This is not always true in other settings, but it is true in this one. *What* is more important than *who*.

## Marketing Your Student

This is a delicate area. Of course, this is what you are doing when you design a killer app, highlight certain aspects of your child, mold your child's social media presence, hire consultants, and put your best foot forward. However, you must be subtle about what you do so it does not come across as too self-serving. Sometimes this is a fine line, and the judgment about what to do and what not to do can be difficult. Use your consultants for this.

A good example of this is the film I made about Max that highlighted some of his accomplishments, had interviews with teachers and students, and showed him giving speeches. I thought this would be a great addition to his resume since he was also a filmmaker. It was done very professionally and in my mind made him look fantastic. However, I was overruled by our consultants and by Max, who declined to submit it. We spent much time, money, and energy on this project, and I was personally invested, so letting it go was not easy. But it was the right decision.

We mentioned this film to the admissions officer who presented Max's application to the committee, and he said it was smart not to include the film. It probably would have led to his rejection since it would have come across as too self-serving and out of the ordinary. We discussed this with him after he was admitted. Admissions officers love meeting parents and the admitted student after the fact. They spend a great deal of time reviewing their application and presenting it to the committee, so it is perfectly okay to search them out, introduce yourself, and thank them for their support. They can be very helpful later on as well.

So, knowing that you can go too far, what can you do to "market" your child? You are, after all, bringing your child to the marketplace of selective schools. You should review and clean up social media posts. I can guarantee you that any Ivy League school that is seriously looking at your child will use Google and Facebook to find out more about him or her. It's easy to do, so make sure your child comes across well.

If you were to google Max, you get two or three pages of links, all good, including some press releases and his websites, awards, etc. Much of this is in the application anyway, but not all of it. It's good for the admissions committee members to come across this stuff on their own. Some parents actually hire a PR firm to orchestrate all this. We did not do this. If this can be done artfully, then I have no objection, but it's risky. Be careful. What looks good to you may not look good to the people making the judgments. I think the admissions committees are looking for potential that they can mold rather than a fully formed and polished finished product, complete with press releases, professionally done resumes, and big Twitter feeds. Thousands of followers may be good for marketing your book, but not your child.

## SCHOLARSHIPS AND FINANCIAL AID

This is a big issue for many families. There are many sources of outside scholarship money, but the big money usually comes from the school itself. The nuances of filling out the Free Application for Federal Student Aid (FAFSA) and College Scholarship Service (CSS) forms are difficult and may require hiring a specialist consultant just for this. Unless you clearly qualify for financial aid or clearly do not qualify for aid, then I would hire one of these consultants.

Many schools state they are "need-blind," and some clearly state they are "need-aware." What does this mean? Theoretically, *need-blind* means that the applications are all judged on their merits alone and not based on ability to pay. However, I suspect that if a school has two applicants with nearly identical applications, but one demonstrates the ability and willingness to pay and the other demonstrates need—it will be the one who can pay that gets the spot. No school can afford to give free tuition to every student, so there must be some control along these lines. It is a business after all. Therefore, I still think that the ability to pay gives an applicant a distinct advantage. I don't have any proof of this. It's a black box. Of course, if the applicant fills a certain need or slot (like a football player, geographical area, etc.), that weighs heavily.

When a school declares themselves as need-aware, then they are telegraphing the fact that they give preference to students who can pay. It's honest. Therefore, if you apply to a need-aware school, be sure and fill out the FAFSA and CSS form anyway even if you don't intend to apply for financial aid since these forms show you can pay. It will give you an edge. We found this out the hard way.

Max applied to a need-aware school for early decision but did not fill out the FAFSA or CSS form since we had not gotten around to it and planned on doing it later. He was rejected, and I think it may have been our lack of attention to this detail which caused this. If you can pay, fill out the FAFSA anyway. It will give you an advantage, especially in need-aware schools.

How do you fill out the FAFSA and or CSS forms to maximize your chances of aid? There are books and a cadre of consultants charging high fees to answer this very question. They can be helpful on occasion, but choose wisely. I know of some families who move money around, use annuities, real estate, or even misrepresent their financial situation. This is tempting for some but a big mistake in my opinion. Be very careful, and above all, be honest.

## **EARLY DECISION, EARLY ACTION, REGULAR DECISION**

Applying early decision (ED) definitely gives you an advantage since most schools accept a higher percentage from ED applicants. However, most legacies and athletes also apply early, so these admission figures may be somewhat misleading. When you factor out the recruited athletes and legacies, the percentage of ED applicants versus regular decision applicants admitted may only be slightly higher, if they are higher at all. The key with ED is that your child is obligated to attend unless there is a pressing financial issue. So unless your child is absolutely sure about which school to attend, then you should probably apply early action or regular decision. You will have better choices in the end when you factor in financial aid.

Many students use their ED card for a reach school, thinking that it's a long shot. Many times their acceptance is deferred, meaning that they will theoretically be considered with the regular decision applicant pool. In reality, deferred ED applicants rarely get in later. The school defers them so the applicant does not feel too let down and so they have more to choose from in April, just in case the applicant pool is weak. It usually isn't.

Some schools, including the Ivies, accept as many as 50 percent of their class via ED. Using or not using the ED card is a personal one which must be made very carefully. In general, if the applicant is strong, then apply regular decision and see what you get. Have confidence. It is very difficult to be objective about your child's chance to be admitted to a given school. Some families act out of fear when they apply ED since they reason that their child is not good enough to get in regular decision and need that extra (likely theoretical) edge. Then, when that student is admitted, everyone will wonder what would have happened if they did not apply ED. Try to project yourself into this situation, and if you even think there is a possibility you would regret the ED choice, then apply regular decision.

Early action is really no advantage at all except that it might give you more of a chance for financial aid in some cases. There are schools that do not have ED since they are confident of filling their spots with quality students. ED is really an advantage for the school since it increases their yield (percent of students matriculating who are offered admission). This in turn raises their ranking, which creates more applicants next year, and so on. Whether or not to rush into ED is really a marker of self-confidence in my opinion. Too many counselors and well-meaning relatives or friends ask where you are applying ED as opposed to if you are applying ED. The latter question should be asked more often.

## Naviance

Most high schools have an online portal called Naviance which shows a graph of each admitted student from that high school to each college. It also graphs GPA and SAT scores. This invaluable information has only been made available recently. It can tell you what your real chances are of getting your child into a given school. It's one thing to look at the published stats from the school itself, but looking at the results from your child's high school gives you a much better idea of where he or she stands and of how the school is valued by the college you are thinking about.

For example, if a given school publishes that their average GPA is 4.2, but the Naviance page of your high school says the average GPA of an accepted student is 4.4, then you know that your high school is not as highly rated by the college in question. On the other hand, if that same college accepts students from your school with a GPA of 4.0, then you know they value your high school more than others. The same analysis can be applied to the SAT scores. Always compare the Naviance averages with the published college stats. This can be very helpful.

Keep in mind, however, that the average GPA or SAT statistics from a given college on their own website is based on thousands of students, and the average GPA and SAT stats on Naviance are based on only a few. This can skew the results. Of course, admissions decisions are based on so many other factors too, so it's really hard to draw any solid conclusions from this data, but it may be an indication of your child's chances. Just another piece of the puzzle— no stone left unturned. In the case of elite schools, the admission decisions are so multifaceted and customized that it's very hard to make conclusions on the handful of students applying to them from each high school. Maybe the admitted student was an athlete of some kind so the Naviance data is a rough guideline, no more. Naviance has great information, but it's rough data, so take it with a grain of salt.

ADMISSIONS TACTICS:

# LION DAD COMMANDMENTS FOR CHAPTER ELEVEN

1. Do not submit too many letters of recommendation.
2. Thank your student's teacher or counselor in writing.
3. Use Naviance and compare stats with the college website.
4. Fill out the FAFSA and CSS early.
5. Think carefully about applying early decision, and don't do it out of fear.
6. Market your child, but be subtle.
7. Clean up any social media sites, and be careful what you post.
8. Develop a personal website that is carefully constructed.
9. Do not submit letters from famous people unless they know your child well.
10. Try to bring all the components together into palatable whole that makes sense.

J K Roark M.D.

# 12

# FILM, TRAVEL & VOLUNTEERING

## A Deep Dive into
## Three Significant Differentiators

*"None of us got where we are solely by pulling ourselves up by our bootstraps. We got here because somebody—a parent, a teacher, an Ivy League crony or a few nuns— bent down and helped us pick up our boots."*
—**Thurgood Marshall, Supreme Court Judge**

When Max was just ten years old, we were horsing around the house one weekend, chasing each other, playing hide and seek, throwing a baseball around in the backyard—just generally having fun. After about thirty minutes, he looked up at me and said: "Dad, sometimes you have to be the parent."

This anecdote, however brief, illustrates the nature of our relationship, which was perhaps unusual. Several friends commented that he was like my best friend. I know some readers would disapprove, but it worked for us. Max always knew I would and could lay down the law if needed, which was rare. I always placed myself on his level, whatever age he was. When he was a toddler, I was on my hands and knees. A few years later, we were on motor scooters. In middle school, on the baseball field. In high school, in his films and at his screenings. I knew every aspect of his classes—not just the courses he took, but the details of the assignments.

I was not, as many parents seem to think is necessary, towering above him as the authority figure he had to obey in an unquestioning manner. I never told him do this with the classic "Because I told you to." Even at a young age, I explained in age-appropriate terms the reasons behind an action. I guided him, but I did not command him. That is why he can guide himself now. He's practiced at making decisions, asserting himself, setting boundaries, and above all, thinking critically. I was the guide on the side, not the sage on the stage. If you harmonize with your child, and they let you into their world, then you can show them the way out into the outer world. That's the real power of Lion Dad parenting, not being a dictator, authority figure, teacher, or sage on the stage.

Contrast this to the way Tiger Mother cubs interact with their parents. The Tiger Mother is the sage on the stage. In many cases, the cubs refer to their parents as Mother and Father, not Mom, Mama, Dad, or Daddy. They are visibly stiff around their parents, being very careful about what they say and do. Tiger Mother cubs learn this behavior early and carry it with them when they meet and interact with other adults. They're respectful but distant. You can see it in their eyes. The recent movie *Crazy Rich Asians* illustrates the East-West dichotomy very well and in an extremely funny way. The East thinks the West values happiness too much, whereas the East values dynasties, strict obedience to authority, and fear-based family structures with well-defined roles. I am not about to criticize cultural norms that took thousands of years to evolve or even state that the Western approach is somehow "better." It is worthwhile, however, to notice these differences, make a conscious choice about what norms to follow, and above all, be flexible enough to see what works in your own environment. The East and Tiger Parents do value older adults as sources of wisdom whereas the West honors their youth. This is the one area that I agree with the East on.

When we are around other children who were raised by Tiger Mothers, they treat me (an adult) the same way they treat their own parents—by being stiff, polite, respectful, and slightly anxious. This is their model. Many of Max's teachers and other adults commented to us that he is as comfortable interacting with adults as with his peers. This is why: he is used to acting that way in front of adults. He's respectful but comfortable at the same time. Children learn how to relate to authority figures by how they relate to their parents. They learn how to relate to their peers by how they relate to their siblings. It's not rocket science.

## Film

This book would not be complete without a section on film, which was such an important part of Max's life starting in elementary school and contributing significantly to his admission to top level schools. Max learned film making on his own before high school, even before middle school. He did this all through trial and error with various cameras, software (including Final Cut Pro and Adobe Premiere—that professional filmmakers use), lenses, microphones, lighting—the works. We spent a fortune on all this stuff, which filled up his office/studio. He made films for many local adults who needed pieces for their websites, businesses, or events. He filmed weddings and had a crew. He had a small business going, but he did not do it for money. He did it out of love and curiosity.

It took many hours of editing once the filming finished, and then the final product was uploaded to YouTube, burned on a DVD, or sometimes broadcast on TV. He still produces films for various entities. It's a great skill. Max went on an overseas trip one summer. Committed to making a film about this event, he brought all his equipment, filmed the entire process in multiple countries, edited the raw footage, and sold copies to the participants, almost paying for the entire trip. The final product was forty minutes, had a soundtrack, titles, credits, and interviews. The kids and parents loved it when we showed it at the reunion and passed out the copies. The best reward for a filmmaker is having an audience with a large screen. We still watch it occasionally.

His film business was not without its problems. One time he arranged to film the wedding of one of his tutors. Max planned this out in detail and even hired an assistant to help him on the day of the event. Considering he was only fifteen years old, it was impressive. He worked very hard on this project, but there was one big problem—the client stiffed him! That's right, even after delivering the raw footage and the finished product, Max did not get paid what he agreed to accept (which was 20 percent of what a professional would charge). I was so angry. It was a learning experience. No contract, no down payment, and handing over the finished product before getting paid were the biggest mistakes. It was so humiliating. An early lesson in business.

Max was also the producer of a TV station at the high school level. They did a twenty-minute story every week, complete with anchors, scripts, filming, editing, etc. It was time consuming but very well done. Most of the students and hundreds of teachers and staff watched it. I have no idea how the students found the time given their busy schedules, AP classes and tests, quarterly courses, and other ECs.

Several of Max's films won awards, including at the state fair. It gave me a deep appreciation of that entire industry and its components—producing, directing, cinematography, editing, post-production, promotional posters, screenings, actors, script writing, etc. This was a great deal more than a kid with his iPhone taking a few videos, and some of the college admission officers fully appreciated it. They understood the deep dive he took, the commitment that it involved, and the extensive time it took away from his other studies. They could also plainly see from the films showcased on his websites, YouTube channels, and screenings that this was not done to polish his resume or get some extrinsic reward. Sure, not all schools recognized this EC for the deep accomplishment it was. There is nothing you can do about that. Max got rejected from a few second-tier schools even though he was accepted at several elite universities. This is a function of the quality of the admissions committees, their own values, luck, and the specific needs of the school. As I said before, the Ivy League looks at students differently than the average school. A smart Lion Dad knows this and works with it.

## THE DEEP DIVE

The deep dive into a particular hobby, skill set, or interest is very important and something most colleges look for, although it's hard to tease out of the resume at times. Some high schools have unique programs that others do not. Maybe it's something in sports, the arts, or a field of academics. Whatever it is, it's worth exploring since whatever your child chooses will help him or her stand out among other applicants. Take advantage of what is right in front of you and make something special out of it. If you visited Yellowstone, would you sit in your room watching TV and look at your phone all day like you do at home, or would you take advantage of the unique opportunity right in front of you to see Old Faithful?

People have asked me, where did Max's interest in film come from? I think it started in kindergarten when I produced and showed a thirty-five-minute film featuring the kindergarten class, teachers, administrators, and school grounds. It was shown in the large, new auditorium at the end of the year, had a wonderful soundtrack, credits, interviews, and special effects. In a way, Max imprinted on this experience much like a wolf cub imprints on its mother. He wanted to pursue film himself and took it much further technically than I ever did.

When high-energy children are motivated internally, they can propel themselves further than you can imagine. When I was making my films and editing them, he would frequently advise me on what to put in and what to leave out, especially if it involved him (as it usually did). Now, as I am writing this book, Max has just started working on a creative writing project for his school. Children automatically mirror what they see around them, good or bad, so take notice.

It was a surprise to many who knew Max that he did not apply to film schools. I think he would have gotten into any one of the top film schools (USC, NYU, UCLA, Chapman) since Max also had excellent grades and test scores, all rare in a film student. Max felt that he would always have film to add to whatever career he chose and wanted a good liberal arts education primarily. He also had other interests. Maybe he will become the first physician filmmaker. At school, he is already filming interviews with key people with the intent of producing a series broadcast to the college. Film is considered the new literature by many, and having deep roots in this skill will serve him well, just as his writing skills will. A picture is worth a thousand words, and a film is worth a thousand pictures.

The Lion Parent approach encourages children to participate in deep and personal ECs. A Tiger Mother would have picked out an activity in advance, usually piano or violin, and made her cub do whatever she said. There is nothing wrong with those activities, which have multiple benefits besides looking good on college applications, but the problem is when the child does not choose it on his or her own. There's no freedom to explore. No Tiger Mother would encourage skateboarding, for example. Yet, skateboarding led to film for Max. The connection emerged from his own mind, from intrinsic, not extrinsic, motivation. Without pressuring him or her, just ask your child what they like to do. From there, you can brainstorm with your child, if necessary, about how to help develop that interest. Kids are controlled enough in school and elsewhere. They should have some sense that their lives are their own. The earlier that realization happens, the better. Some adults never achieve that. How sad. This is one of the basic premises of objectivism, the philosophy of Ayn Rand. Your life is your own. Others have no claim on it unless you voluntarily choose to give it to them.

## VOLUNTEERING

Volunteer experience is another hot item for college admissions, and most students have at least some volunteer work on their resumes. The key is making sure volunteer activities do not appear contrived or meant to polish a resume. They need to be connected to internal motivations. Yes, helping others is nice, but it needs to happen in a way that expresses your child's values and unique background. How deeply is the student involved? Is he or she a leader, or did they just join a group? The former is preferred. Is the organization unique or one of many? Is it done year after year, or is it a one-time activity? Volunteering is, of course, done without compensation and shows what the student does when he is not being rewarded. However, a reward can be looking good to colleges, but if at all possible, try to get that out of the equation while checking the boxes mentioned above.

Max volunteered extensively and deeply. He was specifically honored at a Jewish Federation event, during which the head of the local

Federation announced that Max had volunteered more than any other teen for Jewish events. He started with the Jewish Federation by participating in an amazing teen program, eventually becoming one of the few leaders recognized at an event. Max became involved in Jewish organizations primarily because many of his friends were also involved. I had very little to do with it. Once there, he went the extra mile and produced films for them, which automatically thrust him into a leadership role.

One of the highlights of Max's high school career came from his work at the Jewish Funders Network (JFN), a well-known international organization that raises money for Jewish causes around the globe. They attract many well known and well-heeled people. Max became a spokesperson for some Jewish events and was asked to introduce the keynote speakers. The event attracted six-hundred attendees at a formal luncheon. The mayor of Jerusalem (Nir Barkat) spoke, sat next to Max at the speaker's table, and invited him to visit in Israel. We, of course, got photos, and there was press coverage. There were two large jumbotron screens that had his image as he spoke. His speech was partially prepared for him, but we helped him memorize it, use appropriate body language, and add his own special touches. We rehearsed it over the preceding three days so Max was able to get on stage without notes! He was the only speaker who did that, including the mayor!

When Max was asked to give this introduction, he asked us whether he should do it or not since he already had a busy schedule. I immediately exclaimed, "Absolutely!" I pointed out that this was an honor and that there was no way he should refuse. Without our encouragement, he might not have accepted. This is a reflection of the Lion Dad and Lion Cub relationship. A Tiger Mother cub would not usually ask their parents if they could do something extra since they are typically fully booked by the parent. The foundational relationship established early on between Max and me is still intact. He frequently asks for my opinion and guidance on matters big and small. This is so satisfying to me, and I never take it for granted.

People noticed that he spoke without notes and came up to us with generous congratulations after the event. The famous speaker got onstage after the introduction and said to the entire group, "We will all be working for Max one day." You simply cannot get better PR for colleges than this. I was amazed at Max's composure and his courage to accept the honor in the first place. I was shaking in the audience as I filmed the entire speech. Max has since gained an interest in public speaking and has been asked several times to host events and give other talks. His willingness to put himself out there and present himself as a leader at such a young age is something colleges notice and look for. He even took voice lessons to improve his talks after I researched online tutors. This involved getting up some mornings at 6 a.m. to be coached, but the cub will value what the parent does and advises.

## Travel

Max developed an international perspective from an early age. We traveled as a family to the UK when he was eight and to Canada when he was three. These family travel experiences were not without their challenges. When we traveled as a family to London, I wanted to show Max a part of the world I very much enjoy. On one occasion when we were deep in the London Tube system (the London subway), there were announcements over the PA that all passengers should evacuate ASAP. This was at a time when subway terrorism was frequent. We went up four or five flights on escalators before we finally got above ground, and it was scary to say the least. The next day, I asked Max about this, and he said "I thought, if it was my time, then I'd have to accept it."

I cringed at my eight-year-old having a thought like that, but at the same time, I marveled at his composure under pressure. I truly believe the nurturing he had as a young child prepared him for this stressful event. Since then, Max has been to twenty-four countries, many of them more than once. He has been to Israel four times. He made films in most of those countries, some for his own use and memory, some for profit, and some as a gift to the group he was with. It was a natural activity for him to make films. I have always had a deep interest in international travel, which I got from my parents, so I made a point to pass this on to Max.

Travel is the best education. So many unanticipated events occur, requiring flexibility and being quick on your feet. Those who travel frequently have an advantage in life beyond just sightseeing. The sights, smells, culture, people, architecture, food, events, history, and currency all contribute. What you take to a country, however, is just as important as what you see. Your perspective, attitude, curiosity, grit, and motivation all play into your experience. What have the ultra-rich in society done throughout history? Travel. Now travel is more accessible than ever, so take advantage of the time we live in. Max has taken it to another level, and I have no doubt he will continue this throughout his life and pass it on to his children.

My own parents traveled quite a bit, so I inherited the travel bug from them. When you grow up seeing and hearing about international travel, it becomes a normal event and not so intimidating. This is why I have traveled to over sixty-five countries in my life . . . so far. Max has his own list and dreams along those lines. Our home is filled with mementos from around the world. Some think our collection is like our personal museum. It's not the value of these items that are important (most were not costly), but they represent events to savor and unique items not found elsewhere. It's what they are worth, not what they cost that is important.

This attitude was stressed in our family. We have many photo albums, framed photos on the walls, and even souvenir boards of special tickets and memorabilia scattered throughout our home. These items allow us to savor past events which in all likelihood would be forgotten otherwise. Savoring is akin to gratitude.

My mother had a profound influence on me in many ways. She was a voracious reader. Sometimes I would ask her about a particular book, and she would always know the book I was reading and tell me about the other books this author wrote. She was also the president of her class at Hunter College in NYC at the same time the United Nations had its first meeting, held at her school since the UN building had not been built yet. She was invited to attend, had a police escort, and was mentioned in press releases which I still look at. I was and am so proud of her. I always hoped I could be as good a parent to Max as she was to me. As far as I am concerned, she was the original Lion Dad (Mom). Strong parents can have profound effects on their child which can carry over to succeeding generations. Your child listens and sees everything you do and say. A Lion Dad knows this and is always on the alert for teachable moments and is careful about setting the example.

In the summer between junior and senior year, Max participated in a program that involved travel to Israel. The trip was very different from the usual Israel Birthright trip in that it brought ten US Jewish teens, ten Israeli Jewish teens, and twenty Arabs together to travel in an effort to promote peace and understanding between two groups of people who've traditionally hated one another.

Max had to apply and get accepted into the group for the first year. Then during the trip, the teen leader was selected for the following year. Max was chosen to be the leader, which he was thrilled about. It meant he had to develop the next program for the new participants, take a training trip to Israel in the middle of his senior year, which involved missing some school, and travel back to Israel for a third time with the group of teens he was leading. It was very stressful, and several of the kids got sick, requiring hospitalization. There were two adults involved, but Max had to escort the group home by himself since the adult who was with them had to attend an event in Amsterdam. We coached Max through it, but he largely did all this on his own.

Max also took a trip to India with a small group of high school friends during spring break which coincided with the time they wanted him to travel to Israel for training week. This meant that he could not fly back from India with the school group. He boarded a plane on Qatar Airlines that he arranged on his own to fly from Delhi to Tel Aviv, stopping in Qatar and Cyprus. He flew over Afghanistan, Pakistan, and several other Middle East hotbeds. I was more than a little anxious, but he did it on his own. His leadership skills were vital, and without his calm personality, sophisticated knowledge of travel customs, and confidence, the trip could have turned out far differently.

When we traveled as a family, I taught Max how to navigate various airports, how to stay healthy when traveling, how to select good airport food, and how to search out the unique qualities of each locale. By the time it came for him to travel internationally by himself, I knew he was ready, but I still tracked him with an app on the phone. He is now very comfortable interacting with different cultures and environments. I trust he will pass this on to his children.

## Final Thoughts

When taking six AP classes during his junior year, Max was going to sleep after me and getting up before me. He also made films, had a social life, applied to colleges, applied for scholarships, and maintained his health without taking psychotropic stimulants. He knows how to eat, relax, plan, and execute under pressure. Junior year is the most stressful year in high school, although senior year comes close. Remember, each year builds on the next and cannot not be done well without a solid foundation from the year before. It's important not to lose sight of this if your children are very young. Some even say that pre-K is the most important year. I agree.

Think about what's coming. It has been said that there are two qualities that separate humans from all other life forms: the ability to communicate well and the ability to think about the future. No matter how smart you think dolphins are, I have seen very few books written by them and no evidence that they think about anything except the present. Try to develop those unique human skills.

## LION DAD COMMANDMENTS FOR CHAPTER TWELVE

1. Be your child's best friend.
2. Make your child feel safe enough to tell you the truth.
3. Develop a personal website.
4. Nurture in your child a deep and long-standing interest in something besides school.
5. Be a leader.
6. Start a new group.
7. Volunteer out of passion, not obligation or as a strategy.
8. Travel as much as possible.
9. Say yes to as many new experiences as possible. Experiences are more important than money or collecting expensive things.

J K Roark M.D.

PART C

# HOW WE CHOOSE THE RIGHT SCHOOLS - PRE-K TO COLLEGE

# 13

## WHICH COLLEGE?

### KNOW YOUR VALUES AND BELIEFS, CHANGE YOUR DESTINY

*One's philosophy is not best expressed in words;
it is expressed in the choices one makes . . .
and the choices we make are ultimately our responsibility.*
—**Eleanor Roosevelt, humanitarian**

It seemed like from pre-K on we were deciding which school to go to. Gone are the days when there was only one option, the local public school that students walked to. Now there are multiple private schools competing for your business (and make no mistake about it, no matter how they spin it, it is a business) and many public schools within reach. Private schools of every philosophy, charter schools, home schools (including some exclusively online), parochial schools, government public schools, etc.—all of them are options nowadays, and choosing the right one is a big decision with ramifications not fully known to unprepared parents. These ramifications are dependent on your mindset and your family. In other words, the right choice depends on where you live, deep knowledge of your child, and what options are available. Most parents do not plan on switching schools yearly, but many do, which causes great confusion for the student. Once your child gets used to fellow students, the environment, the curriculum (which builds one year after the other), the teachers, and the culture, it's better to stay put unless there is a pressing reason to change. The choice of which college to attend stems from prior choices and deep knowledge of your particular circumstances.

Our family first thought a private K–12 school was the way to go, especially in comparison to the government public schools available to us. There were only a few private schools near us with any kind of following and reputation, so we chose the one that was considered "the best." It was really just word of mouth and some internet searches. I knew in my heart that homeschooling would be the most efficient, but the cultural experience of classmates, community events, sports, and the feeling of connection won over. This may not be true in every case or for you. Also, online and homeschooling was not as evolved as it is today. Currently about 3–5 percent of students are homeschooled. For the disciplined family, it's a great way to go.

I really do not think that boarding school is good for young children. Taking them away from their roots too early does not give those roots a chance to grow deep. It might be a good choice in high school, especially if the high school feeds into an elite college. I knew one family whose son graduated from a local high school, but he did not get into the Ivy League. His family sent him to a boarding school (that fed into Harvard) to repeat his senior year, just so he could have a chance at the Ivy League. I thought it was a bit extreme at the time, but in the context of an entire life, it does make sense. He is now attending Harvard. Max's frequent school changes during his early years were the result of us feeling our way as an inexperienced family. We did not fully assess the terrain prior to making the first choice.

Max attended four different pre-K programs, two different kindergarten programs, two different elementary schools, one middle school, and one high school. Perhaps that contributed to him struggling in elementary school. The confusion and poor performance I noticed in the early grades was part of the reason we stayed put for middle school and high school. He attended the middle school which fed into the high school seamlessly. There are always factors that influence every switch—such as school reputation, cost, distance, friends, teachers, parental comfort—but most of this was invisible to our son, who just suffered the consequences. We were indecisive, and it hurt Max. Sometimes you can overthink these decisions. It's a balance. Considering every possible consequence, nuance, and outcome can paralyze you at times. I have no easy answer for how to walk the tightrope between too much thinking on the one hand and too little action on the other.

We know families who stayed for their child's entire education at the private school we chose to leave. They were absolutely convinced that this private school was the best choice and that things would have turned out far worse if they left. They were true believers and donated to the school on a regular basis. The school loved them. It reminds me of what people think after consenting to open heart surgery, going through with the surgery, and surviving. They think and say that the surgery "saved" their lives even though that is not true in most cases, according to several studies. When you have your chest opened, your heart stops, and you have a painful recovery, it is very difficult not to justify this horrific experience. So you convince yourself it was necessary and good for you. The same goes for the parents who pay $250,000 for a secondary school education. Even if their child gets into an average school, they become convinced they did the right thing for their child, who—they claim—would not have done better anywhere else. Cognitive dissonance.

Paul Simon famously said: "A man sees what he wants to see and disregards the rest."

What we have learned so far is that continuity matters, stability matters, proximity to home matters, and a small class size up to the sixth grade matters. Curriculum is more important than class size after the sixth grade, and peer groups are also important. We knew children who switched almost yearly because of an argument with a teacher or an administrator, financial reasons, or just because the child was unhappy. On the other end of the spectrum are families who stay with their first choice no matter what and are very averse to change of any kind. This can be as bad for the child as changing yearly if obvious reasons to change are ignored. Deciding whether or not to change schools depends on the parents' judgment about how switching schools will affect their child.

The goal should be to aim for stability if at all possible, especially early on, so make that first choice wisely. By the time you are choosing a college, your thinking should be refined enough to choose appropriately for the next four years or more. Still, I have known several students who switch colleges, which must be very disruptive on a number of levels, but sometimes necessary.

As Thales said in 600 BC: "The most difficult thing in life is to know yourself."

## How to Choose the Right College for Your Child

There are over 4,600 accredited colleges in the US alone, with over 21 million students attending them. That's 5.6 percent of the population and about 35 percent of the 18- to 24-year-olds. If you think globally, there are over 20,000 institutions of higher learning with 37 million students. This is big business. How do you choose? Very simple: values.

What is a value? It's a concept, idea, or judgment about what is important in life, about what is worth your time, money, and energy. A person's values are a major influence on that person's behavior and attitude. They serve as broad guidelines for decisions, both short and long term. If you are clear about your values, you will have no trouble deciding which college to go to and which ones to apply for. The trouble is that most people have no clear sense of their values which are moving targets. Rarely does a student conduct a survey of their own values at a young enough age to guide them in this large decision. Most of the time, values are inherited from parents who inherited their values from their parents, and so on.

Very little conscious attention is placed on these extremely important concepts. Most parents consider only affordability and accreditation. Most students consider only the campus life. I would strongly advise having *happiness* as one of your top values. Would you rather have your child be depressed at Yale or happy at ASU? Given the fact that a full 25 percent of college students take psychotropic *drugs* prescribed by physicians (note that I refer to these substances as drugs and not *medications* since the latter term is a euphemistic misnomer), who really knows what percentage takes them without prescriptions.

Happiness is rarely considered by the Tiger Mother but frequently valued by the Lion Dad. *Excellent Sheep* by Deresiewicz talks about this at length. There are surveys that rate schools by happiness levels, usually based on student input. Those surveys are not always accurate, but determining the percentage of freshman students who continue on to their sophomore year is one way to cross-check these surveys. I think this is a better indicator. Ivy League schools can be very stressful. Cornell, Columbia, and UPenn regularly have students who commit suicide. In fact, the ten most stressful colleges in the country are: Harvard, MIT, UPenn, Tulane, Washington U, Cornell, Northwestern, NYU, Wake Forest, and Stanford. The reasons vary, but common stress factors include an isolated location, crowded conditions, and competition as opposed to collaboration. As a parent, I would not want my cub attending any of these schools.

I am convinced Max is at the right school. Now he needs to select the right path in that school by choosing his direction in life. This is easier said than done, especially in an atmosphere with so many attractive distractions. The Ivy League is like Disneyland for the serious students, so knowing your path and values prior to attending can be very important.

Choosing your profession is even more important than choosing which college to attend. Your values play a big part in this. I have always thought that the expression "find your passion" is a meaningless bromide. Many people are on that quest their entire lives. Your interests usually find you rather than the other way around. A carefully constructed value hierarchy, which of course requires self-knowledge, will inform your direction in life. Once chosen, however, this is not the end of the line. What someone does with that direction is entirely up to them.

A successful person could be happy in several professions. There is no "best" profession for an individual, but it's what a person makes of that choice that counts. Life is flexible and leaves room for many mistakes. That's why persistence, patience, flexibility, grit, curiosity, self-knowledge, and integrity are so important to develop in your child. It's far better to carefully assess your values periodically than to live by the seat of your pants or live by a slogan, as many people do. Slogans like "Find your passion," "Do what you like," "Be a good person," and the like are simplistic and limiting. Think deeper than slogans, which are the fast food of philosophy.

Once you know your values, decisions big and small become easy. This idea comes from another lesson from Tony Robbins. As far as college choice is concerned, it's important to take into consideration both your life values and your specific college values. Life values are things like health, money, family, education, contribution, growth, purpose, work, love, success, and adventure. There are others. I understand that all of these are important, but if you think deeply, you can put them in a hierarchy. Once these values are placed in order of importance (for you), your decisions crystallize.

With your life values in place, they serve as a context for college choice, and then you can do the same prioritizing for college characteristics. Put them in a hierarchy of importance to you.

**Some factors in choosing a college are:**
- Location
- Size
- Public vs. private
- Cost
- School ranking
- Lifetime earning potential
- Campus
- Programs (in general)
- Programs of interest
- Sports
- Dorms
- Student diversity
- Food quality

- Extracurricular activities
- Alumni network
- Weather
- Surrounding town
- Urban vs. rural

There are undoubtedly other factors specific to your own needs. Maybe you need a college that can board your horse, or maybe you don't like to fly, so you need a college close enough to drive to. I am sure you get the idea. List your requirements and put them in order. Please note that all of this should be done before you consider the ease of admissions. It's just a wish list for now. You might even want to put your life values and college values on an index card and carry them around with you. Look at them frequently as far in advance of the actual choice as possible.

The more qualified your student is, the easier it will be to get into any school, so high-achieving students have their options expanded. This could make your decision harder or easier depending on your student's values and how clear he or she is about them. If your student chooses a college based on his or her values, as opposed to other people's values, your student will be much better off. Try to keep that in mind so your child is not swayed by what he or she thinks will look impressive to friends or relatives. Just don't show up on a campus visit, hear your child say "this feels right," and let them make a life-long decision based on a momentary whim. Help them think deeper than that. Some people are so enthralled by a big-name school that they are star struck when admitted. That may lead them to an inappropriate choice of school.

Try not to make this important decision by the seat of your pants, by instinct alone (although instinct can be one of your values), or on a whim. In other words, you can make "gut instinct" one of your values and put that in the hierarchy. Is gut instinct your number-one reason for choosing something, or is it number five? Know yourself.

As Bernard Baruch said, "Only as you know yourself can your brain serve you as a sharp and efficient tool."

No one can count on getting into an Ivy League school, so you need to have a list of five to twenty schools to apply to, which makes this process relevant for even the best students. It is also relevant for choosing between the eight Ivies since they are quite different. If there are other factors you want to consider that are specific to you or your general life value hierarchy, then feel free to add them in the mix. This process can be done with your family, but remember—it's primarily your student's values that should be considered. If done correctly, it will make you and your student much happier, avoid the possibility of a disruptive change, and contribute greatly to success within that institution. There will be fewer surprises. Here is an example:

I will use just five values for simplicity to illustrate the method. However, when this is done for real, you and your student can use as many or as few values as is appropriate for the situation. Let's say someone ranks her overall values when assessing a college as follows:

1. Location
2. Ranking
3. Campus
4. Cost
5. Alumni network

This means that, for this individual, location is more important than ranking, which is more important than campus, which is more important than cost, which is more important than alumni network. All of these values are important (as well as others), but these are the relative importance according to the individual's beliefs and overall life. In this hypothetical case, that person's top five life values are as follows:

1. Family
2. Money
3. Health

4.  Success

5.  Serenity

Again, this list is just the top five values for this individual only. It means this person values family above money, and so on. This list does not mean that nothing else matters, but these are the top five values in hierarchical order. These overall values are always in the background and influence the overall college list.

Looking at these overall college value list and ranking, you can get a picture of who this person might be. Perhaps they want to stay close to home (or strongly prefer a certain area of the country), are very concerned with school reputation and academic excellence, want a pleasant environment for the campus, is moderately (but not overly) concerned with cost, and considers the future alumni network important, but not more than the other factors. Note: please see worksheet on Appendix I.

With this list, this individual can think deeply about a given school. Let's say Harvard. The high school senior goes on a college tour and visits Harvard with his or her family, pen in hand. After taking the tours offered, she sits down and determines how this particular school fits in (or not) with her values. She rates Harvard as a choice based on her college values. Since Harvard is far from home, and location is important to this person, she keeps that factor in mind.

Your mind can do funny things when faced with a decision like this, especially if you are under pressure. Trust me, there will be pressure in April of your student's senior year when acceptances roll in. I truly believe this system, if applied diligently, will work.

## LION DAD COMMANDMENTS FOR CHAPTER THIRTEEN

1. Your choices will shape your destiny.
2. College choice is a big one, so think deeply about it.
3. Make the choice objectively and rationally using value hierarchies.
4. Think about what you value, not what others value.
5. Put your life values and college values in separate hierarchies.
6. Rate each college characteristic while thinking about one school at a time.
7. Sleep on it.

J K Roark M.D.

## PART D

# WHAT WE LEARNED THAT WILL HELP YOU

WHICH COLLEGE?

# 14

# THE THREE MENTAL CAPACITIES FOR SUCCESS

## BALANCE IS BETTER THAN ONE-SIDED

*"When the brain is silent, the executive function, which is this part of the brain that makes decisions, can work much better. So when you get quiet, you make better decisions. You're also more rested - you're not as reactive."*
— **Goldie Hawn, Actress**

I make a point to watch the Scripps National Spelling Bee each year. The most recent competition was so strong that they had to award eight first prizes. It was the first time since 1925 when the Bee began that this was done. Whenever I watch this event, I am always amazed at how eleven- to fifteen-year-old students can know how to spell words that are so long and infrequently used and that have varying origins. I heard that students literally go through the entire dictionary (over 171,000 words) to expose themselves to each word!

How is it possible to do this? The memory capacity, processing speed, and dedication to practice is beyond what most people ever experience. I also think culture, family life (most final contestants are Indian American), values, and age play a critical role. Like the line in the recent movie *Crazy Rich Asians* when the host of the visiting girlfriend is told about the family she was about to meet: "These people are not just rich—they are crazy rich." The top Spelling Bee contestants are *crazy smart*. Or are they? What does it mean to be *smart*? Is the ability to remember vast amounts of information the only requirement for being smart? There's a bit more to it than that.

## The Three Mental Capacities For Success

A student's success in school and in life are dependent on the following three mental capacities: cognitive ability, emotional intelligence, and executive function. Distinguishing these abilities from one another, especially in your child, is vital and usually overlooked by most parents, college admissions officers, teachers, administrators, and employers. Schools usually only focus on cognitive ability and ignore the other two domains. Success in life, however, depends heavily on them. I have alluded to some of this already, but since this is so important, I am dedicating an entire section on these concepts.

When most people think of intelligence or call someone smart, they are only referring to cognitive ability. This is typically measured by an IQ test, a GPA, an AP or SAT score, or other objective evidence (like winning a spelling bee). Cognitive ability allows students to remember a great deal of information, process the information quickly, and make connections adroitly. College admissions usually only take cognitive abilities into consideration when assessing academic potential. This is very much the same as how we determine the worth of a computer via its memory capacity and processing speed.

There is nothing wrong with looking at cognitive ability, recognizing it in an individual, and cultivating it throughout life. It can come in very handy. If it is not consistent with the other mental capacities (emotional intelligence and executive function), however, a student can be led to or choose to get involved with things that are not appropriate for them. The latter two capacities are more difficult to quantify, more "human," and vitally important.

Emotional intelligence involves the absence of affective disorders like depression, anxiety, and insomnia. It also allows people to be comfortable in their own skin, relate to people of all ages, and have a solid nose-up attitude. The qualities of compassion, resilience, ethics, conscious, and extroversion/introversion are all part of emotional intelligence.

Emotional intelligence is centered in the limbic system, specifically the amygdala. To a large degree, emotional intelligence is what will make a person happy, or not. It usually develops in early childhood, is very dependent on environmental influences and exposures, but can be altered later in life as well. Artificial intelligence (AI) will never develop the emotional intelligence humans have as it is uniquely human (thank God). How do you develop emotional intelligence in your child? Just by observing their emotional state under different circumstances, being attentive in the early childhood years, and keeping this vital ability in mind. It is harder to pin down but is at least as important as cognitive ability, if not more so.

Executive function, on the other hand, is centered in the prefrontal cortex, develops maximally between ages twenty-five and thirty, and allows individuals to steer themselves and others toward the most appropriate direction. Executive function is central to the choosing of values described earlier in this book. A CEO has excellent executive function, as does a well-balanced child who knows what they want from an early age. Executive function allows a person to make the big decisions in life correctly—what college to go to, where to live, who to marry, what profession to choose, which classes to take, who to associate with, and many other life choices. Executive function can be applied to yourself as well as others if you are a leader.

Five hundred years ago, the three big decisions in life (where to live, who to marry, and what work to do) were made automatically in most cases. You lived where you were born, you married whoever your parents told you to, and you did what your father did for work. In a way, this reality made executive decisions easy and in some cases irrelevant. Now the three big decisions have many perturbations, are made by the child (usually before age twenty-five), and take a great deal more time to think about.

I would never suggest that it would be better to live in the "good old days" given the amazing variety of experiences available to us thanks to increased longevity, advanced technology, and our interconnected world. Still, it's worth comparing the two eras in order to value the need for executive function development now. The ability to project into the future and communicate are considered by some to be the two skills that only humans have. AI may eventually develop executive function, although will be so far in the future that it's irrelevant for now.

There are a myriad of factors that must be taken into consideration when making executive decisions. For example, the decision about which

## The Three Mental Capacities For Success

college to go to automatically assumes that a student knows himself well enough to instantly know what setting, direction, values, and associates will lead to the brightest future. It is an amazingly complex skill that can only be developed over several years. Most K–12 schools never even mention it or focus on it at all. Yet, executive function is incredibly important. I say it's even more important than cognitive ability.

A given student may make a great physicist but a terrible physician, even if he has the cognitive ability to do both. Or, he may make a great physician but a terrible basic scientist. He may also be very happy living in cold weather but miserable in warm climates. The quality of that student's executive function will determine which path he follows. This kind of self-knowledge and executive function does not come easily for some people. Keep it in mind.

The Ivy League and other elite schools frequently have students with very high cognitive abilities but low executive function and emotional intelligence. This is partly the result of the extreme competitive stress most Ivy applicants go through during their entire childhood. They can jump through all the hoops required on tests, but when they arrive on campus, they need to self-medicate with drugs to assuage their emotional issues, existential discomfort, and lack of direction in life. Even worse, they barely think about their future in any systematic way or are even told how to think about it. College counselors (even private ones) frequently do not measure these abilities in their students, never mind take them into consideration. Executive function involves taking into consideration the emotional qualities of the student in conjunction with their cognitive abilities. A brilliant STEM student who loves being around people may be emotionally miserable sitting in a cubicle all day long as a tech worker and will likely regret that choice if he directs himself into that field, no matter how capable he is cognitively.

How do you develop executive function in a child? It is really just a matter of giving your child more and more responsibility for bigger and bigger choices and keeping the concept of executive decision in mind. This is something a Lion Dad does, but a Tiger Mother does not.

Put simply, cognitive ability gives a student the talent needed to get an A in AP Physics, emotional intelligence allows a student to enjoy

AP Physics, and executive function directs a student to take AP Physics in the first place, assuming it is consistent with their well-thought-out goals and values.

I have known more than one extremely intelligent student who got a perfect SAT score but didn't have a clue about who they were, what they liked, or how to handle their emotions without taking psychotropic drugs. Students like that are unbalanced.

In order for a student to make a holistic decision about college choice, career choice, and other pivotal life directions, the student must know himself or herself within these mental domains. It is far better for an individual to be balanced in each domain than to be skewed with one domain much more developed than the others. The ideal circumstance is to have a student who has exceptional cognitive abilities (the straight-A student) as well as perfect emotional intelligence and highly developed executive function. I have known students like this, although they are rare. They know what they want from an early age, they are emotionally stable and personable, and they have the cognitive abilities to achieve their goals. They hit the home runs in life and are amazing to observe. Where does your child fit in this paradigm? Knowing this as early as possible will direct a Lion Dad to the areas that need the most attention. Schools primarily value cognitive ability, but life values all three. Going further, I believe life values cognitive ability less than the other two domains. There is always someone with greater cognitive ability. The ones with high emotional intelligence and executive function usually achieve much more in life.

Look at the three following profiles of mental functioning. There are many possible combinations. Think about your own child's profile.

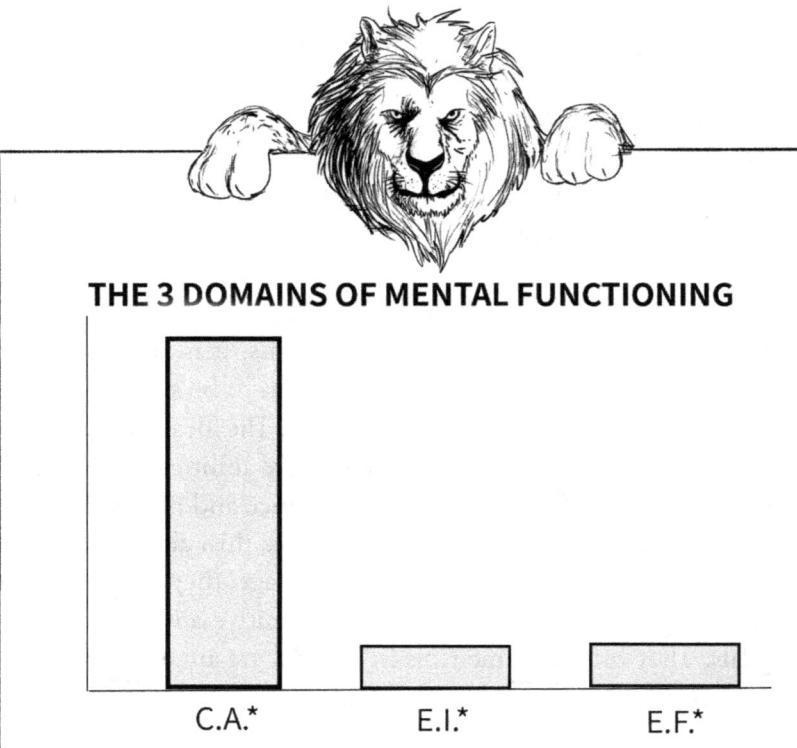

## THE 3 DOMAINS OF MENTAL FUNCTIONING

C.A.*    E.I.*    E.F.*

### Profile 1 - The "smart" child

This profile is typical of an elite school student since the school screens for them. They have high cognitive ability, high GPAs, high SAT/ACT, many AP classes high IQs. They know how to jump through all the necessary hoops but can frequently be emotionally challenged and do not know what they want in life or who they really are (low executive function).

*CA - Cognitive Ability or IQ,
*EI - Emotional Intelligence,
*EF - Executive Function

## THE 3 DOMAINS OF MENTAL FUNCTIONING

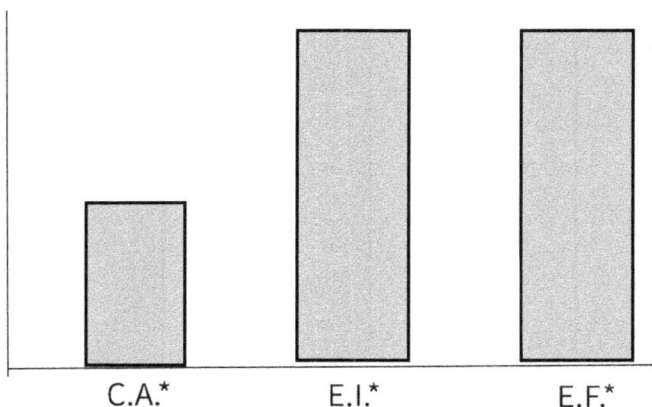

C.A.*　　　　E.I.*　　　　E.F.*

## Profile 2 - The happy child

In this profile executive function is high as is emotional intelligence. The cognitive ability of this student is lower compared to the other two domains but still adequate. These students use this complex knowledge to position themselves in the work place and in life in such a way as to achieve great success financially, with relationships, and make appropriate choices the entire way. They are very happy and others like them. They sail through life easily and achieve more than Profile 1.

*CA - Cognitive Ability or IQ,
*EI - Emotional Intelligence,
*EF - Executive Function

## THE 3 DOMAINS OF MENTAL FUNCTIONING

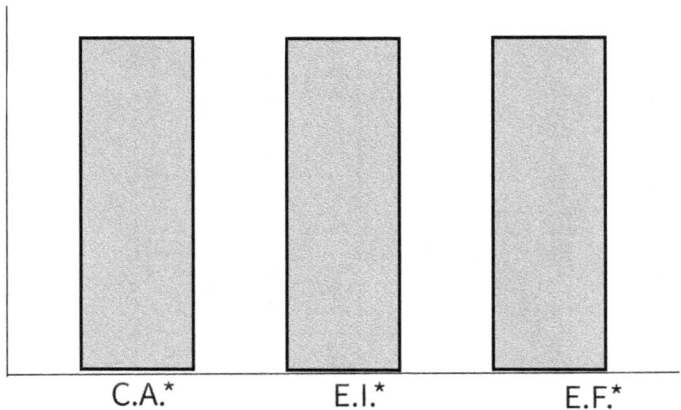

## Profile 3 - The balanced child

This is the rare profile of a student who has all 3 domains in perfect order. They are highly intelligent (cognitive ability), know themselves well, are happy and pleasant to be around. There is no confusion or conflict. Not only do they know what they want in life but are able to plan and execute over a period of years. They not only will achieve great financial success but will be very happy in what they do achieve since it will be consistent with who they are. They make the people around them better. They are the future CEOs, presidents, leaders.

*CA - Cognitive Ability or IQ,
*EI - Emotional Intelligence,
*EF - Executive Function

We are all works in progress, and each of these mental domains can be altered throughout life. The key is recognizing them and where your student stands as early as possible. It will make an enormous difference in the quality of your student's life.

## LION DAD COMMANDMENTS FOR CHAPTER FOURTEEN

1. Rate your student on their level of cognitive ability, emotional intelligence, and executive function, and then work on the weak areas.
2. Happiness is mostly a function of emotional intelligence and executive function.
3. Getting into college is mostly a function of cognitive ability
4. Emotional intelligence primarily develops by age 4 and is governed by the limbic system of the brain
5. Cognitive ability primarily develops by age 25 and is governed by the frontal cortex
6. Executive function develops by age 30 and is focused in the pre-frontal cortex and the number of synaptic connections in the brain
7. All 3 capacities of the brain should be balanced
8. Keep the 3 major life decisions in mind: where you live, who you marry, what work you will do
9. Rate your student on their level of cognitive ability, emotional intelligence, and executive function, and then work on the weak areas.
10. Happiness is mostly a function of emotional intelligence and executive function.
11. Getting into college is mostly a function of cognitive ability.

# 15

# PUTTING IT ALL TOGETHER:

## The Bird's Eye View

*"The whole educational and professional training system is a very elaborate filter, which just weeds out people who are too independent, and who think for themselves, and who don't know how to be submissive, and so on—because they're dysfunctional to the institutions."*
—**Noam Chomsky, philosopher**

There is something in science called reductionism. This is when you attempt to reduce a complex condition or process into its components and then deal with the smallest possible component which, in some cases, can affect everything else downstream. In other words, you go upstream to attempt to find what is theoretically the limiting factor or even the source of everything that follows. Medicine does this all the time. A complex biochemical pathway is laid out and traced back as far as possible. Then a drug is designed to paralyze one component (usually out of hundreds) of the pathway so that everything else is stopped. This is the bread and butter of big pharma.

For example, if you have abdominal pain, you go to a gastroenterologist, who scopes you, scans you, and attempts to relieve your symptoms

## Putting It All Together:

with any number of drugs. If that does not work, then it's off to the surgeon, and you know what they advise—surgery.

The problem with this methodology is that it doesn't work most of the time, and if it does, it's only a short-term solution. By its very nature, reductionism attempts to simplify a complex subject—which is, of course, attractive to a human brain—to find a "magic bullet." Einstein once said, "Everything should be made as simple as possible, but not simpler."

Reductionism in medicine has become as absurd in its attempt for simplicity as it has in education. This is certainly true of education in general and of Ivy League admissions in particular. We have an obsession with reductionism in this country. The throwaway products, the little pink pill, the easy mentality. It's really a psychological and cultural predisposition which simply does not work in many situations. When I grew up in the '50s, one of the most popular TV shows was The Lone Ranger, and sometimes I think shows like that helped to shape the psyche of many Americans. A masked man using silver bullets to kill the bad guys. Now we have masked surgeons wielding scalpels and college counselors with the easy fix. The bullets are made of a rare, precious metal that somehow works better than ordinary lead. Only silver bullets kill vampires and the bad guys, after all.

What does all this have to do with college applications and education? Everything. If only you had the right counselor, the best SAT tutor, the best school, etc.—everything would be efficient, fast, and easy. Never mind the whole person, character, purpose, integrity, and real learning. All that takes time and effort. Never mind executive function or emotional intelligence. Just focus on cognitive ability for the good grades and SAT scores. The silver-bullet consultant perfectly packaged for easy quick use. How convenient. Just nab that silver-bullet SAT prep course that fits into your schedule. Voila. Hi-yo, Silver! Away!

Real brain and thought development does not come in a silver bullet. You cannot reduce education or an application to the Ivy League to an SAT score, GPA, extracurricular activity, or resume. It's a holistic process involving many moving parts. What we are talking about here is optimal brain functioning, which has thousands of components and contributing factors. There are biochemical, neurological, anatomical, cultural, higher-learning, and instructional components that all combine in a yet unknown way to result in a functional, productive adult who contributes to society in a unique way. That is what your child's goal should be—not a score on someone's arbitrary test, not a great essay, not a killer app, not a high GPA. These are all components, not the whole. Keep that in mind. The Ivy League and other top-rated schools look for students with the potential to be well-rounded, successful individuals, because that is what college freshman really are—pure potential.

## Back to Basics

The concept of reductionism hit home for me years ago. I'm reminded of my surgical residency, when I was asked to be a member of the committee that chooses future residents. There were only three people on the committee, including the chairman of the entire program. On one occasion, a candidate was being interviewed who had excellent grades, recommendation letters, and looked great on paper (like so many college applicants do). The chairman of the department (who was a highly intelligent, talented person with a dry sense of humor) asked the candidate what he did in his free time (in other words, the extracurricular profile). The candidate proudly said he was a concert pianist! I was impressed, but the chairman looked him right in the eye and being totally serious said, "Sorry, we are looking for a cellist."

I practically fell off my seat and bit my tongue. It turns out that the chairman was an accomplished violinist and did not care or was not impressed with bragging. The candidate did not get in. As humorous as this true anecdote is, it illustrates a very important point for elite college applicants, as well as in life. Do not brag. Don't do it in your essay, in an interview, or anywhere else on the application. It's the kiss of death most of the time. You are selling yourself. Follow the basic four rules of conduct in business and in life:

1. Say please.
2. Say thank you.

## Putting It All Together:

3. Be on time.
4. Keep your word.

Number five should be "Don't brag."

Sometimes I feel sorry for the admissions directors of top schools who somehow have to ferret out this pure potential from all the noise, hype, promotion, and hoopla. They wield a giant funnel—in one side goes millions of students, and out the narrow exit are the few Ivy League matriculates who somehow manage to get through.

Sometimes admissions committees have to rely on imperfect indications, like standardized tests or grades. At the same time, the applicant has to figure out a way to communicate the many facets of themselves in a concise yet comprehensive manner that sews the many parts together into a pleasing, powerful story. One- or two-sided applicants (no matter how strong those one or two sides are) are not going to get into the Ivy League in the great majority of cases. There are exceptions of course, but I would not bank on it unless you are the daughter of the president (Max's group ran into Malia Obama at a football game recently). You don't say no to someone like that. I have no idea what her other credentials are, and maybe she would have gotten in anyway, but you have to believe her lineage had something to do with it. When your family shows up on campus with Secret Service and the press, that's hard to resist.

## THE MANY PARTS OF BRAIN HEALTH

Reductionism is rampant with nutrition experts who recommend vitamin C supplements instead of eating oranges and other whole foods. The whole food with its myriad of components always trumps the single extract. This has been proven time and time again, yet look at the billion dollar nutraceutical industry. It's much easier to grasp the concept of a single vitamin then it is to carefully balance a diet and eat a variety of fresh whole foods. So what do most people do? Whatever is easier. The same can be said for the pharmaceutical industry or the college admissions industry.

Americans are suckers for reductionism, the quick simple fix for complex problems. Who wouldn't want that? The problem is it does not work. It is much easier to wrap your head around simple components than the entire process. That kind of learning takes many years and dedication to develop, but there comes a time when this must be done. The earlier the better, but better late than never. Is diet, lifestyle, exercise, neuropsychological tests, hormone status, or other components of optimal brain function ever considered for college preparation or admissions?

*No.*

The lawyers would be all over it. Those traits, however, are the foundation of good brain health. As it turns out, I have noticed that the vast majority of college freshmen at Ivy League schools look healthy, at least much healthier than the general population. It simply is not possible to achieve the mental performance necessary to gain admission to these selective institutions otherwise. That is one reason why it pains me to hear that about 70 percent of college students regularly partake in psychotropic drugs (legal and otherwise). Why in the world would an intelligent Ivy League applicant take neurotoxins that kill brain cells? I guess they need the relief from the pressure, but it's certainly counterproductive. People who engage in these activities reveal their emotional intelligence is far behind their cognitive abilities. It also proves that really "smart" people can do stupid things. Being intelligent in one way does not immunize you from stupidity and poor life choices. Sometimes common sense is underrated.

What carries the day over a lifetime are good decisions—consistent with who you are, your talents, passions, and capabilities—positive, nose-up attitudes, grit, curiosity, and support. Cognitive ability is certainly a helpful trait but not the limiting factor. I believe that executive function (the ability to choose what's right for you) and emotional intelligence (the ability to enjoy what you choose) is more valuable than cognitive abilities. Having all three is a home run, but as a parent, a conscious effort should be made to develop these three components of real "intelligence." How many unemployed or underemployed geniuses are out there? Plenty. A good parent strives to instill these values in

Putting It All Together:

their child and groom them. This takes time, intention, and attitude. What's the point of achieving a cognitive goal if it's not appropriate for the individual emotionally and does not fit into their values, talents, or life goals?

A good general college counselor will take the bird's-eye view an admissions committee sees. The last thing committees want to see is an applicant who is a one- or two-trick pony—boring! The more selective the college, the more luxury they have to select the special mix that will become their freshman class. Yes, colleges will brag about their Intel Science Fair winners, football stars, and presidential daughters, but their bread and butter—the students they long for—are well-rounded people who are leaders who also have accomplishments and deep commitments in certain arenas.

## Believing in Belonging

When Max first arrived on campus for orientation and attended a mandatory seminar that reviewed a book he was assigned over the summer, his first reaction was "Dad, there are some really smart people here."

My reply was: "You are one of them, and that's how they see you, so don't forget it."

He was used to being the smartest or one of the smartest in the class, but now he is one in a group of brilliant individuals, as far as intellect and achievement goes. This is an adjustment for most kids, some of whom have "imposter syndrome" until they get used to the company.

Many Ivy League Freshman experience impostor syndrome when they first arrive on campus. They think others are smarter than they are and that they really do not belong in this elite group. Once they make friends, start doing well in their classes, the syndrome evaporates, usually. Sometimes, however, students are not a good fit and have to drop out, but this is very rare since the admissions process is so rigorous. It happens much more often in lower-ranking schools, which collectively have a graduation rate around 50 percent. There is always someone smarter (or with more money, or who is better looking, etc). More times than not, what distinguishes the successful person from the unsuccessful one is not intellect, money, or status. It's personality, emotional stability, and above all, the ability to make good choices for themselves.

The student body is also homogeneous in health and fitness, at least that's how it appears to me. But students differ in terms of country or states of origin, socioeconomic background, race, culture, and interests. The Ivy League is a real melting pot of intelligent, accomplished kids from all over the world. Imagine what will come of this mix! They will establish their lifelong peer group, their standards of excellence, and their goals within a community of superlative peers.

This is perhaps the main reason to try to get admitted to an Ivy League school—the fellow students. Most people will have never encountered a highly intelligent peer group like this, and if they do, they may never encounter it again. More important than the high intelligence, in my opinion, is being with a group of individuals groomed with the right values. This experience will form the basis for future standards, levels of discussions, and achievements. They say it's lonely at the top, but not at an Ivy League school.

It's really important to think about if your student is up for this challenge. Better yet, decide if you are planning early enough to help your child develop into a person of substance. If you are late in the process, and it's the ninth inning, then just put your application together with this in mind. Carefully pick the essay topic that knits together your student's strengths. Craft the resume so it shows a theme. Yes, there can be one or two outstanding accomplishments, but it won't look good if that's all there is, and these great accomplishments will contrast with a poor presentation elsewhere. Think about the whole, not the components. The Ivy League is a dream come true for students and families. Getting in means the entire team has succeeded, and wildly so. It's a worthy goal.

# LION DAD COMMANDMENTS FOR CHAPTER FIFTEEN

1. Take a bird's-eye view on occasion.
2. Think like an admissions officer who has five to fifteen minutes to review the application.
3. Focus intensely on the components with this in mind.
4. Reductionism does not work in this setting.
5. Help your child use the essay to knit components together rationally.
6. The whole is more than the sum of its parts.
7. Start as early as possible.
8. Remember: the Ivy League is really just a metaphor for high achievement, optimal physical and mental functioning, and high standards in life.
9. Choose your peers wisely. This is who you will become.
10. When going through the massive filter of higher education, encourage your child to maintain their individuality and ability to think on his or her own, as Mark Twain said.
11. Remember the three components of intelligence: cognitive ability, emotional intelligence, and executive function.

J K Roark M.D.

# 16

# OUR MISTAKES

*"Experience is simply the name we give to our mistakes."*
—**Oscar Wilde, poet**

*"Those who do not learn from the past
are condemned to repeat it."*
—**George Santayana, philosopher**

Context is king, and it's the job of parents to manage it. Provide a child an excellent context, and they will fill in the content just fine. I certainly did not want to have any reader think that we were perfect parents (if there is such a thing). Far from it. We made plenty of mistakes and lost much sleep over them throughout the years. Some of these mistakes were very painful and associated with all kinds of negative thinking as mistakes tend to be.

As Socrates said, "An unexamined life is not worth living."

Here is my chance to examine what I considered mistakes and what I learned from them. Hopefully the reader will not make these particular mistakes, but you can be sure you will make others. The point is to recognize these errors as soon as possible, mitigate the damages, learn from them, and change your approach.

Generally, it is better to write down your successes rather than failures, but if you make a habit of analyzing your key decisions yearly with complete objectivity, as if someone else is making these decisions, you will learn quite a bit. It should not be shared with your child unless they are very mature or at least thirty years old. Don't linger on these mistakes. Take a positive, forward-looking attitude and move on. The worst thing you can do, however, is not recognize a mistake at all, continue with the same approach out of stubbornness, or be afraid to cut your losses. This is the kiss of death. It's sometimes hard to decide when or if to change course, what to label as a mistake in the first place, and when to persist in an activity to give it time to work itself out. I am certainly no expert on this. Many times these mistakes are only evident in retrospect, but even then they are worth analyzing.

As Einstein said, "Insanity is doing the same thing you have always done over and over and expecting different results."

Know your outcome, take massive action, observe the results, and make appropriate changes along the way. This is exactly what we did. Below you'll catch a glimpse at some of our missteps, each labeled as a felony or misdemeanor depending on their severity.

## FELONY #1: ENROLLING MAX IN THE 'EXCLUSIVE' PRIVATE SCHOOL, STARTING IN PRE-K

Looking back on this decision, it was easy to see why we fell for it. This particular school (I have left the name out for obvious reasons) was touted as the very best in our state. It was populated by children of celebrities, business leaders, physicians, attorneys, and sports stars. We, like so many others, were enamored by the glitz, notoriety, name recognition locally (not so much nationally), and facilities. This was supported by its own self-promotion, flashy brochures, and the well-groomed attitude of the administration, which all were consistent in their presentation of being on the top. The fact that it was a forty minute drive from our home, would only accept Max in pre-K (not kindergarten, which we applied for), and was very expensive was overlooked. We were so flattered that they would "accept" him into their community that we honed our cognitive dissonance and decided to go there.

If I could somehow go back in a time machine, knowing what we now know, I would have enrolled him in the local public school.

These kinds of private schools give the impression that the parents need not be as involved with their child's education since they are getting "the best." This is a great relief to many hard-working parents who found it much easier to write the big check than to actually be hands-on. In a public school, you get the impression that you have to be involved since the teacher-student ratio is lower. In other words, you automatically feel like staying on top of things (homework, curriculum, etc) in a public school. This particular private school even told us that they would make us "better parents" given their vast experience and judgment. Many parents bought into this, so they deferred to them on issues like discipline, values, parenting philosophy, and communication.

In retrospect, it was like Big Brother "newspeak" fostering a collectivist mentality. By the time their child entered the third grade, most parents who stayed began feeling sorry for the families who left, convinced that they were doomed. It was just the opposite. This exemplifies the effect of a peer group, both on the parents and the children. It's still a mystery to me how they were able to do this in spite of the objective evidence to the contrary. Was it Stockholm syndrome, wishful thinking, or something else? I am still not sure. There are private schools that seem to create a mystique around their services, especially for the families currently enrolled.

When we saw what it was like in the public school, I said to myself, "We will have to take much more responsibility here." This felt bad to me at the time since we did not feel as taken care of at the public school, but it turned out to be a blessing since getting deeply involved in Max's education was a primary reason why he did so well. The time spent with him, the attitudes fostered, the family bonding, and the amazing experience of seeing him progress firsthand was worth every minute. Thank you, Exclusive Private School, for creating a situation that led us to leave. Sometimes you have to experience something bad to even know what good is.

We lasted an unbelievable six years (pre-K through grade four) in the private school. One of the things that makes me angry about that, in addition to the money, is that I felt deceived and defrauded. They were not at all what they claimed to be and what we bought into. Private schools like that should be getting at least 20 percent of their students into elite schools, not the 5 to 10 percent they did get in. There are private schools that do that, of course.

But private school offers more than just college prep, at least theoretically. Family experiences, a community of friends—they both come with private schools, but these social advantages can break down if you are not on the same socioeconomic level as the other parents, or for a host of other reasons. Private schools can also become a gossip-mongering Peyton Place that you can't stand to be around. Everybody knows everything. By the time we left, I hated it.

When some of the families from this private school found out Max got into an Ivy League school, they were flabbergasted since his "reputation" was that of an average to below-average student. That reputation would have stuck with him if he stayed there, and he likely would have lived down to it. There is an old saying that says: if you have the reputation of being on time, you can show up late every day. If you have a reputation of being late, then even if you show up on time every day, you are marginalized. People love easy categories. Don't ever accept a negative reputation for your child, ever. Somehow the kids at this private school who enjoyed a "good" reputation always seemed to be the ones whose families donated money—how coincidental! Most of them did not achieve elite school admissions, never mind the Ivy League.

All Max cared about when he was five was taking the big yellow bus to public school like all his neighbors. He had more wisdom than we did at the time. Sometimes it's better to listen to your children. I was very torn about "holding him back," especially at that early age, and he was one of the oldest in his grade. Though there was much angst and self-doubt, this did give him a social and academic advantage right through high school and also gave him an extra year with us. Primarily seen in athletics, "redshirting" is another name for this strategy. Malcolm Gladwell highlights this approach in *Outliers*, pointing out that most highly accomplished student athletes tend to be older. It also applies to academics. We knew nothing about his book or that term at the time.

Every time he met a new friend who was in the same grade (at his school or other schools) who found out he was a year older, I always thought that the other family suspected there was something wrong with Max. It bothered me more than it did him. Now it is irrelevant.

The administration, teachers, and other parents at the private school were accessible, friendly, and warm, at least in the beginning. The classes were small and intimate, which was good for elementary school. They took the kids on expensive trips, the school meetings were lavish, as were the frequent parent fund-raisers. However, they knew nothing about elementary school education, taught subjects in their own bizarre way (they had to be "different"), assigned a lot of homework even though this has been proven to be damaging prior to grade six, and were not at all willing to change. I tried many times to show them the literature that they themselves should have been aware of. It was becoming my opinion that they were unsophisticated academically, intellectually, and pedagogically. They would of course deny this, but one aspect of Lion Dad parenting is the faith in your opinions. Their main focus seemed to be impressing the parents and fundraising. Education seemed secondary to me, although they claimed it was primary. This can be the big lie of many private schools, but not all. They created an atmosphere of finger-pointing and gossip, where everyone attempted to live up to "high standards" and were more than happy to inform the administration of those who did not. It was an oppressive, dark place, more focused on political correctness than academic excellence.

The environment was also clearly competitive and not collaborative. Small cliques formed early, and children were hurt. Most left, including us. I regret not leaving earlier. It left Max thinking he was stupid, and he was academically behind compared to his public school peers. There was frequent administration and faculty turnover. Try to evaluate private school objectively if you can. Delve into the curriculum in as much detail as you can before signing on the dotted line and committing your child to a private school. Ask about faculty and administrative turnover, student dropout rates, fundraising efforts, and expectations beyond tuition. Also, speak to as many current parents as possible. And if possible, speak to parents who left as well. Once you are on this train, it's hard to jump off.

Not all schools are the same, and there are some excellent private schools, but just because a school is private does not mean its good. If there is high teacher or administrator turnover, if many of the students leave, if they do not get a high percentage of the class into elite schools, and if there is a paranoid, finger-pointing atmosphere in the school—beware. It may be hard to get this kind of information, but try. There are private schools that get over ten students per year into several Ivy League schools. Look at Harvard Westlake in LA, for example. Getting inside information about private schools can be difficult, but it is possible if you network with the right people. We did not. Just try to be as objective as possible and ask the hard questions.

In addition to asking about elite college admissions and staff turnover, find out what kind of follow-up they have on their graduates. In other words, how are their graduates doing 1, 5, 10, and 20 years out. It would be so easy for a private school to gather this kind of information, but many of them don't bother. Out of sight, out of mind, I guess. Or perhaps they don't want to know. It's kind of like a doctor writing a prescription for a medication and then not knowing what happened to the patient! If the school is so great, they should have detailed statistics about what happens to their graduates.

Many of these schools feature success stories of exceptional graduates prominently on their website or other publications but avoid hard statistics about classes in general. There are always the superstars, but how did everyone else do? Without long-term follow-up, how do you know the real value? You don't. I suspect this kind of objective analysis is actively avoided by exclusive schools whose main goal is to look good. They are afraid to see what really happens. I can assure you they keep detailed records of who donated money and how much. That shows you what their values are.

Another point to consider is how your particular child will thrive in a school like this as opposed to a public school, given the attitudes projected by the parents and kids. Some children like being in an elitist atmosphere, but I think that is mostly a parental attitude. It's the job of the Lion Dad to know your child well enough to make this and other choices well.

Having a local school is much better in the early years. Less travel, neighborhood peers, friends, and events. Listen to your child. It is true that small classes are beneficial in the early years, but homework should be minimal or nonexistent. This is a time to groom your child's curiosity and passion for learning. Within this context, the content will fall into place eventually. Don't waste your money, your time, and—most of all—your child's precious, early years on pretentious and ostentatious private schools, especially if they have poor results in the end. Some of these private schools are good and do what they claim, but be careful. Much is at stake. How do you know one from the other? This can be difficult since they are not transparent. Go with your gut and your child, and watch carefully. We were not smart enough to avoid this trap, but we were courageous enough to make a change. Max was flexible enough to pull it off. The single best decision we made for Max in his early education was leaving this school. The single worst decision was going to it in the first place.

## Felony #2: Listening to 'Professionals' Who Gave Bad Advice

Professionals in this category include physicians, neuropsychologists, educators, administrators, counselors, and neighbors. We were steered wrong on many occasions, as I have detailed in previous chapters. We listened to them initially, and it caused us great pain, but if there is one quality we are most proud of, it is the fact that we had the confidence and insight to stand up to some of these people and not incorporate their negative messages into our lives. Believe in your child. Have a vision for them, and do not waiver in the face of well-credentialed "experts" who do not know your child as well as you. If you do not stand up for your child, who will? Your child will wind up exactly as these "professionals" paint them. Not all advisors are like this, and it's up to you to figure out who to believe.

How? There is no simple answer. Read as much as you can, keep your antennas up, and err on the side of your child. Encourage them, love them, and believe in them. Your child will prove you right eventually. One indicator is how you feel inside after interacting with advisors. Do you feel optimistic and positive or do you feel pessimistic and insecure? Use this same metric when evaluating physicians. The pre-K teacher who predicted Max would not go to college and wind up as a manual laborer, the third grade teacher who claimed he was in the bottom third of his class, the early testing results which "proved" he was below average, the neuropsychologist who said he would never get into a UC school or any elite school, or the so-called friends who looked upon our child as somehow inferior to theirs—these kinds of negative people and pronouncements should all be ignored and shunned. In most cases, they have more to do with the dysfunctional psychology of those on their soap boxes than anything to do with your child. They all have their agendas which may not be obvious at the time.

I recently attended a lecture by Raun Kaufman, MD, who has developed the Son-Rise program. Son-Rise was inspired by his own experience as a child when he was diagnosed with autism, told he had an IQ of thirty, and was advised by multiple experts to be institutionalized. The experts told his parents that it would be a stretch to even teach him to dress himself. "Normal school" was out of the question.

His heroic parents refused to accept any of it. They developed a way of interacting with their child based on collaboration, understanding, love, and connection. They did not attempt to control his behavior in order to "fix" him. As I listened, I found it was very similar to the Lion Dad philosophy. Kaufman graduated from Brown University with a degree in medical ethics, lectures worldwide, and has contributed greatly to medical knowledge. He finds his way into the mind of the child and then leads them out gently. He does not try to control behavior. Max was never given a diagnosis as severe as Kaufman's, but Kaufman's story exemplifies what this book is about. Believe in your child. Parents have an enormous influence. If it is possible for someone like Dr. Kaufman to overcome the challenges he had, then imagine what your child can do!

How do you know who is who when you are given bad advice? Again, it's very difficult at times. Use common sense, your beliefs, courage, and your knowledge gained through wide reading and life experience. If our story tells you nothing else, remember that you are the main person in your child's life with the most influence. You can guide your child onto the right track. Don't let others derail you. They can have a very negative effect.

You, the parent, have enormous influence and can make or break your child. Max has proven all these negative predictions wrong. He worked hard to do this and most definitely did not focus on negative events. I did not ever say "remember what so-and-so said." I always recalled positive memories and still do. The truth, your truth, the self-fulfilling prophecy is that your child will prove you right, no matter what you feed into their head, good or bad.

In our case, we just repeatedly reinforced Max every time he proved us right and basically ignored anything else. If he made a mistake or did something that was not worthy of him, we never, not once, said to him or ourselves "I guess the psychologist/teacher/friend who made the negative proclamation was right." We could have easily done so. Eventually, Max incorporated this attitude into his own psyche and exceeded even my wildest imagination. Sometimes I feel like I am in a dream when I see the quality of his work and achievements. Sometimes he acts foolish, and I just laugh. Now he is surrounded by wonderful peers who are positive and a joy to be around. They have great attitudes, are friendly, and come from close-knit supportive families. What a gift!

## Felony #3: Frequently Changing Schools

This was insanity and driven by our own lack of knowledge, insight, and judgment. I fully admit it. Fortunately, we corrected this behavior by the time Max got into middle school. The grass is always greener, it seemed, when it came to other schools. The choices are so numerous, especially compared to the past, but the benefits of staying where you are can be great for your child. Clearly a change in school is sometimes necessary, and there's a fine line between the right time to make a change and to stay put. Only time and results will prove if you made the right choice. Parents who move frequently risk hurting their child's education. I know some families who literally changed schools every year. If you are going to make a big change like this, then for heaven's sake make it for a good reason and as early in your child's life as possible. We knew one family who always thought of their child as extremely bright, but they changed schools frequently. Their child never seemed to be as motivated for anything except academics and consequently did not get into an Ivy League school, including the one where they had legacy status. I think the frequent changes had an effect.

Max attended too many pre-K programs, kindergarten programs, and elementary schools (and even too many temples for religious education). Even when he wound up in the public middle school which fed into an excellent public high school, we still applied for another "exclusive" private school in our community. He got accepted into the eighth grade after tests, interviews, and much hoopla. We were smart enough at that point to remember the disastrous experience with the previous private school and considered the fact that Max was thriving where he was at, and turned their offer down. It was possible this private school was better than the one Max previously attended, but I was not going to rock the boat any more. My child was in that boat.

Max gaining admission to one of the world's most elite universities via regular admission, not being a legacy, celebrity, or athlete, and outperforming most of his peers from private school shows that we made some good choices. I am not sure how this new private school would have added to this. Most likely it would have subtracted from Max's success. The problem with choices like this is that you cannot live two parallel lives, playing out both choices. You must make the best prediction based on incomplete knowledge. The more you can accurately project yourself into the future, the better off you will be. If you can do this well, your child will benefit big time.

## The Misdemeanors

There were other mistakes, minor misdemeanors compared to the aforementioned ones, but their effects are still cumulative. Some of them involve choices regarding summer plans, friends, recreation, TV time, program involvement, and living conditions. Max did not really take off academically until we moved out of our big house. The exclusive neighborhood was a negative, especially in retrospect. Coincidence? I think not. I think a child, especially an only child, needs the socialization that an average neighborhood provides, especially early on. Sequestering your child in a fortress, no matter how nice, has its drawbacks, as our experience shows. As soon as we moved to an average neighborhood he had many more friends, played in the street, walked to school, and felt much better.

We also did not listen to Max as much as we should have in regard to some of his preferences in schools, vacation preferences, friends, etc. I am ashamed to say we acted more like a Tiger Mother than a Lion Dad at times. Sometimes we tried to control his behavior instead of thinking more deeply about what was really going on. It was easier. Though a rare occurrence, we punished him for minor things. No, we were not perfect by any stretch, but we were willing to look at our behavior at least as much as his so we eventually got it right, luckily just in time.

## Avoiding Tiger Mother Mistakes

Tiger Mothers will say their children love and respect them despite being treated harshly. The children will eventually figure out that it was for their own good, says the Tiger Mother. In my view, Tiger Mother cubs are afraid of their Tiger Mother and feign respect. They shudder in their parents' presence. Even children who have been severely abused by their parents frequently say they still love them. The need for parental love and approval is a very deep, instinctual need, and even the abused child finds a way to forget. This is not a justification for this abuse or "proof" that such abuse is good. It's a type of Stockholm syndrome. The human brain is remarkably flexible, especially in childhood. It can exhibit selective memory and emotional connection in the worst of circumstances.

The Tiger Mother cub getting into Harvard is not justification for Tiger Mother conduct. Treat your children like real people who you love and respect, not as objects to manipulate for your own self-aggrandizement.

Max had one friend who frequently came over to our rental house and jumped on the trampoline with him. He was also a skateboarding buddy. He was a bright, engaging child. Then his parents got divorced, and he got lost in the shuffle. His mother passed away, and his father told him he did not want anything to do with him for some reason. Maybe he acted out, or maybe he was experimenting with drugs. I'm not sure. But what chance does a child like that have? He wound up in prison, not graduating high school, and is facing a very bleak life. When Max heard about this, he felt very bad and said he really appreciates the kind of parenting he had and could clearly see that this could have been him under different circumstances.

Max knows that our love is not conditional on him performing any skill or behaving in any way. This is a key reason why he is so secure and confident. He knows that even if he were to wind up homeless on the street, drug addicted, or in prison that we would still love him. We would be terribly upset, but it would not change our love of him. We really mean this. We have told Max this many times and are not the least bit afraid it will lead him in the wrong direction. A Tiger Mother would never think like this. Their love is very much conditional on the child's performance, and everyone knows it. The Tiger Mother is the sage on the stage, always there for criticism, insults, and punishment. Not our style.

You can see the effect of our parenting when you speak with Max. When he looks you in the eye, you know you are dealing with a calm, substantial person who has a great deal between his ears. One of our neighbors commented on this when Max was about thirteen. His maturity is well beyond his years. I truly enjoy being around him. At times, I think he has taught me more than I have taught him. Tiger Mother cubs frequently have few social skills, don't know what to say, follow the conversation instead of leading it, and often don't even try to socialize. They stay to themselves. I have observed this more than once. This is despite perfect SATs, grades, etc. Not all are like that, but many are.

This has nothing to do with what race, religion, color, nationality, sex, or socioeconomic status. It has to do with how the parents raised them.

We once had lunch with some of Max's friends. As we were sitting around the table, some of the children were visibly stiff and not at ease. We were the only parents at the table, and it became obvious that they related to us as they related to their own parents. Respectful but afraid. Careful about what they said. Nervous. I suspect they were brought up by Tiger Mothers, and although they were successful academically, they may suffer socially, especially when relating to older people. The die is cast by the parents.

Remember the story about the rich man who purposely decided to live well below his means? He did it to promote good values, a strong work ethic, and promote self-knowledge in his kids. It worked. They are all now successful professionals with full lives. Then he moved into the big house. I have known more than one family who lived in giant fortress-homes. Many times their kids never leave, never make it on their own, and do not have the flexibility to discover their own path. I think it has something to do with the big house. It's truly a tragedy. The parents feel good about providing so well for their children but fail to consider the effect on the child. It's all about them, the parents. That doesn't mean every child growing up rich will wind up like this, but many do.

You need to be future-focused. This may involve sacrifices (if that's what you think they are) for your children's development and the courage to know yourself well enough to project into the future. If you groom your thinking early enough, you can do this as well. How important are the parents? I think it's obvious. It's not possible for a child to pick their parents, but the parents can pick their child by the way they act. There are very few bad seeds (if any), but there are many bad gardeners.

# LION DAD COMMANDMENTS FOR CHAPTER SIXTEEN

1. Keep an eye open for mistakes in parenting.
2. Keep a mistake journal for parental (not child) errors.
3. Have the courage to admit to making a mistake.
4. Have the courage to make a big change if necessary.
5. Favor stability and continuity, but not at all costs.
6. Read, think, and constantly learn.
7. Develop your future-projection skills.
8. We all make mistakes.
9. Don't get stuck.
10. Look to the future. Consider the past. Live in the present.

J K Roark M.D.

# 17

# SUMMARY AND CONCLUSIONS

*"Talent hits a target that no one else can hit,
and genius hits a target that no one else can see."*
—Arthur Schopenhaur, philosopher

*"We pressure students to learn what they do not want to learn,
then punish them when they don't learn it with bad grades."*
—Alfie Kohn, American education author

As I write this, I keep coming back to context, philosophy, attitudes, values, and peer groups. These are the spaces that make the learning of content easier. It's not something I see talked about or written about frequently. It should be. The details previously discussed in this book about SAT, LORS, essays, GPA, ECs, killer apps, diet, etc. are all very important, but only in the right context.

I want my child to design a life, not just earn a living. I want him to be someone with grit, passion, purpose, and intrinsic motivation—not someone who has to be told what to do every minute - a leader, not a cog in a wheel or a factory worker, even if that "factory" is a hospital or a cubicle in a law firm.

It seems as though many jobs today involve sitting in front of a screen all day and doing carefully measured work that is strictly supervised by layers of administrators. I truly hope my child can avoid this. Autonomy and self-regulation are much more satisfying than fitting in the "system" and towing the line. Most individuals start out with this kind of structure, and few break away from it. Going through a very structured educational system for many years can create a person who has to be told what to do most of the time, needs strict metrics to measure progress, and whose life is determined by others. It is one thing to interact with others on some level, but it's another to be controlled by them.

Max is not a trained seal that needs a fish, a horse that needs a carrot and stick, or a dog that is rewarded by a biscuit. He rewards himself by doing what he wants. He has twenty-three pairs of chromosomes, a frontal lobe, free will, his own thoughts, and his own goals. I want to know why he is doing something rather than train him to perform a certain task. This is what a leader does. Most people begin as workers, but if this framework is kept in mind, the chances of becoming a leader who creates rather than follows increases.

In Walter Isaacson's recent book on Leonardo Da Vinci, he reveals that Da Vinci had a great deal of difficulty declaring a painting was finished. He was constantly tinkering with work. In fact, when Da Vinci died, he had the *Mona Lisa* in his room still working on it for five years!

I am no Leonardo, but the challenge of conceptualizing this book was much more satisfying than the chore of declaring it finished. I am always thinking of more things to add, but at some point I had to say it was done. This was difficult since, like any living relationship, it always seemed open-ended with room for improvement. There is much more to say. Perhaps another book or two going deeper is in order.

One very significant event in our lives happened when Max was just beginning high school. I had what was described to me as a "minor" surgical procedure and traveled to another state to have it performed by the best surgeon available. To make a long story short, I wound up being neglected in the recovery room and lost fourteen units of blood before they took me by ambulance to the nearest ER. Once there, they barely saved my life as I was in shock and also needed another emergency surgery to stop the bleeding. I spent several days in intensive care, a clergyman was prompted to speak to me, and I had to be escorted home on the plane.

Somehow, I lived to tell the tale and was given the gift of seeing my son graduate high school and attend an Ivy League university. Given the enormous amount of attention I spent on Max during high school, I believe if I had died, he would not have been as successful. I consider it divine intervention. The lesson in this is the strategic importance parents have on their child's life. Don't ever take it for granted. You are their greatest asset.

As I reflect on Max's evolution from an average, if not below-average, student into a man with razor-sharp intellect, there are some common themes all along the way. We always encouraged Max to be curious about the world around him without being didactic. We also encouraged him to be relentless in his pursuits. Our family values knowledge for knowledge's sake rather than to achieve a goal, but when a goal is chosen, it must be achieved.

It is my hope that Max retains his childlike sense of wonder. This sense of awe, combined with curiosity, gratitude, and a never-ending desire for lifelong learning will lead him further than we can imagine now. I am sure he will go down many rabbit holes, some of which will be dead ends, but some will not. I hope his mind will be filled with connections and that he has the time to adequately digest all that he experiences. I also hope he will be fearless about changing his mind based on new information. This is exactly what we did during his education. There are always difficult but necessary choices to be made along the way.

When I see parents keeping every second of their children's time occupied with homework, busy work, enrichment activities, sports practice, or violin practice, I see a child who will need to be told what to do for the rest of his or her life. I understand these structured activities in part are meant to keep the kids away from media, which is good, but try not to overdo it. "Free time" is definitely not wasted time any more than sleep is wasted time.

During sleep, your unconscious mind is integrating and healing. During wakeful, free, unstructured time, your conscious mind is humming in the background, waiting to pounce on its next target. Try to respect that process in your child and have the faith it will result in something amazing. It did for us. What I mean by amazing is not that Max got admitted to the Ivy League, or that his grades were high, or that his SAT was near perfect. By *amazing*, I mean that he was able to overcome adversity despite negative input along the way, that he managed to define himself despite being told by so many people what to do, and that he maintained his health without artificial substances. That I am proud of. That will allow him to go the distance in life.

A word about collaboration. This is an extremely valuable talent to develop in your child. The big idea may come out of individual minds, but the execution of that idea comes out of collaboration. This is something that Max's current school does very well. The students are encouraged to work, live, and study together. This is in stark contrast to the way it was in high school when individual productivity was rewarded, but art was key here. Max's deep involvement with film served him well in the area of collaboration since he always worked in teams. I have to admit it at times seemed a little fluffy to me as opposed to hitting the STEM books, but now I see the result. He is comfortable in groups and at the same time can sit for hours alone to do his work.

It seems whenever I call Max at school or he calls me, he is with a group of friends. These are definitely quality friends that the school has vetted. I know that whoever he interacts with at this school has impeccable credentials and their own unique story. I've met several of them. This cannot be said about most colleges. As previously stated, this is perhaps the greatest advantage of an Ivy League school. Your peer group will change you, so whatever you can do to assure your child has the best possible peer group is time well spent.

Being admitted means earning a seat at the table. Being able to work with others is such an important skill that is best taught by experience in the early years. The world is full of individual geniuses who cannot work with others, cannot motivate a team, and cannot communicate effectively. They wind up doing very little. Even Steve Jobs, who everybody thought was the epitome of the lone genius, somehow managed to inspire several companies. Without his support group, he would have floundered. Today's high schools and colleges rarely teach this vital skill.

From elementary school through high school, try to be aware of your child's friends are and who their families are. It's not always possible, but try. Every creative genius and person of great accomplishment has a tribe surrounding him. If your child learns to seek out and develop that tribe while contributing something unique, it will lead to rapid success.

# 18

# EDUCATION & PARENTING IN THE PANDEMIC AGE

## How the virus is altering the scene

*"The worst pandemic in modern history was the Spanish Flu of 1918, which killed tens of millions of people. Today, with how interconnected the world is, it would spread faster.*
—**Bill Gates, Founder of Microsoft**

We have moved from the Industrial Age to the Information Age and now, many argue, we are in the Pandemic Age. The current pandemic emanates from factory farming, wet markets, and unsanitary conditions which facilitate the transmission of animal viruses to humans. This is a very brief description of the COVID-19 Pandemic. For a detailed and thoughtful description I strongly recommend Micheal Greger's book entitled *How To Survive a Pandemic* published in June 2020. This book describes in great detail the origin, current status, and likely outcome of the current Pandemic. For an equally riveting book about the Spanish Flu Pandemic of 1918 I recommend John Barry's book entitled *The Great Influenza* published in 2004. My brief description of our current Pandemic is kind of like summarizing *War and Peace* by Tolstoy by saying: "It's about Russia." Any reader who is curious about the past as it relates to the future will read both books immediately. For reasons described herein and in the 2 books just mentioned, this pandemic and future pandemics are not going away anytime soon since the underlying causes are not likely to change. This serious condition is destabilizing every person on the planet, affecting many areas of our lives including the economy, entertainment, and of course education and parenting. This chapter focuses on education and parenting.

## WE FACE NUMEROUS UNKNOWNS INCLUDING:

1. How will this end and when?
2. How will online education compare to in-class learning? See table
3. What is the role of a parent going forward? What is the parent's role in guiding the child through pandemic related decision making?
4. What is the best way to position your child for admission to a good school?
5. How will the pandemic affect admissions?
6. What kind of jobs and education should I encourage in my child? The types of available jobs will change dramatically.
7. Will brick and mortar colleges survive given the huge economic impact of the pandemic

The current trend toward digital education has profound implications for not only education but for our entire way of life. Ray Kurzweil predicts in *The Singularity* that within 20 years we will have our very biology fused to the web. *Homo Deus*, by Noah Harari, also describes the altered nature of human beings in the digital age. I believe the current Pandemic will accelerate both of these scenarios and make life unrecognizable to our current population in ways known and unknown.

It's the nature of pandemics to alter and disrupt and COVID-19, like the Spanish Flu of 1918, is no different. That said, comparing the two pandemics provides a useful perspective.

J K Roark M.D.

| Characteristic | Spanish Flu | Coronavirus |
|---|---|---|
| \multicolumn{3}{c}{SPANISH FLU VS CORONAVIRUS PANDEMICS} | | |
| Time frame | 1918-1920 | 2019-? |
| Age most effected | 20-30 | Over age 60 |
| Number of waves | 3 (#2 was the worst) | 1 so far |
| Deaths when over worldwide | 50-100 million | 387,000 so far |
| Deaths in USA when over | 675,000 | 109,000 and counting |
| Population of world | 2.5 billion | 6.5 billion |
| Reliability of statistics | Poor (underestimation) | Good |
| Treatments | Few | Many |
| Vaccines | None | None so far |
| Significant social contribution | WW1 | Factory farming of animals |
| School closure | Sporadic | 4 months so far |
| Number of k-12 students USA | 20 million (10% graduated) | 60 million (95% graduated) |
| Country worst effected | India | USA |

## How COVID-19 is altering education.

Get ready, it's coming. Education on every level will be effected and like all comprehensive change, it will likely be fought every step of the way. Many resist online classes, for example. Only about 10% of students today prefer online education and for good reasons. So while students in the USA have been sent home to finish the current semester online, studies show that many do not even logon.

The concept of intrinsic motivation referenced in the table that follows suggests that students who learn online will have to demonstrate more internal drive, focus, and motivation than students educated in a physical classroom where educators are on hand to support them. Many students don't develop this drive until late in their education. Some never develop it and can only learn in a physical group setting. We are a social species; there's no getting around it. Advances in education will have to take this into account. Attempting to make tasks more "efficient" that don't consider our social nature won't be successful in the long run. For example, does anyone really like interacting with a phone tree vs. a real person, even though the phone tree provides business efficiencies.

Before the pandemic, only 2% of students attended online classes. Now it's more like 80%, and with the advent of 5G internet, this number is likely to increase. The more digital our lives become, the more isolated people can be. In fact, some consider digital involvement dehumanizing and lacking in the very essence of what it means to be human.

Online education will rapidify changes already occurring in the ways humans interact. After all, we learn how to interact in school. The habits we develop interacting during online classes may morph into the primary mode of human interaction in general. How we learn to socialize as students will carry forward into adult life in the future just as it does now. Social distancing, online education, social media, zoom meetings and zoom parties will produce some hesitancy for human-to-human interaction that could become the norm. The new Amazon Prime series "Upload," offers a cleverly satirical picture of the dystopian society that is the result. Watch it before you support digital education without careful thought. 1.5 billion students in 192 countries are trying to figure all this out now. The rest of the 7 billion people on the planet will follow suit.

| COMPARISON BETWEEN ONLINE AND TRADITIONAL EDUCATION ||
|---|---|
| Online | Traditional |
| Time efficient | Time inefficient |
| Less expensive | More expensive (44 million Americans now have $1.5T in student loans) |
| Little interaction | Much interaction |
| Intrinsic motivation | Extrinsic motivation |
| Lonely | Many friends |
| Good for introvert | Good for extrovert |
| Prepares for solo work | Prepares for group work |
| Prepares for trained worker | Prepares for leadership and entrepreneurs |
| Fights basic human nature | Aligns with basic human nature |

The growth of social media further contributes to our transition to technologically addicted beings. Recent books *Hooked* and *Indistractable* speak to the insidious ways digital companies compete for your attention.

Some think, "So what?" It's the new reality; deal with it. This author believes your humanity is worth fighting for, so try to use technologies rather than be controlled by them. We can control our consumption of technology the same way we, as healthy people, control food consumption. Consuming digital junk food is as detrimental to your emotional and mental health as consuming physical junk food is to your physical health. We can employ technology to fight technology with apps that help students limit their digital addiction. A few apps I have found useful for this are: 1) Stay Focused, 2) App block, 3) Help me focus, and 4) App detox. There are many others. The mere fact that these apps exist speaks to the global change we are now experiencing and how it will continue to affect our brains and inner experience.

## Pandemic effects on elementary, middle school and high school education.

In the USA 130,000 primary schools have been closed, serving 57 million students. School closures especially affect low income students since over 30 million students get free lunches at school. In some cases, it's the student's only meal of the day. Some require disability services as well as internet access and the tech tools they lack at home. The pandemic has implications for healthcare and childcare as well. How can a low income family afford childcare when their children cannot attend a live school?

Yet elementary school children especially may benefit from being around their parents for longer periods of time, provided economic hardships do not overwhelm the family. Lion parents spend as much time as possible with their children, especially in the formative years. Such parental involvement is likely to provide their child with a competitive advantage that makes it easier to successfully transition to an online model.

Middle school and high school students face different challenges since what is thought of as "education" in that age group frequently includes extra-academic pursuits like sports, social activities, music lessons, and related extra-curricular involvements.

> Parents need to think about the difference between:
>
> - **Education** - which is primarily dependent on a curriculum designed by the government,
>
> - **School**, meaning the physical facility in which education occurs,
>
> - **Learning**, which is dependent on the individual's motivation and effort.
>
> - Sometimes all three (education, learning, and school) happen in the same place. But generally this is not true. Involved parents separate these three concepts and monitor them. The ultimate goal is of course "learning" and both "education" and "school" should lead to it.

University education will experience the greatest disruption since over 20 million students go to these institutions in the USA and almost 40 million world-wide. Three-fifths of college students report being so worried about their educational future that most read articles about it every day. The financial implications of the pandemic are enormous. There are 3.6 million people employed by US institutions of higher learning. Tens of billions of endowment dollars are at risk (Harvard has 40 billion) when, because of the pandemic, these students cannot be in a campus classroom. As a result of the virus, 35% of college students are considering taking a gap year. There are also 1.1 million international students attending US institutions, and they are not likely to return anytime soon. These international students usually pay full tuition the loss of which will hurt the US colleges. Seeing these numbers in black and white underscores the enormity of this disruption and the impossibility that University life will proceed as usual.

## How will this end? Here are the possibilities:

*"It's hard to make predictions, especially about the future."*
—Yogi Berra

**Possibility #1-** The pandemic will end abruptly; we all return to our normal pre-pandemic life. Education will occur essentially as before. If so, this episode is a one time aberration. While this would be a wonderful outcome, I consider it is highly unlikely.

**Possibility #2-** There are repeated waves of infection and the virus will taper after 2 years or so. Many schools are designing a hybrid approach that includes both live classes and online classes. In my opinion this will depersonalize the average students experience, decrease a student's extremely important interactions with faculty and fellow students, and devalue any degree.

**Possibility #3-** Repeated pandemics with different viruses will appear since the underlying conditions leading to their occurrence are not being addressed: namely factory animal farming, international travel without restriction, and environmental pollution. We all hope and pray this does not happen. But it could.

Which of these possibilities is most likely? That depends almost entirely on the biology of the virus. The recent attempts to re-open our cities are misguided, and, I believe, wishful thinking. The current statistics do not justify this action. Although the death totals seem to be decreasing, they are easily miscalculated. Mortality is recorded as a COVID-19 death only if the patient tests positive. Given the fact that 30% or more of the subjects have false negative tests (meaning the person really has the virus, but the test missed it), the totals could easily understated by as much as 30%.

On the other hand, some physicians and certainly some hospitals are incentivized to report a death as caused by COVID-19 since they get paid more for taking care of a COVID-19 patient. It is difficult to determine the contribution that COVID-19 had on a heart attack or a stroke, for example. These deaths are not counted as COVID-19-related although the virus undoubtedly affected the patient in some manner. Likewise, you cannot rely on the number of new cases reported when we test only about 3% of the population. If 10% got tested, the numbers go, up of course. Imagine what will happen when students return to college to face mandatory testing. It will look like a new wave of the virus is occurring.

The most valid metric for gauging the prevalence of the virus is the number of hospitalizations from COVID-19. That metric automatically covers the worst cases. When that number goes down, we should be in the clear. Currently this is not the case, and hospital assets remain strained. The World Health Organization (WHO) just reported the highest number of new cases since the pandemic began. Brazil is digging mass graves and predicts their hospitals will collapse from patient overload. The recent worldwide mass gatherings in protest of police aggression (the killing of Mr. Floyd) will likely result in a spike in cases.

Then why are we reopening at all? The rush to reopen countries is more a function of economic pressure than a rational analysis of the facts. For one thing, every 1% rise in unemployment usually results in 40,000 deaths from economic consequences. We now have 20-30% unemployment. This translates to 30 x 40,0000 = 1.2 million deaths. Actually the real unemployment figure in the USA sits at 35% which is an increase of over 30% from pre-pandemic levels. So, 1.2 million deaths is a conservative estimate. If you watched the movie "The Big Short," you understand the 1% figure. It is also formally mentioned in the book, *Corporate Flight: The Causes and Consequences of Economic Dislocation* by Barry Bluestone. A death from poverty, suicide, starvation, or stress is as devastating as a death inflicted from COVID-19. Until we have a vaccine, the balance between saving lives with social distancing and saving lives with a healthy economy will remain a difficult political balancing act.

## College Admissions

In May of 2020, Shaan Harthiramani, of Fast Company asked: "We have to question whether reviving a near-trillion dollar national enterprise where tuition increases eight times faster than wage growth, yet 43% of students graduate underemployed while shouldering $1.7

Trillion in debt should actually be a national priority." Naturally the top heavy and highly paid university administrations think it should but they clearly have a conflict of interest. What about the people paying for all this? What do they say? Most say "no" and will say "no" in the future in even greater numbers. In spite of the deep histories of some of the universities and their impassioned utterances about how "necessary" higher education is to our society, many will recognize the fallacy in this argument and will vote with their feet.

What are the short and long term consequences of COVID-19 on college admissions? For the Fall of 2020, there may be far fewer students willing to attend college and, as noted, some will take gap years. Many will come off the waiting list, and it will be that much easier to gain admission even to elite schools. The school's yield (percentage of admitted students who matriculate) will drop compared to past years. However in the fall of 2021, assuming the virus is no longer a factor, students who took a gap year may return, and the competition for college admission will increase again. Add to this the fact that the current financial squeeze will permanently close hundreds of schools over the next three years, and in the future admissions may be even more competitive.

Currently, universities are cash cows affording multiple levels of administration and faculty cushy lives. What exactly do they produce? More professors? Prestigious degrees? A college "experience"? Given the impact of the pandemic, can schools justify the $1 million plus salaries for administrators and elite faculty that are commonplace? Do the benefits to students justify the money parents are required to spend? For what? To hear a prominent personality speak at commencement? Sooner or later, people will see this and the present system will collapse. Until then, a degree from a good college is an investment that still signals worth to an employer. It it is a personal achievement and allows a student to proceed to the next career step. But ultimately, a student's economic worth will be determined by the choice of profession and by how good he or she is what they choose to do. The best way for a parent to prepare their cub for education in the today's pandemic world is to stay involved so you can plan for their future - even if your planning is based on imperfect information. That is the essence of executive function.

## LION DAD COMMANDMENTS FOR EIGHTEEN

1. Prepare your child for online education
2. As always, stay ahead of the pack. Be proactive. Predict the future
3. Make your own decisions about ending quarantine
4. Learn from history especially regarding pandemics
5. Choose your career with the digital world in mind
6. As a parent, take responsibility for your child's education
7. Understand the difference between school, education, and learning
8. Do not support factory farming
9. Higher education is still important
10. Hands on parenting is more important than ever

# EPILOGUE

> *"The people who think they are crazy enough
> to change the world are the ones who do."*
> —**Steve Jobs, inventor**

What are your goals for your child? The answer to this question requires deep thinking, the earlier the better. You may want your child to have their own goals, but all parents have their dreams, spoken or unspoken. Your child will feel the effects of these dreams and will be shaped by them, especially early on. Be careful what you dream for or what you think, as both very well could materialize. Parents are eyewitnesses to their child's life. Your observations and your testimony will be important in the final result and may even determine it fully. Who you are as parents and people speaks louder than what you say.

What is going on with Max now, and how is he doing? I must confess that I had my inner doubts about sending Max to an elite Ivy League school. How could he possibly succeed without my daily input? How would he remember to do his work and meet his deadlines? Would he be able to arrange his own tutors or even have them at all? How would he mingle with the brightest students in the country? When I was his age, I would have been very intimidated by peers like this, and I probably would not have attempted it if given the chance. What if I pushed him too hard? What if he had to drop out?! These are the kinds of fears I harbored, even as a Lion Dad. I am ashamed to admit it.

This is what happened. Max got straight A's in his first year. He got an email from his professor saying that he got one of the five highest grades in a class of 170 students! He did not need tutors for the first time since he started fifth grade! He is thought of as one of the smartest kids in his class. He is planning on double majoring and has time for activities, volunteering, and a social life that would make your head spin.

After doing the research for this book, I knew I needed to put the straight As and academic accolades in perspective. Max was admitted on the basis of his academic performance in high school plus his total picture. Most of the students admitted in the same year had some kind of hook, like being a legacy, a celebrity, a faculty child, an athlete, or a development case. I think it is safe to assume that between 50 and 70 percent of his class fit into one of those categories. Therefore, right off the bat, he was in the top 30 percent of the class based on academics alone. His study habits, past performance, test prep methods were well honed. He might not do as well academically at schools with fewer preferential admissions, like MIT or CalTech, but this shows that if your child is able to achieve admission to an Ivy League school based primarily on academics, they should thrive when there.

A Lion Dad should consider the "fit" of the school for his cub as part of his value hierarchy. At times, when hearing about all the extra activities Max was involved in, I wondered if the school was too easy for him. Other parents of college kids reported how hard their children worked, leaving them with little time for anything else. Will Max be prepared adequately for the next step? It's a balance. Time will tell. He worked extremely hard in high school (too hard, in my opinion), and that is what got him admitted to great schools.

He got off the plane for winter break smiling from ear to ear. He is having more fun than at any time in his life and never wants it to end. He has a great circle of friends and is planning on bringing five of his fellow students home with him for spring break to stay with us. He has a magnetic personality that people of all ages gravitate toward. He certainly did not get that from me. Probably my wife. I think this developed from the way he was treated as a young child. This proves to me that the way a child is treated when young is more important than the personalities, genetics, or the accomplishments of the parents. The time spent with him and making him happy has truly paid off. He has an enthusiastic attitude, not one of fear, anxiety, depression, or uncertainty. People see that and want it for themselves.

Max was one of the first freshmen to be admitted to the local Jewish fraternity, and he will be rooming with his best friend next year. He now spends much time at the frat. I can't wait to see it. He is also producing a video series in which he interviews key people at school, showcasing these talks on YouTube. This has exposed him to many fascinating fellow students and helped him develop relationships with faculty. Is he up all night, getting drunk, getting high, pushing himself to achieve someone else's goals? No, although he tells me of others doing this. He sleeps eight hours each night, goes to the gym regularly, and handles all of it in stride. Why? Because these are his own goals, not mine. These are the habits groomed in high school. He is not there for the credentials and prestige, or to impress the next gatekeeper. He has harnessed his intrinsic reasons. He has harnessed the Why. The How follows almost effortlessly.

When I talk about this book to other parents, I often hear that they raised their children by following the approach described in this book, although they never really codified it. One word of caution: Please do not use this book as some kind of blueprint for your own child. Yes, there is plenty of good information, but use what is appropriate. No one will use all of it. Every child is different, has different desires, talents, and backgrounds. It's up to you as the Lion Dad to figure out what these unique traits are and to be the guide on the side, not the sage on the stage. This is not a how-to cookbook. If only there was such a thing for Ivy League schools or life. It's just our story and our conclusions about what happened.

You will probably not have the same setbacks we did, but you will also have others. You won't make the same mistakes, but you will make others. You won't have the same good fortune, but fortune will smile on you in other ways. It's all about the consciousness of noticing what you have, the results of your efforts, flexibility, making the right choices, and having the courage to stand up to opposing viewpoints.

As Stephen Hawking said, "Remember to look up at the stars and not at your feet."

## PART E

# QUESTIONNAIRE AND IMPORTANT COMPARISONS

# QUESTIONNAIRE-I

## Are You a Lion Parent or a Tiger Parent?

The following questionnaire may give you some idea of your own parenting style. I have exaggerated some of the responses for effect (and humor). The questionnaire has not been tested so it is distinctly unscientific. It is more of a teaching tool and used to emphasize some of the points I bring up in the book. These are my observations and opinions and they may differ from others' opinions. I do not represent them as facts.

Please answer with your first impression and your true inner feelings (not what you think others would like to hear). Pick the answer that most approximates your attitude. Once the questionnaire is scored, you will see where you fit on the Tiger/Lion scale. This will give you an indication if you are a Tiger Mom or a Lion Dad.

## Parent Questions:

**1. If someone tells you your child got a B in a high school class you would:**

a. look them in the eye and with a straight face say, "What child?"

b. say, "There must be a mistake; I will sue the school."

c. talk to the teacher.

d. casually mention it to my child.

e. do nothing.

**2. If your child asks if they can go on a sleepover you would:**

a. absolutely refuse.

b. consider it after talking to the parents and examining the house.

c. check their recent grades first.

d. question the child completely and probably agree.

e. say, "No problem have a good time."

**3. If your child does not like a teacher you would:**

a. tell them to obey and keep their mouths shut.

b. ask them why.

c. find out others' opinions about the teacher.

d. speak to the teacher.

e. speak to the principal.

**4. The purpose of high school is to:**

a. do well on tests.

b. get into a great college.

c. learn to study.

d. explore interests.

e. develop passions.

**5. Standardized tests like the SAT are:**

a. the most important thing in high school.

b. not as important as grades.

c. prepared for a few months in advance.

d. important and valuable learning experience.

e. opportunity to learn weaknesses.

**6. When working on school matters with your child, you:**

a. tell them what to do.

b. find out what they have to do for the teacher.

c. show them how it's done.

d. hire a tutor and forget about it.

e. work with them slowly and have them figure out why they are doing this.

**7. When picking ECs for/with your child you:**
a. choose something you think would look good and make them do it.
b. persuade them to do what you want.
c. talk to them, but guide them into the right choice.
d. decide with them and give them most of the responsibility.
e. let them decide fully on their own.

**8. Education should be:**
a. controlled by a standard curriculum all over the country from the top.
b. controlled by a standard curriculum locally.
c. customized for each student's unique needs.
d. be primarily driven by student input.
e. decided as a group with the teachers and students.

**9. If the teacher gives an assignment that does not make sense and requires much work you:**
a. tell the child to do it as instructed.
b. do it for the grade, but do it fast.
c. sympathize and ask other parents.
d. question the teacher.
e. protest at the school.

**10. If your student is in a class of forty others you should:**
a. make sure your child is the #1 student.
b. scope out the competition and do what it takes to be on top.

c. hire a tutor.
d. encourage your child to collaborate with other students.
e. go to the school and observe a class.

**11. If your child does really well in a class and gets an A you:**
a. give him extra money.
b. throw him a party.
c. brag to other parents.
d. show no emotion.
e. be happy, but give no reward.

**12. The ideal job for your child to get is:**
a. work in a socially acceptable position making a lot of money.
b. be a doctor.
c. be a lawyer.
d. be an entrepreneur.
e. whatever he or she wants.

**13. The most important thing that school can teach your child is:**
a. a skill.
b. important facts.
c. how to get into college.
d. to learn about themselves and what they like.
e. to develop intrinsic motivations based on their own values.

**14. If you were just told your child is the #2 student out of 500 you would:**
a. say to the child, "Don't you ever humiliate me like that again"

b.  say, "Where did you go wrong?"
c.  say, "Not bad, but you should do better."
d.  say, "Nice job!"
e.  say, "Amazing accomplishment!. I am so proud. I knew you had it in you."

**15. If your child wants to date a member of another culture or race you:**
a.  say, "What is wrong with you?"
b.  say, "You know that is not possible."
c.  discuss it with an open mind.
d.  give your permission right away.
e.  it is understood that this is fine and no discussion necessary.

**16. When choosing classes to take in the junior year you:**

a.  tell them to take the easiest class that also looks good.
b.  carefully investigate the teachers and work load.
c.  ask your child what interests them.
d.  encourage them to take the most challenging course load.
e.  leave it entirely up to them.

**17. Independent travel is:**
a.  a waste of time.
b.  okay only in a carefully supervised group.
c.  nice but not really important.
d.  encouraged.
e.  prioritized.

**18. Self-esteem, self-efficacy, and confidence are:**

a. completely irrelevant.

b. only important if they get good grades.

c. something that develops from success.

d. something the child is born with.

e. specifically monitored and groomed.

**19. The most important aspect of career choice is:**

a. prestige.

b. earning potential.

c. whether or not it is socially acceptable.

d. the ability to contribute to society.

e. whether or not it is a reflection of who the child is.

**20. Your child is primarily:**

a. to be made into your image.

b. a reflection of your heritage and culture.

c. a blank page to be educated.

d. a gift from God.

e. an honor to observe and interact with.

**21. Success is achieved by:**

a. hard work and practice.

b. discipline and sacrifice.

c. Intelligence.

d. doing what you are interested in.

e. doing what you are passionate about.

**Scoring: Assign the following scores for each question and then add the total.**

  A=1

  B=2

  C=3

  D=4

  E=5

YOUR SCORE: _____

If you score **80–105**, you are a Lion Dad. Congratulations!

If you score **21–40**, you are a Tiger Mom at heart.

If you score **40-80**, you are on the fence and can go either way. If you fall into the middle category you have the opportunity to think deeply about your options and choose rather than react.

Keep in mind these are tendencies and subject to change. The Tiger/Lion assessment is a continuum, not black and white in most cases. It is entirely possible to exhibit both extremes under differing circumstances or to change your approach along the way. When faced with culturally predetermined norms of behavior, it is sometimes very difficult to change. It requires a willingness to even look at. It seems to me that the Tiger Mom will usually not have any desire to enter into this conversation. It is the way it has always been done and that is the end of the story. No thought or argument can alter their actions. They have convictions rather than beliefs, which are subject to change depending on changing facts.

A person with a conviction (like the belief in a certain religion) will not change no matter what you tell them, no matter what the evidence shows, and no matter what the effect on their child. A person with a belief will change if logic and evidence shows them it is beneficial to change.

A conviction is linked to your identity and not subject to change. It is important in this self-assessment to be honest with yourself and determine if childhood education is a conviction for you or a belief system. If you conclude that you have a conviction about how to raise and educate your child, then you will likely not change your approach, even though you probably have never thought it through in the beginning. It was most likely inherited from your parents who also never thought it out independently. Same as religious dogma. If, however, you are not bound by predetermined conceptions or cultural rules of behavior, and are willing to consider your options, then you have a belief that is subject to change. Whether or not that change is intelligent and effective depends on many things including your own metaphysics , epistemology, ethics, and aesthetics.

Most times, it's easier to just go along with what is accepted, and that is why cultural norms have the staying power that they do. They are easy, already in place, no work or thought necessary. The problem with that approach is that you will not achieve spectacular individual results by doing what everyone else does. Life is looking for the individual who stands out, not the follower.

# QUESTIONNAIRE - II

## FOR THE CUB TO COMPLETE

Are your parents Tiger Moms or Lion Dads?

What is more important than your own opinion about who you think you are is the opinion of your cub. If you think you are a Lion Dad, but your cub thinks you are a Tiger Mom—guess what? You are a Tiger Mom. Have them take the next set of questions and see the results. Hopefully they will be consistent with your results, but if they are not, learn from this. Try not to influence your cub during the test.

**1. When my parent enters the room I:**

a. am scared.

b. am defensive.

c. expect a criticism.

d. feel good.

e. have much to tell them.

**2. A parent is:**

a. an authority figure.

b. someone to fear.

c. a role model.

d. my guide.

e. my best friend.

**3. My life is:**

a. determined by my parents.

b. strongly influenced by my parents.

c. happy.

d. an expression of who I am.
e. my own responsibility.

## 4. College will be:
a. hard work.
b. a stepping stone for graduate school.
c. fun.
d. something I have earned.
e. an expression of who I am.

## 5. My opinions:
a. don't matter.
b. are my parents opinions.
c. are my cultures opinions.
d. are my own.
e. are well thought out.

## 6. If I tried an illegal drug I would:
a. not tell my parents.
b. tell a sibling or cousin.
c. not tell anyone.
d. eventually tell my parents.
e. immediately tell my parents.

## 7. If I am sick my parents would:
a. tell me to go to school anyway.
b. give me a Motrin and tell me to grin and bear it.
c. have me stay home by myself.

d. stay with me at home.

e. call doctors and take me to them.

**8. Success is:**

a. pleasing my parents.

b. pleasing my teachers.

c. pleasing others.

d. pleasing myself.

e. being harmonious with my peers.

**9. Failure is:**

a. getting a A-.

b. getting a B.

c. not getting into an Ivy.

d. not learning what the course requires.

e. not learning what I want to learn.

**10. I would describe my feelings toward my parents as:**

a. fear.

b. respect.

c. gratitude.

d. love.

e. love and friendship.

**11. My parents:**

a. love me when I do well in school.

b. want to be proud of me.

c. care for me.

d.  love me.

e.  love me as an equal.

**12. My beliefs and values are:**

a.  determined by my parents.

b.  just happen automatically.

c.  things I never think about.

d.  based on my experiences.

e.  systematically worked out with deep thought.

**13. I wish I could:**

a.  have different parents.

b.  have a better relationship with my parents.

c.  be a better child to my parents.

d.  be as good a parent as mine have been.

e.  have all my friends have parents like mine.

**14. My greatest wish is to:**

a.  please my parents.

b.  please my entire family.

c.  please those around me.

d.  expand my mind.

e.  contribute to society and live an ethical, thoughtful life.

**15. I have always been encouraged to:**

a.  obey my elders.

b.  be polite.

c.  do well in school.

d. think about what I am doing.

e. think outside the box.

**Scoring:** Since there are fewer questions in this questionnaire, the scales are different. Assign a (1) for all A's, (2) for all B's, 3 for all C's, (4) for all D's and (5) for all E's.

**Add them up.** A score of **60-75** indicates your child thinks you are a Lion Dad. Congratulations! Not only have you succeeded in being a Lion Dad in your own mind, but your child also thinks that, which is far more important. They will do very well in life. If your child scored between **15-40,** then your child thinks you are a strict Tiger Mom. This may be what you want, but if not, then you have some work to do.

YOUR SCORE: _____

In my opinion, if a child grows up with Tiger Mother attitudes they will likely act the same way to their children, be very repressed emotionally, and have a second-hand life based on conditioning. Unfortunately this appears to be very common. If your child scored between **40-60,** then they can go either way and you have a choice as well as an opportunity to make a big difference in their lives if you act accordingly.

# ACKNOWLEDGMENTS

*"As we express our gratitude we must never forget that the highest appreciation is not to utter words, but to live by them."*
—**John F Kennedy**

For me, this is the most important section of the book since it exemplifies one of the underlying philosophies of the entire manuscript. Gratitude. I always read the acknowledgment section of any book before reading anything else. It gives me a sense of the author and the complexity of the book writing. I am frequently amazed at how many people are involved in the book writing process. I initially thought that a book was primarily written alone as a monastic endeavor with little outside help. I was wrong. Book writing, publishing, and editing are very much team efforts. I drew upon the expertise and stood on the shoulders of experts in several fields. I am eternally grateful for all their help. Some of these helpers were beta readers who spent their time at various stages of the project to give me valuable feedback. Others were formal editors who looked line by line, and still others helped in the publishing and promotion phases. Some were writing coaches, course directors, accomplished authors, lawyers, mentors, tutors, and counselors. I have attempted to separate them into categories as much as possible but there is much overlap

The acknowledgment section of a book is akin to the credits in a movie that show up at the end. I always watch the full credits at the end of a film which frequently makes me the last one to exit the theatre. I gain such an appreciation for the enormous accomplishment of filmmaking by watching the credits roll by. I hope my readers will feel the same way about this section and I hope my team will feel the deep appreciation I have for each and every one of them.

We have consciously attempted to teach Max to be grateful throughout his life and we expressed our gratitude frequently in front of him. This trait is the foundation of his nose-up attitude. I have been greatly influenced by the works of Martin Seligman, Nathaniel Branden, and Mihaly Csikszentmihalyi who have written on positive psychology, self-esteem, and the flow state, respectively. We encouraged Max to keep a gratitude journal, which he did for some time. One trait Max has always has (and still does) is his willingness to listen to us and take our suggestions. This is so gratifying since he usually expands on these initiatives beyond what we suggest. I am convinced that the triad of grit, curiosity, and gratitude have affected Max more than any academic pursuit. These traits greatly contribute to his high emotional intelligence.

Accordingly, it is now my honor to express my gratitude for everyone who participated in the production of this book. I have left out some last names consistent with my attempt to maintain anonymity.

First of all, I thank God every day for the birth of my son, Max. I really mean that. Without Max's birth this book would not exist and our lives would be so much poorer. His miraculous birth occurred later in our lives at a time when we almost had given up on having children altogether.

Without my son's detailed input and agreement, this book would not have been written or published. Of course my wife Mary had much to do with that, and I thank her from the bottom of my heart. Her unique style of parenting balanced me in so many ways. She was always present to support the family. I am eternally grateful to my dear departed mother, who served as my role model for parenting as well as many other things. We were lucky to have her participate in Max's life until she passed away when he was sixteen. I have her picture next to my computer and look at it daily. Max was her only grandchild. My own father passed away from lung cancer when I was fifteen and he was forty-one. I did not have a good relationship with him and I always feared that this same pattern would repeat itself with my own son. It did not. I am so proud to say that our relationship continues to be very close on many levels. This is my greatest achievement. Finally, many of our extended family have read the initial drafts and contributed greatly. I will mention only a few here.

## Editors:

My first editor was Sarah, who carefully annotated the entire manuscript as well as made detailed developmental suggestions which I often used. She also had a school-aged child at home so she found the book particularly relevant. I still refer to her emails. My second round of editing was with James, who is a graduate of Duke University as well as Harvard Law School. He now works in NYC as a human rights attorney, but participates in writing projects on the side as he did with mine. His insights, vocabulary, writing style, and point of view as an Ivy League graduate were invaluable. He was especially helpful with the introduction. I was introduced to James by his father, Mark, also an MD who read parts of this manuscript. Mark is a renaissance man of sorts, travels the world, has written multiple books, and has spoken worldwide. I am grateful he had the time for this. I met him at the gym and we have maintained a strong professional relationship ever since. My wife's cousin, Lewis, another physician, and his wife, Roberta, both read the book and made extensive editorial comments. They themselves have three children who all got perfect or near perfect SAT scores and attended elite universities. If there was ever a couple who knew how to achieve elite school admissions, it's them. Lewis is now a playwright who has had his work performed on stages internationally. This family exemplifies much of what I talk about in this book. Parental and family influences are extremely important. A child develops as his peers do. Danielle, an accomplished author of fiction in her own right, agreed to read multiple versions of my book and spent considerable time, especially with formatting and publishing suggestions. I am so appreciative of her time. She is also my dental hygienist, is a single parent, and very busy.

The final round of editing was done by Qat Wander and Rachel McCracken at chasingkites.com. They were professional and timely as was their entire team. The editing component of this book was especially painful for me as I had to cut out many sections and face my faults. They were so patient with me.

The cover design was by 100 covers and they were very patient with our numerous changes. The index was by devinindexing.com and they did a wonderful, complete job.

Max made several substantive suggestions, factual corrections, and lent moral support to the project. He loved the book and his opinion of this book is THE most important opinion to me. If he winds up being the only person who reads it, it's still worth it. He is a highly critical reader at this point and writes beautifully. Concerns for his privacy, as I previously said in the preface, led me to change his name in the manuscript and remove any identifying details. Many of these details would have added to the narrative, but privacy concerns dominated. Max is very humble, and conservative. He has never liked being the center of attention, but I think he will have to get used to this position given his trajectory in life.

## Mentors and other authors:

I was very much influenced by the work of Alfie Kohn, whose books I reference. His ideas are cutting edge, somewhat counterintuitive, and very much dovetail with my own experience and philosophy. His ideas about homework, rewards, punishment, and grades are so clear. These ideas confirmed my own approach, and hopefully my story will validate his thoroughly researched concepts. I loved the works by Amy Chua, even though the Lion Dad approach seems like the opposite of the Tiger Mother paradigm. I am also critical of her approach in some places. I do not mean any disrespect to her or others who follow this method of parenting, but I wanted to present an alternative approach that may be more palatable to some. Her book on the Triple Package I found much more consistent with our philosophy and experience. I reference both books. I cannot say enough about Tony Robbins and his influence on me, my writing, my attitudes, and parenting. I have attended many of his live seminars, read his books, and listened to many of his tapes. In my opinion, he is the foremost thought leader in personal development, even though he never attended any college.

I was and am highly influenced by Peter Diamandis, M.D. He is a graduate of MIT as well as Harvard medical school, co-founder of Singularity University with Ray Kurzweil (the world's leading futurist), developed the X prize, started Exponential Medicine, and so much more. His books, lectures, and concepts are always on my mind. I have met, interviewed, and talked to him personally. He also has two young children, so I hope he benefits from this book. Peter exemplifies the potential of human accomplishment. I have no idea how he does everything he is involved with. The other authors listed in my reference section should not be ignored, but there is just not enough space to list them all here in detail. Then, locally, I have been influenced by our Rabbi, a Chabad rabbi who I have gotten to know as well as his family. He is a tireless advocate for Jewish teens and was instrumental in helping Max receive a large scholarship. Along those same lines, Garry and Jerrianne, who ran the Israel program mentioned in the book, were influential in my thinking and on Max's development. Darren, who promoted Max within the Jewish community, got Max to introduce Randi Zuckerberg at the JFN national meeting, and strongly advocated for him was very influential in helping him achieve what he has. It takes a village. I am especially grateful to Doug Casey, international author, investor, and true visionary who was kind enough to read the entire manuscript and provide insightful comments.

## COUNSELORS:

Chris was very helpful in the application process and SAT prep. He is a highly intelligent, verbal, and tuned in professional not afraid to take a stand. Adrienne, our college counselor, who saw Max from the 9th grade, helped shape his resume and guide us every step of the way. She served a different role than Chris and complimented him. In retrospect both were vital. There were other counselors we used but these were the two most important. I left their last names out for privacy.

## TUTORS/TEACHERS:

Max had many tutors throughout his K-12 experience. The ones that stand out are Noah, who is now attending University of Chicago Medical School. He is a friend, mentor, and role model for Max. Prior to him was Zach, who is now getting his PhD in English and graduated college in three years. Not an easy feat. He introduced us to other tutors when he left. Other notable tutors/teachers/administrators are Alastair and Kathryn for SAT, several teachers, and administrators in high school, and Jonathan, who is now attending Stanford and who got admitted ED after getting a perfect 2400 on the SAT on his first try. There were others.

## Research Assistant:

This section would not be complete without mentioning Evan Winiger, who was a great help with research, collating references, and article procurement during the writing of this book. He is now getting his PhD in Behavioral Genetics and was a joy to work with. I hope to continue my relationship with him for future books. He has a bright future.

## Consultants:

I used a variety of writing consultants. I met them at a well-known writing course last spring. My illustrator, Jo Yosiuco, Karen Ferreira, and her entire team at Impact Explainers in South Africa, were extremely helpful and patient with me in designing and editing the illustrations and tables.

## Beta Readers:

I truly appreciate the time and efforts of Todd Frank, Debra Dadd (the world's leading authority on environmental home health), Rodney Wallace, Ursula Newman, Cathy Campo Kent, Felice Gersh MD., Mark Tager MD., David Brownstein MD. (who also wrote the Foreword), Doug Krell MD., John White MD., Steven Sinatra MD. (a thought leader in cardiovascular health), Jennette Jacknin MD., Andrew Rouse, Robert Weinreb MD. (the world's leading authority on glaucoma and chairman of the Department of Ophthalmology at UCSD), Laura Freeman MD., William Freeman MD., Todd Scott MD., and Erwin Omens MD. They all gave generously of their time to review my manuscript. Dr. Brownstein has and is a good friend who is a tireless advocate for patient rights, informed consent, and rational effective medical care. He also has written many books and maintains a busy alternative medical practice in Detroit. My discussions with him have been instrumental in my thinking on a number of subjects. There were several other readers.

## Publishers:

I went through many publishers before choosing a method and style. I found the publishing process daunting with all of its many facets. Cover design, formatting, editing, legal vetting, regulatory registrations, marketing, and audio book production, to name a few. I don't think the average reader appreciates how complicated and time consuming this is—I certainly didn't prior to this experience. The Ebook Bakery and Michael Grossman deserve special recognition. I have thoroughly enjoyed working with Michael and our multiple long conversations. He truly understands and resonates with the messages in this book.

# APPENDIX-I

*"Life is not a video game that you get to replay under different scenarios to gain your desired result."*
—Seth Stephens Davidowitz *Everybody Lies*

## VALUE HIERARCHY WORKSHEET - COLLEGE CHOICE

**NOT LISTED IN ANY ORDER:**

1. Cost of attendance (this includes scholarship availability)
2. Ranking (there are several ranking services)
3. Geographical location
4. Size (number of undergrads/grads)
5. Size of campus
6. Rural versus urban
7. Climate
8. Food quality
9. Dorm quality
10. Greek Life
11. Specific majors important to you
12. Campus aesthetics
13. Gut instinct
14. Alumni network
15. Size of typical class
16. Breadth of academic offerings
17. Sports (varsity, intramural, variety)
18. History
19. Earnings of graduates

20. Ease of graduate school admissions
21. Four year graduation rate
22. Quality of peer group

Feel free to add (or subtract) any other things important to the student and the family. Keep in mind these are what is important to you, not necessarily others. This entire process should be done separately by the student and the family. It will be very interesting and food for discussion if the results differ greatly.

## THIS IS YOUR MASTER LIST.

**STEP 1:** Select ten values from this master list that are clearly important to you above the rest. It is possible to rank all your values, but that could get cumbersome since you must compare two at a time, one against the other. I will limit it to ten for this flow sheet but feel free to use as many or as few values as appropriate.

**Top ten values from above list (not in order of importance yet):**

Value #1 ............... Cost
Value #2 ............... Ranking
Value #8 ............... Food quality
Value #12 ............. Campus aesthetics
Value #13 ............. Gut feeling (instinct)
Value #14 ............. Alumni network
Value #17 ............. Sports
Value #20 ............. Ease of graduate school admissions
Value #21 ............. Four year graduation rate
Value #22 ............. Quality of peer group

**STEP 2:** Now that you have narrowed down your value list to the top ten, put them in a hierarchy by comparing each one against every other one on the list by asking yourself: "Which is more important to me? Value number one versus value number two? Value number one versus value number eight? Value number one versus value number twelve? Value number one versus value number twelve? And so on.

**STEP 3:** Fill out the master value hierarchy as you go.

## Hierarchy List of Values:

1. Cost
2. Gut Instinct
3. Ranking
4. Quality of peer group
5. Food quality
6. History
7. Alumni network
8. Campus aesthetics
9. Ease of graduate school admissions
10. Sports

So, for example, if cost is more important to you than any other value on the top ten, then it will be in position number one on you final list. Remember, you have compared cost against each of the other values. Then move on to value number two and compare that to every other value the same way, except you do not need to compare it to "Cost" since you have already done that. Let's say "Ranking" is more important than any other remaining values except "Gut Instinct," which outranks it, but "Gut Instinct" we already know is not as important as "Cost." So "Gut Instinct" goes in position number two. Then just do the same for all the remaining values so you wind up with a true hierarchy that is well thought out (for you). This is very important.

You cannot go by the ranking lists in the various books you can find. For example, I picked up one of those books and they had rankings for a number of categories including campus beauty, and many other categories. I looked at their rankings for campus beauty which was based apparently on interviews, the editors own personal aesthetics, pictures, etc. I had already been on many of these campuses so I knew what I liked and what I considered beautiful. The list in the book in no way resembled my own idea of which campus was the best!! I said to myself, "Are they kidding me? Ranking campus X better than campus Y—no way would I ever say that!" That is why you cannot rely of guide books for these kinds of judgments. The guidebooks can be rough starting points, but no more. This kind of judgment is very personal and requires deep thought—it will pay off.

I have filled in the above list according to my own personal value hierarchy but in no way should you be influenced by this list. Do your own ranking and spend as much time as needed to do so.

In the above hierarchy, this student is saying, for example, that "Alumni Network" is more important than "Campus Aesthetics," which in turn is more important than "Ease of Graduate School Admissions."

Every value higher on the list is more important than all those lower on the list. Remember they are all important and, in fact, out of the over twenty considerations you originally started with, the ten in the final hierarchy are the most important half, so "Sports" is still more important than most of the other twenty-two values originally listed.

**STEP 4**: Assign relative numerical values to each of the master hierarchy in your own custom way starting from ninety. For example, the top value (Cost) would be assigned a ninety. Then assign a lower number for the next value by asking yourself, "How much less important is "Gut Instinct" compared to cost?" If it's close, then assign it an eighty-eight but if it's far from "Cost" in importance to you, then assign it an eighty-two. Then do the same number assignment to each of the values going down. You might wind up with something like this:

## HIERARCHY LIST OF VALUES -(RELATIVE NUMERICAL VALUE):

1. Cost (90)
2. Gut Instinct (88)
3. Ranking (75)
4. Quality of Peer Group (68)
5. Food Quality (62)
6. History (55)
7. Alumni Network (50)
8. Campus Aesthetics (40)
9. Ease of Graduate School Admissions (25)
10. Sports (10)

What you are doing here is drilling down in your own mind to think about the relative importance of each of the top ten values in relation to each other.

**STEP 5:** When you visit or think of a particular college, then you assign a number from one to five next to each of your hierarchy values. You would wind up with something like this:

## HIERARCHY LIST OF VALUES (RELATIVE NUMERICAL VALUE) PRINCETON (1-5):

1. Cost (90) ( 1)
2. Gut Instinct (88) (4)
3. Ranking (75) (5)
4. Quality of Peer Group (68) (5)
5. Food Quality (62) (3)
6. History (55) (5)

7. Alumni Network (50) (4)
8. Campus Aesthetics (40) (4)
9. Ease of Graduate School Admissions (25) (4)
10. Sports (10)(2)

Let me explain my thought process in assigning the one to five numbers to Princeton. When visiting the campus, we had our rating sheet in hand with the top ten values and relative numerical value number starting at ninety. Since Princeton is an Ivy League school they offer no merit financial aid, so the cost will be high, especially compared to other schools. Therefore I rated "Cost" for Princeton as a one (low, as in expensive).

My "Gut Instinct" when visiting the campus was a four since I really liked it, but not as much as I liked the ambiance at Harvard or Brown. The "Ranking" was, of course, a five since Princeton often ranks in the top three schools in the nation. Same with the "Quality of the Peer Group" as far as I could tell. The "Food Quality" was not as good as at Brown for example or at other schools I recently visited, so I rated it a three. In other words the one to five ratings of the individual colleges gives you chance to compare the individual value between schools.

**STEP 6:** Multiply the relative numerical value times the individual school value for each of the top ten in your hierarchy:

For example:
- 90 x 1 = 90
- 88 x 4 = 352
- 75 x 5 = 375
- 68 x 5 = 340
- 62 x 3 = 186
- 55 x 5 = 165
- 50 x 4 = 200
- 40 x 4 = 160
- 25 x 4 = 100
- 10 x 2 = 20

Total = 90 + 352+ 375+ 340+ etc. = 1988

1988 is your personal number for Princeton! Congratulations. You now have an objective number that you can use to realistically compare one of your schools against the other. This is very handy, and once the initial work is done by thinking about your master hierarchy, it becomes a simple matter to compare one school against the other. If one school adds up to 2000 and another one adds up to 1950, they are almost the same, but if one adds up to 1500, you have a real difference to think about. These numbers are very personal and dependent on your own values. You simply cannot do these kinds of complex comparisons by the seat of your pants or on a whim. The stakes are too high, so please put in the work necessary to know your own mind and write it down. Remember this flow sheet is for college values only. Your life value hierarchy is always in the background affecting every one of your decisions.

**FINAL NUMBERS COMPARING SCHOOLS:**

**School 1-**

Notes: _____
_____
_____

**School 2-**

Notes: _____
_____
_____

**School 3-**

Notes: _____
_____
_____

**School 4-**

Notes: _____
_____
_____

**School 5-**

Notes: _____
_____
_____

**School 6-**

Notes: _____

_____

_____

**School 7-**

Notes: _____

_____

_____

**STEP 7**: Fill out your master list with final numbers and think about it. Dive into the specifics if necessary. From there it should be easy to make an appropriate choice based on your values, circumstances, and family input.

# APPENDIX-II

## Max's Essay

These are the actual essays Max used to gain admission to the Ivy League. They were his own creations. You can see many other real essays on **www.Admitsee.com** as I discussed before. The key points in reviewing these essays are that he wrote them himself, the topics coincided with his interests illustrated on the application, and the essays are unique, thoughtful, and intelligent. The essay was redacted to preserve privacy, so all the details are not included.

### Final Common Application Essay

I love to make movies, so I tend to watch a lot of movies. Sometimes I'm interested in their technique or storytelling. When I watched Charlie Kaufman's *Eternal Sunshine of the Spotless Mind*, a film about an experimental procedure that wipes unpleasant memories, I thought Netflix chose the wrong genre: it felt more like Horror than Drama.

The prospect of loss - of memory and life and other things - frightens me. When I was nine and our family was setting out for a vacation, a drunk driver struck our car. My parents were nearly killed, but by chance I was spared, sitting in just the right spot in the back seat. As my parents spent the year recovering, I did what I could to support them, cleaning up around the house and getting groceries. Sometimes this distracted me from trying to comprehend what had happened, from the grief.

At first, I didn't want to preserve my memory of the accident. I wanted to move on, erasing evidence of trauma, just like the characters in Eternal Sunshine. But troubling moments become part of who we are, for better or worse, giving our lives depth and humility. That's one of the reasons I make movies: to preserve moments and capture emotions, even the vulnerable ones.

Since middle school, I've brought my camera along during routine moments and exotic excursions, to make films for surf camps, and to interview my grandmother about her life. When I flip open my Sony cinema recorder, adjust the ISO, and spin the aperture ring, I try to create images that no one will forget.

My public high school has a strong TV/Film program that helped me learn how to frame a shot and design a set—how to control my voice and present my artistic vision.

Film is just one way of investigating the world, one that reminds us that there will always be directions the camera isn't pointing, people whose stories are still silent. I know that in college and beyond, I want to explore new ways of helping memories speak.

*(Note: The remainder of this essay has been deleted for privacy reasons.)*

# RESOURCES & WEBSITES

## Tutoring, College Admissions and Counseling

There are literally thousands of websites with valuable information on the college admissions process, if you include the individual college websites. An applicant should definitely look deeply into the college websites of the schools applied to as well as considered. They have valuable statistics on average SAT scores, average GPA, demographics of admitted students, including where they come from, race, religion, and the percent earning scholarships. There are video tours, photos, information on staff, administration, faculty, programs off shore, and many other things. Any school that warrants your consideration deserves several hours on their website.

Your own high school typically has a website with valuable information including Naviance previously mentioned, which will show you the profiles of students from your exact school in relation to many colleges. High school websites will also offer some scholarship information not available on national databases for local awards, which can amount to a great deal. These high school websites should also be looked at when selecting high schools, of course.

I cannot possibly review all the other websites that are commercially available for test preparation, college counseling, essay advice, student opinions, financial form help, etc. I will, however, list the websites that we found valuable with some editorial comments on each one.

### SAT/ACT prep:

1. **www.khanacademy.org** This free site is important especially with the new SAT, which is supposed to level the playing field for students who cannot afford private tutors. They claim that watching their videos will be as good as a private tutor. Maybe close, but not equal as far as I can tell.

2. **www.kaptest.com** This is an old standard test prep site which is still good with interactive live sessions, videos, cram sessions, and more.

3. **www.princetonreview.com** A paid site which is quite comprehensive and with a long track record. They also offer private tutoring, admissions help, and homework assistance.

4. **www.collegereadiness.collegeboard.org** This has links to free Khan academy videos, registration info, the ability to establish your own account to review test scores.

5. In our city there were at least twenty private services with test prep help. Just use **www.google.com** and search 'SAT prep.' Many of these have ratings which usually cannot be trusted, especially if there are few ratings. The best way to select from your local services is word of mouth and interviews. That is what we did.

6. **www.thecollegewizard.net** We used this service. It was online Skype-based private tutoring. There is a flat fee and Harvey guarantees you will get the score you want if you are willing to put in the time, take enough tests for practice and take as many real tests until you finally succeed. It's the only service I am aware of that makes this guarantee. He also was a previous admissions officer at Dartmouth so he gave us some good advice on getting into elite schools as a bonus. I would advise starting early with him and having the patience to plod through the lessons and tests. Since it is one-on-one tutoring I think it's better than group lessons or video instruction.

7. **www.prepscholar.com** This service offers a customized program depending on budget and goals. They also have their own database of average SAT scores for each school. Please note when I say SAT I am also referring to the ACT. This service exclusively does SAT prep as opposed to many others who offer other services like homework help, subject test prep, AP test prep, etc. Keep in mind that when you use an online service, even though you may have a live tutor on Skype one-on-one, you do not have peers in a class with you or even in the building. This is a big disadvantage. As anyone who has gone through graduate school or a university experience knows, you learn at least as much from your peers as from the professor. Subtle distinctions, collaboration, motivation,

peer pressure, etc. This is the fallacy behind online education in general. Yes, there are online community bulletin boards or the like, but it's not the same as flesh and blood peers any more than Facebook friends are the same as real in-person friends. Still, this is one of the best online programs I have seen, and we did try it. The tutors are good, the tracking system is good, and with the right student it could work. A good online system like this is better than a poor class and live tutor so choose carefully.

8. www.collegevine.com  This is an online system that is full service and offers some unusual items like near-peer mentorship (mentors who are close in age and experience to your student), seven year med coaching, college application coaching, essay editing or coaching, test prep, and even mental health coaching. They advertise carefully screening their tutors and mentors and have an impressive, mostly Ivy League staff with a national organization. There is an excellent blog and articles on a number of subjects. I believe on occasion you can work with your tutor or mentor in person as well.  The parent can be very helpful in screening all these services for your cub. There are simply too many demands on a high school student to digest all this information so that is where their team comes in. As an adult, you also have the maturity and sophistication to judge one service versus the other.  I remember spending many weeks interviewing the various local choices we had for SAT prep. We interviewed, in person, five of them locally since at the time the online offerings were not as robust. Now they are and Collegevine is one of the best. Please keep in mind that the descriptions I offer here should not be thought of as a substitute for your own investigation or examination of their websites. That would be a mistake. There are also many others that you can explore that are not listed here. These services change quality, staffing, and tutor availability regularly, so be careful.  For example, we had a strong local service that I described in this book which hired many tutors and coaches to handle all their business. They can be very variable and are almost never as good as the principal of the company, but some are better for certain things. These

decisions can get tricky and this is where adult supervision and involvement is key. Many of these services advertise certain point increase guarantees or averages. This can be misleading, is largely a marketing tool, and cannot be verified. The point increases are usually calculated from their baseline test which can be much harder than a typical SAT so the baseline appears lower and your increase (for their stats) appears higher. Caveat Emptor. This is big business. It is not unusual for these national or even local services to be making millions of dollars in profits. The industry is changing from the mom and pop shop to big corporations. When big money is on the line you must be especially aware of what is claimed. That said, a good national online service can be great, and better than a mediocre local tutor, even if the tutor comes to your house. There is an online adult service called the Teaching Company (also called the great courses), which offers a series of college level courses on audio or video taught by the best college professors. Essentially you are exposed to the top professors who are voted by their peers and students as great teachers. Many are at Ivy League schools. I have taken several of these courses and they are almost always fabulous. I do not mention them here for your high school student since they do not have time in most cases, but the same screening method is now being offered by test prep companies like Collegevine. This is one of the amazing things that the internet brings to education, so use it if you can.

9. **www.varsitytutors.com** They offer online and in person one-on-one tutors starting at $63/hr. They claim to hand-select their tutors. We used them briefly. The tutor they provided was not that helpful, but maybe it was the luck of the draw. This is still a service worth looking at. Some services will provide bios of their tutors, which are worth looking at in order to screen who you want to interview. Frequently however the best tutors are booked months in advance since everyone wants them, so the earlier you start and the more due diligence you do, the better. Tutors are very important, especially one-on-one. Without the tutors we were lucky enough to find, Max would not be where he is today.

The outside services (for SAT prep, AP test prep, high school work help, mentorship, college counseling help) are becoming a much greater component of a good student's education since no brick and mortar school (even private ones) can provide the level of personal attention a tutor can. They fine-tune the curriculum laid out by the school and fit it to your student. Some of the best tutoring services are not even advertised on the internet! They don't have to since they have more than enough business by word of mouth. This was the case for the one we used—Hamilton prep. Although they do have a website they don't show up on a general search. Being critical about tutor selection and use is good training for your student since it will prepare them to be critical when selecting other services to hire in the future.

10. **www.hamiltoncollegeconsulting.com** Huffington Post calls this service "perhaps the best test prep program in the country" and I agree. We used them for many things. Mr. Hamilton, the CEO, is an former UCLA professor who is passionate about teaching, highly intelligent, and offers a number of services. They have a large whiteboard as you enter the building with their recent college admissions and they produce many perfect SAT scores. The peer group is amazing. You feel like you are entering an Ivy League school. I don't believe they offer online services, however, but if you happen to live near them, I don't see that there is any other choice. When we were looking for test prep and college counseling advice they were just starting out so we did not know how good they really were. We actually interviewed Mr. Hamilton at his house on the weekend. I frankly don't know how he handles everything he offers and unless you purchase the highest level college counseling service you may not have much one-on-one contact with him, but still consider them.

11. **Test prep books**. Barrons, Kaplan, ACT, the college board, all offer excellent test prep manuals year by year. They offer manuals for all the AP subject tests and courses. They are essential. If your student has the focus, discipline, and motivation to carefully go through these manuals, a few pages at a time, take the sample

tests and read the results explanations this is by far the best way to prepare for a standardized test in my opinion. Many Ivy League students will tell you this. This is easier said than done. Make sure you use a manual that has actual past tests in them rather than the company's own questions. It's always best to practice on the real thing. Max has stacks of these manuals in his room, which I can't bring myself to throw out. Opening them now shows his notes, previous practice test attempts, and folded pages. This is real work. The other services I mentioned above are essentially hand holding guidance since the great majority of students need this. Yes, there is the benefit of learning from peers, but the most efficient time use are these manuals, assuming your student can do it and not get distracted by the internet and so many other things.

12. **Flashcards**. There are many offerings for flashcards which we used extensively. They are an excellent way to learn and fun on top of that. Flashcards are best for vocabulary or any fact based knowledge.

13. **Apps**. There are many apps you can download for free although some charge a nominal fee. They can prompt you daily so you can use your free time when waiting in lines or during the commercials when watching Breaking Bad, etc. It's a different medium. As Marshall Mcluhan famously said, "The message is the medium." The more mediums you can use to learn, the better and the more likely you are to succeed. Flashcards, online classes, live classes, tutors, and peers all contribute. Think holistically and use all of them if you can.

14. **TV series**. We used a TV program called SAT prep which had a number of good lectures at various levels. This of course does not substitute for all of the above, but adds to it. It's a familiar medium to many students, so easily palatable. Use everything. The more of your senses that you engage, the more variety in your modalities, the more people you interact with—all contribute to success. Of course you can't take or use everything. Choose based on your

student's personality, budget, and willingness. Remember nothing works if you won't do it.

There are many other services you can look up, which may be better suited to your individual needs so please do not think this is all there is or that these are necessarily the best. The best is what works for you. The best is what will motivate your student to dig in and do the work. You cannot use all of them although you may have to try a few before you get it right. We tried several.

## College Ranking Help:

This is somewhat different than the above category in that their primary focus is determining the differences between various universities as opposed to test prep. There is, of course, overlap, and many test prep services also offer college counseling, essay editing, etc., but I have always felt that it is better to use a company who specializes in one thing rather than many. Some of these sites offer college comparison surveys, which can be useful, but you must be careful. Many times surveys are based on metrics that may not apply to your specific needs. For example if the graduate school quality or number of Fulbright scholars is not something that interests you as an undergraduate then the rankings and comparisons will be skewed. College ranking is something that is actively gamed by the institution to attract more applicants so their admissions rate goes down, which increases their ranking. This can lead to more money for the school. Ranking is a general indication of college worth and no more. That said, you have instant recognition if you attend a name school with a high ranking for whatever that is worth to you. Ranking is one of the college values we talked about earlier.

1. **www.usnews.com** College ranking edition. This edition makes a lot of money for the magazine and is the most referenced ranking list. There are many other ranking lists like **www.niche.com**, which ranks according to student metrics as opposed to difficulty of admissions and other metrics used by **usnews.com**. Similarly,

www.timeshighereducation.com uses student polls with over 200,000 student inputs.

2. **www.forbes.com** Is the college worth the price? This is the main question answered here. They primarily focus on student satisfaction, graduation rates, student debt, earnings of graduates, and career success.

3. **www.princetonreview.com** This is another student-based ranking system based on the best study abroad programs, campus food, dorms, and more. Worth looking at.

4. **www.newyorker.com** has a good article by Malcolm Gladwell on the trouble with college ranking systems.

5. **www.economist.com** has a similar article and take on this flawed system. Whenever there is money involved (and you can be sure money is involved in ranking systems) there is bias, political influence, and lack of objectivity, which as a consumer you must take into consideration.

6. **www.theatlantic.com** has a similar jaded view of college rankings with good articles. Perhaps once you read several of these articles you will be less influenced by college rankings. Keep in mind that most people are like sheep to the slaughter when it comes to college rankings and are passively influenced by them, use them to guide applications, and build their egos on where their school fits in. This is a very easy trap to fall into and distracts from what should be your student's main objective—to attend a school that is most appropriate for their individual needs, values, and goals. Sounds so simple, but this is rarely done and even more rarely done right. It's so tempting to go to Harvard, for example, just for the bragging rights your entire life, even if you are miserable there. I have noticed that Harvard graduates frequently ask me where I went to school (hoping I will ask them).

7. **www.thebestschools.org** is an alternative site that focuses on worldwide schools and breaks their rankings down by country. There are many good universities offshore, most of which are considerably less expensive.

8. **www.topuniversities.com** Also a worldwide approach. Keep in mind that many of the above ranking systems also have a worldwide ranking list.

9. **www.cnbc.com** Even they weigh in on college rankings. You will see Ivy League schools on all these lists consistently, although there are several others that achieve higher rankings than Ivy Leagues do. If you can figure out all these ranking systems and compare one to the other, you are more intelligent than I.

10. **www.thebestcolleges.org** makes a list of the top 50 and takes other ranking systems into account. With so many ranking systems, you get the idea that there is money involved in creating and marketing the ranking systems.

11. There are ranking systems that focus on individual sports, individual countries, earnings after graduation, campus quality, dorm quality, food quality, and almost any other college characteristic you can think of. Again, this is why your individual goals and values are vital to narrow down your choices. There is really no other rational way to choose.

12. **www.time.com/money/best-colleges/rankings** This is worth looking at since it focuses on ROI which is rarely discussed for some reason.

13. **www.businessinsider.com** another money-oriented ranking system

14. **www.ivywise.com** is a site that allows you to build your own custom ranking list very much like the value system I propose. **www.collegefactual.com** does the same as does **www.parentscountdowntocollege.com**, which has an interactive spreadsheet. **www.diycollegerankings.com** does the same.

What do most students do? If anything they glance at U.S. News rankings and decide by the seat of their pants or by a whim. Then when the admissions letters start coming in they have a defined group to think deeper about. This is such an important decision that time spent on it will pay off not only for four years but for a lifetime.

Why don't they teach this skill in high school? Again, I believe I have made a dent in this discussion but you can take it much deeper as you should. We did not do this as well as we could have, did not look at many helpful sites but more importantly did not do a formal values hierarchy. This was one of our mistakes.

## COLLEGE BLOGS AND OTHER HELPFUL SITES

These are generally informal sites that focus on high school student opinions of a host of issues. You can enter two or more schools and compare them to each other. This can be useful once you have narrowed down your lists. We used them frequently.

1. **www.collegeconfidential.com** offers side by side comparisons which we found very useful. There are many tools on this site, as well as ongoing blogs about everything you can imagine. Too many cooks. Given there are about 4000 schools in the U.S. alone, imagine being able to compare any two side by side. The number of comparisons is enormous as is the database.
2. **www.collegescorecard.com**
3. **www.collegefactual.com**
4. **www.parchment.com**
5. **www.cappex.com**
6. **www.noodle.com**
7. **www.collegdata.com**

There are many more sites. Who has the time to look at all these—nobody! Most, however, look at some of them but usually in a shallow way. The two characteristics that separate humans from every other living being is 1) the ability to communicate so well and 2) the ability to project into the future. These sites help with both human qualities and are extensions of our very nature. Before the internet it was much harder to gather this kind of information, but successful people do this all the time. Take advantage.

## Scholarship Sites:

This book is not primarily focused on how to pay for college, but any book like this would be incomplete without mentioning this imperative. In many cases paying for college is a rate limiting step that dictates where you should apply and ranks #1 in the family's value hierarchy. There are two kinds of financial aid—merit and need-based. The big money aid comes from each university so look on the individual college sites for that. Ivy League schools offer no merit aid, only need-based, which can be quite generous if you qualify. How to qualify is quite a large subject and not the primary subject of this book, but well worth investigating and doing so years in advance. I will list sites that I found useful in this regard. Some are specific to certain demographics like scholarships for veterans, certain religions, state wide scholarships if you live in the state, and every imaginable category. I will not list these as they can be found in the guidebooks which are readily available. Please do not consider this anything close to a comprehensive list of sites. That would easily double the length of this book. I hope to whet your appetite for this subject, nothing more. These are sites we used.

1. **www.fastweb.com** This is a comprehensive site that boasts over 1.5 million scholarships to choose from. You can set it up to receive regular emails that tell you about scholarships as they present. There are other services offered like career advice, college search, plus much more. You could spend years on this site alone. There is so much money available for college today, it's absurd and there is almost no reason to pay full price if you have the patience to wade through all this, even if your family can afford to pay. My experience, which matches that of many other families, is that a student is most motivated to apply to all these scholarships while still in high school. Once in college, they seem to lose interest in this aspect of their education, unfortunately. It takes a very organized, dedicated student to keep track of individual scholarship applications on top of everything else they are doing once they get to college, and it's not like they have nothing to do in high school either. Some college students have written books on

how they earned millions in scholarship money by systematically going through these sites, keeping on top of the applications, and carefully selecting which ones to apply to. In my opinion the time spent on scholarship applications is much more cost effective than getting a job for $10/hour in the dining hall. This is true even if you only are successful five percent of the time. I also think that a student who can navigate the scholarship maze is showing that they understand the value of a dollar and will likely be very financially successful in the future. This is my opinion and not based on any study. The kids with the eye of the tiger in regard to money will maintain that trait. I knew several fellow students like that and they are all multi-millionaires today. It's just a matter of focus and priorities. Nothing magical. This is kind of a litmus test for future wealth if you ask me. There will never be an easier way for a student to earn money than they have right now—as a high school or college student. Try to motivate your student to understand this and take advantage of it. I have to admit I have not been successful doing this with Max. He seems content to rely on the Bank of Dad at least so far. I am sure this will change.

2. www.collegescholarships.org Another massive site that also has a section on loans and grants. Keep in mind there are many scholarships offered all along the way in college and beyond. Again, motivation, organization, grit, and perseverance. That's all it takes. The trick is doing this at the same time as doing all the other things in college—academics, athletics, fraternities, lectures, events, and everything else the Disneyland that college education has become. When you start looking at all this money being offered and all these sites, you wonder why anyone pays full price. It seems to me that a focus on money skips generations. In other words, if the parents always pay for everything since they can afford to, the children in that family seem to be less interested in money. Then they might not do as well financially so their children become interested in money. Every other generation. Of course, this is a massive generalization with many exceptions, but I have seen it often play out like this. In some ways, like I mentioned earlier in

the book, growing up with money can be a handicap insofar as developing financial knowledge and focus is concerned. Perhaps another book is in order—Tiger Dad and Money: How to Teach your Cub How to be Wealthy.

3. **www.scholarships.com** They offer millions of scholarships, scholarships by major, sports, state, and any other categories. Makes my mouth water. Unfortunately the parents cannot complete these applications for their child. Many of them require essays, personal statements, and access to all kinds of data. This entire area is something we neglected although we did give it a try, and Max did receive some merit money as I mentioned before. We were so focused on the admissions process that there was not enough time for this, or we were not organized enough for it. The game is still not over however. **Note**: Many of the sites (if not all of them) that I mentioned in the other resource sections have advice and sites on scholarships that are very good. Please don't ignore them.

4. **http://studentaid.ed.gov** lists government sources, which may not be listed in the commercial sites. When I hear college students or high school students complain about not being able to pay for college I think, "Are you kidding?" Just open your eyes. If you are not willing to do the work, you will not get the money—big surprise. It's not a matter of luck; its real work so dig in.

5. **Books** like the *Ultimate Scholarship Book, Confessions of a Scholarship Winner, Debt Free U, Winning Scholarships for College, Free Money for College for Dummies, Scholarships 101, How to Submit Winning Scholarship Applications*, and many more. There are far more books on scholarships than there are books on how to get into college in the first place! What does that tell you?? There is a lot of money out there for the asking. So what are you waiting for?

6. **Apps** for scholarship searches are also available. The best one, in my opinion, is Scholly. Very handy. You can enter your specific qualifications and background information and viola—your list with links to the application. How easy can it get? As I said before, no reason to pay full price.

7. There are individual **consultants** that do nothing but help you navigate the scholarship maze. You fill out a simple questionnaire and they have ways of optimizing your search and even apply for you. One I like is www.withfrank.org

8. www.collegescholarships.com This is a comprehensive site available since 1995 which is easy to navigate, has many subdivisions. Given the plethora of sites, how do you choose? I would recommend spending about three to four hours just browsing the various sites and deciding one or two sites to focus on. Once that key decision is made, then spend several days drilling down on these sites to choose your target application goals. Take into consideration how many awards the individual entity offers and how large the awards are. Also, think about how involved the application is. For example, if a scholarship gives away one $500 award per year and they have 1000 applicants, don't waste your time. You are not likely to win this. If the application is lengthy and difficult, this may be an advantage since most students will pass it up. It's just like choosing a career in a way. The professions with the highest entry barriers (like medicine, requiring much time and work) may be hard to get into, but once you are in, you are set. The jobs with the easiest barriers that take little training (like working at a fast food restaurant, which can train you in about five minutes) may be easy jobs to land but lead nowhere. Hard is not necessarily bad. Cross check this with the number of applicants if that information is available. Some scholarships will not print the number of applicants on their website, but that information can be obtained from the large scholarship directories in manuals. This kind of strategy will very much increase your odds. There are so many scholarships offered these days that there are many who have no applicants!! It's your job to find those and be the only applicant. Just like applying to the Ivy League. If you don't apply, you won't get in or get the scholarship.

9. www.collegexpress.com They list some off-beat scholarships not listed elsewhere. Worth looking at. Many of these scholarships go unclaimed as I said before. When they're awarded, there can

be lavish presentation ceremonies complete with press coverage. If won early enough, this can help with a college application. It always looks good to the admissions committees to have won a merit scholarship. It shows initiative. An obvious conclusion after even a casual look at the scholarship landscape is that this takes a lot of time, focus, and commitment. Most students will not do it. It's the same concept as outrunning the grizzly bear in the woods. You just have to outrun your competition. Just like in real life.

10. **www.studentscholarships.org** Another comprehensive site. Of course there are duplications in many of these sites, which is why you should spend some time selecting the sites to concentrate on.

11. **www.superscholar.org** They list the top fifty scholarships. I have no idea how they arrive at this but these scholarships are for large amounts and therefore have many applicants.

## OTHER MISCELLANEOUS HELPFUL SITES:

1. **www.admitsee.com** This is a paid site that I found very useful. You can see what real students needed to get admitted. There are actual profiles of real students with their full essays, GPAs, SAT scores, schools applied to, admitted to, and more. How much better can it get if you want to see your chances of getting in and hearing the thoughts of the students who did. Again, studying success can help you model others to achieve the same.

2. **www.collegeessaymentor.com** This provides help for essays.

3. **http://studentshare.net** This is primarily a database for shared student essays. Good for ideas.

4. **https://try.collegewise.com** Elite college admissions counselors who claim five out of six of their clients get into one of their top three choices.

5. **www.ivycoach.com** This is a very deep college admissions service with many levels of service, some of which are expensive. They offer updated, almost real-time blogs, and if you start with them early (ninth grade) you will have a distinct advantage. Some of

these exclusive private coaching services can cost almost $1000/hour.

6. **www.ivyselect.com, www.toptieradmissons.com, www.ivyedge.com, https://ttlearning.com.** More of the same but if you can afford this kind of expertise then look at all of them. Some have refund guarantees, others have lawsuits against them, and prices vary wildly. Is it better to hire a remote counselor like this? In my opinion, no. Not only can it be very expensive, but the time spent with them is time not spent on other activities. Also, local counselors who meet face-to-face are better and that is what did. We were not in a position to spring for this much money. Perhaps if I was a multi-millionaire or billionaire I would think differently, but the same principle applies here as does with private schools in general. You cannot just write a big check and delegate this. The parent must be involved every step. Yes, you can use consultants, but the tendency to hand the whole matter to the consultant (especially high priced ones) is strong. This is counterproductive from my experience.

7. **www.glassdoor.com** This is a site with reviews on many companies including college-related ones. Of course, you could always just Google the company name/reviews and look for the independent ones not just the ones posted on their own websites.

8. **Info.getintocollege.com** This offers middle of the line college coaching.

9. **https://veritasprep.com** has an admissions calculator, free resources, test prep, and grad school admissions prep. These calculators are rough guides at best. Several sites offer calculators. People seem to like this kind of simplicity. It's kind of like the lifespan calculators you can find online—put in one or two characteristics of your health and out pops the age when you will die. It's absurd.

10. **https://nces.ed.gov** This federal site has a wealth of information and is independent

11. **www.collegeresults.org** provides data on graduation rates for colleges. This is better than getting this info from the individual college website since it is objective.
12. **www.chegg.com** is great for homework help, even last minute.
13. **https://collegemajors101.com** gives great information on over 150 college majors and where they can lead.
14. **www.collegeinsight.com** Great independent website.
15. **www.collegeboard.com** has more than just test scores including scholarship search, planning etc.

## MORE COMMENTS ON SCHOLARSHIPS

A student and their family must be extremely organized and willing to put in the time for these scholarships and frequently you can be successful. We spent any months doing this and did have some success. As the second half of the senior year progresses and especially during college itself many students drop this lucrative activity since the student has other seemingly more important responsibilities. In my opinion, a student must have some skin in the game and participate in one way or another with paying for college rather than rely on the Bank of Dad. The ones who do pay for their own education probably make more money in life. There are also apps that can screen for scholarships you may qualify for. Just search the app store for these. I have not included an exhaustive review of scholarships in this book, either merit or need-based, except to make some general comments. However, please do not assume that I do not think this is important. The general attitude your student has in regard to money, self-sufficiency, earning their keep, independence, and managing their assets are extremely important lessons in life. Unfortunately, this is severely neglected in today's high schools and colleges. Why? This must be taught by the parents, mentors, or self-taught by the student themselves. Sometimes it seems as though some students are born with this instinct and others just ignore it. They all want to make a lot of money; they just don't want to bother doing the planning, making the sacrifices, or doing the work necessary. Books like *Think and Grow Rich* and many others in the same genre are so valuable but ignored. It must appear to many students that accumulation of money is by good luck, a good stock pick, or inheritance. How wrong they are. A subscription to money magazine or Forbes might be in order starting in the ninth grade but the main influence is that of the parent—what they themselves do and how money is approached when your child is young. *The Rich Dad, Poor Dad* series is well worth looking at.

I have just scratched the surface with the above list. Please do not infer that I endorse any of these sites, although I did know about them and use a few. A good approach would be to peruse these sites and others over one or two weeks and try to determine which ones are appropriate for your child and budget (time, money, and energy budgets). If you want to ask other students which sites they found valuable, be sure and ask successful students only. See what they did and model it.

# NOTES ON SELECT CHAPTERS

## CHAPTER 1 - WHY THE IVY LEAGUE

1. **Rumberger, Russell W., and Gregory J. Palardy. "Test Scores, Dropout Rates, and Transfer Rates as Alternative Indicators of High School Performance." American Educational Research Journal 42, no. 1 (2005): 3-42.** This study investigated the relationships among several different indicators of high school performance: test scores, dropout rates, transfer rates, and attrition rates. Hierarchical linear models were used to analyze panel data from a sample of 14,199 students who took part in the National Education Longitudinal Survey of 1988. The results generally support the notion of an alternative as opposed to a common view of school effectiveness. Schools that are effective in promoting student learning (growth in achievement) are not necessarily effective in reducing dropout or transfer rates. In fact, after control for student inputs, high schools exhibit relatively little variability in dropout rates but considerable variation in transfer rates. In addition, characteristics of schools that contributed to performance in one area often did not contribute to performance in another. Given these findings, the authors suggest that, along with test scores, dropout and transfer rates should be used to judge school performance.

2. **Cancian, Maria. "Race-based Versus Class-based Affirmative Action in College Admissions." Journal of Policy Analysis and Management: The Journal of the Association for Public Policy Analysis and Management 17, no. 1 (1998): 94-105.** Affirmative action is increasingly under attack. Some argue that racism is no longer a problem, that compensation for past wrongs is inappropriate, and that the ultimate goal of a color-blind society cannot be reached by means of a race-based policy. Others concede the need for some sort of affirmative-action program but argue for a broader definition of disadvantage, often focusing on socioeconomic status variables other than race or ethnicity. According to this perspective, "class-based" affirmative action is a fairer and more politically palatable means to similar ends. Proposals for class-based affirmative action policies have become particularly important in college admissions in the wake of recent court decisions that suggest that race-based scholarships and admissions policies may be unconstitutional. A number of institutions, including the University of California system, have moved to

eliminate programs based on race and ethnicity and replace them with programs based on alternative definitions of disadvantage. This article does not attempt to address the issues of the appropriate justifications for affirmative action based on race or class. Documenting the extent and impact of historical and contemporary racism is beyond the scope of this analysis. Instead, the potential impact of a move from race-based to class-based affirmative action is simulated in an effort to begin to answer two questions. First, is class-based affirmative action just another means to the same end? In other words, are racial and ethnic minorities so frequently socioeconomically disadvantaged that most minority youth would be eligible for a class-based program? Second, how would eligibility for class-based affirmative action be determined and what are the implications for the administration of such a program?

3. **Avery, Christopher, Mark Glickman, Caroline Hoxby, and Andrew Metrick. A Revealed Preference Ranking of U.S. Colleges and Universities. No. w10803. National Bureau of Economic Research, 2004.** We present a method of ranking U.S. undergraduate programs based on students' revealed preferences. When a student chooses a college among those that have admitted him, that college "wins" his "tournament." Our method efficiently integrates the information from thousands of such tournaments. We implement the method using data from a national sample of high-achieving students. We demonstrate that this ranking method has strong theoretical properties, eliminating incentives for colleges to adopt strategic, inefficient admissions policies to improve their rankings. We also show empirically that our ranking is (1) not vulnerable to strategic manipulation; (2) similar regardless of whether we control for variables, such as net cost, that vary among a college's admits; (3) similar regardless of whether we account for students selecting where to apply, including Early Decision. We exemplify multiple rankings for different types of students who have preferences that vary systematically.

4. **Golden, Daniel. The Price of Admission: How America's Ruling Class Buys Its Way into Elite Colleges—and Who Gets Left Outside the Gates. Crown Publishing Group/Random House, 2006.** Every spring thousands of middle-class and lower-income high-school seniors learn that they have been rejected by America's most exclusive colleges. What they may never learn is how many candidates like themselves have been passed over in favor of wealthy white students with lesser credentials—children of alumni, big donors, or celebrities.

This book argues that America, the so-called land of opportunity, is rapidly becoming an aristocracy in which America's richest families receive special access to elite higher education—enabling them to give their children even more of a head start. Based on two years of investigative reporting and hundreds of interviews with students, parents, school administrators, and admissions personnel, this book exposes the corrupt admissions practices that favor the wealthy, the powerful, and the famous. He explores favoritism at many institutions. He reveals that colleges hold Asian American students to a higher standard than whites; comply with Title IX by giving scholarships to rich women in "patrician sports" like horseback riding, squash, and crew; and repay congressmen for favors by admitting their children. This book explodes the myth of an American meritocracy—the belief that no matter what your background, if you are smart and diligent enough, you will have access to the nation's most elite universities. It is must reading not only for parents and students with a personal stake in college admissions, but also for those disturbed by the growing divide between ordinary and privileged Americans.

5. **Hernandez, Michele A. A Is for Admission: The Insider's Guide to Getting into the Ivy League and Other Top Colleges. Grand Central Publishing, 2010.** For generations, the admissions process of the Ivy League schools has been cloaked in mystery and myth. Now Michele A. Hernandez, a former admissions officer at Dartmouth College, finally breaks the ancient code of silence to reveal how the world's most highly selective schools really make their decisions. With absolute candor, she tells you all the hard truths, how officials factor in every extenuating circumstance and, most importantly, how to make this complex, high-stakes system work for you. Thorough, direct, and written for results, *A Is for Admission* answers the questions asked by countless student

6. **Greene, Jay P., and Greg Forster. "Public High School Graduation and College Readiness Rates in the United States. Education Working Paper No. 3." Center for Civic Innovation (2003).** Students who fail to graduate high school prepared to attend a four-year college are much less likely to gain full access to our country's economic, political, and social opportunities. In this study we estimate the percentage of students in the public high school class of 2001 who actually possess the minimum qualifications for applying to four-year colleges. To be "college ready" students must pass three crucial hurdles: they must graduate from high school, they must have taken certain courses in

high school that colleges require for the acquisition of necessary skills, and they must demonstrate basic literacy skills. Using data from the U.S. Department of Education we are able to estimate the percentage of students who graduate high school as well as the percentage that finish high school ready to attend a four-year college. We are also able to produce these estimates by racial/ethnic group as well as by region and state.

7. **Bowen, Howard R. "The Costs of Higher Education: How Much Do Colleges and Universities Spend per Student and How Much Should They Spend?" (1980).** The question of what American colleges and universities should spend to educate their students is addressed. Both societal and institutional factors that determine the costs of colleges' educating their students and longitudinal changes in the unit cost of higher education are examined. The following issues are considered: long-term trends in unit cost, faculty and staff compensation as a major element of cost, costs that have been socially imposed as the nation has tried to protect and enhance social welfare, and under maintenance of assets. In addition to examining the higher education system as a whole, a sample of institutions are also assessed. Cost differences among institutions, institutional affluence and patterns of resource allocation, effect of institutional affluence on educational outcomes, and economies and diseconomies of scale are analyzed. Implications of the study of national trends and of the study of individual institutions are discussed. Appended materials concern: sources and methods for allocating total expenditures, historical trends in the costs of higher education institutions, and sources and methods of analysis for data on institutional costs. References are included.

8. **Miller, Danny, Xiaowei Xu, and Vikas Mehrotra. "When is Human Capital a Valuable Resource? The Performance Effects of Ivy League Selection Among Celebrated CEOs." Strategic Management Journal 36, no. 6 (2015): 930-944.** We investigate whether and when highly trained human capital constitutes a rent-sustaining resource. Our study of 444 CEOs celebrated on the covers of major U.S. business magazines found an advantage accruing to graduates of selective universities. Such CEOs led firms with higher and more sustained market valuations. The advantage was strongest for undergraduate programs as these related to the kinds of talent demanded of a CEO. The advantage also was greatest in smaller firms where CEO discretion might be highest and for younger CEOs who may benefit most from college and are less able to

appropriate rents. Finally, the advantage accrued to graduates of more recent years, when selective schools had become less socially elitist and increasingly meritocratic, thus favoring human versus social capital.

9. **Martelli, Joseph, and Patricia Abels. "The Education of a Leader: Educational Credentials and Other Characteristics of Chief Executive Officers." Journal of Education for Business 85, no. 4 (2010): 209-217.** The authors identified and described the CEOs of Fortune 500 companies in terms of several education-related and other demographic variables. Specifically, they identified the type and level of degrees earned, including specific majors, and additionally explored several demographic variables, including age, gender and ethnicity. They also identified trends among CEOs and across industries in order to further understand the educational profile of these leaders. Secondary data covering more than 50 variables and 500 cases were collected from various business-related and research databases.

10. **Birley, Sue, and David Norburn. "Owners and Managers: The Venture 100 vs. the Fortune 500." Journal of Business Venturing 2, no. 4 (1987): 351-363.** A steady supply of entrepreneurs who will build the growth firms of the future has always been seen as fundamental to the economic health of a country. However, as companies have grown to the point where many have balance sheets larger than many countries, the role of the Top Management Team in managing these corporate giants has also received more prominence. Unfortunately, research into the two groups of current entrepreneurs and large corporation managers has been both sparse, and has followed different, though parallel, paths. This research examines their backgrounds and asks the question whether the basic assumption that they are, in fact, different is correct—who are the high-flying entrepreneurs, and are they any different from successful corporate leaders? Data was drawn from three sources. A questionnaire was sent to the 167 founders listed in the July 1984 edition of Venture Magazine as the "Venture 100"—"the nation's top entrepreneurs who run the companies they founded in the past ten years." Sixty-seven useable replies were received from 40% of the founders and 52% of the companies. Comparative data was extracted from the "Korn Ferry's International Executive Profile: A Survey of Corporate Leaders," which surveyed five senior executives from each of the Fortune 500 companies. A response rate of 47% was received from a survey of 3640 executives. Further comparative analysis was extracted from the characteristics of senior executives

of all firms in five selected industries (Dairy, Mobile Homes, Tires, Footwear, and Machine Tools) as listed in Duns Reference Book of Corporate Management 1983/1984. Data was collected on personal characteristics (age, family background, and education), previous employment experience, managerial style, and work patterns. The null hypothesis of there being no significant difference between high-flying entrepreneurs and their counterparts in the largest U.S. corporations was not sustained. Whereas certain characteristics showed similar patterning—previous employment experience, managerial success traits—the remaining variables demonstrated significant differences. The entrepreneurs were younger, better educated, had more international experience, and worked harder than their corporate colleagues. If replicated elsewhere, the results of this study have particular implications for the type of educational and employment experience necessary to affect the supply of the entrepreneurs of the future.

11. **Zajac, Edward J., and James D. Westphal. "Who Shall Succeed? How CEO/board Preferences and Power Affect the Choice of New CEOs." Academy of Management Journal 39, no. 1 (1996): 64-90.** This study shows how social psychological and sociopolitical factors can create divergence in the preferences of an incumbent CEO and existing board regarding the desired characteristics of a new CEO, and how relative CEO/board power can predict whose preferences are realized. Using extensive longitudinal data, we found that more powerful boards are more likely to change CEO characteristics in the direction of their own demographic profile. Outside successors are also typically demographically different from their CEO predecessors but demographically similar to the boards.

## CHAPTER2 - BIRTH THROUGH PK: THE FOUNDATION

12. **Nelson, Charles A. Romania's Abandoned Children. Harvard University Press, 2014.** The implications of early experience for children's brain development, behavior, and psychological functioning have long absorbed caregivers, researchers, and clinicians. The 1989 fall of Romania's Ceausescu regime left approximately 170,000 children in 700 overcrowded, impoverished institutions across Romania, and prompted the most comprehensive study to date on the effects of institutionalization on children's wellbeing. *Romania's Abandoned Children*, the authoritative account of this landmark study, documents the devastating toll paid by children who are deprived of responsive care, social

interaction, stimulation, and psychological comfort. Launched in 2000, the Bucharest Early Intervention Project (BEIP) was a rigorously controlled investigation of foster care as an alternative to institutionalization. Researchers included 136 abandoned infants and toddlers in the study and randomly assigned half of them to foster care created specifically for the project. The other half stayed in Romanian institutions, where conditions remained substandard. Over a twelve-year span, both groups were assessed for physical growth, cognitive functioning, brain development, and social behavior. Data from a third group of children raised by their birth families were collected for comparison. The study found that the institutionalized children were severely impaired in IQ and manifested a variety of social and emotional disorders, as well as changes in brain development. However, the earlier an institutionalized child was placed into foster care, the better the recovery. Combining scientific, historical, and personal narratives in a gripping, often heartbreaking, account, Romania's *Abandoned Children* highlights the urgency of efforts to help the millions of parentless children living in institutions throughout the world.

13. **Chugani, Harry T., Michael E. Behen, Otto Muzik, Csaba Juhász, Ferenc Nagy, and Diane C. Chugani.** "Local Brain Functional Activity Following Early Deprivation: A Study of Post Institutionalized Romanian Orphans." *Neuroimage* 14, no. 6 (2001): 1290-1301. Early global deprivation of institutionalized children may result in persistent specific cognitive and behavioral deficits. In order to examine brain dysfunction underlying these deficits, we have applied positron emission tomography using 2-deoxy-2-[18F] fluoroglucose in 10 children (6 males, 4 females, mean age 8.8 years) adopted from Romanian orphanages. Using statistical parametric mapping (SPM), the pattern of brain glucose metabolism in the orphans was compared to the patterns obtained from two control groups: (i) a group of 17 normal adults (9 males, 8 females, mean age 27.6 years) and (ii) a group of 7 children (5 males and 2 females, mean age 10.7 years) with medically refractory focal epilepsy, but normal glucose metabolism pattern in the contralateral hemisphere. Consistent with previous studies of children adopted from Romanian orphanages, neuropsychological assessment of Romanian orphans in the present study showed mild neurocognitive impairment, impulsivity, and attention and social deficits. Comparing the normalized glucose metabolic rates to those of normal adults, the Romanian orphans showed significantly decreased metabolism bilaterally in the orbital

frontal gyrus, the infralimbic prefrontal cortex, the medial temporal structures (amygdala and head of hippocampus), the lateral temporal cortex, and the brain stem. These findings were confirmed using a region-of-interest approach. SPM analysis showed significantly decreased glucose metabolism in the same brain regions comparing the orphans to the nonepileptic hemisphere of the childhood epilepsy controls. Dysfunction of these brain regions may result from the stress of early global deprivation and may be involved in the long-term cognitive and behavioral deficits displayed by some Romanian orphans.

14. **Fisher, Lianne, Elinor W. Ames, Kim Chisholm, and Lynn Savoie. "Problems Reported by Parents of Romanian Orphans Adopted to British Columbia." International Journal of Behavioral Development 20, no. 1 (1997): 67-82.** Behavior problems in Romanian orphans adopted to Canada were examined through parents' interview reports of specific problems, and children's scores on the Child Behavior Checklist (CBCL) (Achenbach, Edelbrock, & Howell, 1987) completed by their parents. Three groups of children were studied. Romanian orphanage (RO) children had spent at least 8 months in a Romanian orphanage. Parents' reports of RO children's problems were compared to parent reports from 2 comparison groups: (1) Canadian-born children (CB) who were not adopted and never institutionalized; and (2) children who would have gone to a Romanian orphanage had they not been adopted before 4 months of age (Romanian Comparison: RC). RO children scored higher than CB and RC children for Total problems and Internalizing problems on the CBCL. No significant differences were found for any group comparison on Externalizing problems. CBCL scores were positively correlated with RO children's total time in orphanage. According to parent interview, RO children had more eating problems, medical problems, and stereotyped behavior problems than both CB and RC children. These problems were distinctive ones, rarely if ever being reported for CB or RC children. It is suggested that these distinctive RO problems arise out of a normal developmental base, and reflect either continuations of orphanage behaviors, reactions to stimuli different from those experienced in orphanage, or lack of opportunity for development or learning within the orphanage.

15. **Kaler, Sandra R., and B. J. Freeman. "Analysis of Environmental Deprivation: Cognitive and Social Development in Romanian Orphans." Journal of Child Psychology and Psychiatry 35, no. 4 (1994): 769-781.** The cognitive

and social developmental status of a representative: group of Romanian orphans between the ages of 23 and 50 months living in the Leagan de Copii in Timisoara, Romania was assessed using a variety of traditional and nontraditional measures. Results indicated that the orphanage sample all exhibited deficits in cognitive and social functioning; the majority were severely delayed. Correlations between the traditional and nontraditional measures indicated that children's delays occurred across domains. Deficits were not related to length of time in the orphanage, age at entrance, Apgar scores, or birthweight. The children's greatest capability was in peer social interaction.

16. **O'Connor, Thomas G., Diana Bredenkamp, Michael Rutter, and English and Romanian Adoptees (ERA) Study Team. "Attachment Disturbances and Disorders in Children Exposed to Early Severe Deprivation." Infant Mental Health Journal 20, no. 1 (1999): 10-29.** Attachment disorder has garnered considerable attention in recent years. Despite the clear clinical and theoretical importance of attachment disorder, however, there are remarkably few systematic studies of attachment disorder behaviors or their etiology, course, and associated features. Evidence of attachment disorder behaviors was examined in a sample of 111 children who experienced institutional upbringing and were later adopted into the United Kingdom, and a comparison sample of 52 intracountry adopted children not exposed to early deprivation. All children were 4 years of age at the time of assessment. Information was obtained from a semi-structured interview with the parent, questionnaires, and direct assessment of the children. Results indicated that attachment disorder behaviors were positively associated with duration of severe deprivation, but a substantial number of children exposed to even prolonged severe early privation did not exhibit these symptoms. Retrospective parental reports further indicated that children with concurrent disturbances in attachment behavior were likely to have displayed disturbances early on (i.e., at placement), but there was also considerable evidence for discontinuity. The discussion focuses on how these findings address conceptual and diagnostic issues of attachment disorder. In addition, case illustrations are offered to extend the empirical findings and to highlight central aspects of attachment disorder that require further attention.

17. **Wilson, Samantha L. "Post-institutionalization: The Effects of Early Deprivation on Development of Romanian Adoptees."** *Child and Adolescent Social Work Journal* 20, no. 6 (2003): 473-483. Accounts of childhood adversity and extreme

deprivation are not new to psychological literature. Intensive case studies of children raised in isolation or extreme deprivation have provided developmental psychologists a better understanding of the effects of early environment on later development (see Curtiss, 1977, for a detailed account of the developmental sequelae of Genie, a girl rescued from 13 years of restraint and isolation). The influx of children adopted from impoverished institutional care has provided a more recent opportunity to investigate the long-term adjustment and outcome of children who endured a circumscribed period of deprivation (Gunnar, Bruce, & Grotevant, 2000). The following paper will review the research concerning the physical, cognitive, and emotional development of children adopted from Romanian institutions within the last 15 years. Understanding this population is not only important for helping these children and their families, but also to delineate the effects of early deprivation and elucidate potential outcomes for other populations that experience early adverse life events.

18. **Burley, Mason, and Mina Halpern. "Educational Attainment of Foster Youth: Achievement and Graduation Outcomes for Children in State Care." (2001).** This report summarizes findings from a statewide analysis of the educational attainment of foster youth in Washington's public-school system. It analyzes various factors related to educational success, comparing the outcomes of youth in long-term foster care with the state's school-age population. The report merges data from the child welfare system and the public schools to detail the educational experience of students, including foster youth, from elementary school through high school completion. On average, foster youth score 15 to 20 percentile points below non-foster youth on statewide achievement tests. Only 59 percent of foster youth enrolled in 11th grade complete high school by the end of grade 12. The completion rate for non-foster youth is 86 percent. At both the elementary and secondary levels, twice as many foster youth have repeated a grade, changed schools during the year, or enrolled in special education programs compared with non-foster youth. A youth's length of stay in foster care and other placement characteristics do not appear to relate to educational attainment. Three appendices present regression results for schoolwide assessments, long-term foster youth assessments, and grade 11 high school completion.

19. **Pecora, Peter J., Jason Williams, Ronald C. Kessler, Eva Hiripi, Kirk O'Brien, John Emerson, Mary A. Herrick, and Dan Torres. "Assessing the

Educational Achievements of Adults Who Were Formerly Placed in Family Foster Care." Child & Family Social Work 11, no. 3 (2006): 220-231. Case records and interviews concerning educational achievements of 1087 foster care alumni are presented. Youth were served by a voluntary agency in 23 communities across the USA between 1966 and 1998. Because the alumni were older than most foster care follow-up studies, a more extensive picture of educational achievement was possible. High school graduation and college enrolment rates were comparable to or even greater than those of the general population, but the number of alumni completing high school with a Graduate Equivalency Diploma and the college dropout rates were a concern. Predictors of high school completion while in foster care, such as fewer placement changes, extracurricular activities and independent living training, are presented, along with recommendations for improving educational and vocational preparation.

20. **Harden, Brenda Jones. "Safety and Stability for Foster Children: A Developmental Perspective." The Future of Children (2004): 31-47.** Children in foster care face a challenging journey through childhood. In addition to the troubling family circumstances that bring them into state care, they face additional difficulties within the child welfare system that may further compromise their healthy development. This article discusses the importance of safety and stability to healthy child development and reviews the research on the risks associated with maltreatment and the foster care experience. It finds that family stability is best viewed as a process of caregiving practices that, when present, can greatly facilitate healthy child development. Children in foster care, as a result of exposure to risk factors such as poverty, maltreatment, and the foster care experience, face multiple threats to their healthy development, including poor physical health, attachment disorders, compromised brain functioning, inadequate social skills, and mental health difficulties. Providing stable and nurturing families can bolster the resilience of children in care and ameliorate negative impacts on their developmental outcomes. The author concludes that developmentally-sensitive child welfare policies and practices designed to promote the well-being of the whole child, such as ongoing screening and assessment and coordinated systems of care, are needed to facilitate the healthy development of children in foster care.

21. **Hansen, Robin L., Fatema Lakhani Mawjee, Keith Barton, Mary B. Metcalf, and Nancy R. Joye. "Comparing the Health Status of Low-income Children**

**In and Out of Foster Care." Child Welfare 83, no. 4 (2004): 367.** Children in foster care face poverty, family dysfunction, neglect, and abuse, with high rates of chronic health, emotional, and developmental problems. This study compared the overall health status of a group of children entering foster care with a group of Medicaid-eligible children living with their parents, matched for age and gender. It identified significantly more health and developmental problems in children in foster care than in the comparison group. Possible contributors to the higher percentage of problems among foster care children may be that the foster children have more problems related to the underlying risk factors resulting in placement, or that the foster care physicians conducted a more comprehensive assessment or had lower clinical thresholds. Further research is necessary to identify and treat the problems of this high-risk group.

De Fabrique, Nathalie, Stephen J. Romano, Gregory M. Vecchi, and Vincent B. Van Hasselt. "Understanding Stockholm Syndrome." *FBI L. Enforcement Bull.* 76 (2007): 10. The term "Stockholm syndrome" was initially used to explain the phenomenon that emerged during the 1973 robbery of a bank in Stockholm, Sweden. The two robbers held four bank employees hostage in a bank vault from August 23 to 28. During their ordeal, the hostages became emotionally attached to their captors and even defended them after the incident was resolved without any deaths or serious injuries. The Stockholm syndrome occurs when hostages have positive feelings for their captors; hostages show fear, mistrust, and anger toward the authorities; and perpetrators develop positive feelings toward hostages. Most psychologists agree on the conditions necessary for the Stockholm syndrome to occur. First, a hostage cannot escape and depends on the hostage-taker for life. Second, the hostage is isolated from other people and is exposed only to the captor's perspective of the situation. Third, the hostage-taker threatens to kill the hostage, and the hostage takes the threat seriously. Fourth, the hostage views the hostage-taker as kind so long as the hostage-taker is not abusive to the hostage. Although these conditions necessary for Stockholm syndrome rarely occur, hostage negotiators should attempt to manipulate barricaded hostage situations, so hostage-takers develop positive attitudes toward the hostages. In order to strike the balance necessary for successful negotiations, negotiators should show concern for the hostage-taker's welfare first before seeking to develop the hostage-taker's positive feelings for the hostages.

## Chapter 3 - Elementary school

22. **Lane, John, Andrew M. Lane, and Anna Kyprianou. "Self-efficacy, Self-esteem and their Impact on Academic Performance." Social Behavior and Personality: an International Journal 32, no. 3 (2004): 247-256.** This study investigated relationships between self-efficacy, self-esteem, previous performance accomplishments, and academic performance among a sample of 205 postgraduate students. Participants completed measures of past performance accomplishments, self-esteem, and self-efficacy at the start of a 15-week course. Each student's average grade from modules studied was used as the performance measure. Correlation results indicated significant relationships between self-efficacy and self-esteem. Multiple regression results indicated that self-efficacy mediated the relationship between performance accomplishments and academic performance. Findings lend support to the predictive effectiveness of self-efficacy measures in academic settings.

23. **Tauer, John M., and Judith M. Harackiewicz. "The Effects of Cooperation and Competition on Intrinsic Motivation and Performance." Journal of Personality and Social Psychology 86, no. 6 (2004): 849.** The authors examined the effects of competition and cooperation on intrinsic motivation and performance in 4 studies. Across 3 behavioral studies that involved shooting a basketball, no differences were observed between competition and cooperation on task enjoyment or performance. However, the combination of competition and cooperation (intergroup competition) consistently led to higher levels of intrinsic motivation, and in 2 of the 3 studies, performance. In a questionnaire study, the authors replicated the positive effects of intergroup competition on enjoyment and examined process measures that might account for these effects. These findings suggest that competition and cooperation both have positive aspects and that structuring recreational activities to include both can facilitate high levels of both intrinsic motivation and performance.

24. **Michaels, James W. "Classroom Reward Structures and Academic Performance." Review of Educational Research 47, no. 1 (1977): 87-98.** Four general classroom reward structures were identified (individual reward contingencies, group reward contingencies, individual competition and group competition) and studies comparing their effectiveness in strengthening the

independent academic performance of students were reviewed. The most striking finding was the consistent superiority of individual competition.

25. **Medlin, Richard G. "Homeschooling and the Question of Socialization Revisited." Peabody Journal of Education 88, no. 3 (2013): 284-297.** This article reviews recent research on homeschooled children's socialization. The research indicates that homeschooling parents expect their children to respect and get along with people of diverse backgrounds, provide their children with a variety of social opportunities outside the family, and believe their children's social skills are at least as good as those of other children. What homeschooled children think about their own social skills is less clear. Compared to children attending conventional schools, however, research suggests that they have higher quality friendships and better relationships with their parents and other adults. They are happy, optimistic, and satisfied with their lives. Their moral reasoning is at least as advanced as that of other children, and they may be more likely to act unselfishly. As adolescents, they have a strong sense of social responsibility and exhibit less emotional turmoil and problem behaviors than their peers. Those who go on to college are socially involved and open to new experiences. Adults who were homeschooled as children are civically engaged and functioning competently in every way measured so far. An alarmist view of homeschooling, therefore, is not supported by empirical research. It is suggested that future studies focus not on outcomes of socialization but on the process itself.

26. **Gathercole, Rachel. The Well-adjusted Child: The Social Benefits of Homeschooling. Mapletree Publishing Company, 2007.** Socialization may well be the single most important aspect of education today. With high and rising rates of divorce, drug abuse, youth violence, alcoholism, teen promiscuity, and so forth, we cannot afford to let this issue go unexamined. To cling to the idea that what we, as a culture, are doing now is the right and best way for all children simply because it is what we are used to is to shut our eyes and minds to other possibilities—possibilities that may well afford greater happiness, success, peace, and safety to our own children. At a time when people feel more disconnected than ever before, we cannot afford to overlook or allow ourselves to be blinded to an option which offers great benefits, including a rich, fulfilling, and healthy social life, that our children may well need for the future. Homeschooling offers

great social benefits to kids and parents. And when we understand them, our children are the ones who will win.

27. **Romanowski, Michael H. "Revisiting the Common Myths about Homeschooling." The Clearing House: A Journal of Educational Strategies, Issues and Ideas 79, no. 3 (2006): 125-129** The author examines four common myths that still influence individuals regarding their perspective and understanding of the role homeschooling plays in the education of American children. Myth 1 is that homeschooling produces social misfits, stemming from the belief that homeschooled students lack the socialization skills necessary for normal functioning in today's society. Myth 2 is that homeschooling fails to prepare good citizens by "isolating" students from the world, including political and social involvement. Myth 3 is that students who are homeschooled have difficulty entering college due to not having a high school diploma, grades, and SAT or ACT scores and might be at a disadvantage with their postsecondary studies. Myth 4 is that most people homeschool for religious reasons. In each case, realities are presented dispelling these myths. The author concludes that the expectation that public education should adequately serve the needs of children from broad and diverse backgrounds needs reconsideration. Public schools do not, cannot, and probably should not be expected to meet the needs of every child in the community. Instead, parents, schools, and the community need to work together to educate all children and maximize their potential, regardless of what form of education parents choose. Murphy, Joseph. "The Social and Educational Outcomes of Homeschooling." *Sociological Spectrum* 34, no. 3 (2014): 244-272. In this article, we provide a comprehensive review and analysis of the outcomes of homeschooling in America. We ground the work in an examination of the importance of homeschooling in society in general and education in particular. We provide an analysis of the strengths and weaknesses of the existing research base on homeschooling. With an eye on methodological weaknesses in the homeschool research, we compile data on what is known about the outcomes of this social movement and educational reform. We document the impact of homeschooling on the social fabric of the nation (e.g., families) and the institution of schooling (e.g., student learning outcomes).

## Chapter 4 - Middle school

28. **Dempster, Robert, Beth Wildman, and Adam Keating. "The Role of Stigma in Parental Help-seeking for Child Behavior Problems." Journal of Clinical Child & Adolescent Psychology 42, no. 1 (2013): 56-67.** The present study examined the relationship between stigma and parental help-seeking after controlling for demographics, child behavior, and barriers to treatment. One hundred fifteen parents of children ages 4 to 8 years were surveyed during well-child visits in a rural pediatric primary care practice. Parental perceptions of stigma toward parents and children were both assessed. Parents believe that children are more likely to be stigmatized by the public and personally impacted by stigma. In linear regression analyses, parents rated themselves as more likely to attend parenting classes with lower levels of self-stigma and greater levels of personal impact of stigma. Stigma toward the child was not associated with help-seeking. Child behavior moderated the relationship between stigma and parental help-seeking. When referring parents to treatment, providers should address potential stigma concerns. Future research should assess both the impact of the stigma of attending treatment and the stigma of having a child with behavior problems.

29. **Block, Mary Ann. No More Ritalin: Treating ADHD Without Drugs. Kensington Books, 1996.** Outlines why Ritalin may be dangerous to children while offering parents safer and more effective alternatives for treating ADHD, providing accompanying case histories and research.

30. **Safer, Daniel J. "Are Stimulants Overprescribed for Youths with ADHD?." Annals of Clinical Psychiatry 12, no. 1 (2000): 55-62.** Critics of stimulant treatment for youths with attention deficit hyperactivity disorder (ADHD) have increased their rhetoric of late, contending that the leading medication for it, Ritalin®, is vastly overprescribed. Additionally, they claim that Ritalin (methylphenidate) is inherently dangerous and that the entire system of the diagnosis and treatment of ADHD is seriously flawed. The critics view the underlying reason for the "epidemic" as societal, due to our modern pace of living, our competitive society, and our consumer emphasis. Rejoinders to and clarifications of the more tangible points of the critics are presented, followed by a discussion of some more practical and legitimate concerns for researchers in this area. These concerns include changes within the ADHD category, the clinical need for multiple sources of diagnostic data, infrequent teacher–physician

communication, problematic ADHD/conduct disorder comorbidity in adolescence, and the limited amount of community-based research.

31. **Jensen, Peter S., Lori Kettle, Margaret T. Roper, Michael T. Sloan, Mina K. Dulcan, Christina Hoven, Hector R. Bird, Jose J. Bauermeister, and Jennifer D. Payne. "Are Stimulants Overprescribed? Treatment of ADHD in Four U.S. Communities." Journal of the American Academy of Child & Adolescent Psychiatry 38, no. 7 (1999): 797-804.** To address rising concerns about the possible over-diagnosis of attention-deficit hyperactivity disorder (ADHD) and overtreatment with stimulants. To date, almost no studies have examined ADHD in unbiased community-based studies, ascertaining both the prevalence of the diagnosis within non-refereed populations and the extent to which various treatments (i.e., stimulant medication, mental health treatments, and educational interventions) are used. As a part of the Methods for the Epidemiology of Child and Adolescent Mental Disorders (MECA) Study, the authors examined epidemiological survey data obtained from 1,285 children and their parents across 4 U.S. communities. Analyses examined the frequency of children's ADHD diagnosis, the extent to which medications were prescribed, as well as the provision of other services (e.g., psychosocial treatments, school-based educational interventions). Findings indicated that 5.1% of children met full DSM-III-RADHD criteria across the pooled sample. Only 12.5% of children meeting ADHD criteria had been treated with stimulants during the previous 12 months. Some children who had been prescribed stimulants did not meet full ADHD diagnostic criteria, but these children manifested high levels of ADHD symptoms, suggesting that the medication had been appropriately prescribed. Children with ADHD were generally more likely to receive mental health counseling and/or school-based interventions than medication. Medication treatments are often not used in treating ADHD children identified in the community, suggesting the need for better education of parents, physicians, and mental health professionals about the effectiveness of these treatments. On the basis of these data it cannot be concluded that substantial "overtreatment" with stimulants is occurring across communities in general.

32. **Svetlov, Stanislav I., Firas H. Kobeissy, and Mark S. Gold. "Performance Enhancing, Non-prescription Use of Ritalin: A Comparison with Amphetamines and Cocaine." Journal of Addictive Diseases 26, no. 4 (2007): 1-6.** Ritalin, known under chemical name methylphenidate (MPH), is a

psychostimulant prescribed to treat attention-deficit/hyperactivity disorder (ADHD) and other conditions. Psychotropic effects and pharmacological pathways evoked by MPH are similar, but not identical to those produced by amphetamines and cocaine. Although not completely understood in detail, MPH psychostimulation is mediated by the increase of central dopamine (DA) and possibly norepinephrine (NE) and serotonin (ST) due to decrease of their re-uptake via binding to and inhibition of DA, NE, and ST transporters. Despite similarity in psychopharmacological effects, the rewarding/reinforcing ability of MPH appears to be significantly lower than amphetamines and especially cocaine. MPH and similar medications have been widely used on college campuses and by students preparing for exams. Nicknamed 'steroids for SATs,' MPH and related medications are purchased without prescription and their use may even be encouraged by parents and tutors. However, while widely and safely used and administered for over forty years, Ritalin generated significant controversy including MPH abuse and addiction, and adverse reactions. It is now clear that treatment of ADD/ADHD with psychostimulants prevents drug abuse and addictions. Use by those without any medical or psychiatric diagnosis is increasing. In this mini-review, we discuss psychopharmacological and behavioral aspects, and outline neurochemical mechanisms that may provoke Ritalin abuse, addiction and adverse effects compared to amphetamines and cocaine.

33. **Breggin, Peter. Talking Back to Ritalin: What Doctors Aren't Telling You About Stimulants and ADHD. Da Capo Press, 2007.** Millions of children take Ritalin for Attention-Deficit Hyperactivity Disorder. The drug's manufacturer, Novartis, claims that Ritalin is the "solution" to this widespread problem. But hidden behind the well-oiled public-relations machine is a potentially devastating reality: children are being given a drug that can cause the same bad effects as amphetamine and cocaine, including behavioral disorders, growth suppression, neurological tics, agitation, addiction, and psychosis. Talking Back to Ritalin uncovers these and other startling facts and translates the research findings for parents and doctors alike. An advocate for education not medication, Dr. Breggin empowers parents to channel distracted, disenchanted, and energetic children into powerful, confident, and brilliant members of the family and society.

34. **Harpin, Valerie A. "The Effect of ADHD on the Life of an Individual, Their Family, and Community from Preschool to Adult Life." Archives of Disease**

in Childhood 90, no. suppl 1 (2005): i2-i7. Attention deficit/hyperactivity disorder (ADHD) may affect all aspects of a child's life. Indeed, it impacts not only on the child, but also on parents and siblings, causing disturbances to family and marital functioning. The adverse effects of ADHD upon children and their families changes from the preschool years to primary school and adolescence, with varying aspects of the disorder being more prominent at different stages. ADHD may persist into adulthood causing disruptions to both professional and personal life. In addition, ADHD has been associated with increased healthcare costs for patients and their family members.

35. **Volkow, Nora D., and James M. Swanson. "Does Childhood Treatment of ADHD with Stimulant Medication Affect Substance Abuse in Adulthood?." (2008): 553-555.** One of the most controversial issues in childhood psychiatry is whether the wide-spread use of stimulant medications to treat children with attention deficit hyperactivity disorder (ADHD) increases the risk of substance abuse in adulthood. Part of the rationale for this concern is that stimulant medications (methylphenidate and amphetamine) share with drugs of abuse the ability to increase dopamine concentration in the nucleus accumbens, which is the neural mechanism considered crucial for their reinforcing effects (1). Indeed, methylphenidate and amphetamine are sometimes abused in some settings (2). This misuse can produce dependence. Another reason for concern is the timing of exposure. Human epidemiological studies have shown that the earlier an individual is exposed to substances with abuse potential, such as alcohol and nicotine, the greater the risk of drug abuse and dependence in adulthood (3). However, the opposite perspective has also been proposed—that stimulant treatment of children and adolescents with ADHD may reduce the risk of later substance abuse (4). Considering that individuals with ADHD are at higher-than-normal risk for substance abuse (5), it is urgent that these two perspectives be addressed properly, yet relatively few clinical studies have done so.

36. **Robertson, Donald, and James Symons. "Do Peer Groups Matter? Peer Group Versus Schooling Effects on Academic Attainment." Economica 70, no. 277 (2003): 31-53.** This paper estimates an educational production function. Educational attainment is a function of peer group, parental input and schooling. Conventional measures of school quality are not good predictors for academic attainment, once we control for peer group effects; parental qualities

also have strong effects on academic attainment. This academic attainment is a then a key determinant of subsequent labor market success, as measured by earnings. The main methodological innovation in this paper is the nomination of a set of instruments, very broad regions of birth, which, as a whole, pass close scrutiny for validity and permit unbiased estimation of the production function.

37. **McEwan, Patrick J. "Peer Effects on Student Achievement: Evidence from Chile." Economics of Education Review 22, no. 2 (2003): 131-141.** This paper reports estimates of peer effects on student achievement, using a 1997 census of eighth-grade achievement in Chile. The data allow detailed measures of peer characteristics to be constructed for each classroom within a school. The paper addresses the endogeneity of peer variables by including school fixed effects that control for unobserved family and student characteristics. The estimates suggest that the classroom mean of mothers' education is an important determinant of individual achievement, though subject to diminishing marginal returns. Additional specifications using family fixed effects are not suggestive that estimates are biased by within-school sorting.

38. **Zimmerman, David J. "Peer Effects in Academic Outcomes: Evidence from a Natural Experiment." Review of Economics and Statistics 85, no. 1 (2003): 9-23.** I use data from Williams College to implement a quasi-experimental empirical strategy aimed at measuring peer effects in academic outcomes. In particular, I use data on individual students' grades, their SAT scores, and the SAT scores of their roommates. I argue that first-year roommates are assigned randomly with respect to academic ability. This allows me to measure differences in grades of high-, medium-, or low-SAT students living with high-, medium-, or low-SAT roommates. With random assignment these estimates would provide compelling estimates of the effect of roommates' academic characteristics on an individual's grades. I also consider the effect of peers at somewhat more aggregated levels. In particular, I consider the effects associated with different academic environments in clusters of rooms that define distinct social units. The results suggest that peer effects are almost always linked more strongly with verbal SAT scores than with math SAT scores. Students in the middle of the SAT distribution may have somewhat worse grades if they share a room with a student who is in the bottom 15% of the verbal SAT distribution. The effects are not large but are statistically significant in many models.

## Chapter 5 - High school - Boot camp

39. **Kohn, Alfie. "The Dangerous Myth of Grade Inflation." Chronicle of Higher Education 49, no. 11 (2002): B7.** Examines public worries about grade inflation. States that these concerns are neither new nor well-founded. Asserts that these "myths" perpetuate a tendency to confuse quality with difficulty.

40. **Mulvenon, Sean, and Dan Ferritor. "Grade Inflation in Higher Education: Isolated or Systemic?." International Journal of Learning 12, no. 6 (2005).** An issue of gaining relevance in higher education is the steady increase in grades during the last four decades. Numerous postsecondary institutions have examined the effect of increasing grades and have implemented or are investigating strategies to mitigate this current phenomenon. Many questions and theories exist regarding the impact of what has been referred to as "grade inflation" and the purpose of this study was to empirically examine the impact of increasing grades at a major southern AAU research institution, the University of Arkansas. More specifically, to determine the effect, if any, of increasing grades on the academic quality of degrees.

41. **Hunt, Lester H., ed. Grade inflation: Academic Standards in Higher Education. Suny Press, 2008.** This book provides a provocative look at the issues and controversies surrounding grade inflation, and, more generally, grading practices in American higher education. The contributors confront the issues from a number of different disciplines and varying points of view. Topics explored include empirical evidence for and against the claim that there is a general upward trend in grading, whether grade inflation (if it exists) is a problem, which ethical considerations are relevant to grading, and whether heavy reliance on anonymous student evaluations of teaching excellence has a distorting effect on grading practices. Finally, the contributors offer contrasting perspectives on the prospects for reform.

42. **Tucker, Jan, and Bari Courts. "Grade Inflation in the College Classroom." Foresight 12, no. 1 (2010): 45-53.** The purpose of this article is to assess the concept of grade inflation in higher education institutions in an effort to determine its prevalence, causes, and strategies that can be implemented to curtail it. A literature review of the problem is presented along with several strategies as possible solutions to restraining the problem of escalating grades in the college classroom. The problem of grade inflation has been a topic of concern for over

a century and there are no quick fixes or simple methods of reversing this trend but there are several alternatives presented which could help curtail this trend. Most of the research is based on anecdotal research. Very little has been written on how to fix this problem. This paper brings this issue to the forefront in an effort to engage the reader, college administrators and educators. Originality/value – The paper begins with an overview of previous research in this area and then moves on to what is currently being implemented to curb grade inflation. The authors then propose several methods and possible solutions that could be implemented to deal with this problem.

43. **Finefter-Rosenbluh, Ilana, and Meira L. Levinson. "What Is Wrong with Grade Inflation (If Anything)?." (2015)**. Grade inflation is a global phenomenon that has garnered widespread condemnation among educators, researchers, and the public. Yet, few have deliberated over the ethics of grading, let alone the ethics of grade inflation. The purpose of this paper is to map out and examine the ethics of grade inflation. By way of beginning, we clarify why grade inflation is a problem of practical ethics embedded in contemporary social practice. Then, we illuminate three different aspects of grade inflation—longitudinal, compressed, and comparative—and explore the ethical dilemmas that each one raises. We demonstrate how these three aspects may be seen as corresponding to three different victims of grade inflation—individuals, institutions, and society—and hence also to three potential agents of harm—teachers, schools, and educational systems. Next, we reflect upon various compelling reasons that these agents inflate grades, whether from an ethic of care, fiduciary responsibility, or simple self-preservation. Subsequently, we consider a variety of means of combatting grade inflation and invite more educators and philosophers to delve into the complex practical ethics of grade inflation.

44. **Chan, William, Li Hao, and Wing Suen. "A Signaling Theory of Grade Inflation." International Economic Review 48, no. 3 (2007): 1065-1090.**

45. **Ziomek, Robert L., and Joseph C. Svec. "High School Grades and Achievement: Evidence of Grade Inflation." NASSP Bulletin 81, no. 587 (1997): 105-113.**

46. **Woodruff, David J., and Robert L. Ziomek. "High School Grade Inflation from 1991 to 2003. Research Report Series 2004-04."** *ACT Inc* (2004). This report presents the results of a study investigating inflation in high school

grade point average (HSGPA). Inflation was measured by comparing HSGPA to ACT Assessment (ACT) scores over the years 1991 to 2003. The results indicate the presence of grade inflation over the 13 years. That is, HSGPAs increased without a concomitant increase in achievement, as measured by the ACT. Both the marginal analyses and the conditional analyses reveal the presence of grade inflation. Depending on the subject area, the average amount of grade inflation over the 13 years varied between 0.20 and 0.26 on a HSGPA scale of 0 (F) to 4 (A).

## CHAPTER 6 - HIGH SCHOOL: HOW TO KNOCK IT OUT OF THE PARK

47. **Vogel, Sarah A. "The Politics of Plastics: The Making and Unmaking of Bisphenol a "Safety"." American Journal of Public Health 99, no. S3 (2009): S559-S566. Bisphenol A (BPA),** a synthetic chemical used in the production of plastics since the 1950s and a known endocrine disruptor, is a ubiquitous component of the material environment and human body. New research on very-low-dose exposure to BPA suggests an association with adverse health effects, including breast and prostate cancer, obesity, neurobehavioral problems, and reproductive abnormalities. These findings challenge the long-standing scientific and legal presumption of BPA's safety. The history of how BPA's safety was defined and defended provides critical insight into the questions now facing lawmakers and regulators: is BPA safe, and if not, what steps must be taken to protect the public's health?

48. **Lanphear, Bruce P., Charles V. Vorhees, and David C. Bellinger. "Protecting Children from Environmental Toxins." PLoS medicine 2, no. 3 (2005): e61.** Epidemics of overt toxicity following widespread environmental contamination from commercial toxins heralded the discovery of children's enhanced vulnerability to lead, methyl mercury, polychlorinated biphenyls (PCBs), and tobacco. Over the past three decades, researchers have found that remarkably low-level exposures to these toxins are linked with less overt symptoms of toxicity—intellectual impairments, behavioral problems, spontaneous abortions, or preterm births. Moreover, there is emerging evidence that decrements in intellectual abilities and low birth weight linked with lead or tobacco are, for a given increment of exposure, greater at lower levels than those found at higher levels.

49. **McDonald, Libby. The Toxic Sandbox: The Truth about Environmental Toxins and Our Children's Health. Penguin, 2007.** From pesticides to PCBs—what's a threat, what's not, and what to do about it? Mercury. Lead. Pesticides. Plastics. Air pollution. PCBs. How can parents' sort through the hype, propaganda, and misinformation—and find out what is and isn't a threat to children's health? Investigative journalist, advocate, and concerned parent Libby McDonald separates the facts from the alarmist myths. Based on the latest research along with interviews with top medical, toxicological, and environmental experts, *The Toxic Sandbox* covers a wide range of essential concerns, including:

    i. How can kids be protected from mercury poisoning?

    ii. What are the sources of lead poisoning, and how can they be avoided?

    iii. What pesticides are children ingesting, and does eating organic keep them safe?

    iv. Which teenage beauty products contain carcinogenic phthalates?

    v. What are PCBs and PBDEs and why are they found in breast milk?

    vi. What can be done to stop the childhood asthma epidemic?

50. **Buka, Irena, Alvaro Osornio-Vargas, and Robin Walker. "Canada Declares Bisphenol A a 'Dangerous Substance': Questioning the Safety of Plastics." Pediatrics & Child Health 14, no. 1 (2009): 11-13.** The Canadian government has recently taken a bold step in becoming the first country to declare bisphenol A (BPA) a 'dangerous substance,' thereby raising strong consideration for its banning (1). It is a synthetic petroleum-based chemical present in a variety of hard plastic products (eg, baby bottles, food storage containers, plastic drinking bottles, food can linings and dental sealants), and has the potential to leach into food. Leaching is accelerated particularly by heating (2). To date, no longitudinal human health effect epidemiological studies have been published. BPA is an endocrine disruptor and may mimic the hormone estrogen. A recently published review (3) of the literature identified 115 published animal

studies, 81% of which found significant effects at low levels of exposure to BPA, meaning that the effects were observed when using less than 50 mg/kg of body weight/day – the accepted 'no observed adverse effect' level for BPA (3). Approximately one third of those studies found effects when testing concentrations below 50 ug/kg/day.

51. **Jacobson, Joseph L., Sandra W. Jacobson, Pamela M. Schwartz, Greta G. Fein, and Jeffrey K. Dowler. "Prenatal Exposure to Environmental Toxin: A Test of the Multiple Effects Model." Developmental Psychology 20, no. 4 (1984): 523.** The multiple effects model of teratological exposure predicts that neonatal deficits associated with intrauterine exposure to small doses of a potentially teratogenic agent will vary considerably across individuals. This hypothesis was tested in a sample of 242 newborns exposed prenatally to low levels of polychlorinated biphenyls (PCBs) from maternal consumption of contaminated lake fish and 71 control infants whose mothers did not eat these fish. Behavioral outcomes were assessed using the Brazelton Neonatal Behavioral Assessment Scale (NABS). Contaminated fish consumption predicted motoric immaturity, poorer lability of states, a greater amount of startle, and more abnormally weak (hypoactive) reflexes. The most highly exposed Ss were more likely than controls to be classified as "worrisome" on 3 NBAS clusters. Results from a stepwise regression analysis are consistent with the multiple effects model, indicating that some affected Ss were born small and/or early, whereas others exhibited one or another of the behavioral deficits. The analysis indicated that 12.2% of the variance in contaminated fish consumption was associated with measurable neonatal deficits.

52. **Bruce, Nigel, Rogelio Perez-Padilla, and Rachel Albalak. "Indoor Air Pollution in Developing Countries: A Major Environmental and Public Health Challenge." Bulletin of the World Health Organization 78 (2000): 1078-1092.** Around 50% of people, almost all in developing countries, rely on coal and biomass in the form of wood, dung, and crop residues for domestic energy. These materials are typically burnt in simple stoves with very incomplete combustion. Consequently, women and young children are exposed to high levels of indoor air pollution every day. There is consistent evidence that indoor air pollution increases the risk of chronic obstructive pulmonary disease and of acute respiratory infections in childhood, the most important cause of death among children under 5 years of age in developing countries. Evidence

also exists of associations with low birth weight, increased infant and perinatal mortality, pulmonary tuberculosis, nasopharyngeal and laryngeal cancer, cataract, and, specifically in respect of the use of coal, with lung cancer. Conflicting evidence exists with regard to asthma. All studies are observational and very few have measured exposure directly, while a substantial proportion have not dealt with confounding. As a result, risk estimates are poorly quantified and may be biased. Exposure to indoor air pollution may be responsible for nearly 2 million excess deaths in developing countries and for some 4% of the global burden of disease. Indoor air pollution is a major global public health threat requiring greatly increased efforts in the areas of research and policy-making. Research on its health effects should be strengthened, particularly in relation to tuberculosis and acute lower respiratory infections. A more systematic approach to the development and evaluation of interventions is desirable, with clearer recognition of the interrelationships between poverty and dependence on polluting fuels.

53. **Viraraghavan, T., K. S. Subramanian, and J. A. Aruldoss. "Arsenic in Drinking Water—Problems and Solutions." Water Science and Technology 40, no. 2 (1999): 69.** The current United States maximum contaminant level for arsenic in drinking water is set at 50 ug/l. Because of the cancer risks involved, Canada has already lowered the maximum contaminant level to 25 ug/l; the United States Environmental Protection Agency is reviewing the current allowable level for arsenic with a view of lowering it significantly. Various treatment methods have been adopted to remove arsenic from drinking water. These methods include 1) adsorption-coprecipitation using iron and aluminum salts, 2) adsorption on activated alumina, activated carbon, and activated bauxite, 3) reverse osmosis, 4) ion exchange and 5) oxidation followed by filtration. Because of the promise of oxidation-filtration systems, column studies were conducted at the University of Regina to examine oxidation with $KMnO_4$ followed by filtration using manganese greensand and iron-oxide coated sand to examine the removal of arsenic from drinking water; these results were compared with the data from ion exchange studies. These studies demonstrated that As (III) could be reduced from 200 ug/l to below 25 ug/l by the manganese greensand system. In the case of manganese greensand filtration, addition of iron in the ratio of 20:1 was found necessary to achieve this removal.

54. **McCabe, Sean Esteban, John R. Knight, Christian J. Teter, and Henry Wechsler. "Non-medical Use of Prescription Stimulants Among U.S.**

College Students: Prevalence and Correlates from a National Survey." **Addiction 100, no. 1 (2005): 96-106.** The life-time prevalence of non-medical prescription stimulant use was 6.9%, past year prevalence was 4.1% and past month prevalence was 2.1%. Past year rates of non-medical use ranged from zero to 25% at individual colleges. Multivariate regression analyses indicated non-medical use was higher among college students who were male, white, members of fraternities and sororities and earned lower grade point averages. Rates were higher at colleges located in the north-eastern region of the US and colleges with more competitive admission standards. Non-medical prescription stimulant users were more likely to report use of alcohol, cigarettes, marijuana, ecstasy, cocaine and other risky behaviors. The findings of the present study provide evidence that non-medical use of prescription stimulants is more prevalent among particular subgroups of U.S. college students and types of colleges. The non-medical use of prescription stimulants represents a high-risk behavior that should be monitored further and intervention efforts are needed to curb this form of drug use.

55. **Low, K. Graff, and A. E. Gendaszek. "Illicit Use of Psychostimulants Among College Students: A Preliminary Study." Psychology, Health & Medicine 7, no. 3 (2002): 283-287.** There is little recent research on the illicit use of prescription stimulants such as methylphenidate on college campuses. Given the increasing number of amphetamine prescriptions for attention deficit-hyperactivity disorder in older adolescents, non-medical use seems likely to occur. The present study surveyed undergraduates at a small college in the USA on their use of both legal and illegal stimulants; 35.5% of undergraduates who were convenience-sampled had used prescription amphetamines illicitly (defined as use without a prescription), with men reporting more use than women. Motivations were primarily academic, but 19.3% of students reported using prescription stimulants in combination with alcohol for recreational reasons. In addition, 34% of the sample reported using either cocaine or MDMA in the previous year. Motivations for use of illegal stimulants were primarily recreational. Sensation seeking appears to be a correlate of both types of stimulant use; for abuse of prescription drugs, being both high in sensation seeking and more perfectionistic is associated with greater use. Abuse of prescription and illegal stimulants appears to be widespread in this college sample.

56. Hall, Kristina M., Melissa M. Irwin, Krista A. Bowman, William Frankenberger, and David C. Jewett. "Illicit Use of Prescribed Stimulant Medication Among College Students." *Journal of American College Health* 53, no. 4 (2005): 167-174. The authors investigated illicit use of stimulant medications at a Midwestern university. They used a questionnaire to (a) examine the extent to which university students illicitly used stimulant medications prescribed for attention-deficit hyperactivity disorder; (b) determine why college students abused such drugs; and (c) identify the factors that predicted illicit use of prescribed stimulant medication. Findings revealed that 17% of 179 surveyed men and 11% of 202 women reported illicit use of prescribed stimulant medication. Forty-four percent of surveyed students stated that they knew students who used stimulant medication illicitly for both academic and recreational reasons. Students reported they experienced time pressures associated with college life and that stimulants were said to increase alertness and energy. Regression analysis revealed that the factor that predicted men's use was knowing where to get easily acquired stimulant medication, whereas the main predictor for women was whether another student had offered the prescribed stimulants.

57. Teter, Christian J., Sean Esteban McCabe, James A. Cranford, Carol J. Boyd, and Saliy K. Guthrie. "Prevalence and Motives for Illicit Use of Prescription Stimulants in an Undergraduate Student Sample." *Journal of American College Health* 53, no. 6 (2005): 253-262. To assess the prevalence and motives for illicit use of prescription stimulants and alcohol and other drugs (AODs), associated with these motives, the authors distributed a self-administered Web survey to a random sample of 9,161 undergraduate college students. Of the study participants, 8.1% reported lifetime and 5.4% reported past-year illicit use of prescription stimulants. The most prevalent motives given for illicit use of prescription stimulants were to (1) help with concentration, (2) increase alertness, and (3) provide a high. Although men were more likely than women were to report illicit use of prescription stimulants, the authors found no gender differences in motives. Regardless of motive, illicit use of prescription stimulants was associated with elevated rates of AOD use, and number of motives endorsed and AOD use were positively related. Students appear to be using these prescription drugs non-medically, mainly to enhance performance or get high.

58. **Lucier, C., Rosofsky, A., London, B., Scharber, H., & Shandra, J. M. (2011). "Toxic Pollution and School Performance Scores: Environmental Ascription in East Baton Rouge Parish, Louisiana." Organization & Environment, 24(4), 423-443.** The current study adds to the literature linking environmental pollution and disparities in educational outcomes among vulnerable populations by measuring variations in school performance scores in East Baton Rouge (EBR) Parish, Louisiana. The authors ask whether the unique, place-specific, results of a study such as the 2004 study by Pastor, Sadd, and Morello-Frosch, specifically the finding that schools' academic performance scores are negatively related to proximity to major polluters, can be made somewhat more "general" by examining a similar relationship in another location. The authors closely approximate the model and methodology used by Pastor et al. and then re-specify that model by including new independent variables with a particular focus on alternative and more nuanced measures of proximity to polluters as indicators of potential human exposure. Furthermore, they analyze the relationship between proximity and achievement in terms of disproportionate effects on human capital experienced by vulnerable populations. The findings provide evidence of "environmental ascription," the idea that "place" (especially, attending school in polluted places) has ascriptive properties. The authors find that, all else equal, their several measures of proximity (to Toxics Release Inventory facilities in general, to high concentrations of toxic emissions, and to high-volume polluters of developmental neurotoxins) are significantly related to school performance scores throughout EBR Parish.

59. **Mohai, Paul, Byoung-Suk Kweon, Sangyun Lee, and Kerry Ard. "Air Pollution Around Schools is Linked to Poorer Student Health and Academic Performance." Health Affairs 30, no. 5 (2011): 852-862.** Exposing children to environmental pollutants during important times of physiological development can lead to long-lasting health problems, dysfunction, and disease. The location of children's schools can increase their exposure. We examined the extent of air pollution from industrial sources around public schools in Michigan to find out whether air pollution jeopardizes children's health and academic success. We found that schools located in areas with the highest air pollution levels had the lowest attendance rates—a potential indicator of poor health—and the highest proportions of students who failed to meet state educational testing standards. Michigan and many other states currently do not

require officials considering a site for a new school to analyze its environmental quality. Our results show that such requirements are needed. For schools already in existence, we recommend that their environmental quality should be investigated and improved if necessary.

## CHAPTER 7 - STANDARDIZED TESTS

60. **Atkinson, Richard C., and Saul Geiser. "Reflections on a Century of College Admissions Tests." Educational Researcher 38, no. 9 (2009): 665-676.** The College Boards started as achievement tests designed to measure students' mastery of college preparatory subjects. Admissions testing has significantly changed since then with the introduction of the Scholastic Aptitude Test, Lindquist's creation of the ACT, renewed interest in subject-specific assessments, and current efforts to adapt K–12 standards-based tests for use in college admissions. We have come full circle to a renewed appreciation for the value of achievement tests. Curriculum-based achievement tests are more valid indicators of college readiness than other tests and have important incentive or signaling effects for K–12 schools as well: They help reinforce a rigorous academic curriculum and create better alignment of teaching, learning, and assessment along the pathway from high school to college.

61. **Zwick, Rebecca, and Jeffrey C. Sklar. "Predicting College Grades and Degree Completion Using High School Grades and SAT Scores: The Role of Student Ethnicity and First Language." American Educational Research Journal 42, no. 3 (2005): 439-464.** The degree to which SAT scores and high school grade-point average (GPA) predicted first-year college GPA (FGPA) and college graduation was examined for four groups: Hispanic students whose first language was Spanish and Hispanic, Black, and White students whose first language was English. The percentage of variance in FGPA jointly explained by high school GPA and SAT score varied from 7% to 20% across groups. Survival analyses showed that high school GPA had a statistically significant influence on graduation in the White/English group; SAT had a significant effect in the Hispanic/English and White/English groups. The regression and survival analyses revealed interesting differences in achievement patterns between the Hispanic/Spanish and Hispanic/English groups, demonstrating the value of taking language background into consideration in educational research.

62. **Sawyer, R. (2013). "Beyond Correlations: Usefulness of High School GPA and Test Scores in Making College Admissions Decisions. Applied Measurement in Education, 26(2), 89-112.** Correlational evidence suggests that high school GPA is better than admission test scores in predicting first-year college GPA, although test scores have incremental predictive validity. The usefulness of a selection variable in making admission decisions depends in part on its predictive validity, but also on institutions' selectivity and definition of success. Analyses of data from 192 institutions suggest that high school GPA is more useful than admission test scores in situations involving low selectivity in admissions and minimal to average academic performance in college. In contrast, test scores are more useful than high school GPA in situations involving high selectivity and high academic performance. In nearly all contexts, test scores have incremental usefulness beyond high school GPA. Moreover, high school GPA by test score interactions are important in predicting academic success. (Contains 5 figures, 4 tables, and 4 footnotes.)

63. **Tucker, Jan, and Bari Courts. "Grade Inflation in the College Classroom." Foresight 12, no. 1 (2010): 45-53.** Purpose–The purpose of this article is to assess the concept of grade inflation in higher education institutions in an effort to determine its prevalence, causes, and strategies that can be implemented to curtail it. Design/methodology/approach—A literature review of the problem is presented along with several strategies as possible solutions to restraining the problem of escalating grades in the college classroom. Findings—The problem of grade inflation has been a topic of concern for over a century and there are no quick fixes or simple methods of reversing this trend but there are several alternatives presented which could help curtail this trend. Research limitations/implications—Most of the research is based on anecdotal research. Very little has been written on how to fix this problem. Practical implications—This paper brings this issue to the forefront in an effort to engage the reader, college administrators and educators. Originality/value—The paper begins with an overview of previous research in this area and then moves on to what is currently being implemented to curb grade inflation. The authors then propose several methods and possible solutions that could be implemented to deal with this problem.

64. **Ziomek, Robert L., and Joseph C. Svec. "High School Grades and Achievement: Evidence of Grade Inflation." NASSP Bulletin 81, no. 587 (1997): 105-113.**

65. **Geiser, Saul, and Veronica Santelices. "The Role of Advanced Placement and Honors Courses in College Admissions." Expanding Opportunity in Higher Education: Leveraging Promise 75114 (2006).** This study examines the role of Advanced Placement (AP) and other honors-level courses as a criterion for admission at a leading public university, the University of California, and finds that the number of AP and honors courses taken in high school bears little or no relationship to student's later performance in college. AP is increasingly emphasized as a factor in admissions, particularly at selective colleges and universities. But while student performance on AP examinations is strongly related to college performance, merely taking AP or other honors-level courses in high school is not a valid indicator of the likelihood that students will perform well in college. These findings suggest that institutions may need to reconsider the use of AP as a criterion in admissions, particularly given the marked disparity in access to AP and honors courses among disadvantaged and underrepresented minority students.

66. **Santoli, Susan P. "Is There an Advanced Placement Advantage?." American Secondary Education (2002): 23-35.** Examines potential advantages of Advance Placement (AP) courses for students and schools. Reviews literature on the effects of AP courses on students, AP implications for college admissions, AP implications for college attendance, AP economic implications, and AP program concerns. Concludes that AP program advantages for students, schools, and colleges outweigh concerns.

67. **Schneider, Jack. "Privilege, Equity, and the Advanced Placement Program: Tug of War." Journal of Curriculum Studies 41, no. 6 (2009): 813-831.** The Advanced Placement Program is growing at a striking rate in U.S. high schools and at the same time being abandoned by high-status schools. This paper explores the history of the Advanced Placement Program, from its roots in the 1950s as a program for challenging high-achieving students at high-status schools, through its equity-motivated expansion in the latter decades of the 20th century, up to the present as it faces threats to its credibility and prestige. In so doing, it also explores the difficulty of combating inequality with school reform, particularly in light of continuing moves by privileged groups to gain a measure of distinction. In the case of the Advanced Placement Program, a greater push for equity has, ironically, incited a reaction that may, in the end, result in greater inequity.

68. **Hernandez, Michele A. A is for Admission: The Insider's Guide to Getting into the Ivy League and Other Top Colleges. Grand Central Publishing, 2010**. A former admissions officer at Dartmouth College reveals how the world's most highly selective schools really make their decisions.

69. **Hughes, Chuck W., and Charles W. II Hughes. What It Really Takes to Get into the ivy league & Other Highly Selective Colleges. McGraw-Hill, 2003.** The ultimate insider's guide to getting into the nation's most competitive colleges. Written by a former senior admissions officer at Harvard University, this book provides keen insights into what it takes to get into America's top schools. With the help of case studies of successful Harvard applicants, Charles Hughes II defines the goals and mission of highly selective schools. He explains the relative weight given to: Academics, Extra-curricular activities, Personal qualities, and Intangibles in the admission process. Hughes breaks down the components of the application, explaining the significance of each and how they are evaluated.

70. **Mullen, Ann L. "Elite Destinations: Pathways to Aattending an Ivy League University." British Journal of Sociology of Education 30, no. 1 (2009): 15-27.** As higher education expands and becomes more differentiated, patterns of class stratification remain deeply entrenched, in part due to class-based differences in college choice. A qualitative study of 50 Yale students shows the effects of social class, high schools and peers on students' pathways to college. For students from wealthy and highly educated families, the choice of an Ivy League institution becomes normalized through the inculcated expectations of families, the explicit positioning of schools, and the peer culture. Without these advantages, less-privileged students more often place elite institutions outside the realm of the possible—in part because of concerns of elitism. These findings suggest that even low-socioeconomic status students with exceptional academic credentials must overcome substantial hurdles to arrive at an Ivy League university.

71. **E Moll, Richard. "Playing the Private College Admissions Game." (1979).** Truths and myths involved with student admission to Ivy League colleges are revealed by a director of admissions whose experience includes admission work at Vassar, Bowdoin, Harvard and Yale. Several basic concepts are offered as fact: most private colleges in America today are not highly selective; many colleges pose as being more selective than they really are hoping to attract the cream of

the crop; few undergraduate institutions in America today are as highly selective as they ever have been; nothing speaks louder than a strong high school record; and given the (rare) highly selective college situation, "other considerations" can indeed enter the picture, some of which the candidate can capitalize on. Myths are centered on such factors as name, location, size, major, social type, and cost. Examples are described rebutting the following myths: the more prestigious the college, the better the college; the smaller the college, the more personal the education; the middle class has been squeezed out of Ivy-type colleges; and single-sex colleges are dead. Other chapters in the book discuss the criteria for admission, how colleges sell themselves, and how a student should choose a college. Five appendices are provided that examine such areas as how financial aid is determined, application procedures, transfer patterns, the Statement of Principles of Good Practice as adopted by the National Association of College Admissions Counselors, and some humorous admission experiences as told by directors of admissions.

72. **Murphy, Michael, Mark Harrold, Seán Carey, and Mark Mulrooney. "A Survey of the Level of Learning Disability Among the Prison Population in Ireland." Dublin: Department of Justice, Equality and Law Reform (2000).** This study reports the results of a survey on the level of learning disability in Irish prisons commissioned by the Department of Justice, Equality and Law Reform of the Irish Government commissioned in 1999. The authors completed psychological assessment on 264 prisoners, which represented 10% of the total prisoner population in Ireland at the time of the study. In each of the fourteen prisons ten percent of inmates were randomly selected for inclusion in the study. Assessments included the Kaufman Brief Intelligence Test (KBIT), the Wide Range Achievement Test (WRAT), the Vocabulary sub test from the Weschler Adult Intelligence Scale-Revised (WAIS-R), and the National Adult Prisoner Survey (NAPS). Results showed that 28.8% of the sample population scored below 70 on the KBIT, which is suggestive of a significant degree of intellectual disability/mental handicap. Results from other tests were consistent with those of the KBIT. The implications of these findings are discussed.

73. **Craig, Hugh. "Shakespeare's Vocabulary: Myth and Reality." Shakespeare Quarterly 62, no. 1 (2011): 53-74.** One of the staples of Shakespeare commentary for the past century and more has been the idea that Shakespeare had an exceptionally large vocabulary. Now that electronic texts of early modern

English drama are available in quantity, it is possible to check this claim. Comparing Shakespeare's plays to a large group of plays by other writers from the period shows that his vocabulary is indeed large, but this would seem to be only because his canon of surviving single-author plays is larger than his contemporaries. Play for play, Shakespeare's dramatic works fit well with the pattern of others in the number of different words used. The same can be said of the number of new words he introduces into successive plays. Looking at a different measure—the extent to which a playwright's rate of use of individual words deviates from the average—Shakespeare is remarkable for the closeness of his practice to that of his peers. Whatever quantitative measures reflecting Shakespeare's acknowledged exceptional status are explored in the future, the evidence of vocabulary size and word-use frequency places Shakespeare with his contemporaries, rather than apart from them.

74. **Elliott, Ward EY, and Robert J. Valenza. "Shakespeare's Vocabulary: Did It Dwarf All Others?."** Shakespeare, who displayed a greater variety of expression than probably any writer in any language, produced all his plays with about 15,000 words. Milton's works are built up with 8,000 and the Old Testament says all that it has to say with 5,642 words." *Stylistics and Shakespeare's Language: Transdisciplinary Approaches* (2011): 34-57.

## CHAPTER 9 - EXTRACURRICULAR ACTIVITIES

75. **Tyler, Steven, and David Dalton. Does the Noise in My Head Bother You?. Edel: Books, 2012.** *Does the Noise in My Head Bother You?* is the rock memoir to end all rock memoirs—the straight-up, no-holds-barred story of Grammy Award-winning, Rock 'n' Roll Hall of Fame inductee, and all around superstar legend Steven Tyler, lead singer of Aerosmith (and celebrity judge on American Idol). The rock and roll epic that is Tyler's life begins with Tyler's youth in the Bronx, tracing his early music career and influences, his legendary partnership with Joe Perry, the meteoric rise, fall, and rise of Aerosmith over the last three decades, their music, Tyler's battles with substance abuse, his epic romantic life, his relationship with his four children (including actress Liv Tyler), life on the road and in the spotlight, the economics of the rock star business—and all the sex, drugs, and rock and roll that anyone could ask for. In Tyler's own words: "I've been mythicized, Mickcized, eulogized and fooligized, I've been Cole-Portered and farmer's-daughtered, I've been Led Zepped and 12-stepped.

I'm a rhyming fool and so cool that me, Fritz the Cat, and Mohair Sam are the baddest cats that am. I have so many outrageous stories, too many, and I'm gonna tell 'em all. All the unexpurgated, brain-jangling tales of debauchery, sex & drugs, transcendence & chemical dependence you will ever want to hear. And this is not just my take, this is the unbridled truth, the in-your-face, up-close and prodigious tale of Steven Tyler straight from the horse's lips."

76. **Rivera, Lauren A. "Ivies, Extracurriculars, and Exclusion: Elite Employers' Use of Educational Credentials." Research in Social Stratification and Mobility 29, no. 1 (2011): 71-90** Although a robust literature has demonstrated a positive relationship between education and socio-economic attainment, the processes through which formal schooling yields enhanced economic and social rewards remain less clear. Employers play a crucial role in explaining the returns to formal schooling, yet little is known about how employers, particularly elite employers, use and interpret educational credentials. In this article, I analyze how elite professional service employers use and interpret educational credentials in real-life hiring decisions. I find that educational credentials were the most common criteria employers used to solicit and screen resumes. However, it was not the content of education that elite employers valued but rather its prestige. Contrary to common sociological measures of institutional prestige, employers privileged candidates who possessed a super-elite (e.g., top four) rather than selective university affiliation. They restricted competition to students with elite affiliations and attributed superior abilities to candidates who had been admitted to super-elite institutions, regardless of their actual performance once there. However, a super-elite university affiliation was insufficient on its own. Importing the logic of university admissions, firms performed a strong secondary screen on candidates' extracurricular accomplishments, favoring high status, resource-intensive activities that resonated with white, upper-middle class culture. I discuss these findings in terms of the changing nature of educational credentialism to suggest that (a) extracurricular activities have become credentials of social and moral character that have monetary conversion value in labor markets and (b) the way employers use and interpret educational credentials contributes to a social closure of elite jobs based on socio-economic status.

77. **Swanson, Christopher B. "Spending Time or Investing Time? Involvement in High School Curricular and Extracurricular Activities as Strategic Action." Rationality and Society 14, no. 4 (2002): 431-471.** A rational choice

perspective on social behavior implies that individuals engage in purposive action with the intention of maximizing their interests in valued objectives. Although adolescents have more often been viewed as products of their environments than as rational actors, the choices they face in allocating time and effort among different activities can influence their ability to achieve important life goals. This article develops a conceptual model of involvement as investment to characterize participation in high school curricular and extracurricular activities and the returns they yield for college matriculation. Data from a national sample of students and schools and multi-level statistical methods are used to explore a set of empirical questions derived from this model. Findings demonstrate that activity involvement displays properties characteristic of social exchange and investment. Involvement in both the formal curriculum and school extracurriculars yields significant returns for college matriculation while also showing evidence of diminishing returns associated with overinvesting. Results further show that the point of diminishing returns to investment in formal curricular activities comes at higher levels of involvement for progressively more competitive outcomes and that rates of curricular returns are linked to an actor's goal specificity. Comparisons between actual and optimal patterns of investment suggest that high school students are relatively strategic in their activity involvement.

## Chapter 10 - The essay

78. **Freire, Paulo. "The Importance of the Act of Reading." Journal of Education 165, no. 1 (1983): 5-11.** The question of the importance of reading is addressed by considering the ways in which experience itself is read through the interaction of the self and the world. Through examining memories of childhood, it is possible to view objects and experiences as texts, words, and letters and to see the growing awareness of the world as a kind of reading through which the self learns and changes. The actual act of reading literary texts is seen as part of a wider process of human development and growth based on understanding both one's own experience and the social world. Learning to read must be seen as one aspect of the act of knowing and as a creative act. Reading the world thus precedes reading the word and writing a new text must be seen as one means of transforming the world.

79. **Cox, Brian. Literacy Is Not Enough: Essays on the Importance of Reading. Manchester University Press, 1999.** The last two decades have witnessed a considerable reaction to the progressive utopianism of the 1960s. In education debates all over the English-speaking world, the talk is now of competition, back to basics, league tables, the demands of the market. This reaction has gone too far. Children need to be helped not only to achieve basic literacy but to read "critically," to discriminate, to evaluate, to enjoy great literature. It is not enough to help children to achieve literacy if this simply means they read only sufficiently well to be seduced by advertisers and tabloid newspapers. The essays in this book are by people engaged in the "promotion" of English, be they primary teachers or university lecturers, novelists or poets, publishers or social commentators, politicians or professors.

80. **Ross, Catherine Sheldrick, Lynne McKechnie, and Paulette M. Rothbauer. Reading Matters: What the Research Reveals About Reading, Libraries, and Community. Westport, CT: Libraries Unlimited, 2006.** Drawing upon data published in a variety of scholarly journals, monographs in education, cultural studies, media studies, and libraries and information studies, as well as their own research findings, these authors shatter some of the popular myths about reading and offer a cogent case for the library's vital role in the life of a reader. By providing a road map to research findings on reading, reader-response, audiences, genres, the value of popular culture, the social nature of reading, and the role of libraries in promoting literacy and reading, this guide offers a clear rationale for making pleasure reading a priority in the library and in schools. The authors assert that reading for pleasure is as vital as ever; and that it is, and should be, woven into the majority of activities librarians consider fundamental: reference, collection building, provision of leisure materials, readers' advisory services, storytelling programs, adult literacy programs, and the like. Reading Matters covers myths about reading, the boy problem, reading and identity, how readers select books, and reading as a social activity. An essential resource for library administrators and personnel, the book will help them convey a message about the importance of reading to grant-funding agencies and others. It contains powerful proof that can be used to justify the establishment, maintenance, and growth of fiction (and other pleasure reading) collections, and of readers' advisory services. It is also of interest to LIS faculty who wish to establish/maintain courses in readers' advisory and can be used as

supplemental reading in these classes. Finally, it is a great model and aide for additional research on this topic.

81. **Daiute, Colette, and Bridget Dalton. "Collaboration Between Children Learning to Write: Can Novices Be masters?." Cognition and Instruction 10, no. 4 (1993): 281-333.** This study describes social aspects of the literacy learning process among young peers and synthesizes distinct strands of research on socially constructed literacy. Fourteen 7- to 9-year-old children in a third-grade urban classroom wrote four stories individually and three stories collaboratively with a partner over a 3-month period. Analyses of the children's individual and collaborative stories and transcripts of their collaboration processes as they composed together were done to identify children's expertise as writers and to trace any transfer of knowledge about the structure of stories between partners. Analyses of the 7,512 talk turns in the collaborative composing sessions showed that 95 % of the story elements added after collaboration had been the focus of children's talk as they composed together. Furthermore, children who demonstrated even minimal ability to write stories transferred basic aspects of story structure to each other. To learn more about the social nature of literacy development, we related these children's collaboration processes to those identified as important in teacher-student collaborations (Collins, Brown, & Newman, 1989). Like expert-novice pairs, young peers used generative processes and reflective processes, yet they also did considerable repeating, which seemed to serve them well. This study shows that the literacy learning process involves intense engagement among young peers who share their relative expertise as they focus intellectual and social energies on the text they create together.

82. **Teasley, Stephanie D. "Talking About Reasoning: How Important Is the Peer in Peer Collaboration?." In Discourse, Tools and Reasoning, pp. 361-384. Springer, Berlin, Heidelberg, 1997.** Using data from two studies of scientific reasoning, this chapter explores whether transactive discussion is the basis of productive peer collaborations and questions what role the partner plays in the apparent effectiveness of this type of discussion. In the first study, dyads who engaged in transactive discussion showed more improvement than dyads who did not have transactive discussions. In the second study, both dyads and children working alone showed improvement related to talk in general. However, dyads produced more transactive types of talk and showed a more

complex understanding of the problem that they generated more quickly. Having a partner was not a necessary or sufficient condition for producing transactive talk but increased likelihood that it would occur. The data from these studies suggest that the value of peer collaborations may be that the presence of a partner provides a natural context for elaborating one's own reasoning.

83. **O'Malley, Patrick M., and Lloyd D. Johnston. "Epidemiology of Alcohol and Other Drug Use Among American College Students." Journal of Studies on Alcohol, Supplement 14 (2002): 23-39.** This article provides information on the extent of alcohol use and other drug use among American college students. Five different sources of data are examined for estimating recent levels of alcohol (and other drug) use among college students: Harvard School of Public Health College Alcohol Study (CAS), the Core Institute (CORE), Monitoring the Future (MTF), National College Health Risk Behavior Survey (NCHRBS) and National Household Survey on Drug Abuse (NHSDA). Alcohol use rates are very high among college students. Approximately two of five American college students were heavy drinkers, defined as having had five or more drinks in a row in the past 2 weeks. Alcohol use is higher among male than female students. White students are highest in heavy drinking, black students are lowest and Hispanic students are intermediate. Use of alcohol—but not cigarettes, marijuana and cocaine—is higher among college students than among non-college age-mates. Longitudinal data show that, while in high school, students who go on to attend college have lower rates of heavy drinking than do those who will not attend college. Both groups increase their heavy drinking after high school graduation, but the college students increase distinctly more and actually surpass their nonstudent age-mates. Trend data from 1980 to 1999 show some slight improvement in recent years. Despite improvements in the past 20 years, colleges need to do more to reduce heavy alcohol use among students.

84. **Furr, Susan R., John S. Westefeld, Gaye N. McConnell, and J. Marshall Jenkins. "Suicide and Depression Among College Students: A Decade Later." Professional Psychology: Research and Practice 32, no. 1 (2001): 97.** Are suicidal thoughts and depression increasing or decreasing among college students? What life circumstances are the most critical to explore with depressed or suicidal college students? This article focuses on the rate of self-assessed depression and suicide among college students and examines contributing factors and help-seeking behavior. Results of the study indicated that 53% of the

sample stated that they experienced depression since beginning college, with 9% reporting that they had considered committing suicide since beginning college. Suggestions for college mental health practitioners related to programming, prevention, and psychoeducation are described.

85. **Hunt, Justin, and Daniel Eisenberg. "Mental Health Problems and Help-seeking Behavior Among College Students." Journal of Adolescent Health 46, no. 1 (2010): 3-10.** Mental disorders are as prevalent among college students as same-aged non-students, and these disorders appear to be increasing in number and severity. The purpose of this report is to review the research literature on college student mental health, while also drawing comparisons to the parallel literature on the broader adolescent and young adult populations.

## CHAPTER 13 - WHICH COLLEGE?

86. **Goldring, Ellen B., and Kristie JR Phillips. "Parent Preferences and Parent Choices: The Public–private Decision About School Choice." Journal of Education Policy 23, no. 3 (2008): 209-230.** School choice survey data from the Metropolitan Nashville Public Schools, a large county-wide school district, is analyzed to examine the characteristics of parents who consider choosing private schools for their children and those who do not. We examine differences in background, including race, educational attainment and socioeconomic status, as well as differences in parent satisfaction with their child's previous school, parent involvement in school, parents' priorities in school choice, as well as parents' social networks. After controlling for background characteristics, we find that parent satisfaction with their child's previous school was not a predictor of considering a private school. Rather, parent involvement seems to be a more important indicator of whether or not a parent would consider sending their child to a private school. In this case, parents are not 'pushed' away from public schools, contrary to much public rhetoric that suggests private schools are somehow inherently 'better' than public schools and parents who are dissatisfied with their public schools will opt for private schools. Instead, these findings suggest a 'pull' towards private schools. Parents may perceive that parent involvement and parent communication are more easily facilitated and valued in private schools.

87. **Holmes, George M., Jeff DeSimone, and Nicholas G. Rupp. "Does School Choice Increase School Quality? Evidence from North Carolina Charter**

Schools." In Improving School Accountability, pp. 131-155. Emerald Group Publishing Limited, 2006. Federal "No Child Left Behind" legislation, which enables students of low-performing schools to exercise public school choice, exemplifies a widespread belief that competing for students will spur public schools to higher achievement. We investigate how the introduction of school choice in North Carolina, via a dramatic increase in the number of charter schools, affects student performance on statewide end-of-year testing at traditional public schools. We find test score gains from competition that are robust to a variety of specifications. Charter school competition causes an approximately one percent increase in the score, which constitutes about one quarter of the average yearly growth.

88. Belfield, Clive R., and Henry M. Levin. "—Modeling School Choice: A Comparison of Public, Private–Independent, Private–Religious, and Home-Schooled Students." In Privatizing Educational Choice, pp. 89-102. Routledge, 2015. U.S. students now have four choices of schooling: public schooling, private–religious schooling, private–independent schooling, and home-schooling. Of these, home-schooling is the most novel: since legalization across the states in the last few decades, it has grown in importance and legitimacy as an alternative choice. Thus, it is now possible to investigate the motivation for home-schooling, relative to the other schooling options. Here, we use two recent large-scale datasets to assess the school enrollment decision: the first is the National Household Expenditure Survey (1999), and the second is micro-data on SAT test-takers in 2001. We find that, generally, families with home-schoolers have similar characteristics to those with children at other types of school, but mother's characteristics—specifically, her employment status—have a strong influence on the decision to home-school. Plausibly, religious belief has an important influence on the schooling decision, not only for Catholic students, but also those of other faiths.

## Chapter 17- Putting it all together

89. McCabe, Sean Esteban, John R. Knight, Christian J. Teter, and Henry Wechsler. "Non-medical Use of Prescription Stimulants Among U.S. College Students: Prevalence and Correlates from a National Survey." Addiction 100, no. 1 (2005): 96-106. The life-time prevalence of non-medical prescription stimulant use was 6.9%, past year prevalence was 4.1% and past

month prevalence was 2.1%. Past year rates of non-medical use ranged from zero to 25% at individual colleges. Multivariate regression analyses indicated non-medical use was higher among college students who were male, white, members of fraternities and sororities and earned lower grade point averages. Rates were higher at colleges located in the north-eastern region of the U.S. and colleges with more competitive admission standards. Non-medical prescription stimulant users were more likely to report use of alcohol, cigarettes, marijuana, ecstasy, cocaine and other risky behaviors. The findings of the present study provide evidence that non-medical use of prescription stimulants is more prevalent among particular subgroups of US college students and types of colleges. The non-medical use of prescription stimulants represents a high-risk behavior that should be monitored further and intervention efforts are needed to curb this form of drug use.

90. **O'Malley, Patrick M., and Lloyd D. Johnston. "Epidemiology of Alcohol and Other Drug Use Among American College Students." Journal of Studies on Alcohol, Supplement 14 (2002): 23-39.** Alcohol use rates are very high among college students. Approximately two of five American college students were heavy drinkers, defined as having had five or more drinks in a row in the past 2 weeks. Alcohol use is higher among male than female students. White students are highest in heavy drinking, black students are lowest and Hispanic students are intermediate. Use of alcohol—but not cigarettes, marijuana and cocaine—is higher among college students than among non-college age-mates. Longitudinal data show that, while in high school, students who go on to attend college have lower rates of heavy drinking than do those who will not attend college. Both groups increase their heavy drinking after high school graduation, but the college students increase distinctly more and actually surpass their nonstudent age-mates. Trend data from 1980 to 1999 show some slight improvement in recent years. Despite improvements in the past 20 years, colleges need to do more to reduce heavy alcohol use among students.

91. **Cope-Watson, Georgann, and Andrea Smith Betts. "Confronting Otherness: An E-conversation Between Doctoral Students Living with the Imposter Syndrome." Canadian Journal for New Scholars in Education/Revue canadienne des jeunes chercheures et chercheurs en éducation 3, no. 1 (2010).** This qualitative research study is about two women doctoral students who are experiencing The Imposter Syndrome, (Clance & Imes, 1978), a phenomenon

characterized by an inability to internalize academic success. The purpose of this study is to connect the theoretical frameworks around this phenomenon to our experiences as women graduate students in a doctoral program. The research question for this study is: Do our email conversations provide us with clues to explain our imposter feelings? The methodology for this study is autoethnography (Ellis, 1997). Emails collected over an eight-month period provide the data for this study. To analyze the data we used thematic analysis. The data reveal three predominant themes: fear, family and fellowship. The findings of this study provoke an extension into the experiences of other doctoral students as they meet the challenges of self-concepts in their course of study.

92. **Chapman, Amanda. "Using the Assessment Process to Overcome Impostor Syndrome in Mature Students." Journal of Further and Higher Education 41, no. 2 (2017): 112-119.** This research draws on the experience of a group of mature students' studies during their first year at university. All experienced varying degrees of impostor syndrome, feelings of fraudulence and a lack of confidence in their ability. The process of "becoming" a mature student is one of identity change and risk. Gaining a sense of belonging to the institution and academia is an important part of the transition year, but the assimilation into the culture of university life can be problematic. The first assessment for all students can be seen as a "rite of passage" on the journey of "belonging." So for mature students who may have had a substantial gap in their education, this can be a critical moment in their progression through the transition year. Negotiation through the culture and language of academia can lead to misunderstanding and self-doubt, and the process of assessment can be an emotional journey for some students. In this article the students describe their experiences of the assessment process and their need for feedback. Facing the judgement of their peer group and the academic staff was a particular fear of most of the students, as was the difficulty in both "getting started" on and "letting go" of their written work. The article concludes with a discussion of the role of assessment in relation to confidence building and to overcoming Imposter Syndrome.

93. **Clance, Pauline Rose, and Maureen Ann O'Toole. "The Impostor Phenomenon: An Internal Barrier to Empowerment and Achievement." Women & Therapy 6, no. 3 (1987): 51-64.** Discusses the impostor phenomenon (IP), a term used by P. R. Clance and S. A. Imes to designate an internal experience of phoniness, which seemed particularly prevalent among their sample of 150

high achieving women. It is asserted that IP sufferers do not have a realistic sense of their own competence and are not fully empowered to internalize their strengths, accept their deficits, and function with joy. It is suggested that impostor fears may interfere more with women's functioning than men's (e.g., decreasing their striving for high academic achievement). Ten features that accompany IP beliefs in the typical female clients are listed; IP treatment issues are discussed. A copyrighted IP questionnaire is included.

94. **Topping, Mary E., and Ellen B. Kimmel. "The Impostor Phenomenon: Feeling Phony." Academic Psychology Bulletin (1985).** Examined the construct validity of the impostor phenomenon (IP) using J. C. Harvey's (1982) measure of IP. IP is defined as an internal experience of intellectual phoniness. A modified version of the IP scale and 7 additional instruments (e.g., a sex-role behavior index, a self-esteem scale) were also administered to 285 university faculty (128 men, 157 women). Men earned a significantly higher mean IP scale score than women. For both sexes, level of faculty rank, self-esteem, and attributing success to effort were negatively related to IP and trait anxiety was positively related to IP. Attributing success to ability was negatively related to IP for men; across sexes there was a moderate, positive relationship between IP and self-monitoring behavior. It is concluded that if experiencing the IP is a barrier to fulfilling one's potential, as is posited by some, then there is a need to refine methods for its early identification and possible intervention.

# REFERENCES

1. "The 10 Best Public Universities in America." *U.S. News & World Report.* Accessed June 10, 2018. https://www.usnews.com/best-colleges/rankings/national-universities/top-public.

2. Ivy League Admissions Statistics; Ivy Coach. Accessed June 10, 2018. https://www.ivycoach com/2020-ivy-league-admissions-statistics/.

3. The 50 Most Stressful Colleges; CollegeXpress. Accessed June 10, 2018. https://www.collegexpress.com/lists/list/the-50-most-stressful-colleges/1480/.

4. Adams, Mike. *Food Forensics: The Hidden Toxins Lurking in Your Food and How You Can Avoid Them for Lifelong Health.* Dallas, TX: BenBella Books, 2016.

5. Admission Statistics | Princeton University Admission." Accessed June 10, 2018. https://admission.princeton.edu/how-apply/admission-statistics.

6. Alexander, Karl L., Doris R. Entwisle, and Susan L. Dauber. "First-Grade Classroom Behavior: Its Short-and Long-Term Consequences for School Performance." *Child Development* 64, no. 3 (1993): 801-814.

7. Amen, Daniel G. *Change Your Brain, Change Your Life: The Breakthrough Programme for Conquering Anxiety, Depression, Anger and Obsessiveness.* London: Piatkus, 2016.

8. Amen, Daniel G. Making a Good Brain Great: *The Amen Clinic Program for Achieving and Sustaining Optimal Mental Performance.* New York: Three Rivers Press, 2006.

9. Appleton, Nancy, and G. N. Jacobs. *Suicide by Sugar: A Startling Look at Our National Addiction.* Garden City Park, NY: Square One Publishers, 2009.

10. Atkinson, Richard C., and Saul Geiser. "Reflections on a Century of College Admissions Tests." *Educational Researcher* 38, no. 9 (2009): 665-676.

11. Avery, Christopher. "The Effects of College Counseling on High-achieving, Low-income Students." Cambridge, MA: National Bureau of Economic Research (2010).

12. Avery, Christopher, Mark Glickman, Caroline Hoxby, and Andrew Metrick. "A Revealed Preference Ranking of US Colleges and Universities." No. w10803. National Bureau of Economic Research, 2004.

13. 14. Award for Jewish Teen Leaders - Diller Teen Tikkun Olam Awards; Diller Teen Awards. Accessed June 10, 2018. http://www.dillerteenawards.org/.
14. Bagley, Gerald H. *Detox or Die*. Salt Lake City, UT: Publishers Press, 1988.
15. Barnard, Wendy Miedel. "Parent Involvement in Elementary School and Educational Attainment." *Children and Youth Services Review* 26, no. 1 (2004): 39-62.
16. Barnett, W. Steven, and Jason T. Hustedt. "Preschool: The Most Important Grade." *Educational Leadership* 60, no. 7 (2003): 54-57.
17. Barnett, W. Steven. *Preschool education and its lasting effects: Research and Policy Implications*, 2008.
18. Bauman, Dan, Tyler Davis, and Brian O'Leary. "Executive Compensation at Private and Public Colleges." (2018): Accessed July 30, 2018. Chronicle.com. https://www.chronicle.com/interactives/executive- compensation#id=table_private_2015.
19. Belfield, Clive R., and Henry M. Levin. "Modeling School Choice: A Comparison of Public, Private–Independent, Private–Religious, and Home-Schooled Students." *Privatizing Educational Choice* (2015). 89-102.
20. Bergman, Dave. "Is There a Private School Advantage in College Admissions?" (July 2017). Accessed June 10, 2018. https://www.collegetransitions.com/blog/private-vs-public-hs/.
21. "Best Universities and Colleges by Salary Potential." PayScale. Accessed June 10, 2018. https://www.payscale.com/college-salary-report/bachelors?page=101.
22. Birley, Sue, and David Norburn. "The Venture 100 vs the Fortune 500." *Journal of Business Venturing* 2, no. 4 (1987): 351-363.
23. Biskupic, Joan. "Race Case against Harvard Moves Forward." CNN. April 10, 2018. Accessed June 10, 2018. https://www.cnn.com/2018/04/10/politics/harvard-asian-american-students/index.html.
24. Biskupic, Joan. "Suit Accusing Harvard of Capping Asian-Americans Admissions Could Be Tried This Summer." CNN. March 10, 2018. Accessed June 10, 2018. https://www.cnn.com/2018/03/10/politics/harvard-college-lawsuit-asian-americans- trial/index.html.
25. Blaylock, Russell L. Excitotoxins: *The Taste That Kills*. Santa Fe, NM: Health Press, 1998.

26. Block, Mary Ann. *No More Ritalin: Treating ADHD without Drugs*. New York: Kensington Books, 199.

27. Board of Governors of the Federal Reserve System. FRB: IFDP Notes: The Effects of Demographic Change on GDP Growth in OECD Economies. Accessed June 10, 2018. https://www.federalreserve.gov/releases/g19/HIST/cc_hist_memo_levels.html.

28. Booth, Barbara. "What Would You Pay to Get Your Kid into Harvard?" CNBC. April 16, 2015. Accessed June 10, 2018. https://www.cnbc.com/2014/11/10/is-a-college-planner-really-worth-it.html.

29. Bowen, Howard R. *The Costs of Higher Education: How Much Do Colleges and Universities Spend per Student and How Much Should They Spend?* (1980).

30. Boyd, John, and Philip Zimbardo. *The Time Paradox: Using the new psychology of time to your advantage*. Random House, 2012.

31. Branden, Nathaniel. *Power of Self Esteem*. Barnes & Noble Books, 1992.

32. Breggin, Peter. *Talking back to Ritalin: What Doctors Aren't Telling You about Stimulants and ADHD*. Da Capo Press, 2007.

33. Brewer, D. J., Eide, E., and Ehrenberg, R. G. (1996). Does it pay to attend an elite private college? Cross cohort evidence on the effects of college quality on earnings (No. w5613). National Bureau of Economic Research.

34. Ibid.

35. Bronson, Po, and Ashley Merryman. NurtureShock: New thinking about children. Hachette UK, 2009.

36. Brooks, Robert, and Sam Goldstein. *Raising Resilient Children: Fostering Strength, Hope, and Optimism in Your Child*. Lincolnwood, IL: Contemporary, 2002.

37. Brownstein, David. *Overcoming Thyroid Disorders*. Medical Alternatives Press, 2008.

38. Bruce, Nigel, Rogelio Perez-Padilla, and Rachel Albalak. "Indoor Air Pollution in Developing Countries: A Major Environmental and Public Health Challenge." *Bulletin of The World Health organization* 78, no. 9 (2000): 1078-1092.

39. Bruer, John T. *The Myth of the First Three Years: A New Understanding of Early Brain Development and Lifelong Learning*. Simon and Schuster, 1999.

40. Bruni, Frank. Where You Go Is Not Who You'll Be: *An Antidote to the College Admissions Mania*. Grand Central Publishing, 2015.
41. Ibid.
42. Buchmann, Claudia, Dennis J. Condron, and Vincent J. Roscigno. "Shadow Education, American style: Test preparation, the SAT and college enrollment." *Social Forces* 89, no. 2 (2010): 435-461.
43. Buettner, Dan. *The Blue Zones: 9 lessons for Living Longer From the People Who've Lived the Longest*. National Geographic Books, 2012.
44. Buka, Irena, Alvaro Osornio-Vargas, and Robin Walker. "Canada Declares Bisphenol a 'Dangerous Substance': Questioning the Safety of Plastics." *Pediatrics & Child Health* 14, no. 1 (2009): 11-13.
45. Burchinal, Margaret R., Ellen Peisner-Feinberg, Robert Pianta, and Carollee Howes. "Development of Academic Skills from Preschool through Second Grade: Family and Classroom Predictors of Developmental Trajectories." *Journal of school Psychology* 40, no. 5 (2002): 415-436.
46. Burley, Mason, and Mina Halpern. Educational Attainment of Foster Youth: Achievement and Graduation Outcomes for Children in State Care (2001).
47. Branden, Nathaniel. *The Psychology of Self-Esteem: A New Concept of Man's Psychological Nature*. Bantam Books, 1971.
48. Camara, Wayne J., and Gary Echternacht. The SAT [R] I and High School Grades: Utility in Predicting Success in College. Research Notes. (2000).
49. Camilli, Gregory, Sadako Vargas, Sharon Ryan, and W. Steven Barnett. Meta-analysis of the Effects of Early Education Interventions on Cognitive and Social Development. *Teachers College Record* 112, no. 3 (2010): 579-620.
50. Campbell, Don. *The Mozart Effect: Tapping the Power of Music to Heal the Body, Strengthen the Mind and Unlock the Creative Spirit*. Hodder Headline Australia Pty Ltd., Rydalmere, NSW (1997).
51. Carnegie, D. *How to Develop Self-Confidence and Influence People by Public Speaking*. New York: Simon and Schuster, 2017.
52. Carnegie, Dale. *How to Win Friends & Influence People*. Musaicum Books, 2017.
53. Carter, Philip J., and Kenneth Russell *The Great IQ Challenge*. New York: Barnes & Noble Books, 1996.

54. Chan, William, Li Hao, and Wing Suen. "A Signaling Theory of Grade Inflation." *International Economic Review* 48, no. 3 (2007): 1065-1090.

55. Chapman, Chris, Jennifer Laird, Nicole Ifill, and Angelina KewalRamani. "Trends in High School Dropout and Completion Rates in the United States: 1972-2009."

56. Compendium Report. NCES 2012-006. National Center for Education Statistics (2011). Chomsky, Noam, and David Barsamian. Secrets, Lies, and Democracy. Tucson, Arizona: Odonian Press, 1994.

57. Christopher, Glickman, Mark E., Hoxby, Caroline M., Metrick, and Andrew. "A Revealed Preference Ranking of U.S. Colleges and Universities." By John Cigno: SSRN. October 11, 2004. Accessed June 10, 2018. https://papers.ssrn.com/sol3/papers.cfm?abstract_id=601105#PaperDownload.

58. Chua, Amy, and Jed Rubenfeld. *The Triple Package: How Three Unlikely Traits Explain the Rise and Fall of Cultural Groups in America.* Penguin, 2014.

59. Chua, Amy. *Battle Hymn of the Tiger Mother.* Bloomsbury Publishing, 2011.

60. Chu, Lenora. *Little Soldiers: An American Boy, a Chinese School and the Global Race to Achieve.* Hachette UK, 2017.

61. Chugani, Harry T., Michael E. Behen, Otto Muzik, Csaba Juhász, Ferenc Nagy, and Diane C. Chugani. "Local Brain Functional Activity Following Early Deprivation: a Study of Post Institutionalized Romanian Orphans." *Neuroimage* 14, no. 6 (2001): 1290-1301.

62. Cohen, Elizabeth S. *The Empowered Patient: How to Get the Right Diagnosis, Buy the Cheapest Drugs, Beat Your Insurance Company, and Get the Best Medical Care Every Time.* Ballantine Books, 2010.

63. Cohen, Jay S. *Over Dose: the Case Against the Drug Companies: Prescription Drugs, Side Effects, and Your Health.* Jeremy P Tarcher/Putnam, 2001.

64. Cohen, Kat. "The Truth About Need-Aware Admissions." *The Huffington Post.* April 28, 2013. Accessed June 10, 2018. https://www.huffingtonpost.com/kat-cohen/the-truth-about-needaware_b_2758566.html.

65. Cohen, Shawn, and Laura Italiano. "Stress, Isolation Blamed for Suicide Cluster Rocking Ivy League Campus." New York Post

February 03, 2017. Accessed June 10,https://nypost.com/2017/02/03/stress-and-isolation-blamed-for-string-of- suicides-at-columbia/.

66. Colby, Brandon. Outsmart Your Genes: *How Understanding Your DNA Will Empower You to Protect Yourself Against Cancer, Alzheimer's, Heart Disease, Obesity, and Many Other Conditions*. Penguin, 2010.

67. Coleman, Rachel. "How Can I Socialize My Homeschooled Child?" Coalition for Responsible Home Education. February 13, 2017. Accessed June 10, 2018. https://www.responsiblehomeschooling.org/how-can-i-socialize-my-homeschooled-child/.

68. College Accreditation List. Office of Secondary Education. Accessed June 10, 2018. https://ope.ed.gov/accreditation/GetDownLoadFile.aspx.

69. The Condition of Education - Preprimary, Elementary, and Secondary Education High School Completion - Public High School Graduation Rates - Indicator May (2018). Revenues and Expenditures for Public Elementary and Secondary Education: School Year 2001-2002, E.D. Tab. Accessed June 10, 2018. https://nces.ed.gov/programs/coe/indicator_coi.asp.

70. Cooper, Morton. *Change Your Voice, Change Your Life: A Quick, Simple Plan for Finding and Using Your Natural, Dynamic Voice*. Barnes & Noble, 1984.

71. Cox, Brian. *Literacy Is Not Enough: Essays on the Importance of Reading*. Manchester University Press, 1999.

72. Craig, Hugh. "Shakespeare's Vocabulary: Myth and Reality." *Shakespeare Quarterly* 62, no. 1 (2011): 53-74.

73. Crawford, Lacy. *Early Decision: Based on a True Frenzy*. Harper Collins, 2013.

74. Csikszentmihalyi, Mihaly. *Flow and the Psychology of Discovery and Invention*. New York: Harper Perennial, 1997.

75. Dadd, Debra Lynn. *Home Safe Home: Protecting Yourself and Your Family from Everyday Toxics and Harmful Household Products*. Jeremy P. Tarcher/Putnam, 1997.

76. Dadd, Debra Lynn. Toxic Free: *How to Protect Your Health and Home from the Chemicals That Are Making You Sick*. Penguin, 2011.

77. Daiute, Colette, and Bridget Dalton. Collaboration Between Children Learning to Write: Can Novices Be Masters? *Cognition and Instruction* 10, no. 4 (1993): 281-333.

78. Dale, Stacy Berg, and Alan B. Krueger. "Estimating the Payoff to Attending a More Selective College: An Application of Selection on Observables and Unobservable." *The Quarterly Journal of Economics* 117, no. 4 (2002): 1491-1527.

79. Danielson, Melissa L., Rebecca H. Bitsko, Reem M. Ghandour, Joseph R. Holbrook, Michael D. Kogan, and Stephen J. Blumberg. "Prevalence of Parent-reported ADHD Diagnosis and Associated Treatment among US Children and Adolescents." *Journal of Clinical Child & Adolescent Psychology* 47, no. 2 (2018): 199-212.

80. Data Dashboard. Complete College America. https://completecollege.org/data-dashboard/. Common College Completion Metrics for the country and states.

81. De Fabrique, Nathalie, Stephen J. Romano, Gregory M. Vecchi, and Vincent B. Van Hasselt. "Understanding Stockholm Syndrome." FBI L. Enforcement Bull. 76 (2007):

82. Dean, Carolyn. T*he Magnesium Miracle*. Ballantine Books, 2017.

83. DeBerard, M. Scott, Glen Spielmans, and Deana Julka. "Predictors of Academic Achievement and Retention among College Freshmen: A Longitudinal Study." College *Student Journal* 38, no. 1 (2004): 66-80.

84. Dempster, Robert, Beth Wildman, and Adam Keating. "The Role of Stigma in Parental Help-Seeking for Child Behavior Problems." *Journal of Clinical Child & Adolescent Psychology* 42, no. 1 (2013): 56-67.

85. DeNinno, Nadine. "Madison Holleran Suicide: UPenn Freshman Jumps to Death Over Grades at Ivy League College." *International Business Times,* Jan 21 (2014).

86. Deresiewicz, William. *Excellent Sheep: The Miseducation of the American Elite and the Way to a Meaningful Life*. Simon and Schuster, 2014.

87. Despres, Joseph, Frank Brady, and A. Scott McGowan. "Understanding the Culture of the Student-Athlete: *Implications for College Counselors."* *The Journal of Humanistic Counseling* 47, no. 2 (2008): 200-211.

88. Desrochers, Donna M., and Steven Hurlburt. Trends in College Spending: 2001-2011. A Delta Data Update. Delta Cost Project at American Institutes for Research (2014).

89. Diamandis, Peter H., and Steven Kotler. *Bold: How to Go Big, Create Wealth and Impact the World*. Simon and Schuster, 2015.

90. Digest of Education Statistics, 2016. Revenues and Expenditures for Public Elementary and Secondary Education: School Year 2001-2002, E.D. Tab. Accessed June 10, 2018. https://nces.ed.gov/programs/digest/d16/tables/dt16_219.10.asp.

91. Doidge, Norman. *The Brain that Changes Itself: Stories of Personal Triumph from the Frontiers of Brain Science*. Penguin, 2007.

92. Dunne, Carey. "Millennials Took Adderall to Get through School. Now They've Taken Their Addiction to the Workplace." Quartz. October 19, 2016. Accessed June 10, 2018. https://qz.com/812604/millennials-took-adderall-to-get-through-school-now- theyve-taken-their-addiction-to-the-workplace/.

93. Edward, M., and E. M. Hallowell. *CrazyBusy: Overstretched, Overbooked, and about to Snap! Strategies for Coping in a World Gone* ADD. (2006).

94. Eide, Eric, Dominic J. Brewer, and Ronald G. Ehrenberg. Does It Pay to Attend an Elite Private College? Evidence on the Effects of Undergraduate College Quality on Graduate School Attendance." *Economics of Education Review* 17, no. 4 (1998): 371-376.

95. El Nokali, Nermeen E., Heather J. Bachman, and Elizabeth Votruba-Drzal. "Parent Involvement and Children's Academic and Social Development in Elementary School." *Child development* 81, no. 3 (2010): 988-1005.

96. Elliott, Carl. *White Coat, Black Hat: Adventures on the Dark Side of Medicine*. Beacon Press, 2010.

97. Elliott, Ward EY, and Robert J. Valenza. Shakespeare's Vocabulary: Did It Dwarf All Others? Stylistics and Shakespeare's Language: Transdisciplinary Approaches (2011): 34-57.

98. Ellis, Kristina. *Confessions of a Scholarship Winner: The Secrets that Helped Me Win $500,000 in Free Money for College*. Brentwood, TN: Worthy Pub., 2013.

99. Emerson, John, and Thomas Lovitt. "The Educational Plight of Foster Children in Schools and What Can Be Done about It." *Remedial and Special Education* 24, no. 4 (2003): 199-203.

100. Emmons, Robert A., and Charles M. Shelton. "Gratitude and the Science of Positive Psychology." *Handbook of Positive Psychology* 18 (2002): 459-471.

101. Emmons, Robert A., and Anjali Mishra. "Why Gratitude Enhances Well-Being: What We Know, What We Need to Know." *Designing Positive Psychology: Taking Stock and Moving Forward* (2011): 248-262.

102. Englund, Michelle M., Amy E. Luckner, Gloria JL Whaley, and Byron Egeland. "Children's Achievement in Early Elementary School: Longitudinal Effects of Parental Involvement, Expectations, and Quality of Assistance." *Journal of Educational Psychology* 96, no. 4 (2004): 723.

103. Entwisle, Doris R., and Leslie Alec Hayduk. "Lasting Effects of Elementary School." *Sociology of Education* (1988): 147-159.

104. Epple, Dennis, and Richard E. Romano. "Competition between Private and Public Schools, Vouchers, and Peer-Group Effects." *American Economic Review* (1998): 33-62.

105. Eysenck, H. J., and Doctor Glenn Wilson. *Know Your Own IQ*. Harmondsworth: Penguin Books, 1962.

106. Fabes, Richard A. "Effects of Reward Contexts on Young Children's Task Interest. T*he Journal of Psychology* 121, no. 1 (1987): 5-19.

107. Farmanfarmaian, Robin. The Patient as CEO: How Technology Empowers the Healthcare Consumer. San Bernardino, CA: Lioncrest Publishing, 2015.

108. Ferriss, Timothy. *The 4-Hour Workweek: Escape 9–5, Live Anywhere, and Join the New Rich*. New York: Crown (2007).

109. Ferriss, Timothy. *The 4-hour body: An Uncommon Guide to Rapid Fat-Loss, Incredible Sex, and Becoming Superhuman*. Harmony, 2010.

110. Finder, Alan. "Rejected by Harvard? You Have Lots of Company." *The New York Times*. April 01, 2008. Accessed June 10, 2018. https://www.nytimes.com/2008/04/01/world/americas/01iht-college.1.11581684.html.

111. Finefter-Rosenbluh, Ilana, and Meira Levinson. 2015. "What Is Wrong with Grade Inflation (If Anything)." *Philosophical Inquiry in Education* 23, no. 1 (2015): 3-21

112. Fisher, Lianne, Elinor W. Ames, Kim Chisholm, and Lynn Savoie. "Problems Reported by Parents of Romanian Orphans Adopted to British Columbia." *International Journal of Behavioral Development* 20, no. 1 (1997): 67-82.

113. Fisher, Lisa. *Admissions by Design: Stop the Madness and Find the Best College for You*. Boise, ID: Elevate, 2015.

114. Fitzgerald, Randall. *The Hundred-Year Lie: How to Protect Yourself from the Chemicals That Are Destroying Your Health*. Penguin, 2007.

115. Norris, Floyd. "Fewer U.S. Graduates Opt for College After High School." *The New York Times*. April 25, 2014. https://www.nytimes.com/2014/04/26/business/fewer-us- high-school-graduates-opt-for-college.html.

116. Fox, D. R. "Practical, Effective, and Advanced Treatments for the Environmental Factors that Contribute to Chronic Illnesses." October 21–24, 2010, California, USA. *The International Journal of Occupational and Environmental Medicine* 2, no. 1 January (2010).

117. Fox, Marc. "Is It a Good Investment to Attend an Elite Private College?" *Economics of Education Review* 12, no. 2 (1993): 137-151.

118. Frankl, Viktor E. *Man's Search for Meaning*. Simon and Schuster, 1985.

119. Freire, Paulo. "The Importance of the Act of Reading." *Journal of Education* 165, no. 1 (1983): 5-11.

120. Furr, Susan R., John S. Westefeld, Gaye N. McConnell, and J. Marshall Jenkins. "Suicide and Depression among College Students: A Decade Later." *Professional Psychology: Research and Practice* 32, no. 1 (2001): 97.

121. Gaby, Alan R. *Nutritional Medicine*. Vol. 265. Fritz Perlberg Publishing, 2011.

122. Gathercole, Rachel. *The Well-Adjusted Child: The Social Benefits of Homeschooling*. Mapletree Publishing Company, 2007.

123. Geiser, Saul, and Veronica Santelices. "The Role of Advanced Placement and Honors Courses in College Admissions." Expanding opportunity in higher education: Leveraging promise 75114 (2006).

124. Gendlin, Eugene T. *Focusing*. Bantam, 1982.

125. Golden, Daniel. "Many Colleges Bend Rules To Admit Rich Applicants." *The Wall Street Journal*. February 20, 2003. Accessed June 11, 2018. http://online.wsj.com/public/resources/documents/Polk_Rich_Applicants.htm.

126. Golden, Daniel. *The Price of Admission: How America's Ruling Class Buys Its Way into Elite Colleges--and Who Gets Left Outside the Gates*. Crown Publishing Group/RandomHouse, 2006.

127. Goldring, Ellen B., and Kristie JR Phillips. "Parent Preferences and Parent Choices: The Public–Private Decision about School Choice." *Journal of Education* Policy 23, no. 3 (2008): 209-230.

128. Gore, Al. *An Inconvenient Truth: The Planetary Emergency of Global Warming and What We Can Do about It*. Rodale, 2006.

129. Greene, Jay P., and Greg Forster. Public High School Graduation and College Readiness Rates in the United States. Education Working Paper No. 3. Center for Civic Innovation (2003).

130. Green Peter, H. R., and Rory Jones. *Celiac Disease: A Hidden Epidemic*. (2010).

131. Greger, Michael, and Gene Stone. *How Not to Die: Discover the Foods scientifically Proven to Prevent and Reverse Disease*. Pan Macmillan, 2016.

132. Gurian, Michael. *The Wonder of Boys: What Parents, Mentors and Educators Can Do to Shape Boys into Exceptional Men*. Penguin, 2006.

133. Gustafson, Craig. Michael Greger, MD: "Reversing Chronic Disease Through Diet; Addressing the 2015 USDA Dietary Guidelines Committee." *Integrative Medicine: A Clinician's Journal* 13, no. 2 (2014): 22.

134. Hadler, Nortin M. *Last Well Person: How to Stay Well Despite the Health-Care System*. McGill-Queen's Press-MQUP, 2004.

135. Hadler, Nortin M. *Worried Sick—A Prescription for Health in an Overtreated America*. Paperback edition. Univ of North Carolina Press, 2012.

136. Hallowell, Edward M. *The Childhood Roots of Adult Happiness: Five Steps to Help Kids Create and Sustain Lifelong Joy*. Ballantine Books, 2002.

137. Hallowell, Edward M. Worry: *Hope and Help for a Common Condition*. Random House Digital, Inc., 1998.

138. Hallowell, Edward M., and John J. Ratey. *Answers to Distraction*. Anchor, 2010.

139. Hallowell, Edward. *Driven to Distraction: Recognizing and Coping with Attention Deficit Disorder from Childhood through Adulthood*. Tappan. (1994).

140. Hamre, Bridget K., and Robert C. Pianta. "Early Teacher–Child Relationships and the Trajectory of Children's School Outcomes through Eighth Grade." *Child Development* 72, no. 2 (2001): 625-638.

141. Hansen, Robin L., Fatema Lakhani Mawjee, Keith Barton, Mary B. Metcalf, and Nancy R. Joye. "Comparing the Health Status of Low-Income Children in and out of Foster Care." *Child Welfare* 83, no. 4 (2004): 367.

142. Harden, Brenda Jones. "Safety and Stability for Foster Children: A Developmental Perspective." *The Future of Children* (2004): 31-47. 144.

143. Harpin, Valerie A. "The Effect of ADHD on the Life of an Individual, Their Family, and Community from Preschool to Adult Life." *Archives of Disease in Childhood* 90, no. suppl 1 (2005): i2-i7.

144. Hart, Betsy. *It Takes a Parent: How the Culture of Pushover Parenting Is Hurting Our Kids--and What to Do about It*. Penguin, 2006.

145. Hartocollis, Anemona. "Asian-Americans Suing Harvard Say Admissions Files Show Discrimination." *The New York Times*. April 04, 2018. Accessed June 10, 2018. https://www.nytimes.com/2018/04/04/us/harvard-asian-admission.html.

146. Hébert, Thomas P. "Reflections at Graduation: The Long-Term Impact of Elementary School Experiences in Creative Productivity." *Roeper Review* 16, no. 1 (1993): 22-28.

147. Hécaen, Henry, and Martin L. Albert. *Human Neuropsychology*. New York: Wiley, 1978.

148. Hernández, Michele A. *A Is for Admission: The Insider's Guide to Getting into the Ivy League and Other Top Colleges*. Grand Central Publishing, 2010.

149. Hersey, Jane. *Why Can't My Child Behave? Why Can't She Cope? Why Can't He Learn?* Pear Tree Press, 1996.

150. Hill, Kashmir. "What College Admission Officers Don't Like Seeing on Facebook: Vulgarity, Drinking Photos & Illegal Activities." Forbes. October 12, 2012. Accessed June 10, 2018. https://www.forbes.com/sites/kashmirhill/2012/10/12/what-college- admission-officers-dont-like-seeing-on-facebook-profiles-vulgarity-drinking-photos-and- illegal-activities/#63b339002170.

151. Hill, Napoleon. *The Law of Success Deluxe Edition*. Penguin, 2017.

152. Hill, Napoleon. *Think and Grow Rich*. Hachette UK, 2011.

153. Holmes, George M., Jeff DeSimone, and Nicholas G. Rupp. "Does School Choice Increase School Quality? Evidence from North Carolina Charter schools in Improving School Accountability," pp. 131-155. Emerald Group Publishing Limited, 2006.

154. *Homeless to Harvard: The Liz Murray Story*. Directed by Peter Levin. April 7, 2003.

155. Hoover, Eric. "Application Inflation: When Is Enough Enough?" *The New York Times*. November 05, 2010. Accessed June 10, 2018. https://www.nytimes.com/2010/11/07/education/edlife/07HOOVER-t.html.

156. Hughes, Chuck W., and Charles W. II Hughes. *What It Really Takes to Get into the Ivy League & Other Highly Selective Colleges*. McGraw-Hill, 2003.

157. Hunt, Justin, and Daniel Eisenberg. "Mental Health Problems and Help-Seeking Behavior among College Students." *Journal of Adolescent Health* 46, no. 1 (2010): 3-10.

158. Hunt, Lester H., ed. *Grade Inflation: Academic Standards in Higher Education*. Suny Press, 2008.

159. Hyman, Mark, and Mark Liponis. *Ultra Prevention: The 6-Week Plan That Will Make You Healthy for Life*. Simon and Schuster, 2003.

160. Ingraham, Christopher. "This Chart Shows How Much More Ivy League Grads Make than You." *The Washington Post*. September 14, 2015. Accessed June 10, 2018. https://www.washingtonpost.com/news/wonk/wp/2015/09/14this-chart-shows-why- parents-push-their-kids-so-hard-to-get-into-ivy-league-schools/?utm_term=.0fed2f7830bd.

161. Isaacson, Walter, and Engelbert L. Schucking. "Einstein: His Life and Universe." *Physics Today* 60, no. 11 (2007): 59.

162. Jackson, Abby. "The Ivy League Has Released Early-application Acceptance Rates - Here's Where They All Stand." *Business Insider*. December 19, 2017. Accessed June 10, 2018. http://www.businessinsider.com/harvard-yale-princeton-ivy-league-early- acceptance-rate-2017-12.

163. Jacobs, Peter. "How Much Each Ivy League University President Makes in A Year." *Business Insider*. December 16, 2014. Accessed June 10, 2018. http://www.businessinsider.com/ivy-league-president-compensation-ranked-2014-12.

164. Jacobs, Peter. "The 10 Highest-Paid College Presidents." *Business Insider*. December 07, 2014. Accessed June 10, 2018. http://www.businessinsider.com/highest- paid-college-presidents-2014-12.

165. Jacobson, Joseph L., Sandra W. Jacobson, Pamela M. Schwartz, Greta G. Fein, and Jeffrey K. Dowler. "Prenatal exposure to Environmental Toxin: A Test of the Multiple Effects Model." *Developmental Psychology* 20, no. 4 (1984): 523.

166. Jager-Hyman, Joie. *Fat Envelope Frenzy: One Year, Five Promising Students, and the Pursuit of the Ivy League Prize*. HarperCollins, 2008.

167. Jena, Lalatendu Kesari, and Eeman Basu. "Deep Work: Rules for Focused Success in a Distracted World." *Vikalpa* 43, no. 1 (2018): 58-60.

168. Jensen, Peter S., Lori Kettle, Margaret T. Roper, Michael T. Sloan, Mina K. Dulcan, Christina Hoven, Hector R. Bird, Jose J. Bauermeister, and Jennifer D. Payne. "Are Stimulants Overprescribed? Treatment of ADHD in Four US Communities." *Journal of the American Academy of Child & Adolescent Psychiatry* 38, no. 7 (1999): 797-804.

169. Jimerson, Shane, Byron Egeland, L. Alan Sroufe, and Betty Carlson. "A Prospective Longitudinal Study of High School Dropouts Examining Multiple Predictors across Development." *Journal of School Psychology* 38, no. 6 (2000): 525-549.

170. Johnson, Paul. *History of the Jews*. Hachette UK, 2013.

171. Jones, David Scott. *Textbook of Functional Medicine. Institute for Functional Medicine*, 2010.

172. Kaler, Sandra R., and B. J. Freeman. "Analysis of Environmental Deprivation: Cognitive and Social Development in Romanian Orphans." *Journal of Child Psychology and Psychiatry* 35, no. 4 (1994): 769-781.

173. Karabel, Jerome. *The Chosen: The Hidden History of Admission and Exclusion at Harvard, Yale, and Princeton*. Houghton Mifflin Harcourt, 2006.

174. Kids Pushing Too Hard? Prescription Stimulants Abuse in Private Schools - ISM. The Only Private School Consulting, Insurance, and Software Group in

the US. Accessed June 10, 2018. https://isminc.com/blog/school-heads/vol-10/no-10/kids-pushing-too-hard-prescription-stimulants-abuse-in-private-schools.

175. Kingston, Paul William, and John C. Smart. *The Economic Pay-Off of Prestigious Colleges. The high status track* (1990): 147-174.

176. Kirsch, Irving. *The Emperor's New Drugs: Exploding the Antidepressant Myth*. ReadHowYouWant.com, 2010.

177. Klicka, Chris. HSLDA Socialization: Homeschoolers Are in the Real World. Home School Legal Defense Association. March 2007. Accessed June 10, 2018. https://hslda.org/content/docs/nche/000000/00000068.asp.

178. Knott, J. Eugene. Campus suicide in America. OMEGA-Journal of Death and Dying 4, no. 1 (1973): 65-71.

179. Kohn, Alfie. "The Dangerous Myth of Grade Inflation." *Chronicle of Higher Education* 49, no. 11 (2002): B7.

180. Kohn, Alfie. *Punished by rewards: The Trouble with Gold Stars, Incentive Plans, A's, Praise, and Other Bribes*. Houghton Mifflin Harcourt, 1999.

181. Kohn, Alfie. *Schooling beyond Measure & Other Unorthodox Essays about Education*. Heinemann, 2015.

182. Kohn, Alfie. *The Homework Myth: Why Our Kids Get too Much of a Bad Thing*. Da Capo Lifelong Books, 2006.

183. Kohn, Alfie. *The Myth of the Spoiled Child*. Beacon Press, 2016.

184. Kohn, Alfie. *Unconditional Parenting: Moving from Rewards and Punishments to Love and Reason*. Simon and Schuster, 2006.

185. Kurzweil, Ray, and Terry Grossman. *Fantastic Voyage: Live Long Enough to Live Forever*. Rodale, 2005.

186. 187. Kurzweil, Ray, and Terry Grossman. *Transcend: Nine Steps to Living Well Forever*. Rodale, 2010.

187. Lane, John, Andrew M. Lane, and Anna Kyprianou. "Self-Efficacy, Self-Esteem and Their Impact on Academic Performance." *Social Behavior and Personality: An International Journal* 32, no. 3 (2004): 247-256.

188. Laneri, Raquel. "No. 12: Harvard-Westlake." Forbes. July 11, 2012. Accessed June 10, 2018. https://www.forbes.com/2010/04/29/best-prep-schools-2010-opinions-harvard-westlake.html#64756d5650d9.

189. Lanphear, Bruce P., Charles V. Vorhees, and David C. Bellinger. "Protecting Children from Environmental Toxins." *PLoS Medicine* 2, no. 3 (2005): e61.

190. Lawlis, Frank, and G. Frank Lawlis. *The IQ Answer: Maximizing Your Child's Potential*. Penguin, 2007.

191. Lazar, Irving, Richard Darlington, Harry Murray, Jacqueline Royce, Ann Snipper, and Craig T. Ramey. Lasting effects of early education: A report from the Consortium for Longitudinal Studies. Monographs of the Society for Research in Child Development (1982): i-151.

192. Leamer, Laurence. *Fantastic: The Life of Arnold Schwarzenegger*. Macmillan, 2005.

193. Levine, Mel. *A Mind at a Time: How Every Child Can Succeed*. Simon and Schuster, 2012.

194. Levitt, B. Blake. *Electromagnetic Fields: A Consumer's Guide to the Issues and How to Protect Ourselves*. Harvest Books, 1995.

195. Ley, Terry C., Barbara B. Schaer, and Betsy W. Dismukes. "Longitudinal Study of the Reading Attitudes and Behaviors of Middle School Students." *Reading Psychology: An International Quarterly* 15, no. 1 (1994): 11-38.

196. Lloyd, Dee Norman. "Prediction of School Failure from Third-Grade Data." *Educational and Psychological Measurement* 38, no. 4 (1978): 1193-1200.

197. Loe, Irene M., and Heidi M. Feldman. "Academic and Educational Outcomes of Children with ADHD." *Journal of Pediatric Psychology* 32, no. 6 (2007): 643-654.

198. London, Michael. *The New Rules of College Admissions: Ten Former Admissions Officers Reveal What It Takes to Get into College Today*. Simon and Schuster, 2006.

199. Lord, Richard S., and J. Alexander Bralley, eds. *Laboratory evaluations for integrative and functional medicine*. Metametrix Institute, 2008.

200. Low, K. Graff, and A. E. Gendaszek. "Illicit Use of Psychostimulants among College Students: A Preliminary Study." *Psychology, Health, & Medicine* 7, no. 3 (2002): 283-287.

201. Lucier, Cristina, Anna Rosofsky, Bruce London, Helen Scharber, and John M. Shandra. "Toxic Pollution and School Performance Scores: Environmental Ascription in East Baton Rouge Parish, Louisiana." *Organization & Environment* 24, no. 4 (2011): 423-

202. Lythcott-Haims, Julie. *How to Raise an Adult: Break Free of the Overparenting Trap And Prepare Your Kid for Success.* Henry Holt and Company, 2015.

203. Makary, Marty. *Unaccountable: What Hospitals Won't Tell You and How Transparency Can Revolutionize Health Care.* Bloomsbury Publishing USA, 2013.

204. Malatesta, Matt. "Need Blind Vs Need Aware." Union College. https://www.union.edu/admissions/school-counselor/resources/needblind-needaware/

205. Maroon, Joseph C., and Jeffrey Bost. *Fish oil: The Natural Anti-Inflammatory.* Basic Health Publications, Inc., 2006.

206. Maroon, Joseph. *The Longevity Factor: How Resveratrol and Red Wine Activate Genes for a Longer and Healthier Life.* Simon and Schuster, 2008.

207. Martelli, Joseph, and Patricia Abels. "The Education of a Leader: Educational Credentials and Other Characteristics of Chief Executive Officers." *Journal of Education for Business* 85, no. 4 (2010): 209-217.

208. McCabe, Sean Esteban, John R. Knight, Christian J. Teter, and Henry Wechsler. "Non-Medical Use of Prescription Stimulants among US College Students: Prevalence and Correlates from a National Survey." *Addiction 100*, no. 1 (2005): 96-106.

209. McCullough, Michael E., Marcia B. Kimeldorf, and Adam D. Cohen. "An Adaptation for Altruism: The Social Causes, Social Effects, and Social Evolution of Gratitude." *Current Directions in Psychological Science* 17, no. 4 (2008): 281-285.

210. McDonald, Libby. *The Toxic Sandbox: The Truth about Environmental Toxins and Our Children's Health.* Penguin, 2007.

211. McDonough, Patricia M. "Counseling and College Counseling in America's High Schools." *State of College Admission* (2005): 107-121.

212. McEwan, Patrick J. "Peer Effects on Student Achievement: Evidence from Chile." *Economics of Education Review* 22, no. 2 (2003): 131-141.

213. McFarland, Joel, Patrick Stark, and Jiashan Cui. Trends in High School Dropout and Completion Rates in the United States: 2014. Revenues and Expenditures for Public Elementary and Secondary Education: School Year 2001-2002, E.D. Tab. February 22, 2018. Accessed July 30, 2018. https://nces.ed.gov/pubsearch/pubsinfo.asp?pubid=2018117.

214. Medlin, Richard G. "Homeschooling and the Question of socialization." *Peabody Journal of Education* 75, no. 1-2 (2000): 107-123.

215. Michaels, James W. "Classroom Reward Structures and Academic Performance." Review of Educational Research 47, no. 1 (1977): 87-98.

216. Miller, Danny, Xiaowei Xu, and Vikas Mehrotra. "When Is Human Capital a Valuable Resource? The Performance Effects of Ivy League Selection among Celebrated CEOs." *Strategic Management Journal* 36, no. 6 (2015): 930-944.

217. Miller, Neil Z. *Miller's Review of Critical Vaccine Studies: 400 Important Scientific Papers Summarized for Parents and Researchers.* New Atlantean Press, 2016.

218. Moffic, H. Steven. *The Citizen Patient: Reforming Health Care for the Sake of the Patient, Not the System.* (2014): e03-e03.

219. Mohai, Paul, Byoung-Suk Kweon, Sangyun Lee, and Kerry Ard. "Air Pollution around Schools Is Linked to Poorer Student Health and Academic Performance." *Health Affairs* 30, no. 5 (2011): 852-862.

220. Moll, Richard. *Playing the Private College Admissions Game.* (1979).

221. Moore, Justine. "Connections to University Can Affect Admissions Decision." *Stanford Daily*. March 12, 2013. Accessed June 11, 2018. https://www.stanforddaily.com/2013/03/12/connections-to-university-can-affect-admissions-decision/.

222. Moore, Thomas J. *Prescription for Disaster: The Hidden Dangers in Your Medicine Cabinet.* New York: Simon & Schuster, 1998.

223. Moyad, Mark, and Janet Lee. *The Supplement Handbook: A Trusted Expert's Guide to What Works & What's Worthless for More Than 100 Conditions.* Rodale, 2014.

224. Mullen, Ann L. "Elite Destinations: Pathways to Attending an Ivy League University." *British Journal of Sociology of Education* 30, no. 1 (2009): 15-27.

225. Mulvenon, Sean, and Dan Ferritor. "Grade Inflation in Higher Education: Isolated or Systemic?" *International Journal of Learning* 12, no. 6 (2005).

226. Murphy, Joseph. "The Social and Educational Outcomes of Homeschooling." *Sociological Spectrum* 34, no. 3 (2014): 244-272.

227. Murphy, Michael, Mark Harrold, Seán Carey, and Mark Mulrooney. A survey of the level of learning disability among the prison population in Ireland. Dublin: Department of Justice, Equality and Law Reform (2000).

228. Murray, Charles. *Human Accomplishment: The Pursuit of Excellence in the Arts and Sciences, 800 BC to 1950.* Harper Collins, 2003.

229. National Collegiate Athletic Association. Estimated Probability of Competing in College Athletics. (2016).

230. National Merit Scholarship Corporation: 2016–17 Annual Report. Nationalmerit.org. October 31, 2017. Accessed June 10, 2018. https://www.nationalmerit.org/s/1758/images/gid2/editor_documents/annual_report.pdf?gid=2&pgid=61.

231. The NCES Fast Facts Tool Provides Quick Answers to Many Education Questions (National Center for Education Statistics). Revenues and Expenditures for Public Elementary and Secondary Education: School Year 2001-2002, E.D. Tab. Accessed June 10, 2018. https://nces.ed.gov/fastfacts/display.asp?id=75.

232. The NCES Fast Facts Tool Provides Quick Answers to Many Education Questions (National Center for Education Statistics). Revenues and Expenditures for Public Elementary and Secondary Education: School Year 2001-2002, E.D. Tab. Accessed June 10, 2018. https://nces.ed.gov/fastfacts/display.asp?id=98.

233. The NCES Fast Facts Tool Provides Quick Answers to Many Education Questions (National Center for Education Statistics). Revenues and Expenditures for Public Elementary and Secondary Education: School Year 2001-2002, E.D. Tab. Accessed June 10, 2018. https://nces.ed.gov/fastfacts/display.asp?id=91.

234. The NCES Fast Facts Tool Provides Quick Answers to Many Education Questions (National Center for Education Statistics). Revenues and Expenditures for Public Elementary and Secondary Education: School Year 2001-2002, E.D. Tab. Accessed June 10, 2018. https://nces.ed.gov/fastfacts/display.asp?id=372.

235. The NCES Fast Facts Tool Provides Quick Answers to Many Education Questions (National Center for Education Statistics). Revenues and Expenditures for Public Elementary and Secondary Education: School Year 2001-2002, E.D. Tab. Accessed June 10, 2018. https://nces.ed.gov/fastfacts/display.asp?id=16.

236. Nelson, Charles A. *Romanian Abandoned Children.* Harvard University Press,

237. NMSC History and Facts. National Merit Scholarship Corporation - National Merit® Scholarship Program. Accessed June 10, 2018. https://www.nationalmerit.org/s/1758/interior.aspx?sid=1758&gid=2&pgid=451.

238. Connor, Thomas G., Diana Bredenkamp, Michael Rutter, and English and Romanian Adoptees (ERA) Study Team. "Attachment Disturbances and Disorders in Children Exposed to Early Severe Deprivation." *Infant Mental Health Journal* 20, no. 1 (1999): 10-29.

239. O'Malley, Patrick M., and Lloyd D. Johnston. "Epidemiology of Alcohol and Other Drug Use among American College Students." *Journal of Studies on Alcohol,* Supplement 14 (2002): 23-39.

240. Oreilly, Bill. *Old School : Life in the Sane Lane.* S.1.: Griffen, 2018.

241. Pangborn, Jon, and Sidney M. Baker. Autism: Effective Biomedical Treatments: Have We Done Everything We Can Do for this Child?: Individuality in an Autism Epidemic. *Autism Research Institute*, 2005.

242. Pauling, Linus. "Vitamin C and the Common Cold." *Canadian Medical Association Journal* 105, no. 5 (1971): 448.

243. Peale, Norman Vincent. *The Power of Positive Thinking.* Random House, 2012.

244. Percentage of High School Dropouts among Persons 16 to 24 Years Old (status Dropout Rate), by Income Level, and Percentage Distribution of Status Dropouts, by Labor Force Status and Years of School Completed: 1970 through 2015. Revenues and Expenditures for Public Elementary and Secondary Education: School Year 2001-2002, E.D. Tab. Accessed July 30, 2018. https://nces.ed.gov/programs/digest/d16/tables/dt16_219.75.asp?current=yes.

245. Pecora, Peter J., Jason Williams, Ronald C. Kessler, Eva Hiripi, Kirk O'Brien, John Emerson, Mary A. Herrick, and Dan Torres. "Assessing the Educational Achievements of Adults Who Were Formerly Placed in Family Foster Care." *Child & Family Social Work* 11, no. 3 (2006): 220-231.

246. Perlmutter, David. *Grain Brain: The Surprising Truth about Wheat, Carbs, and Sugar-Your Brain & Silent Killers*. Hachette UK, 2014.

247. Perlmutter, David. *Power up Your Brain*. Hay House, Inc, 2011.

248. Perna, Laura W., Heather T. Rowan-Kenyon, Scott Loring Thomas, Angela Bell, Robert Anderson, and Chunyan Li. "The Role of College Counseling in Shaping College Opportunity: Variations across High Schools." *The Review of Higher Education* 31, no. 2 (2008): 131-159.

249. Perry, Luddene, and Dan Schultz. *A Field Guide to Buying Organic: An Aisle-by-Aisle Guide to Every Organic Product*. Bantam, 2008.

250. Population 16 to 24 Years Old and Number of 16- to 24-year-old High School Dropouts (status Dropouts), by Sex and Race/ethnicity: 1970 through 2015. Revenues and Expenditures for Public Elementary and Secondary Education: School Year 2001- 2002, E.D. Tab. Accessed July 30, 2018. https://nces.ed.gov/programs/digest/d16/tables/dt16_219.71.asp?current=yes.

251. 252. *Race to Nowhere*. Directed by Vicki Abeles and Jessica Congdon. September 10, 2009.

252. Rachael Pells, Education Correspondent. "Top Private School Pupils More Likely to End up with Drug and Alcohol Addictions, New Research Reveals." *The Independent*. June 01, 2017. Accessed June 10, 2018. https://www.independent.co.uk/news/education/education-news/private-school- pupils-drug-alcohol-addictions-more-likely-new-research-money-fake-id-a7766951.html.

253. Radlauer, Steve, and Ellis Weiner. *Monsters of the Ivy League*. New York, NY: Little, Brown and, 2017.

254. Raggio, Randle D., and Judith Anne Garretson Folse. "Gratitude Works: Its Impact and the Mediating Role of Affective Commitment in Driving Positive Outcomes." *Journal of the Academy of Marketing Science* 37, no. 4 (2009): 455.

255. Rapp, Doris J. *Is This Your Child's World? How You Can Fix the Schools and Homes That Are Making Your Children Sick*. Bantam Books, 1540 Broadway, New York, NY 10036.(Out-of-print), 1996.

256. Rapp, Doris J. "Our Toxic World, a Wake Up Call: How to Keep Yourself and Your Loved Ones Out of Harm's Way: Chemicals Damage Your Body, Brain, Behavior and Sex." *Environmental Medical Research Foundation*, 2004.

257. Redford, J., Battle, D., and Bielick, S. (2017). Homeschooling in the United States: 2012 (NCES 2016-096.REV). National Center for Education Statistics, Institute of Education Sciences, U.S. Department of Education. Washington, DC.

258. Redwood, Daniel, and C. Norman Shealy. "The China Study: The Most Comprehensive Study of Nutrition Ever Conducted and the Startling Implications for Diet, Weight Loss and Long-Term Health. Two Reviews." *Journal of Alternative Complementary Medicine: Research on Paradigm, Practice, and Policy* 11, no. 6 (2005): 1117-1119.

259. Reyna, R., Reindl, T., Witham, K., & Stanley, J. (2010). *Complete to Compete: Common College Completion Metrics. Technical Guide.* NGA Center for Best Practices.

260. Rivera, Lauren A. "Ivies, Extracurriculars, and Exclusion: Elite Employers' Use of Educational Credentials." *Research in Social Stratification and Mobility* 29, no. 1 (2011): 71-90.

261. Robbins, Tony. *Awaken the Giant Within: How to Take Immediate Control of Your Mental, Emotional, Physical and Financial Destiny.* Simon and Schuster, 2007

262. Robertson, Donald, and James Symons. "Do Peer Groups Matter? Peer Group Versus Schooling Effects on Academic Attainment." *Economica* 70, no. 277 (2003): 31-53.

263. Robins, Antonay. *Unlimited Power: The New Science of Personal Achievement.* (1986).

264. Robinson, Ken. *The element: How Finding Your Passion Changes Everything.* Penguin, 2009.

265. Roeser, Robert W., Jacquelynne S. Eccles, and Arnold J. Sameroff. "School As a Context of Early Adolescents Academic and Social-Emotional Development: A Summary Of Research Findings." *The Elementary School Journal* 100, no. 5 (2000): 443-471.

266. Rogers, Abby. "The Most Expensive Preschools in New York City." *Business Insider.* October 10, 2011. Accessed June 10, 2018. http://www.businessinsider.com/most-expensive-preschools-in-new-york-city-2011-9.

267. Rogers, Sherry A. *Chemical Sensitivity: Environmental Diseases and Pollutants, How They Hurt Us, How to Deal with Them.* New Canaan, CT: Keats, 1995.

268. Rogers, Sherry A. *The Cure Is in the Kitchen: A Guide to Healthy Eating.* Syracuse, NY: Prestige Publishers, 1999.

269. Romanowski, Michael H. "Revisiting the Common Myths about Homeschooling." *The Clearing House: Journal of Educational Strategies, Issues and Ideas* 79, no. 3 (2006): 125-129.

270. Ross, Catherine Sheldrick, Lynne McKechnie, and Paulette M. Rothbauer. *Reading Matters: What the Research Reveals about Reading, Libraries, and Community.* Westport, CT: Libraries Unlimited, 2006.

271. Rouse, Kathryn E. "The Impact of High School Leadership on Subsequent Educational Attainment." *Social Science Quarterly* 93, no. 1 (2012): 110-129.

272. Rumberger, Russell W., and Gregory J. Palardy. "Test Scores, Dropout Rates, and Transfer Rates As Alternative Indicators of High School Performance." *American Educational Research Journal* 42, no. 1 (2005): 3-42.

273. Safer, Daniel J. "Are Stimulants Overprescribed for Youths with ADHD?" *Annals of Clinical Psychiatry* 12, no. 1 (2000): 55-62.

274. Sansone, Randy A., and Lori A. Sansone. "Gratitude and Well Being: The Benefits of Appreciation." *Psychiatry* (Edgmont) 7, no. 11 (2010): 18.

275. Santoli, Susan P. "Is there an Advanced Placement advantage?" *American Secondary Education* (2002): 23-35.

276. Sapolsky, Robert M. Behave: *The Biology of Humans at Your Best and Worst.* Penguin, 2017.

277. Saveth, Edward N. "Suicide of an Elite?" *Commentary* 92, no. 2 (1991): 44.

278. Sawyer, Richard. "Beyond Correlations: Usefulness of High School GPA and Test Scores in Making College Admissions Decisions." *Applied Measurement in Education* 26, no. 2 (2013): 89-112.

279. Seligman, Martin EP. *Flourish: A Visionary New Understanding of Happiness and Well-Being.* Simon and Schuster, 2012.

280. Sheldon, Kennon M., and Sonja Lyubomirsky. "How to Increase and Sustain Positive Emotion: The Effects of Expressing Gratitude and Visualizing Best Possible Selves." *The Journal of Positive Psychology* 1, no. 2 (2006): 73-82.

281. Schneider, Jack. "Privilege, Equity, and the Advanced Placement Program: Tug of War." *Journal of Curriculum Studies* 41, no. 6 (2009): 813-831.

282. Schwartz, David Joseph. *The Magic of Getting What You Want*. W. Morrow, 1983.

283. Schwartz, David S. *Magic of Self Direction*. Simon & Schuster, 1975.

284. Schwarz, Alan. "Risky Rise of the Good-Grade Pill." *The New York Times*. June 09, 2012. Accessed June 10, 2018. https://www.nytimes.com/2012/06/10/education/seeking-academic-edge-teenagers-abuse-stimulants.html?pagewanted=all&mtrref=undefined&gwh=D30BD3E91266E66AEAAB344087333526&gwt=pay.

285. Schwartz, Yishai. "For Parents Willing to Pay Thousands, College Counselors Promise to Make Ivy League Dreams a Reality." *Town & Country*. June 28, 2017. https://www.townandcountrymag.com/leisure/a10202220/college-counseling-services/.

286. Shapiro, Doug, Afet Dundar, Phoebe Khasiala Wakhungu, Xin Yuan, Angel Nathan, and Youngsik Hwang. Time to Degree: A National View of the Time Enrolled and Elapsed for Associate and Bachelor's Degree Earners. (Signature Report No. 11). National Student Clearinghouse (2016).

287. Siler, Todd. *Think like a Genius: Use Your Creativity in Ways That Will Enrich Your Life*. New York: Bantam Books, 1999

288. Smith, Jeffrey M. *Seeds of Deception. Exposing Industry and Government Lies about the Safety of the Genetically Engineered Food You're Eating*. Fairfield, Iowa: Yes (2003).

289. SOCA-Executive Summary. National Association for College Admission Counseling. Accessed June 10, 2018. https://www.nacacnet.org/news-publications/publications/state-of-college-admission/soca-download/.

290. Somers, Darian. "Do Colleges Look at Your Social Media Accounts?" *U.S. News & World Report*. Accessed June 10, 2018. https://

www.usnews.com/education/best- colleges/articles/2017-02-10/colleges-really-are-looking-at-your-social-media-accounts.

291. Somers, Suzanne. *Tox-Sick: From Toxic to Not Sick*. Harmony, 2016.

292. Spinath, Birgit, and Frank M. Spinath. "Longitudinal Analysis of the Link between Learning Motivation and Competence Beliefs among Elementary School Children." *Learning and Instruction* 15, no. 2 (2005): 87-102.

293. The State of College Admission Report. National Association for College Admission Counseling. Accessed June 11, 2018. https://www.nacacnet.org/news-publications/publications/state-of-college-admission/.

294. Statistics about Non-Public Education in the United States. The National Household Education Surveys (NHES) Program of 2012. March 01, 2017. Accessed June 10, 2018. https://www2.ed.gov/about/offices/list/oii/nonpublic/statistics.html#homeschl.

295. Steinberg, Jacques. Before College, Costly Advice Just on Getting In. *The New York Times*. July 18, 2009. Accessed June 10, 2018. https://www.nytimes.com/2009/07/19/education/19counselor.html.

296. Steinberg, Jacques. *The Gatekeepers: Inside the Admissions Process of a Premier College*. Penguin, 2003.

297. Stern, William. *The Psychological Methods of Testing Intelligence*. No. 13. Warwick & York, 1914.

298. Strand, Ray. *Death by prescription: The Shocking Truth Behind an Overmedicated Nation*. Thomas Nelson, 2006.

299. Strauss, Karsten. "The Highest-Paid Private College Presidents." Forbes. December 05, 2016. Accessed July 30, 2018. https://www.forbes.com/sites/karstenstrauss/2016/12/05/the-highest-paid-private-college-presidents/#3f15e610444e.

300. Sulek, Julia Prodis. "Perfect ACT, SAT Scores Don't Mean Admission to Top Universities." *The Mercury News*. April 03, 2018. Accessed June 10, 2018. https://www.mercurynews.com/2018/04/02/perfect-act-sat-scores-dont-mean- admission-to-top-universities/.

301. Svetlov, Stanislav I., Firas H. Kobeissy, and Mark S. Gold. "Performance Enhancing, Non-Prescription Use of Ritalin: A Comparison with Amphetamines and Cocaine." *Journal of Addictive Diseases* 26, no. 4 (2007): 1-6.

302. Swanson, Christopher B. "Spending Time or Investing Time? Involvement in High School Curricular and Extracurricular Activities As Strategic Action." *Rationality and Society* 14, no. 4 (2002): 431-471.

303. Sweeney, Michael S. Brain: *The Complete Mind*. National Geographic Books, 2009.

304. Tauer, John M., and Judith M. Harackiewicz."The Effects of Cooperation and Competition on Intrinsic Motivation and Performance." *Journal of Personality and Social Psychology* 86, no. 6 (2004): 849.

305. 306. Team, MainStreet. "Top US Private Schools with the Most Graduates Getting into Ivy League Universities." The Street. October 15, 2015. Accessed June 10, 2018. https://www.thestreet.com/story/13325695/1/top-us-private-schools-with-the-most-graduates-getting-into-ivy-league-universities.html.

306. Teasley, Stephanie D. "Talking about Reasoning: How Important Is the Peer in Peer Collaboration?" *Discourse, Tools and Reasoning*, pp. 361-384. Springer, Berlin, Heidelberg, 1997.

307. Teter, Christian J., Sean Esteban McCabe, James A. Cranford, Carol J. Boyd, and Saliy K. Guthrie. "Prevalence and Motives for Illicit Use of Prescription Stimulants in an Undergraduate Student Sample." *Journal of American College Health* 53, no. 6 (2005): 253-262.

308. Thia Garajan, Maya. *Beyond the Tiger Mom: East-West Parenting for the Global Age*. S.l.: Tuttle Publishing, 2018.

309. Toepfer, Steven M., Kelly Cichy, and Patti Peters. "Letters of Gratitude: Further Evidence for Author Benefits." Journal of Happiness Studies 13, no. 1 (2012): 187-201.

310. Top Tier Admissions. "Do Public Schools Trump Private Schools in College Admissions?" November 01, 2016. Accessed June 10, 2018. http://www.toptieradmissions.com/do-public-schools-trump-private-schools-in-college- admissions/.

311. Topol, Eric J. *The Patient Will See You Now: The Future of Medicine Is in Your Hands*. Tantor Media, 2015.

312. Tough, Paul. *How Children Succeed.* Random House, 2013.

313. Tremblay, Christopher W. "Earning Admission: Real Strategies for Getting into Highly Selective Colleges." *College and University* 93, no. 1 (2018): 55-60.

314. "Trends in High School Dropout and Completion Rates in the United States: 2014." Revenues and Expenditures for Public Elementary and Secondary Education: School Year 2001-2002, E.D. Tab. February 22, 2018. Accessed June 10, 2018. https://nces.ed.gov/pubsearch/pubsinfo.asp?pubid=2018117.

315. Tucker, Jan, and Bari Courts. "Grade Inflation in the College Classroom." *Foresight 12*, no. 1 (2010): 45-53.

316. Tyler, Steven, and David Dalton. *Does the Noise in My Head Bother You? A Rock N Roll Memoir.* New York: Ecco Press, 2012.

317. 318. Viraraghavan, T., K. S. Subramanian, and J. A. Aruldoss. "Arsenic in Drinking Water-Problems and Solutions." *Water Science and Technology* 40, no. 2 (1999): 69-76.

318. Vogel, Sarah A. "The Politics of Plastics: The Making and Unmaking of Bisphenol a safety.'" *American Journal of Public Health* 99, no. S3 (2009): S559-S566.

319. Volkow, Nora D., and James M. Swanson. "Does Childhood Treatment of ADHD with Stimulant Medication Affect Substance Abuse in Adulthood?" (2008): 553-555.

320. Watson, Thomas J., and Peter Petre. Father, Son & Co. *My Life at IBM and Beyond.* Bantam, 2013.

321. Weil, Andrew. *Why Our Health Matters: A Vision of Medicine That Can Transform Our Future.* Blackstone Audio, Incorporated, 2009.

322. Weiss, Gabrielle, and Lily Trokenberg Hechtman. *Hyperactive Children Grown Up: ADHD in Children, Adolescents, and Adults.* Guilford Press, 1993.

323. Welch, H. Gilbert, Lisa Schwartz, and Steve Woloshin. *Overdiagnoses: Making People Sick in the Pursuit of Health.* Beacon Press, 2011.

324. Welch, H. Gilbert. *Less Medicine, More Health: 7 Assumptions That Drive Too Much Medical Care.* Beacon Press, 2015.

325. Wentzel, Kathryn R. "Social Relationships and Motivation in Middle School: The Role of Parents, Teachers, and Peers." *Journal of Educational Psychology* 90, no. 2 (1998): 202.

326. Wesley, Joseph C. "Effects of Ability, High School Achievement, and Procrastinatory Behavior on College Performance." *Educational and Psychological Measurement* 54, no. 2 (1994): 404-408.

327. Whitaker, Robert. "Anatomy of an Epidemic: Psychiatric Drugs and the Astonishing Rise of Mental Illness in America." *Ethical Human Sciences and Services* 7, no. 1 (2005): 23-35.

328. Whitaker, Robert. Mad in America: *Bad Science, Bad Medicine, and the Enduring Mistreatment of the Mentally Ill*. Basic Books, 2001.

329. White, Martha C. "Do Colleges Look Up Students Facebook During Admissions?" *Time*. March 09, 2016. Accessed June 11, 2018. http://time.com/money/4252541/colleges-facebook-social-media-students-admissions/.

330. Wigfield, Allan, and Jacquelynne S. Eccles. "Children's Competence Beliefs, Achievement Values, and General Self-Esteem: Change across Elementary and Middle School." *The Journal of Early Adolescence* 14, no. 2 (1994): 107-138.

331. Wilson, Glenn Daniel, ed. *Your personality & Potential*. Salem House Pub, 1989.

332. Wilson, Samantha L. "Post-institutionalization: The Effects of Early Deprivation on Development of Romanian Adoptees." *Child and Adolescent Social Work Journal* 20, no. 6 (2003): 473-483.

333. Winget, Larry. *Your Kids Are Your Own Fault: A Fix-the-Way-You-Parent Guide to Raising Responsible, Productive Adults*. New York: Gotham, 2011.

334. Wolfe, Raymond N., and Scott D. Johnson. "Personality As a Predictor of College Performance." *Educational and Psychological Measurement* 55, no. 2 (1995): 177-185.

335. Wolraich, Mark, and Howard Schubiner. "Clinical Diagnosis and Management of Attention-Deficit/Hyperactivity Disorder (ADHD)." *Professional Communications*, 2008.

336. Woodruff, David J., and Robert L. Ziomek. "High School Grade Inflation from 1991 to 2003." *Research Report Series* 2004-04. ACT Inc (2004).

337. Wurtman, Judith J., and Margaret Danbrot. *Managing your Mind and Mood through Food*. 1986.

338. Yale College Class of 2021 First-Year Class Profile. https://admissions.yale.edu/sites/default/files/files/class_profile_2021_final.pdf.

339. Zajac, Edward J., and James D. Westphal. "Who Shall Succeed? How CEO/Board Preferences and Power Affect the Choice of New CEOs." *Academy of Management Journal* 39, no. 1 (1996): 64-90.

340. Zimmer, Ron W., and Eugenia F. Toma. "Peer Effects in Private and Public Schools across Countries." *Journal of Policy Analysis and Management* (2000): 75-92.

341. Zimmerman, David J. "Peer Effects in Academic Outcomes: Evidence from a Natural Experiment." *Review of Economics and Statistics* 85, no. 1 (2003): 9-23.

342. Ziomek, Robert L., and Joseph C. Svec. "High School Grades and Achievement: Evidence of Grade Inflation." NASSP *Bulletin 81*, no. 587 (1997): 105-113.

343. Zwick, Rebecca, and Jeffrey C. Sklar. "Predicting College Grades and Degree Completion Using High School Grades and SAT Scores: The Role of Student Ethnicity and First Language." *American Educational Research Journal* 42, no. 3 (2005): 439-464.

344. "Adverse Consequences of School Closures." UNESCO, May 13, 2020. https://en.unesco.org/themes/education-emergencies/coronavirus-school-closures/consequences.

345. "How Will the Pandemic Change Higher Education?" *The Chronicle of Higher Education*. April 2020. https://store.chronicle.com/products/how-will-the-pandemic-change-higher-education.

346. "Impact of the 2019–20 Coronavirus Pandemic on Education." Wikipedia. Wikimedia Foundation, May 4, 2020. https://en.wikipedia.org/wiki/Impact_of_the_2019–20_coronavirus_pandemic_on_education.

347. Azoulay, Audrey. "290 Million Students out of School Due to COVID-19: UNESCO Releases First Global Numbers and Mobilizes Response." UNESCO, March 30, 2020. https://en.unesco.org/news/290-million-students-out-school-due-covid-19-unesco-releases-first-global-numbers-and-mobilizes.

348. Bao, Xue, Hang Qu, Ruixiong Zhang, and Tiffany P. Hogan. "Literacy Loss in Kindergarten Children during COVID-19 School Closures." *SocArXiv*, April 15, 2020. https://doi.org/10.31235/osf.io/nbv79.

349. Frankfurt, Tal. "Council Post: How The Pandemic Could Forever Change Higher Education." Forbes. Forbes Magazine, May 8, 2020.

350. https://www.forbes.com/sites/forbestechcouncil/2020/05/08/how-the-pandemic-could-forever-change-higher-education/#2c0ec69e7b93.

351. Goldstein, Dana, Adam Popescu, and Nikole Hannah-jones. "As School Moves Online, Many Students Stay Logged Out." The New York Times. The New York Times, April 6, 2020. https://www.nytimes.com/2020/04/06/us/coronavirus-schools-attendance-absent.html.

352. Darby, Whitney R., Richard B. Doane, Philip A. Cook, and Sandra K. Garrett. "College student knowledge and behavior concerning novel H1N1 influenza." In IIE Annual Conference. Proceedings, p. 1. Institute of Industrial and Systems Engineers (IISE), 2010.

353. Hall, Stephanie. "A Global View of the Pandemic's Effect on Higher Education." The Century Foundation, April 27, 2020. https://tcf.org/content/commentary/global-view-pandemics-effect-higher-education

354. Hoover, Eric. "How Is Covid-19 Changing Prospective Students' Plans? Here's an Early Look." *The Chronicle of Higher Education*, March 25, 2020. https://www.chronicle.com/article/How-Is-Covid-19-Changing/248316.

355. Kandri, Salah-Eddine. "COVID-19 Is Sparking a Revolution in Higher Education." *World Economic Forum*. Accessed May 18, 2020. https://www.weforum.org/agenda/2020/05/how-covid-19-is-sparking-a-revolution-in-higher-education/.

356. Krupnick, Matt. "Universities Face Another Challenge amid Coronavirus Crisis: Fewer Graduate Students." NBCNews.com. NBCUniversal News Group, May 13, 2020. https://www.nbcnews.com/news/education/universities-face-another-challenge-amid-coronavirus-crisis-fewer-graduate-students-n1205611.

357. Marcus, Jon. "Universities Now Face Tens of Billions in Losses for University Endowments." *The Hechinger Report,* March 30, 2020. https://hechingerreport.org/already-stretched-universities-now-face-tens-of-billions-in-endowment-losses/.

358. Massa, Robert. "5 Ways That the Coronavirus Will Change College Admissions This Fall." *The Conversation*, April 2, 2020. https://theconversation.com/5-ways-that-the-coronavirus-will-change-college-admissions-this-fall-135152.

359. Mineo, Liz. "The Pandemic's Impact on Education." *Harvard Gazette*, April 10, 2020. https://news.harvard.edu/gazette/story/2020/04/the-pandemics-impact-on-education/.

360. Nesbit, Joanna. "Here's How College Admissions Are Changing This Year - and What High School Seniors Need to Know." *Money*. Accessed May 18, 2020. https://money.com/college-admissions-coronavirus/.

361. Newton, Derek. "Five Ways COVID-19 Will Impact Fall College Enrollments." *Forbes* Magazine, March 30, 2020. https://www.forbes.com/sites/dereknewton/2020/03/30/five-ways-covid-19-will-impact-fall-college-enrollments/#7b4302966114.

362. Patch, Will. "Impact of Coronavirus on Students' Academic Progress and College Plans." Niche, May 8, 2020. https://www.niche.com/about/enrollment-insights/impact-of-coronavirus-on-students-academic-progress-and-college-plans/. Snyder, Thomas D. *120 Years of American education: A statistical portrait.* US Department of Education, Office of Educational Research and Improvement, National Center for Education Statistics, 1993.

# INDEX

A
abuse, 30, 227
acceptance
    and affirmative action, 12, 13
    nd athletics, 10, 11, 13, 89, 117
    bribery scandal, 1, 12–14, 82
    and celebrities, 10, 11, 12, 13, 210
    challenges to, 9–15
    deferred, 159
    discrimination lawsuits, 96
    early decision, 15, 159–60, 162
    and extracurricular activities, 95–96, 97, 132–36, 236
    gaming, 39
    and geographic diversity, 22
    and hooks, 10, 11–15, 251
    Ivy League rates, 9, 10, 15
    and number of applications, 14
    private high school rates of, 14, 38–39, 219, 222
    regular decision, 15, 159, 160
    at strictly merit schools, 11–12
    accommodations, 65
ACT
    "good enough" score, 116
    importance of, 103–7, 116, 118
    resources on, 287–93
    vs. SAT, 109
ADD (attention deficit disorder), 62, 64, 65
admissions officers, meeting with, 157
admitsee.com, 149, 285, 301
Advanced Placement (AP), 78, 79, 110, 291
adverse childhood experiences, 24–26
adversity score, 77, 106
Aeries, 81–82, 83
affirmative action, 12, 13
affluenza, 42–45, 138, 229
age
    advantages of being older than

classmates, 2, 37–38, 59, 220
    respect for, 94, 166
alcohol use, 71, 87, 88, 93
alumni
    benefits of Ivy League, 5, 88
    as factor in selecting college, 187, 188, 276
analytical skills and benefits of testing, 115
Anatomy of an Epidemic (Whitaker), 64
AP (Advanced Placement), 78, 79, 110, 291
apologies, xxxix, 44–45
applications
    avoiding additional materials in, 126, 129, 147, 157
    bird's eye view of, 214
    bragging in, 126, 147, 148, 209, 210
    Common App, 14
    need for parental involvement, 2, 16
    numbers of, 14
    peers, 126, 127, 154
    See also essays
app (phone and computer) resources, 292, 299–300
AP Scholar, 110
AP Scholar of Distinction, 110
artificial intelligence, 196–97
athletics
    acceptance rates, 10, 11, 13, 89, 117
    early decision, 159
    as factor in selecting college, 186, 276
    high school, 89–90, 100
Tiger Mother model, xxviii, xxix, xxxiv
The Atlantic, 294
attachment parenting, 30
attention deficit disorder (ADD), 62, 64, 65
authority, parental, xxxvi, xxxvii, 50, 165–67
Awesome, Jar of, 66

# B

babysitters, 32
Bar Mitzvah, 69
Barry, John, 239
*The Battle Hymn of the Tiger Mother* (Chua), xxv
Berea College, 12
*Beyond the Tiger Mom* (Thiagarajan), xxvi
blogs, 296

Bluestone, Barry, 247
boarding schools, 55, 182
bonuses, tutor, 56, 59, 80
books
    in home, 116
    test prep books, 110, 111, 116, 118, 291–92
bragging, avoiding, 126, 147, 148, 151, 209, 210
brag sheets, 156
brain
    development, 25, 30, 32
    frontal cortex, 204
    health of, 211
    limbic system, 22, 196, 204
    prefrontal cortex, 197, 204
    technology's effect on, 104–5
*See also* intelligence
breastfeeding, 30, 35
bribery scandal, 1, 12–14, 82
Bruni, Frank, 3
businessinsider.com, 295

# C

calculators, college, 302
CalTech, 11
campus, as factor in selecting college, 186, 188, 276
Caplan, Barry, 5, 123
cappex.com, 296
Carr, Nicolas, 104–5
*The Case Against Education* (Caplan), 5, 123
celebrities
    acceptance rates for children of, 10, 11, 12, 13, 210
    letters of recommendation by, 155, 162
Chatterjee, Pria, 105–6
chegg.com, 303
child
    acceptance rates for children of faculty, 10, 11, 12, 13
    foster children, 25–26
    goals of, xxxvi, xxxviii, xxxix, 49, 75
    importance of spending time with, 40–42, 55
    need for understanding, xxx–xxxi
    questionnaire for, 264–68
    trust in, 59, 64, 71, 223–25

*See also* childhood, early; happiness; intrinsic motivation
child abuse, 30, 227
childhood, early
    attachment parenting, 30
    attitude and potential, 28–31, 40
    brain development, 25, 30, 32
    happiness, 24–28, 31
    importance of, 34–35
    *See also* pre-Kindergarten education
Chu, Lenora, xxvi
Chua, Amy, xxv, 70
classes
    AP, 78, 79, 110
    class size as factor in selecting college, 276
    selecting in high school, 77–78, 124
cnbc.com, 295
cognitive ability, 196–204, 211, 214
collaboration, xxviii, 80–81, 236
collegdata.com, 296
college
    attendance rates, 7, 121–22
    and COVID-19, 240, 245, 247–48
    extracurricular activities in, 4, 186, 251–52
    graduation rates, 3, 7, 25, 122, 212, 276
    and imposter syndrome, 212–13
    intrinsic motivation at, 242, 252
    number of institutions, 10, 184
    selecting, 3, 6, 16, 190, 251, 276–84, 297
    selecting professors, 80
    stress of, 185
    switching schools, 184
    value of, 2–3, 122–23
    visiting, 16
    websites as resources, 287
    *See also* alumni; financial aid and scholarships; Ivy League; rankings and ratings, colleges
collegeboard.com, 303
collegeconfidential.com, 296
college counselors, See counselors, college
collegeessaymentor.com, 301
collegefactual.com, 295, 296
collegeinsight.com, 303
collegemajors101.com, 303
collegereadiness.collegeboard.org, 288

collegeresults.org, 303
collegescholarships.com, 300
College Scholarship Service (CSS), 158, 162
collegescholarships.org, 298
collegescorecard.com, 296
collegevine.com, 289
collegexpress.com, 301
Common App, 14
communication, xxix, xxxix, 59
commutes, 76, 218
competition
    college, 185
    early childhood education, 21–22
    grade school, 38, 221
    high school, 72, 73–74
    self-efficacy, 46
    Tiger Mother model, xxxvi
confidence, xxx, xxxix, 228
consequences vs. punishment, 50
consultants, college, See counselors, college
Cooper Union, 11
*Corporate Flight* (Bluestone), 247
costs
    college counselors, 44
    and COVID-19, 245, 247–48
    debt, 122–23
    as factor in selecting college, 16, 186, 188, 276, 297
    Ivy League, 3, 4
    Lion Dad model, xxxix
    test preparation, 44
    travel, 44
    tutors, 44, 56–57, 59, 80–81
counselors, college
    bird's eye view of application, 212
    costs, 44
    essays, 126, 127, 145, 146–47, 148, 151
    executive function and emotional intelligence, 198
    financial aid, 158, 300
    general, 123, 124, 126, 129
    letters of recommendation by, 156
    need for, 123, 125–26, 148
    reductionism, 208
    remote, 125, 127, 302
    resources for, 302

    selecting, 94, 124–29
    selecting high school courses, 77, 85, 124
    specialists, 123, 126, 129
    test preparation, 124, 126, 127
    vs. tutors, 146
    using, 93–94, 100, 121–29
counselors, guidance, 156, 162
courses, See classes
COVID-19, 239–49
*Crazy Rich Asians* (2018), 166, 195
CSS (College Scholarship Service), 158, 162
culture and rites of passage, 69–70
curriculum
    college, 186, 276
    grade school, 53, 54
    high school, 53, 54, 75, 116, 183, 221
    tests, 116

# D

Da Vinci, Leonardo, 234
deaths from COVID-19, 246–47
debt, 122
deferred acceptance, 159
Deresiewicz, William, 2, 185
desk and study area, 68
Diamandis, Peter, 77
diet, 87–88, 100, 110, 111. See also supplements
*Digital Minimalism* (Newport), 105
discipline
    Lion Dad vs. Tiger Mother model, xxvi, xxviii, xxx, xxxvi–xxxvii, 30, 46, 49–51
    punishment vs. consequences, 50
    time outs, 50, 51
discrimination lawsuits, 96
diversity
    as factor in acceptance, 12, 13, 22
    as factor in selecting college, 186
    geographic, 22
diycollegerankings.com, 295
donors and donations
    acceptance rates, 10, 11, 12, 13
    focus on in private schools, 38, 53, 54, 220, 221
    grades, 82
dropout rates, 212, 221

drug use, 71, 87, 88, 93, 198, 211

**E**
early childhood education, See pre-Kindergarten education
early decision, 15, 159–60, 162
*The Economist,* 294
education
    boarding schools, 55, 182
    vs. learning, 2, 51–52, 245, 249
    middle school, 61–71, 182–83, 226, 245
    rewards in, 47
    school closures, 244–45
    switching schools, 39–40, 53, 181–83, 184, 225–26
    travel as, 172
    *See also* college; educators; grade school; high school; homeschooling; Ivy League; pre-Kindergarten education; private schools; public schools; tests; tutors
education, higher, See college; Ivy League
educators
    goals, xxxix
    grade pressure, 107–8
    interacting with, 78, 79, 83, 85, 155, 183
    letters of recommendation by, 155–57, 162
    negative assessments from, 33–34, 35, 52–53, 59, 220, 223–25
    quality of as factor in selecting schools, 54, 75, 76, 221
    selecting in college, 80
    selecting in high school, 78–80
emotional intelligence, 30, 108, 196–204, 211–13, 214
emotions, xxvi. See also emotional intelligence; happiness; unhappiness
*The Emperor's New Drugs* (Kirsch), 64
employment
    and COVID-19 pandemic, 240, 246, 247, 248, 249
    goals, xxxi, xxxix
    and online learning, 243
    passion, 185–86
    recruitment and Ivy League, 5
    salary and earnings potential, 5, 186, 276
    selecting, 185–86
energy, as commodity, 83–84
environmental exposure, 30, 32, 35, 90–91, 100
essays, 126, 127, 143–51, 213, 214, 285–86

*Excellent Sheep* (Deresiewicz), 2, 185
executive function, 108, 196–204, 211–12, 213, 214, 248
exercise, 87, 89–90, 110, 111
extracurricular activities
    college, 251–52
    depth of, 55, 97, 100, 134–35, 168–71, 176
    as factor in acceptance, 95–96, 97, 132–36, 236
    as factor in selecting college, 4, 186
    intrinsic motivation, xxxviii, 97–98, 100, 132, 133, 138–40, 167, 169–70, 176
    passion, 96, 97–98, 133, 134–35, 138–39, 140
    peers, 136–37
    questions on, 134–35
    summer activities, 98–99
    Tiger Mother model, xxvi, xxxviii, 139, 170
    volunteering, 170–72, 176
*Extraordinary and Popular Delusions and the Madness of Crowds* (Mackay), 2

# E
early childhood education, See pre-Kindergarten education
early decision, 12, 159–60, 162
*The Economist*, 294
education
    boarding schools, 55, 182
    vs. learning, 52, 245, 249
    middle school, 61–71, 182–83, 226, 245
    rewards in, 47
    school closures, 244–45
    switching schools, 39–40, 53, 181–83, 184, 225–26
    travel as, 172
    See also college; educators; grade school; high school; homeschooling; Ivy League; pre-Kindergarten education; private schools; public schools; tests; tutors
education, higher, See college; Ivy League
educators
    goals, xxxix
    grade pressure, 107–8
    interacting with, 78, 79, 83, 85, 155, 183
    letters of recommendation by, 155–57, 162
    negative assessments from, 33–34, 35, 52–53, 59, 197, 199, 220, 223–25
    quality of as factor in selecting schools, 54, 75, 76, 221
    selecting in college, 80

    selecting in high school, 78–80
emotional intelligence, 30, 108, 196–204, 211–13, 214
emotions, xxvi. See also emotional intelligence; happiness; unhappiness
*The Emperor's New Drugs* (Kirsch), 64
employment
    and COVID-19 pandemic, 240, 246, 247, 248, 249
    goals, xxxi, xxxix
    and online learning, 243
    passion, 185–86
    recruitment and Ivy League, 2
    salary and earnings potential, 5, 186, 276
    selecting, 185–86
energy, as commodity, 83–84
environmental exposure, 30, 32, 35, 90–91, 100
essays, 126, 127, 143–51, 213, 214, 285–86
*Excellent Sheep* (Deresiewicz), 185
executive function, 108, 196–204, 211–12, 213, 214, 248
exercise, 87, 89–90, 110
extracurricular activities
    college, 251–52
    depth of, 55, 97, 100, 134–35, 168–71, 176
    as factor in acceptance, 95–96, 97, 132–36, 236
    as factor in selecting college, 4, 186
    intrinsic motivation, xxxviii, 97–98, 100, 132, 133, 138–40, 167, 169–70, 176
    passion, 96, 97–98, 133, 134–35, 138–39, 140
    peers, 136–37
    questions on, 134–35
    summer activities, 98–99
    Tiger Mother model, xxvi, xxxviii, 139, 170
    volunteering, 170–72, 176

# F

factory farming, 239, 246, 249
faculty
    acceptance rates for children of, 10, 11, 12, 13
    Ivy League advantages, 5
    selecting professors in college, 80
FAFSA (Free Application for Federal Student Aid), 158–59, 162
faith in child, 59, 64, 71, 223–25
fastweb.com, 297

film, as Max's extracurricular activity, 67, 97, 98, 132, 138–39, 167–68, 236, 251–52
financial aid and scholarships
    and acceptance, 158–59, 162
    athletic scholarships, 89
    college counselors for, 126, 300
    early action, 160
    FAFSA forms, 158–59, 162
    National Merit Scholarship awards, 109
    need-based, 12, 297
    need-blind vs. need-aware, 158–59
    pursuing, 297–98, 303–4
    resources on, 159, 287, 297–301
flash cards, 113, 114, 292
food
    diet and health, 87–88, 100, 110, 111
    as factor in selecting college, 186, 276
forbes.com, 294
foster children, 25–26
fraternities, 251, 276
Free Application for Federal Student Aid (FAFSA), 158–59, 162
friendships, xxv, xxvi, xxxvii, 227, 236, 243. See also peers
frontal cortex, 204

# G
Gaby, Alan, 92
gap year, 245
geography
    admissions and diversity of, 22
    as factor in selecting college, 186, 187, 188, 276
    as factor in selecting schools, 75–76, 222
    friendships, 227
    as stress factor in college, 185
*Getting into a Top College* (Chatterjee), 105–6
gifted children programs, 22
Gladwell, Malcolm, xxviii, 220, 294
glassdoor.com, 302
goals
    child's, xxxvi, xxxviii, xxxix, 49, 75
    educator's, xxxix
    parents', xxxvi, 49, 250
grades

acceptance rates, 15
AP classes and GPA, 110
donations, 82
grade inflation, 5, 81–82, 107
homeschooling, 55, 79
intrinsic motivation, 47, 108
Lion Dad model vs. Tiger Mother model, xxxviii
monitoring and managing, 81–83, 85
on Naviance, 160–61
resources on GPAs, 301
grade school
    advantages of being older than classmates, 2, 37–38, 59
    boarding schools, 55
    COVID-19 closures, 244
    homework in, 221, 223
    parental involvement in, 40–42, 244
    rewards in, 47
    selecting, 37–40, 53–55, 181–83, 218–23
    self-efficacy, 45–46, 53
    switching schools, 39–40, 182
    tutors, 55–57
graduate school, 4, 5, 122, 276
graduation rates
    college, 3, 10, 25, 122, 212, 277
    foster children, 25–26
    high school, 9, 10, 25, 121, 122
    Ivy League, 5
gratitude, 65–66, 71, 173
*The Great Influenza* (Barry), 239
Greger, Michael, 88, 239
guidance counselors, 156, 162

# H
Hadler, Nortin, 64
hamiltoncollegeconsulting.com, 291
happiness
    early childhood, 24–28, 31
    emotional intelligence, 201, 204
    executive function, 201, 204
    Lion Dad model vs. Tiger Mother model, xxvi, xxix, xxx–xxxi, xxxvi
    selecting school, 184–86
    success, 251

Harari, Noah, 240
Harthiramani, Shaan, 247–48
Harvard Westlake, 38, 222
health
    of author, 234–35
    COVID-19 pandemic, 239–41, 246–49
    diet, 87–88, 100, 110
    environmental exposure, 30, 32, 35, 90–91, 100
    exercise, 87, 89–90
    and school closures, 244
    supplements, 92–93, 100, 110, 210
    vaccines, 91–92
high school
    acceptance rates and private schools, 14, 38–39, 219, 222
    athletics in, 89–90, 100
    competition in, 72, 73–74
    COVID-19 closures, 245
    curriculum, 53, 54, 75, 116, 183, 221
        graduation rates, 9, 10, 25, 121, 122
        health, 87–93
        numbers of students, 10
        rankings and ratings, 75, 137, 160–61
        resources, 81, 83, 85, 160–61, 287
        selecting, 67, 71, 75–77, 85, 137–38, 181–83, 221–22
        selecting courses, 77–78, 85, 124
        selecting teachers, 78–80
        summer activities, 98–99
    *See also* extracurricular activities; tests; tutors
*Homeless to Harvard* (2003), 77
homeschooling, 54–55, 66, 77, 79, 138, 182
homework in grade school, 221, 223
*Homo Deus* (Noah Harari), 240
honors courses, 78
hormone deficiencies, 91
housing, as factor in selecting college, 186, 276
*How to Survive a Pandemic* (Greger), 239

# I

identity and rites of passage, 69–70
imposter syndrome, 212–13
impulse control, 70
income, child's potential, 5, 186, 276

info.getintocollege.com, 302
insecurity and exceptionalism, 70
intelligence
    artificial intelligence, 196–97
    tests, 23–24, 196
    *See also* cognitive ability; emotional intelligence; executive function
internet
    online education, 240, 242–45, 246, 249
    social media, 98, 157–58, 162, 244
intrinsic motivation
    at college, 242, 252
    extracurricular activities, xxxviii, 97–98, 100, 132, 133, 138–40, 167, 169–70, 176
    grades, 47, 108
    for learning, 49, 52, 77, 116, 223, 242, 243
    and online learning, 242, 243
    in overview, xxix, xxxvi
    rewards, xxviii, 47, 56, 59, 234
    volunteering, 170, 176
IQ tests, 23–24, 196
Isaacson, Walter, 234
ivycoach.com, 302
ivy-edge.com, 302
Ivy League
    acceptance rates, general, 9, 10, 15
    acceptance rates and private schools, 14, 38–39, 219, 222
    advantages of, 3, 4–9, 88
    costs, 3, 4
    disadvantages of, 3, 6
    graduation rates, 5
    list of schools in, 4
    peers at, 6, 67, 126, 127, 213, 214, 236
    rankings, 9
    selecting among, 16
    stress at, 185
ivyselect.com, 302
ivywise.com, 295

# J

Jar of Awesome, 66
Jewish Federation, 170–71
Jewish Funders Network, 171

Jobs, Steve, 236
journals, 65–66, 230

## K
kaptest.com, 287
Kaufman, Raun, 224
khanacademy.org, 287, 288
Kirsch, Irving, 64
Kohn, Alfie, xxviii, 47
Kurzweil, Ray, 77, 240

## L
leadership
    early in life, 2, 37
    and executive function, 197
    extracurricular activities, 97, 98, 135, 170–71, 172, 174, 176
    and online learning, 243
    self-direction, 233, 234
    writing skills, 144
learning
    vs. education, 2, 51–52, 245, 249
    intrinsic motivation for, 49, 52, 77, 116, 223, 242
    by parent, 230
    preferences, xxxviii
legacy applicants, 10, 11, 13, 117, 159
letters of recommendation, 155–57, 162
limbic system, 22, 196, 204
listening v. talking, xxxix
*Little Soldiers* (Chu), xxvi
location, See geography
love, xxx, xxxvi, 46–47, 51, 59, 227, 228

## M
Mackay, Charles, 2
manners, 209–10
marketing, 157–58, 162
math, xxxviii, 50, 104
medications
    neuropsychology, 64–65, 93, 184–85, 211
    nutritional/hormone deficiencies, 91
    psychostimulants, 93, 100

middle school, 61–71, 182–83, 226, 245
mistakes
    admitting, 230
    analyzing, 217–18
    journal, 230
money
    attitudes toward, 298–99, 303–4
    as commodity, 83–84
    *See also* costs
motivation
    grades, 47, 108
    Lion Dad model vs. Tiger Mother model, xxix, xxxvi, xxxvii
    *See also* intrinsic motivation
music, 32

## N

National Merit Scholarship awards, 109
Natural Medicine Comprehensive Database, 92
Naviance, 160–61, 287
nces.ed.gov, 303
negativity
    educators, 33–34, 35, 52–53, 59, 220, 223–25
    "experts," 23–24, 62–65, 71, 223–25
    self-talk, 100
neuropsychology
    medications, 64–65, 93, 184–85, 211
    negativity from psychologists, 62–65, 71, 224
Newport, Cal, 105
*The New Yorker,* 294
niche.com, 293
noise, exposure to, 32
noodle.com, 296
numeracy, 104
nutrition
    diet, 87–88, 100, 110, 111
    supplements, 92–93, 100, 210
*Nutritional Medicine* (Gaby), 92
Nutritionfacts.org, 88

## O

obedience, xxv, xxvi, xxx, xxxvii, 166
obesity, 88, 90
online education, 240, 242–45, 246, 249.

*See also* social media; websites
orphans, 25
*Outliers* (Gladwell), 220

# P

Pacific Ridge, 38
pandemics, 239–49
parchment.com, 296
parenting, attachment, 30
parents
    attitudes toward school, xxxviii
    authority of, xxxvi, xxxvii, 50, 165–67
    goals of, xxxvi, 2, 49, 250
    involvement in application process, 2, 16
    involvement in college, 94–95
    involvement in grade school, 40–42
    involvement in high school, 74, 75, 95
    involvement in middle school, 71
    involvement in private schools, 219
    learning by, 230
    names for, xxvi, 166
    other parents as resource, 153–54, 221
    positioning of, xxxvi
    *See also* Tiger Mother model
parentscountdowntocollege.com, 295
passion
employment, 185–86
    extracurricular activities, 96, 97–98, 133, 134–35, 138–39, 140
    volunteering, 176
peers
    application process, 126, 127, 154
    extracurricular activities, 136–37
    as factor in selecting college, 277
    grade school, 32, 39, 219
    high school, 75–76, 183
    imposter syndrome, 212–13
    Ivy League benefits, 6, 67, 126, 127, 213, 214, 236
    Lion Dad vs. Tiger Mother model, xxxvii
    middle school, 67, 69, 71, 183
    outrunning, 72, 73–74
    test preparation, 116, 288–89
physicians, evaluating, 223

pollution, 90
poverty, 26
practice tests, 109, 111, 116, 118, 291–92
praise, 46–47
prefrontal cortex and executive function, 197, 204
pre-Kindergarten education, 1–2, 21–22, 32–34, 37, 175, 182, 218–23
prenatal development, 32
prepscholar.com, 288–89
primary education, See grade school
princetonreview.com, 288, 294
printing press, 144
prison, 25, 114
private schools
    AP classes, 110
    as factor in selecting college, 186
    focus on donations, 38, 53, 54, 82, 220, 221
    graduation rates, 10
    Ivy League acceptance rates, 14, 38–39, 219, 222
    vs. public schools, 37–40, 53–55, 67, 76, 181–82, 218–23, 226
    rankings, 137
    *See also* grade school; high school; middle school
profession, See employment
PSAT, 109
psychology, See neuropsychology
psychostimulants, 93, 100
public schools
    as factor in selecting college, 186
    graduation rates, 10
    Ivy League acceptance rates, 14
    parental involvement in, 219
    vs. private schools, 37–40, 53–55, 67, 76, 181–82, 218–23, 226
    rankings, 137
    *See also* grade school; high school; middle school
public speaking, 171–72
Puerto Rico, 38–39
punishment, *See also* discipline

# Q

questionnaires, 256–68

## R

*Race to Nowhere* (2009), 2
rankings and ratings, colleges
    adversity scores, 106
    early decision, 160
    as factor in selecting college, 186, 188, 277, 278–79
    Ivy League in, 9
    merit-only schools, 12
    resources on, 293–96
rankings and ratings, high schools, 75, 137, 160–61
rankings and ratings, teachers, 78–79
rankings and ratings, test prep services, 288
reading, xxxviii, 116
recommendation, letters of, 155–57, 162
redshirting, 220. See also age
reductionism, 207–11, 214
regular decision, 15, 159, 160
religion and rites of passage, 69–70
resources
    apps, 292, 299–300
    blogs, 296
    on college counselors, 302
    college websites, 287
    essays, 149, 285, 301
    financial aid, 159, 287, 297–301
    GPAs, 301
    high school, 81, 83, 85, 160–61, 287
    Ivy League students as, 149, 199
    list of, 287–304
    Naviance, 160–61, 287
    other applicants as, 154
    other parents as, 153–54, 221
    rankings and ratings, 293–96
    tests, 287–93, 301
    tutors, 290–91
resumes, 97, 124, 213
rewards
    athletics, 90
    grades, 108
    intrinsic motivation, xxviii, 47, 56, 59, 234
    Lion Dad vs. Tiger Mother model, xxvi, xxviii, xxx–xxxi, xxxvi, xxxvi–xxxvii, 46, 49–51
    self-efficacy, 45–46

*Rich Dad, Poor Dad* (Kiyosaki), 304
Ritalin, 65
rites of passage, 69–70
Robbins, Tony, 40–42, 186
Robinson, Ken, xxvii

**S**
safety, xxx, xxxiv, 28, 31, 176
salary and earnings potential, 5, 186, 276
SAT
    vs. ACT, 109
    adversity score, 77, 106
    benefits of, 114–15
    college counselors for, 126, 127
    essay, 145
    "good enough" score, 112, 116
    importance of, 103–7, 116, 118
    as metric, 105–6
    number of times to take, 112–14
    resources on, 287–93, 301
    SAT II tests, 110
    scores and acceptance rates, 15
    scores on Naviance, 160–61
    as superscored, 109, 112
*SAT prep* (television program), 292
scheduling, xxxv, 56
scholarships, See financial aid and scholarships
scholarships.com, 299
Scholly, 299
school
    attitudes towards, xxxviii
    homeschooling, 54–55, 66, 77, 79, 138, 182
    school closures, 244–45
    *See also* education; educators; grade school; high school; middle school; pre-Kindergarten education; private schools; public schools
Schwarzenegger, Arnold, 26
Scripps National Spelling Bee, 195
self-direction as goal, 233–34
self-efficacy, 45–46, 53, 68
self-esteem, 45–46, 53
self-image
    advantage of being older than classmates, 37
    comfort with, xxxix

negativity, 53
self-efficacy, 46, 68
self-improvement formula, 40–42, 59, 127
self-knowledge, 185, 198, 199
*The Shallows* (Carr), 105
signaling effect, 5
size, as factor in selecting college, 186, 276
sleep, 235–36
sleep, 110, 111
social media, 98, 157–58, 162, 244
social skills
    and technology, 242–43
    in Tiger Mother model, xxvi, 229
Son-Rise, 224
Spanish flu pandemic, 239, 240–41
spelling bees, 195
sports, See athletics
standardized tests, See ACT; SAT; tests
Stockholm syndrome, 30, 219, 227
studentaid.ed.gov, 299
student debt, 122
studentscholarships.org, 301
studentshare.net, 301
study area, 68
study styles, xxxviii
success
    assessing, xxxix
    avoiding surprise at, xxxi, 68, 71
    celebrating vs. rewarding, xxx–xxxi
    collaboration, xxviii
    "easier" schools, 4
    happiness, 251
    interest vs. practice, xxviii
    learning from, 154
    mental functioning, 196–204, 213
    in overview, xxxvi
    self-improvement formula, 40–42, 59, 127
suffering, in Tiger Mother model, xxvii
suicide, 185
summer activities, 98–99
superscholar.org, 301
supplements, 92–93, 100, 110, 210
surprise, xxxi, 68, 71
switching schools, 39–40, 53, 181–83, 184, 225–26

# T

talking vs. listening, xxxix
Tallarico, Steven, 131–32
teachers, See educators
Teaching Company, 290
technology
    effect on brain, 104–5
    online education, 240, 242–45, 246, 249
    and social skills, 242–43
test preparation
    AP tests, 111
    classes, 116, 118
    college counselors, 124, 126, 127
    costs, 44
    need for, 107, 111–14, 116–17
    peers, 116, 288–89
    practice tests, 109, 111, 116, 118, 291–92
    resources on, 287–93
    review books, 111, 116, 118, 291–92
    selecting services, 288–90
    strategies for, 111–14
    tutors, 111, 118
    videos, 287, 288, 292–93
    *See also* ACT; SAT; tests
tests
    AP, 109, 291
    benefits of, 114–15
    cognitive ability, 196
    importance of, 103–7, 115, 118
    intelligence, 23–24, 196
    in other countries, 103–4
    problems with, 23
    PSAT, 110
    resources on, 287–93, 301
    selecting, 109
    *See also* ACT; SAT; test preparation
thebestcolleges.org, 295
thebestschools.org, 294
thecollegewizard.net, 288
Thiagarajan, Maya, xxvi
thinking
    encouraging independent, 2
    vs. grades, 108
    in overview, xxx, xxxv, xxxix

Tiger Mother model
- authority in, xxxvi, xxxvii, 50, 166–67
- discipline in, xxvi, xxviii, xxxvi–xxxvii, 30, 49–50
- extracurricular activities in, xxvi, xxxviii, 139, 170
- mistakes, 227–29
- overview, xxxvi–xxxix
- questionnaires, 256–63
- respect for age, 94, 166
- rewards in, xxvi, xxviii, xxx, xxxvi–xxxvii
- social skills in, xxvi, 229
- unhappiness in, xxvi, xxviii, xxxiv, 30, 49

time
- athletics, 89
- as commodity, 83–84
- importance of spending with child, 40–42, 55
- spending together as family, 51–52

*Time,* 295
time outs, 50, 51
timeshighereducation.com, 293
titles, essay, 148
tobacco use, 71, 87
toptieradmissons.com, 302
topuniversities.com, 295
tours, 16
transfers, 39–40, 53, 181–83, 184, 225–26
travel, 44, 51, 98–99, 172–75, 176
The Triple Package (Chua), 70
trust, 51, 59, 64, 70
try.collegewise.com, 301
ttlearning.com, 302

tuition
- and COVID-19, 245, 247–48
- debt, 122–23
- as factor in selecting college, 16, 186, 188, 276, 297
- Ivy League, 3, 4
- *See also* costs

tutors
- vs. college counselors, 146
- costs, 44, 56–57, 59, 80–81
- grade school, 55–57
- high school, 76–77, 80–81, 85, 111
- online, 111
- resources, 290–91
- selecting, 59, 76–77, 81, 118, 290–91

Tiger Mother model, 49
    utilizing, 80–81, 111, 118, 138
Tyler, Steven, 131–32

## U

unhappiness in Tiger Mother model, xxvi, xxviii, xxxiv, 30, 49
*U.S. News & World Report*, 9, 293, 295

## V

vaccines, 91–92
values
    core competencies and, xxvii
    executive function, 197
    in overview, xxx, xxxv, xxxvi–xxxix
    selecting college, 16, 184–86, 190, 251, 276–84, 297
    selecting profession, 185–86
    worksheet, 276–83
varsitytutors.com, 290–91
veritasprep.com, 302
videos
    in applications, 126, 147, 157
    test preparation, 287, 288, 292–93
visits, college, 16
vocabulary
    as benefit of testing, 114
    essays, 148, 149, 151
voice lessons, 126, 172
volunteering, 170–72, 176

## W

water quality, 90
weather, as factor in selecting college, 187, 276
websites
    college, 287
    high school, 287
personal, 158, 162, 168, 176
Welch, Gilbert, 64
*Where You Go Is Not Who You'll Be* (Bruni), 3
Whitaker, Robert, 64
withfrank.org, 300
wonder, sense of, 66, 70, 235

Wright, Jonathan, 92
writing skills, 115, 144, 151. *See also* essays
www.admitsee.com, 149, 285, 301
www.businessinsider.com, 295
www.cappex.com, 296
www.chegg.com, 303
www.cnbc.com, 295
www.collegdata.com, 296
www.collegeboard.com, 303
www.collegeconfidential.com, 296
www.collegeessaymentor.com, 301
www.collegefactual.com, 295, 296
www.collegeinsight.com, 303
www.collegereadiness.collegeboard.org, 288
www.collegeresults.org, 303
www.collegescholarships.com, 300
www.collegescholarships.org, 298
www.collegescorecard.com, 296
www.collegevine.com, 289
www.collegexpress.com, 301
www.diycollegerankings.com, 295
www.economist.com, 294
www.fastweb.com, 297
www.forbes.com, 294
www.glassdoor.com, 302
www.hamiltoncollegeconsulting.com, 291
www.ivycoach.com, 302
www.ivy-edge.com, 302
www.ivyselect.com, 302
www.ivywise.com, 295
www.kaptest.com, 287
www.khanacademy.org, 287
www.newyorker.com, 294
www.niche.com, 293
www.noodle.com, 296
www.parchment.com, 296
www.parentscountdowntocollege.com, 295
www.prepscholar.com, 288–89
www.princetonreview.com, 288, 294
www.scholarships.com, 299
www.studentscholarships.org, 301
www.superscholar.org, 301
www.theatlantic.com, 294
www.thebestcolleges.org, 295

www.thebestschools.org, 294
www.thecollegewizard.net, 288
www.time.com, 295
www.timeshighereducation.com, 293
www.toptieradmissons.com, 302
www.topuniversities.com, 295
www.usnews.com, 293
www.varsitytutors.com, 290–91
www.withfrank.org, 300

# Y
*Your Child and School* (Robinson). xxvii

*Please take a moment to review Dr. Roark's Lion Dad at Amazon.com. Your review will help parents and students seeking a healtier approach to learning. It will also help promote Lion Dad parenting.
Thank you.*

# ABOUT THE AUTHOR

Details about Dr. Roark are purposefully left out or changed to preserve his anonymity as well as that of his son, Max.

Dr. Roark is a physician, Board certified in three specialties. He has written several articles and chapters for medical journals. Dr. Roark has always been a voracious reader and maintains a library of over 6,000 books, tapes, CDs, and mp3s, including a full set of the Encyclopedia Brittanica given to him when he was ten by his grandparents.

He has traveled to over 65 countries and lectured worldwide. He has volunteered in several countries to perform needed surgery including Nigeria, India, Guatemala, Honduras, and Mexico.

His interest, expertise, and passion for parenting, childhood education, and psychology were developed after the birth of his only child, Max. If there is one lesson to remember from this book, it's the difference a deeply involved parent can make with their child.

Dr. Roark has a reputation for thinking outside the box, and looking at things from a fresh perspective. He maintains contact with a wide variety of friends and colleagues across the globe, some of whom contributed to this book. He lives somewhere on the West Coast with his wife, Mary.

Visit LionDad.com

www.ingramcontent.com/pod-product-compliance
Lightning Source LLC
Chambersburg PA
CBHW071959150426
43194CB00008B/930